OUTSIDERS LOOKING IN: THE ROSSETTIS THEN AND NOW

Anthem Nineteenth Century Studies

Series Editor: Robert Douglas-Fairhurst

Other titles in the series:

Simon James, *Unsettled Accounts: Money and Narrative in the Novels of George Gissing* (2003)

Bharat Tandon, *Jane Austen and the Morality of Conversation* (2003)

OUTSIDERS LOOKING IN: THE ROSSETTIS THEN AND NOW

edited by
David Clifford
and
Laurence Roussillon

Anthem Press

This edition first published by Anthem Press 2004

Anthem Press is an imprint of
Wimbledon Publishing Company
75–76 Blackfriars Road
London SE1 8HA

British Library Cataloguing in Publication Data
Data available

Library of Congress Cataloging in Publication Data
A catalogue record has been applied for

1 3 5 7 9 10 8 6 4 2

ISBN 1 84331 105 4 (hbk)
ISBN 1 84331 106 2 (pbk)

Typeset by Regent Typesetting, London
Printed by Interpress, Hungary

CONTENTS

PART IV. Radical Poetics

PART V. Literary Tradition and the Rossetti Legacy

LIST OF ILLUSTRATIONS

ACKNOWLEDGEMENTS

In the period since this volume was first conceived we have been fortunate in our network of support, expertise and encouragement. The foremost name to whom we must acknowledge our debt is Wei-Wei Yeo, without whom there might be be no such volume at all. We should also offer our gratitude here to the series editor and editor at Anthem Press, Robert Douglas-Fairhurst and Tom Penn respectively, for making the final stages of publication the positive experience it has turned out to be.

At various stages we have been assisted financially, and wish here to express our gratitude to Isabelle Joyau of the Délégation Culturelle Française, Cambridge, the Judith E Wilson Fund of the Faculty of English, Cambridge University, and to St John's and Trinity Colleges, Cambridge.

Others have contributed in various small or large, but always significant, ways, and we record our thanks here to Barrie Bullen, Julia Grella, Jean Khalfa, Angela Leighton, David Midgley and Jan-Melissa Schramm.

David Clifford, Cambridge UK
Laurence Roussillon, Lyon
September 2003

CONTRIBUTORS

Mary Arseneau, Associate Professor of English at the University of Ottawa, is the author of articles on Christina Rossetti, the Rossetti family and John Keats. With Antony H Harrison and Lorraine Janzen Kooistra, she is a co-editor of *The Culture of Christina Rossetti: Female Poetics and Victorian Contexts* (Athens: Ohio University Press, 1999). Her book, *Recovering Christina Rossetti: Female Community and Incarnational Poetics* is forthcoming from Palgrave Macmillan.

Florence S Boos is Professor of English at the University of Iowa. She has published books on Dante Rossetti (1976) and William Morris (1991), and edited with full apparatus Morris' *Socialist Diary* (1985) and *Earthly Paradise* (in two volumes, 2001). Her current projects include an anthology of poetry of Victorian working-class women, and a critical study of their Scottish sisters.

Gavin Budge has been Lecturer in English Literature at the University of Central England in Birmingham since 1995. He has published papers on the Whitechapel Exhibitions in the journal *Visual Culture in Britain* (2000), on Realism and Typology in Charlotte M Yonge in *Nineteenth Century Literature and Culture* (2003), and two anthologies for Thoemmes Press, *Aesthetics and the Picturesque, 1795–1840* (2001) and *Aesthetics and Religion in Nineteenth-Century Britain* (2003). He is currently editing a collection of essays on Romantic Empiricism for Bucknell University Press, and working on a book about Romanticism and nineteenth-century medicine.

David Clifford is a College Teaching Officer in English and Fellow of Homerton College, Cambridge. He gained his doctorate from Cambridge in 2000 and is the author of *Reform, the Novel and the Origins of Neo-Lamarckism* (Ashgate, 2003). He is also editor of volume V of Chatto & Pickering's *Literature and Science 1660–1834* series, an annotated anthology of primary texts on Fauna to be published in January 2004.

Mariaconcetta Costantini is Associate Professor of English at the University 'G d'Annunzio' of Chieti-Pescara. She has published extensively on Victorian literature (Dickens, Gaskell, Hopkins, Christina Rossetti, Hardy and others), on twentieth-century fiction and on the postcolonial novel. She is the author of *Poesia e sovversione: Christina Rossetti, Gerard Manley Hopkins* (2000) and of *Behind the Mask. A Study of Ben Okri's Fiction* (2002).

Michelle Hawley is Assistant Professor in English Literature at California State University in Los Angeles. She is currently working on a project about Victorian poetry and aesthetic citizenship between 1868 and 1876.

John Holmes is Lecturer in English Literature at the University of Reading. His research interests include the sonnet sequence, the Victorian crisis of belief, spiritualism, colonialism and the literature of science.

Lorraine Janzen Kooistra is Professor of English at Nipissing University in North Bay, Canada. She is the author of *Christina Rossetti and Illustration: A Publishing History* and *The Artist as Critic: Bitextuality in Fin-de-Siècle Illustrated Books* and co-editor, along with Mary Arseneau and Antony H Harrison, of *The Culture of Christina Rossetti: Female Poetics and Victorian Contexts*. She is currently working on a book-length study of Victorian Poetry and Illustration.

Maria Keaton is a PhD candidate at Marquette University, Milwaukee. Her previous publications include 'The Mother's Tale: The Empowerment of Juno in *Juno and the Paycock*' in *The New Hibernian Review*. Her scholarly interests lie in the analysis of technique, in discourse and in poetry.

Jerome McGann is the John Stewart Bryan University Professor, University of Virginia. He has been building the online *Complete Writings and Pictures of Dante Gabriel Rossetti: A Hypermedia Research Archive* since 1993, a project which should eventually mutate into a comprehensive online research archive for studying the Pre-Raphaelite and Aesthetic movements in general. His *Dante Gabriel Rossetti and the Game that Must be Lost* was published in 2000, and a collected edition of key writings, based on *The Rossetti Archive*, is scheduled for publication in 2003 (both from Yale University Press).

Peter Mandler is University Lecturer in History and Fellow of Gonville and Caius College, Cambridge. He is the author of, among other books, *The Fall and Rise of the Stately Home* (1997; paperback edition 1999) and *History and National Life* (2002), and is currently completing a history of the idea of the English national character.

Jan Marsh is a Fellow of the Royal Historical Society and an honorary Professor at the University of Sussex. She has published extensively on the Rossetti family and the pre-Raphaelite movement, including biographies of Dante Gabriel Rossetti (1999) and Christina Rossetti (1996). Other major publications include *Pre-Raphaelite Women Artists* (1999), *The Pre-Raphaelite Sisterhood* (1989) and *The Legend of Elizabeth Siddal* (1989).

Emma Mason is Lecturer in Nineteenth-Century Poetry at the University of Warwick. She is the author of Women Poets of the Nineteenth Century (2003) for the Writers and their Work Series, and has published articles in Victorian Literature and Culture, Victorian Poetry, The Journal of Victorian Culture and Romanticism on the Net. She is editor of the British Association for Victorian Studies Newsletter and an annual reviewer for The Year's Work in English Studies. Her current book is a study of affection and Romantic religious poetry.

Catherine Maxwell is Senior Lecturer in the School of English and Drama at Queen Mary, University of London. She is the editor of *Algernon Charles Swinburne* (1997) and author of *The Female Sublime from Milton to Swinburne: Bearing Blindness* (2001). Her volume on Swinburne for the series Writers and their Work is published early in 2004. She has published articles on Dante Gabriel and Christina Rossetti, George Eliot, Ruskin, Robert Browning, Swinburne, Hardy and Vernon Lee. She is presently editing a collection of Vernon Lee's short stories for Broadview Press.

Laurence Roussillon is 'maître de conférence' in English Literature at the University 'Louis Lumière, Lyon 2' (France). She recently completed a French doctorate entitled 'In Medusa's Mirror: Dante Gabriel Rossetti's Art of Looking (Painting and Poetry)'. Her main field of research is nineteenth century literature (Thomas Hardy, Gerard Manley Hopkins) and her other interests include aesthetics, art history and the relationship between text and image. She is currently working on a translation project of Ruskin's writings on aesthetics.

Angela Thirlwell's biography *William and Lucy: The Other Rossettis*, about William Michael Rossetti and Lucy Madox Brown, was published by Yale University Press at the end of 2003. She edited *The Folio Anthology of Autobiography* (1994) and *The Pre-Raphaelites and their World* (1995) for The Folio Society. She has taught literature for many years for the Faculty of Continuing Education, Birkbeck College, London University.

Valeria Tinkler-Villani is Senior Lecturer in the department of English, University of Leiden, the Netherlands. She is the author of *Visions of Dante in English Poetry* (1989), co-editor of *Exhibited by Candlelight: Sources and Developments in the Gothic Tradition* (1995), and has published numerous articles on Dante, Italian historical figures in English literature and the Rossettis.

Clive Wilmer, poet, translator, critic and broadcaster, is Associate Teaching Officer at Fitzwilliam and Sidney Sussex Colleges, Cambridge, and an Honorary Fellow of Anglia Polytechnic University. He has edited Dante Gabriel Rossetti's *Selected Poems and Translations* (1991) as well as Penguin selections of John Ruskin and William Morris.

INTRODUCTION

David Clifford and Laurence Roussillon

Towards the end of his life Dante Gabriel Rossetti wrote in a letter to a friend: 'I am one of those whose very little is their own.' Is this to be read as a lucid statement on his lack of achievement or originality? Or is this simply a rhetorical stance from someone who knew that the 'very little' was what really mattered? To a contemporary reader it seems that both hypotheses are equally true of Dante Gabriel: in painting and in poetry he did not so much create as reveal what were underlying ideas and ideals of Victorian society. At the same time, the way he dressed familiar thoughts in strange and new guises – such as those expressed in *The Blessed Damozel* – definitely allotted him a singular niche in the intellectual landscape of his time.

Like his father Gabriele before him, Dante Gabriel was to occupy such a marginal position in the world he inhabited that his ambiguous statement can appear to qualify the role that not only he, but the entire Rossetti family, played during their lifetime and through their interaction with their contemporaries. Indeed, outsiders though they were, being half-Italian and half-English, the various members of the Rossetti family – Gabriele and his wife Maria Frances and their four children – were at one point at the centre of a bustling intellectual life: following his exile from Italy, the *paterfamilias* Gabriele pursued his career as a professor of Italian and remained a political activist while publishing controversial writings on Dante. His home became famous for being a refuge for Italian expatriates with whom he discussed the politics of his native land. With the early publication of her poetry, his eldest daughter Christina was soon regarded as a major female poet, at once devotional and highly sensual, or even at times *engagée*.

Her brother Dante Gabriel, a poet and a painter, found himself at the head of the Pre-Raphaelite movement, which was to be championed by the highly influential art critic John Ruskin. In his London home of Chatham, Dante Gabriel was renowned for entertaining his literary and artistic guests until the small hours, talking about the arts and reciting poetry. Surrounded by a loyal group that he compared to Dante's circle of poet friends, he inspired many into action, such as William Morris, who followed his advice and founded the William Morris Company that was to lead to the Arts and Crafts Movement.

Following in his path, Dante Gabriel's younger brother William Michael also tried his hand at poetry, but instead made a name for himself as the editor of works by romantic poets such as Keats and Shelley. A faithful recorder of the Pre-Raphaelite Brotherhood, William Michael also edited their short-lived journal, *The Germ*, and later worked on editing Christina and Dante Gabriel's poetical works. As Peter Mandler argues in this volume, William Michael, who worked as a taxman for the State, was able to influence the artistic canon of the time through a combination of his editorial, critical and professional skills. Finally, the youngest of the Rossetti siblings, Maria Francesca, together with her mother Frances and sister Christina, played an active part in High Church politics and was also committed to knowledge and to her cultural heritage. As a teacher of Italian who never actually visited Italy, Maria exemplifies the liminal position the Rossettis held in Victorian London, with her strong but idealistic attachment to the Italian fatherland, and a deep spiritual commitment to the adoptive country in which she and her siblings were born.

Beyond their individual idiosyncrasies and personal achievements, it seems that the members of the Rossetti family shared a common sense of Italian identity as well as a desire to be fully recognized as British. Being perfectly bilingual, the four Rossetti siblings all used their linguistic skills at some point to instil a foreign or exotic element from one culture into the other. Through translation, they were not only able to share part of their heritage but also to tune their ear to the rhythm and sound of English. The best examples of this are probably to be found in Christina Rossetti's beautiful nursery poems, such as *Sing-Song*, in which the lilting rhythm is quintessentially English and yet retains the lulling quality of an Italian sonata. Another instance, as Jan Marsh remarks in her essay, is the way the family name Rossetti was uttered, the 's' being pronounced like the soft English 'z', which made it sound at the same time definitely English, yet exotically foreign.

In the same fashion, the Rossettis treated their knowledge of Dante's writings almost as a personal literary heritage from their father which they made their own through writing or translation, or even painting: Dante Gabriel's depiction of Beatrice in his most famous painting, *Beata Beatrix*, with the red-haired silhouette of Elizabeth Siddal cut against the golden landscape of Florence, is a 'dream beyond' the original version of Dante's vision of Beatrice's death. On the one hand, it captures the moment that Dante himself deliberately avoided describing in *La Vita Nuova* – the (literally) awful moment of transition between life and death where all energies converge towards one last instant of ecstasy. On the other, it translates the sentiment of loss to another time and place, as we read into the painting Dante Gabriel's tragic marriage with his English wife, and become aware of the intense personal emotion that pervades the picture. Receding in the background, the ghostly presence of Dante is at the same time superfluous and essential to the atmosphere of the scene. 'In the Shadow of Dante', an essay written by Maria, the youngest of the siblings, appears in this instance an appropriate title to Gabriel's endeavour.

To a considerable degree, it might also have provided a definition of their life and family ethic. Like Dante, who surrounded himself with a community of artists and poets, it appears in the family letters that the Rossettis were always supportive of one another's work and committed to the success of the whole family. What they brought to the London intellectual stage was indeed a sense of community or 'brotherhood' that looked beyond individual interest and promoted interaction between the various arts and skills each member possessed. At a time when industrialization could be seen as a threat to individual talent and personal venture, the Rossettis managed to cross the divide between writers and editors, models and artists, poets and printers, and bring together their various talents in the service of their art. In the case of Christina Rossetti's poetry for example, both Dante Gabriel and William Michael worked as intermediaries between their sister and her potential publishers, advertising the quality of her verse. More specifically, the illustrations that Dante Gabriel drew for *Goblin Market* also contributed to the success of her books and encouraged her readers to enter the realms of both siblings' imaginations.

Moreover, the Rossettis' interaction with major public figures of the time – John Ruskin, Walter Pater, Alfred Tennyson, the Brownings – placed them at the core of the London literary scene and allowed them to bring their vision of the arts into the public sphere. Without the publicity that Ruskin gave the Pre-Raphaelite artists, and more specifically to the work of Dante Gabriel, his career might have been much less successful. Conversely, Dante Gabriel's dream of a Victorian Quattrocento – a kind of English revival of Italian renaissance painting – doubtless influenced the ideas Pater developed in *The Renaissance* and initiated the *fin-de-siècle* movement which was to put an end to the Victorian age.

Whether considered as a whole, or through its various members, the Rossetti family acted as a sounding board against which resonated many themes and ideas that were rarely voiced in the society they lived in. Their dual nationality and ambivalent desire to belong to two empires, one of the British Crown and the other of the mind, found resonance in the way

Victorian society was divided between tradition and modernity, religious belief and science, prudery and erotic longing. Given this, it is to be expected that they should have attracted so many admirers and followers both in their own lifetimes and subsequently, as this volume aims to demonstrate.

The present collection is the result of much consideration and collaboration over several years – as well as across different hemispheres. The issues it addresses are reflected in the nature of its organization. We intended, foremost, that it should be concerned with the Rossettis' position as outsiders engaged with the bustling, cosmopolitan intellectual life of their adopted homeland. It seemed that there was much to be explored regarding the various siblings and their relations with their peers, in the light of modern critical approaches. Frances Winsar gave us a helpful insight into the dynamics of these relationship in *The Rossettis and their Circle* (1934), and the present collection aims to augment that classic work.

In its first incarnation papers on these aspects of the Rossettis were called for presentation at a conference, *The Rossettis: Cosmopolitans in Victorian London*, which was duly held in Cambridge in July 2001. In true cosmopolitan and interdisciplinary spirit, it attracted scholars from ten countries across four continents, with interests ranging from literary criticism and art history to musicology, church history and the history of science. The shape of the eventual conference well reflected the cultural cross-pollination between its organizers, the delegates who attended and the family at its centre.

In spirit, this collection is the result of much reworking, revising and restructuring of the more innovative conclusions drawn from the debates held at the conference. What emerged confirmed our initial intuition that the life and writings of the Rossetti family exemplified the way the Italian community made a home and a name for themselves in Victorian London, using Italy as a source of inspiration and an imaginary haven away from the bustle of the city and the quarrels of their peers. Every panel revealed how each member of the Rossetti family voiced specific criticisms of the Victorian era, while at the same time bringing their own personal answers to dilemmas on religion, social issues or artistic practice, informed by their status as outsiders. As a group, they captured some aspects of the Victorian way of thinking and offered a kaleidoscopic view on complex issues such as the relation between art and commerce, religion and politics. On a more analytical level, the *parti pris* of interdisciplinary viewpoints led to a fruitful confrontation of ideas and a whole range of new ones. Compared to the criticism on the Rossettis written in the 1970s, the commentaries written today benefit from new methodological approaches brought about by the development of critical, cultural and gender studies. In the case of the female members of the family, these recent developments shed new light on their work and roles in the domestic and artistic economy of the household, as well as on their engagement with wider social and religious concerns, such as pew-rents and Anglo-Catholic practices.

The contributors to this volume have sought to find new correspondences between different areas of research, resulting in a richer and more interdisciplinary approach to the Rossetti family. For example, one of the things that is striking to many of the contributors, as well as to the editors, was the importance to the Rossettis of the relationship between science and faith. The history of Victorian science and culture has proven to be an area of considerable academic interest over the past couple of decades. While the Rossettis were as informed about these debates as anyone else of their time, by seeing them as a family group with at times radically varied concerns, their engagement with these questions takes on new dimensions.

As a whole, the essays published in this volume fall into four sections giving a dynamic view of the Rossettis' cultural and literary achievements. It opens on cultural, more general, aspects of their identity and gradually moves on towards more complex issues of aesthetics, faith and literary legacy.

The first section of the book looks at how the family saw themselves in relation to Italy, their 'fatherland'. Beginning with the complex ways in which they regarded the nature of 'Italianness', its cultural heritage and its physical existence as a place to visit (always denying the status of 'home' either to Italy or England), this collection draws attention to the overwhelming importance of Italy in the siblings' lives – to say nothing of their émigré father.

The studies of the artistic Rossettis included in this volume are firmly located in the context of both the intellectual and commercial culture of their age, and highlight how the importance of the mechanics of producing, presenting and consuming art in the period obviously played on all the Rossettis' minds. In part two, 'Aesthetics in a Commercial World', the particulars of cultural production cast new light on familiar images and poetry. No study of the Rossettis, however, can isolate one aspect or other from the rest if it seeks to present a cohesive and representative picture of the cosmopolitan lives they lived. Dante Gabriel's poetry in particular provokes energetic critical discussion, and the three essays in the third section, 'Radical Poetics', offer important insights both into how he created his art and how it was received by his contemporaries.

Many readers will not be surprised to find that the fourth section, 'Faith in an Age of Science', focuses heavily, though not exclusively, on Christina. Religion was of profound importance for the Rossetti women, and their engagement went beyond even Christina's devout poetry. She and Maria were active in the 'free and open church movement', the details of which are uncovered by Mary Arseneau's researches, and her exploration of some of the deeper questions about science are enlightening.

Finally the last section, 'Literary Tradition and the Rossetti Legacy', shows in original ways where Dante Gabriel Rossetti's poetry stands in relation to classical myth and English literary tradition, Thomas Hardy, and later, less well-known female sonneteers. These simultaneously backward- and forward-looking views will provide a clearer picture of the poet's true position in the Victorian literary scene, and of his influence on those who came after him – including ourselves.

To complete this overview of the contents of the volume, one should mention that examining the achievement of the Rossettis as a whole allowed the authors of these essays to get some sense of the atmosphere that probably reigned in the Rossetti home. What started as a student's joking observation that during their evenings of entertainment, the Rossettis must have looked pretty different from the rest of their rosy-cheeked companions, as Max Beerbohm's drawings in *Rossetti and his Circle* testify, was what, to our eyes, made the success of this venture. Just as with a new circle of friends, it brought together people of varied nationalities and interests and tried to revive the spirit of a fraternal community, where ideas shone and passed, converged or parted, and are now allowed to survive on paper.

What 'very little of their own' was distinctly the Rossettis', we hope to have captured in this collection.

PART I

ITALY AND ITALIANNESS

1

SIBLING CULTURES

Jan Marsh

The children of exile stand in very complex relation to their countries of birth and ancestry. While critical and biographical writing on the Rossettis has tended to portray their Italian inheritance in a simple and generally positive light, a close reading of their responses suggests a more ambivalent and certainly more nuanced picture.

The four Rossetti siblings were born between 1826 and 1830 in London to an Italian who found political asylum in Britain, and his wife, daughter of an Italian expatriate and a British mother. Thus the children were three-quarters Italian by blood – if that has any meaning – and one-quarter British.[1] Throughout life, this dual national identity was as important to all four as their siblingship.

They grew up bilingual, speaking Italian with their father, English with their mother, aunts and servants – an experience encapsulated by *SingSong*, the nursery poems Christina composed in English and subsequently translated back into Italian as *NinnaNanna*, thereby enacting the linguistic simultaneity of her infancy.[2]

> Koorookookoo!
> Crows the cock before the morn
> Cuccurruccu!
> All' alba il gallo canta
>
> If a pig wore a wig....
> Porco la zucca fitta in parucca!

The family socialized within the small world of the Italian community in London, which valued and promoted 'Italianità'. The language, the culture, the music, the customs, the food: all were Italian. But on all sides they were surrounded by the British world. Pronunciation is a small symbol of this: at home the name was Ross/etti, outside it was Roze/etti (as commonly said in Britain today.) The outside world also anglicized Gabriele and Cristina into Gabriel and Christina,[3] although even at home William prevailed over Guglielmo with all except their father.

Their early education was in English.[4] However, as John Schad remarks in his essay on Christina Rossetti and Luce Irigaray, 'Of course, coming from an Anglo-Italian family, Christina is always, in a sense, doing something other than writing in English – hers is an Italicized English in more senses than one.'[5] And, through the thicket of senses, this must be true of all four siblings: behind or within use of one language is knowledge of the other. A truly dual linguistic inheritance, the languages standing in sibling relation to each other, with continual exchange.

That the world outside was British was impressed on the boys at school where they were first made to feel their difference. Neither flourished as they should, and neither joined in the playground rough-and-tumble. The fact that both kept their distance from classmates to me at least suggests name-calling by chronically xenophobic schoolboys.[6] A faint echo of juvenile insults may inform the 'rank words' addressed to Dante in Dante Gabriel's poem on the humiliations of exile, *Dante at Verona*.

On the London streets, Italians were conspicuous as members of the indigent underclass.[7] The more visible economic migrants sold carved figurines and played barrel organs, and as quasi-beggars aroused concern and complaint among the host community. According to a *Times* leader in 1856, Italian organ-grinders were a 'gratuitous aggravation' of 'urban disagreeables' comparable to 'dirt and vermin'. When not thus insulted, the buskers were pitied, as was illustrated in a popular painting of 1858 entitled 'Charity', which showed a ragged Italian musician receiving alms from a British woman and her child, and thereby underlined the message that as a nation 'England' was rich and benevolent towards less fortunate foreigners.[8] Even the educated élite, who worked as professional musicians, artists, linguists and teachers, experienced condescension. This was especially true of the political refugees, like Gabriele Rossetti *père*, who were dependent on British goodwill for asylum and livelihood. Although many were socially well connected to the British élite, they were also objects of pity, patronage, pecuniary assistance.

A series of binary oppositions characterized the connotations of the two nations in this era. 'Italy' signified poverty, 'England' prosperity. Italy was backward and unmodernized, whereas Britain was economically and politically advanced, as foreign visitors remarked and natives boasted. To the latter, 'England' was strong, industrious[9] and honest, whereas 'Italy' was weak and, in the words of Thomas Macaulay, 'corrupted by a bad government and a bad religion'.[10] Being under foreign domination, Italy occupied a servile, quasi-colonial position, while Britain's vaunted attributes were freedom and mastery.

'Honest Englishmen', as Charles Kingsley wrote in 'Letter to Thomas Hughes':

do the work that's nearest,
Though it's dull at whiles
Helping, when we meet them
Lame dogs over stiles.

To many Britons, Italy and Italians were effectively lame dogs, and un-hygienic into the bargain. Generations of British travellers stressed English cleanliness versus Italian squalor. In the words of Kingsley's doggerel:

Leave to Robert Browning
Beggars, fleas and vines;
Leave to squeamish Ruskin
Popish Appenines,
Dirty stones of Venice...

In *Vanna's Twins*, Christina has her English narrator explicitly contest this prejudice with an allusion to 'what we, in our insularity, term the English love of soap and water'.

Furthermore, in popular notations of 'national character', Italians were portrayed as lazy, dishonest and 'sly'. A small example of this is the remark attributed to Millais's mother when the press attacked the Pre-Raphaelite Brotherhood in 1850. 'I don't like the look of him,' she is quoted as saying of Dante Gabriel; 'he's a sly Italian and his forestalling you deceitfully [...] was quite un-English and unpardonable.'[11]

So while in the Rossetti home being Italian was a wholly positive experi-ence, reinforced by the fervent patriotism of the exile community, the child-ren stepped over the threshold into a world where Italian identity carried very different resonances.

But the Rossettis were also British citizens by birth at a time when to be British was to be privileged, when the nation was on the cusp of a rising pride and patriotism that was vocal, pervasive and frequently figured on military heroes. As the storytelling aunt in *Speaking Likenesses* admonishes one of her listeners: 'Oh Clara, you an English girl and not know Lord Nelson!' Even Dante Gabriel was sufficiently patriotic to visit the Waterloo battlefield at age twenty, to compose an ode on the death of Wellington and at fifty to respond to 'the Last Three from Trafalgar'.

England was their daily reality. Generally speaking, in Britain the critical emphasis tends to focus on the Rossettis' Italianness, while from an Italian perspective one might remark more forcefully on their essential Englishness, although to apply the football test no doubt all would have supported Italy in any contest against England.

In the rhetorical realm, 'Italy' was a land of imagination reached through figure, not in terms of actuality nor even travel destination. And as, owing to their father's proscription, the Rossettis grew up knowing they were unable to visit the country, its imaginative allure was if anything enhanced. They devoured 'Italy' in several guises: as Gothic romance through their juvenile playacting, theatre-going and comic books featuring brigands and banditti, outlaws and endangered heroines (in which Italy resembled the Wild West of early-twentieth-century entertainment); in the popular fictions of Ann Radcliffe and Letitia Landon; and in the work of major poets, where the idea or myth of 'Italy' held a prominent position in the repertoire of Romanticism. Here Italy is conventionally the poetic, beautiful, ruined past.[12] In a famous passage, Byron wrote:

> And now, fair Italy!
> Thou art the garden of the world,
> Even in thy desert, what is like to thee?
> Thy very weeds are beautiful, thy waste
> More rich than other climes' fertility.
> Thy wreck a glory and thy ruin graced
> With an immaculate charm that cannot be defaced.[13]

Desert, weeds, wreck, waste, simultaneously with beauty, glory, grace: the lines illustrate the Romantic valorization of picturesque decline. And in the letter prefacing this Italian canto of *Childe Harold's Pilgrimage*, Byron also praised 'the extraordinary capacity of this people […] the rapidity of their conceptions, the fire of their genius, their sense of beauty amidst all the disadvantages […] and the despair of ages, their still unquenched "longing after immortality" – the immortality of independence.'[14]

But even here, the picture is ambivalent. Indeed, more Italian connotations were negative than positive. 'Italy' had a dual aspect, Shelley bluntly told Leigh Hunt:

> There are two Italies: one composed of the green earth & transparent sea and the mighty ruins of antient times, and aerial mountains & the warm and radiant atmosphere which is interfused through all things. The other consists of the Italians of the present day, their words and ways. The one

is the most sublime & lovely contemplation that can be conceived by the imagination of man; the other the most degraded, disgusting & odious.[15]

Italian men, he added, looked 'like a tribe of stupid and shrivelled slaves' while the women were 'ignorant [...] disgusting [...] bigoted [and] filthy'.

These poets had of course a special significance to the Rossettis thanks to their uncle Dr John Polidori, who had travelled with them as Byron's physician. He too had a dual aspect. As William Michael later explained to the National Portrait Gallery, John Polidori had been 'born in London of an Italian father and English mother'. However, William continued emphatically, perhaps betraying some familial anxiety, his uncle was 'not a foreigner' but a British subject.[16]

In this, he was unlike their father, who constituted the overwhelming presence of Italy in the family and who brought Italy to England together with his reputation as a poet and patriot and the stirring account of his escape from tyranny. Refusing to speak English on principle, he was a patriarchal figure in the Italian mode, temporarily transported, who one day would take his family 'back home.' Temperamentally, he was also emphatically 'Italian': warm, voluble, volatile, demonstrative, in contrast to their mother Frances, who is always described as typically 'English': self-controlled, firm, reserved.[17] One can go further: in gender terms, thanks to their grandfather Gaetano and grandmother Anne Mary Pierce, as well as the three Polidori aunts and the Rossetti cousin Teodorico, in the family landscape Italy was figured as male/paternal, England as female/maternal. Literally, so to speak, fatherland and motherland.

This was a reversal of the cultural dimension where Italy – l'Italia – was strongly figured as feminine. In poetry such as Hemans' *Dying Improvisator* or Browning's *An Englishman in Italy* Italy is represented as a feminine country of beauty, grace, allure. In de Stael's *Corinne* and Barrett Browning's *Aurora Leigh,* key texts with Anglo-Italian protagonists, the heroine's father is English, her mother Italian, and in both the latter is held to have seduced the former from his sterner duties. England was thus contrastingly figured as masculine: its qualities being strength, silence, staunchness and pugnacity when incarnated as John Bull. While the oppositions are not always consistent, they maintain an inflexible contrast and division. As Aurora Leigh declares, 'Italy/ is one thing, England one.'

So what did it mean to live in England as part-Italian, part-English?

William's daughter Helen Angeli, who reversed the family migration, interpreted Dante Gabriel's life as one 'incident in [the] age-long national tragedy [...] of Italian emigration [...] which has scattered abroad such inestimable treasures of genius, labour and beauty, and turned so many of Italy's sons into 'displaced persons'.[18] But if migrants are displaced persons, those born in exile can be unplaced persons, with no homeland, or two-placed persons, with twin or sibling homelands, a dual, equal but different heritage. It's sometimes a shock when such people travel to their parents' country; this place called 'home' can be alien to the next generation. 'Wherefore art thou strange and not my mother?' asked Christina poetically, at the very moment of 'return', on her one encounter with the actual land of Italy.

For half their lives, England was the actual homeland, Italy the 'lost' homeland they could not visit. However, for a brief moment in 1848 it looked likely that the family would 'return' when their father was summoned home. At this date Maria was 21, Dante Gabriel nearly 20, William 18, Christina 17. There's no documented reference to any response – a silence whose meaning is opaque and puzzling. If Italy was indeed a 'homeland of the heart', one wants to know how they all responded to the possibility of 'return'. They were all caught up that year in the politics of hope and disappointment, yet none but their father appears to have contemplated leaving Britain, even in fantasy.

When his hope of return was extinguished, Professor Rossetti wrote his autobiography, describing his children as free-born in contrast to his own servile status and adding

> Voi siete in patria, ed in esiglio io sono
> You are in fatherland, I am in exile.[19]

Here England features as his exile, and as their homeland. But it might simultaneously be said that the younger generation were also in exile from Italy, their ancestral fatherland. Citing this passage, Valeria Tinkler-Villani translated 'patria' as 'motherland',[20] which is doubly accurate in so far as Britain was the land of their mother's birth as well as their own but forfeits the irony of 'patria', which forces attention to the fact that the children's fatherland was not the same as their father's.

In her essay 'Italy and the Maternal in Christina Rossetti's Poetry', Alison Chapman explores what is called the problematic trope of Christina's conceptualization of Italy as 'a focal point for explorations of identity and heritage that emerge in multiple configurations'.[21] Something of the same complexity can be seen in the responses of each of the four siblings, which point up the multiplicity of positions and ambiguities of feeling.

Dante Gabriel was quoted as declaring around 1870: 'I am an Italian who has never seen Italy'– a statement modified slightly when telling Barbara Bodichon that he was 'an inveterate southerner though I fear no particular patriot'.[22] Many people saw him as Italian in looks, but very English in demeanour – bluff, forthright, often dogmatic, summed up by a regular dinner guest as his 'bluntly cordial, John Bullish manner'.[23] This aspect is underlined by William's use of the same image of English patriotism in regard to Dante Gabriel's 'ultra-John-Bullish opinions and ways'. Nonetheless William summed up his brother 'as more an Italian than an Englishman [...] in temper of mind [and] in general tone of moral perception.' Yet, he added, Dante Gabriel was 'very far from being like his Italian father, and was wholly unlike his Italian grandfather'.[24]

When in 1909 the Italian government proposed to award William a national honour, he replied with a finely modulated account of his own sense of identity. Declining politely, he told the ambassador that he regarded Italy as being 'my native country almost in equal degree with England'. This 'almost' is not equal, however: William presents himself as a British subject, like his uncle. Moreover, he wrote his letter in English, and reminded his correspondent that Italy had banished their father, making him *'esule e proscritto* in the cause of his country', as if to imply that the country could not so easily claim the son of a man so ill-treated, as and when it wished. In this exchange, William and the Marchese de San Giuliano do not share the same 'native country'.[25] Yet the use of this one phrase – 'esule e proscritto' – in Italian also subtly undercuts the assertion of British nationality. William was a very precise writer, and this letter demonstrates his exact understanding of dual inheritance.

To point the subtleties further, however, William is most easily characterized as 'English' in Kingsley's terms: reliable, hardworking, even dull – the very reverse of Italian ebullience.[26] But he was the sibling most familiar with, most at home in, most knowledgeable about, most drawn to Italy. In 1864, when Garibaldi arrived in London to an overwhelming popular response, it was William who escorted their mother to join the welcoming crowd at Vauxhall station. And he was full of patriotic pride when telling Walt Whitman that he was three-quarters Italian in blood, adding: 'it is often a pleasure to reflect that, with all the miserable oppression and depression under which she has so long been labouring, Italy has after all produced the 3 greatest public men [...] of the last 100 years in Europe': Napoleon, Mazzini and Garibaldi.[27] He visited Italy at the first opportunity, as soon as it was politically possible, in 1860, recording this as a landmark in his life and returning more or less annually. The others did not. Maria Francesca and Dante Gabriel chose never to visit their ancestral land, while Christina went once, with William and their mother, to Lombardy in 1865. William was therefore the only one to know both the lands he was heir to, comfortable in his dual role as English gentleman and Italian expatriate.

Once, in London, Dante Gabriel sent on an unwanted visitor to William saying 'I dare say he is a nice fellow, and you like Italians, so I have the less remorse in sending him to you'.[28]

'You like Italians'. If William liked meeting Italians, is the inference that Dante Gabriel did not? There were few if any among his adult friends.

What of Maria Francesca? the most enigmatic of the Rossettis, because we have so little information. We do know she was deemed very Italian in looks,[29] with black hair, olive skin, 'dark Italian countenance and rapt eyes'.[30] Despite their father's famous division of the children into the calms and the storms – 'se volessi cambiare *due calme* per *due tempeste*'[31] – Maria Francesca was passionate by temperament, fervent in her enthusiasms, warm and energetic. I don't allot nationality to those qualities but it's worth insisting that Maria Francesca was not one of the cold, phlegmatic Englishwomen of her sister's poem, *Enrica*.

Baulked of her chosen profession in the religious life, Maria Francesca took over her father's role teaching Italian. Loyally Christina described her sister as a born teacher, though to our minds Maria's teaching text, *Exercises in Idiomatic Italian*, with extracts done into English using Italian constructions, to be rendered back into the original, speaks of some desperation in the face of Britons' linguistic incompetence. And surprisingly for a language teacher, she never visited Italy, though she might have gone at various times with William. How is this to be interpreted? She was not devotionally opposed to holidays as such. At the least, her decision not to go with the others in 1865 suggests that ardent curiosity and commitment to the ancestral land were lacking. So, if one had to place Maria on one side of the fence only, she seems to sit better on the English side, with her mother and aunts, although her linguistic roles ought to favour the Italian.

Her extant works reach across the fence. As well as the *Exercises in Idiomatic Italian* there is her early translation of *In Morte di Guendalina Talbot* (by CP Campana), which puts into English some Italian verses on the English-born woman who married Prince Borghese, thus rendering the obituary back into the deceased's native tongue.

Likewise, Maria's 1871 book *The Shadow of Dante* represents a peculiarly English engagement with the Italian classic. Dante's name was universally known, Maria announced; but how many English readers were actually familiar with his masterpiece, the *Divine Comedy*? Her task was to elucidate the dense and difficult text for them, and the resulting plain person's exposition is, one might say, very English in its approach. She admired Dante's poetic style as much as his transcendental subject, but was forthright in stating where the text was hard, ambiguous or downright baffling.

As for Christina, on return from her sole, short visit to Italy, she declared: 'I am glad of my Italian blood';[32] while in a later letter to William's wife Lucy, she declared of herself that 'it is enough to be half an Italian.'[33]

The phrase suggests other literary figures, including the heroines of Romanticism who combine both nations in their parentage. Both Corinne and Aurora Leigh are poets, and one would dearly like to know how Christina felt about the way in which the latter (as it were) usurps her own story of an Anglo-Italian girl in England with poetic ambitions. Her affinity with the former is signalled by the use of de Stael's famous quotation '*Italia, Io Ti Saluto!*' as the title for her own poetic tribute to 'the country half my own'.

Enrica 1865, on the same theme, rehearses the familiar dichotomies in a double trajectory built on comparing the eponymous woman from Italy with 'we Englishwomen'. 'She', 'South', 'Italy' are bright, smiling, sweet, glowing, liberal, ample, blooming, summer, naturally courteous, graceful, warm-hearted, cordial, adventurous. By contrast 'North,' 'England,' 'we' are characterized as chill, dwarfed, pale, trim, correct, all the same, coldly polite out of self-regard, trammelled, rigid, colourless, chill (again), rocky. As first published, the original title *An English Drawing-Room* gave the piece a domestic setting that allows us to read 'we Englishwomen' as including the Rossetti sisters, their aunts, cousin Henrietta and friends. It adds weight to the English side of the balance, otherwise in Italy's favour, leading to the turn at the end, which, after praising Italy full-heartedly, comes down firmly for England: 'deep at our deepest, strong and free.' This is surely the land of noble Lord Nelson, of whom no English girl should be ignorant.

Telling a friend about her one visit to Italy, Christina proclaimed that it was 'enjoyable beyond words', which is a pity as we only have words to go on. Several phrases are similarly conceived: 'not one drawback occurred', 'no pen could put on paper', 'I need not exert myself to tell you', and so on.[34] As it progresses, however, this account enacts an emotional movement, beginning from an initial fear that she would not enjoy the trip at all – hence the apprehensive depression that overcame her in Switzerland, as they approached Italy. Then came the Alpine afterglow, followed by the carpet of 'unforgotten, never-to-be-forgotten' forget-me-nots on the St Gotthard, both of which in her Pentecostal manner Christina took as signs, emblems, before they 'plunged down' 'all Italy before us', and fears vanished.[35] Indeed, she and her mother were so eager to like Italy that laughingly Christina challenged Shelley by declaring 'its people are a noble people' and parodied Byron with 'its very cattle are of high born aspect'.[36] Never mind the weeds, the cattle were 'grand and beautiful beyond our English wont'.[37]

The most magical moment was the evening on Lake Como, when in the warm air she listened to nightingales singing as the boatman shipped his oars and chatted to William about Italian affairs, thereby blending the natural beauties, the language and the history of Italy into a harmony that enveloped herself, until 'that night glowed like a doubled June'.[38] This was an epiphanic moment that made its way into an important sonnet, but if it made her feel 'at home' in Italy, she also knew that she belonged to Britain. Another observation from this journey relates surprise that 'our English wild scarlet poppies excelled the Italian poppies in gorgeous colour'[39]. Both here and with the cattle, the possessive pronoun 'our English' is explicit; it is the traveller's habit of comparing abroad with home – that is, England. Worse than the poppies (and unlike the cattle), Italian pigs were also 'exceptionally mean and repulsive'; not everything in that 'characteristically lovely land' was fair.[40]

William felt that since she so much liked Italian 'amenity, naturalness and freedom from self-centred stiffness' (surely his own view), it would have suited Christina to settle in Italy.[41] She herself knew better, expressly including in *Time Flies* the moral tale of an artist who sought 'far and wide' for the perfect place to paint, settled in Italy and promptly died.[42] And while in his essay Schad refers quite casually to events in Christina's 'native Italy',[43] the poet herself, in *Italia, Io Ti Saluto!*, states plainly that 'the bleak North' is where she was born, bred and expects to die, insistently endorsing this with repeated 'Amens'. It is however a complex relation, for as fast as the 'Amens' register acceptance of a Northern birthplace, even more numerous invocations protest at the 'sweet South' being 'out of reach'. Both here and in *Enrica* the fortuitous rhyming of 'south' and 'mouth' carries great semantic value, returning us to the bilinguality of infancy.

The English aspect of the Rossettis' dual literary heritage needs only to be sketched in – to a large extent it is also ours today, starting with Chaucer and Shakespeare and leading to Scott and the Brownings. This, the literary culture on which they drew, was given expression by William Michael's editions of various English poets as well as his work on Shelley. The English literary heritage is also visible throughout the poetry of his brother and sister, though with Dante Gabriel it is more properly described as Scottish, being so much based on Walter Scott and Border Ballads, which form the matrix for *Rose Mary* and *The King's Tragedy* as well as many shorter pieces.

However, alongside this dominantly influential literary strand, and unlike most of their contemporaries, the Rossettis had a strong Italian literary heritage: Dante obviously, others of his century, Petrarca, Tasso, Ariosto, through to Metastasio, Leopardi and writers of their father's generation. Italy was hardly lacking in cultural giants: William could have augmented his political pantheon by claiming Italian poets among the 'immortals' of Europe. Apart from the Rossettis' especial relation to Dante this dual literary background has been relatively neglected by English-speaking critics, but there is scope for scholarship here, starting with the Rossettis' juvenile reading and including the essays on Italian personages that William and Christina contributed to an international dictionary of biography, published in Britain.

In regard to Dante Gabriel's own literary works, the dual political inheritance has also been relatively ignored. Politically, in his youth, England stood

for stability, constitutional rule, rational debate, national and individual freedom, while Italy was subjugated, unstable, incapable of unity, in thrall to
superstitious religion, but nevertheless and above all engaged in an exciting
political struggle for identity, freedom and unity, which as a national liber-
ation struggle demanded fervour and idealism. Indeed, many young Britons
adopted Italy's cause, for example in the Friends of Italy support group.[44]

Because in adulthood Dante Gabriel disclaimed all interest in political
matters, it is easy to overlook his passionate response to the events of 1848,
which built on those of 1831 and his father's glorious hour in 1820. It is possible to read *The Blessed Damozel*, Dante Gabriel's first major poem, as oblique-
ly referring to the Italian political struggle. His father's celebrated poem at the
time of the Carbonari resistance had been a hymn to Italian freedom from
foreign domination in which Liberty is figured as a beautiful woman with
stars in her hair and lilies in her crown, a fragrant bosom and a 'smile of realized desire'. Dante Gabriel's Damozel is cast in the same mould, with a warm
bosom, three lilies in her arms and seven stars in her hair, loosely standing
for Italy's regions. Like that of her forerunner, her desire is fulfilled only in
fantasy, as she yearns for union with the beloved.

Dante Gabriel was a child of 1848. Unlike his student friends, he was contemptuous of the contemporary Chartist demonstrators, characterizing them
as typical English cowards. Although as British citizens, the Rossetti brothers
could not join Mazzini's militant youth organization Italia Giovine, this cause
claimed their hearts, expressed in sonnets and in Dante Gabriel's most openly
political poem, the dramatic monologue *A Last Confession*, in which the young
hero boasts of killing Austrian soldiers, and plainly declares his idealism:

Italy, / The weeping desolate mother, long has claimed
Her sons' strong arms to lean on, and their hands...
And from her need / Had grown the fashion of my whole poor life
Which I was proud to yield her, as my father / Had yielded his.

The poem is a direct response to Browning's *An Italian in England*, which
features a similar hero speaking in exile:

That second time they hunted me
From hill to plain, from shore to sea,
And Austria, hounding far and wide
Her bloodhounds through the countryside
Breathed hot and instant on my trace

It must have been somewhat curious to see one's own history, the history of
one's father and compatriots, thus appropriated by an English poet. But both

poems contain a motif of idealism betrayed. Browning's narrator has brothers who 'live in Austria's pay', in contrast to the girl who helped him evade capture and who represents the Cause, her 'calm simplicity of grace' being 'our Italy's own attitude'. In *A Last Confession* the girl likewise personifies the national struggle, and the poem hinges on her betrayal of that cause, as she turns from the old Madonna, linked to the symbolic Iron Crown of Italy, to a tinselled Madonna, 'a slight German toy'. When she disdains the hero's gift, a pledge of love and patriotism, he turns the knife on her, killing his own disappointed hopes of and for 'Italy'.

'With hope deluded, valiant effort gone/ to nothingness[…]/ The cause ungained/ of Italy flickered dim: yearning and pained/ her broken voice despaired almost of dawn.' William would later write thus of the collapse of the revolutionary movement ('the temporary collapse we now know it to have been', as he added.[45]) He kept faith, but from this date Dante Gabriel was 'no particular patriot'.[46]

Some of Dante Gabriel's feeling was displaced into *Dante at Verona*, another response to Browning, as well as a tribute to Dante Gabriel's actual father, as an exiled and humiliated poet and patriot, 'esule e proscritto',[47] who similarly led 'a twofold life' physically in exile but always mentally in his native land.

> Even through the body's prison bars
> His soul possessed the sun and stars.

Looking at the Dantean elements that moved his nineteenth-century namesake to literary expression, we see firstly (and predictably) the poet-lover of *La Vita Nuova*; secondly the sonnet-swapping Florentine gallant; and thirdly the embittered exile. In *Dante at Verona*, the insults and inferior employment Dante endures from Can Grande della Scala have counterparts in Professor Rossetti's experience, while his proud refusal to return to Florence 'with humbled face', in exchange for a pardon, is an image of the Victorian exiles' staunch ideals.

If for William 'Italy' began as fantasy land of brigands and outlaws, drawn from books and paternal exploits, it matured as a site for radical political engagement with events and issues. After unification, the idea of 'Italy' ceased to hold its ideal aspect. By no means blind to this, William nonetheless retained his radical idealism, which found expression in *Democratic Sonnets*, composed in 1881–2. As the by then politically conservative Dante Gabriel remarked with alarm, these were quite incendiary, praising the assassin Orsini as well as Mazzini and Garibaldi and commemorating the Risorgimento in rousing terms:

> Red like the dripping hands of Italy

Bathed sacred in the drops her martyred sons
Have shed.[48]

Dante Gabriel's most ignored declaration of Italian identity was the magnum opus that became *Early Italian Poets*, published in 1861 but in progress since the mid-1840s. In the eventual preface, he described the book as 'the only contribution I expect to make to our English knowledge of old Italy', while modestly concluding that there was 'no great stir to be made by launching afresh on high seas busy with new traffic, the ships which have been long outstripped.' Both are significant statements in relation to a sense of dual identity, the first quite plainly so, the second illuminated by the defensive tone of the assertion that the originals possessed 'beauties of a kind' and treasures of grace and metre, despite their 'monotony', limited subject range and 'continual obscurity', with 'corrupt dialect and imperfect expression.'[49]

Here, 'old Italy' is backward, imperfect, corrupt and 'outstripped', rather in the manner of modern Italy in Dante Gabriel's youth. His translation project implicitly contested this. If Chaucer was part of England's proud heritage, Italy could comparably claim Dante and his contemporaries.

Although after the deaths of their grandfather and father in the early 1850s, none of the Rossettis inhabited an Italian-speaking environment, all continued to read and write easily in both languages; certainly Maria must have been equally fluent in both. Both Dante Gabriel and Christina chose to compose sometimes in Italian. Dante Gabriel's Italian compositions included original pieces like the song that begins '*È giovine il signore*', and two sonnets for his own pictures. Standing together with sonnets in English, the latter exercise produces a triple work of art, a painting and two poems, rather like different but related siblings. Taking into account his translations, Dante Gabriel's whole oeuvre – painting, poetry and poetic translation – forms another triad, each art form sibling to the others, different but not more favoured offspring of the same *genitore*.

It is not necessary to be a literary critic to notice how the sibling motif – brothers and sisters literal and metaphorical, together with surrogate siblings like cousins and pairs – runs through the Rossettis' lives and works. There was, to start with, their actual familial relationship, followed by the sisterhoods and brotherhoods they joined and created. By virtue of Christina's literal relation to Dante Gabriel and William, she was for instance literary sister to the PRB, within the pages of the *Germ*, and in her sonnets on the Brotherhood. In their literary work siblings proliferate – in *Goblin Market*, *The Lowest Room*, *My Sister's Sleep*, *The Bride's Prelude*, *Sister Helen*, *The White Ship*, with cousins in *Maude*, *Maggie A Lady*, *Cousin Kate* and especially *Jenny*, where the narrator's relation to his cousin Nell is matched by Nell's symbolic pairing with Jenny.

I want to end by considering Italy and England not as oppositional elements, nor exclusively as parental elements, but rather as sibling cultures, uniting the Rossettis through similarity and difference. Their sense of national identity was complex, shifting, contradictory, contingent – all those things so popular with critical theorists – but simultaneously strong, assured, always double but never in doubt.

In her aptly titled essay 'Exiles at Home', Tinkler-Villani notes how Christina inserts Italian proverbs into her devotional volume *Time Flies*, saying she is thereby present in the text 'in her own voice, which is an Italian voice.'[50] I would rather say that Christina is present in two voices, two languages and in a combined 'Anglo-Italian' voice; and that this doubling, the intermingling of Italian and English, the coexistence of work in both, and a range of allusions that no doubt eludes all but the most cosmopolitan scholar, is found throughout Christina's writing.

Her writings encompass both languages – *Singsong*, *Ninna–Nanna*, *Uomibatto*, *Il Rosseggiar dell'Oriente* – the last being the enigmatic unpublished sequence supposedly addressed to Charles Cayley. Her fiction plays with combined, complementary or opposed Anglo-Italian identities. Take the early unfinished epistolary novel *Corrispondenzia Famigliare*[51], written in Italian for English readers. The chief correspondents are Angela-Maria de' Ruggieri and her English cousin Emma Ward. Angela is the daughter of a political exile, still dangerously active: 'I'm very afraid that some political affair has obliged him to leave England', she says, 'and who knows whether some impulsive plan has not taken him to Italy?' Emma is more cautious and pragmatic, while also admiring Angela's Romantic notions. And of course *Corrispondenzia Famigliare* is a punning title – Family Correspondence – drawing attention to the fact that Italy and England are corresponding female cousins, complementing each other like surrogate siblings. What more apt for the articulation of a dual heritage?

Christina's other stories also draw on this dyad. The northern child Hero, daughter of Peter Grump (a really Northern name), who desires to be the object of supreme admiration, is duly metamorphosed into the evidently Italian singer Melice Rapta. In *Vanna's Twins*, the narrator is an English spinster who takes lodgings with an Italian couple. To begin with, the couple are introduced to her as Cole and Fanny, their actual names having been anglicized out of recognition. Really named Nicola and Giovanna, their history is partly that of their author's father:

They were both Neapolitans of the ex-kingdom, though not the city, of Naples; whenever I asked either of them after the name of their native place, they invariably answered me in a tone of endearment, by what

sounded more like 'Vascitammò' than aught else I knew how to spell; but
when my English tongue uttered 'Vascitammò' after them, they would
shake their heads and repeat the uncatchable word; at last it grew to be a
standing joke between us that when I became a millionaire my courier
Cola and my maid Vanna should take the twins and me to see
Vascitammò.

I find this deeply emotional: the 'native place' whose name is 'uncatchable' –
unspellable and unpronounceable by an English tongue – which is also a
motif of wishful desire for the Englishwoman who, when she became a millionaire – i.e. never – would visit Vascitammò, not a million miles from the
author's paternal birthplace of Vasto, in the ex-kingdom of Naples.

The narrator is a solitary, nervous, invalid and fastidious Englishwoman,
whose qualities are thrown into relief by the warm good nature of her Italian
hosts and their delightful infants – one strand of this supremely sentimental
tale being the familiar trope of the emotional refreshment of the frigid North
by the cordial South. It is also as if the characters dramatize their author's
divided identity. Or rather, the story both separates and plaits together the
two elements by incorporating the stiff narrator, with typical English prejudice against foreign food – she acquires a taste for oven-hot pasta but can't
face fried squid – into the welcoming Italian family, becoming united in the
happy fantasy of 'returning' to Vascitammò together.

Of course, this day never comes. The twins die like babes in the wood, and
Nicola and Vanna go home alone. The Englishwoman bids them farewell at
the station, on their way through London to Vascitammò, 'which now neither
the twins nor I shall ever see.' This is the unbridgeable gulf for those born in
exile: the unreachable, uncatchable knowledge of the 'native place' they have
never had, which belongs not to the real world of travel and trains, but the
inner landscape of the heart, where desires cannot be attained.

On her own return journey in 1865 – home to England – Christina was
already articulating, en route, her complex Anglo–Italian identity in the
sequence of poems that soon emerged in manuscript. The textual history of
these is a little complicated, but they tend to be run together, as they were
evidently composed.[52]

The first to be published was that on Enrica, with its oppositional elements.
The altered title when republished a little while later dilutes the emphasis on
stereotypes by giving an actual name and date and enabling William to tell
readers that Enrica Filopanti was an acquaintance who had been deserted by
her husband, an enthusiastic but somewhat cracked follower of Garibaldi.[53]
'Very agreeable, bright-natured' and young, she attracted notice for her
extempore public salute to Garibaldi when he came to London in 1864.[54] By

that act, of course, Enrica did personify Italy, speaking before the English masses at Vauxhall station.

In their movement between the two nations, the verses under her name rehearse the same bringing together and pulling apart as the narrative in *Vanna's Twins* and the epistolary exchange between cousins in *Corrispondenzia Famigliare*. Here too, England and Italy are counterparts. But with its occupation of an English room or realm, the poem at the same time unifies the binary elements. Both author and subject share the identity of the Italian woman in England. Making her home there, her presence renders the country brighter, the English language sweeter.[55] Reciprocally, she discovers in Englishness the warm hearts concealed by a cold demeanour, and of course, the national strength and depth figured as rocks and sea, the crossing places that separate and unite. In this configuration, Enrica is a surrogate sibling: England and Italy are brought together through difference.

The title of *En Route* was appended by William[56] to make a discrete poem out of three stanzas whose siblings were used by Christina for another composition. Nonetheless, it is a good title and a good poem (I am not one who deplores sibling interventions in the final forms of Christina's works) which articulates many complexities of the dual identity. And, having created it, William glossed *En Route* as expressing his sister's 'passionate delight in Italy', which suggested to him that 'she was almost an alien – or, like her father, an exile – in the North.'[57] His commentary suggests to me how powerfully, after fifty years, exile could still be invoked among the siblings as also in her text:

> Wherefore art thou strange and not my mother?
> Thou hast taken my heart and broken it:
> Would that I might call thy sons 'My brother'
> Call thy daughters 'Sisters sweet'
> ...
> Farewell, land of love, Italy,
> Sister-land of Paradise:
> With my own feet I have trodden thee,
> Have seen thee with mine own eyes:
> I remember, thou forgettest me
> I remember thee.

The feeling is one of passion and delight, but the words fail to cover the complexity of the poem's thought. Italy is blessed, kindly, cordial, sweet (as ever) and in keeping with these maternal attributes (Italy also has a lap) it claims the poet's heart and tears, all the tenderest emotions. However, this is not an effusion in the manner of Felicia Hemans or Christina's other poetic foremothers. If maternal, Italy is 'not my mother'. Indeed, like a false lover, Italy has 'stolen my heart and broken it'. Moreover, although the poet has visited the country and trod its ground, Italy has not registered this: 'thou forgettest me.' It is as if Italy were the true mother, England an adoptive one, and that on remeeting, the birth mother disclaims her daughter.

The strongest desire here is for siblings: for Italian brothers and sisters, for Italy as a sibling country. The poet says 'farewell, land of love, Italy, sister land' and only after that sequence of identities do we become aware that, in the transfiguration of earthly relation to the heavenly realm, it is sister-land not to the poet but to paradise. This is intended devotionally, but also expresses the unreachableness of the country, that unattainable Italy of the heart and imagination formed in exile.

The paradisal invocation prefigures the starting point of *Mother Country* – the title that leads us to expect a poem about national identity, not devotional yearning – which with a similar verbal shift offers itself to this same sequence.[58]

> Oh what is that country,
> And where can it be,
> Not mine own country,
> But dearer far to me.

Knowing the other pieces, we expect the Mother Country to be Italy, but here is no overt link, only a submerged connection provided by other texts, and that inferred from the congruence of dating and motifs.

Moreover, 'Not mine own country' is echoed in *Italia, Io Ti Saluto!*, where the country is 'half my own', while the language is 'half–familiar' – one of those subtle shifts around repetition so characteristic of Christina's writing. The syntax suggests a simple analogy between land and language; but 'half my own' oscillates semantically between a part claim to Italy and a division of the self into two halves. Half-familiar speech is a different register, playing both on the division of the linguistic self and on the 'familial'. The concepts combine, separate, come together again.

I am always reminded, when reading Christina's elegantly complex verbal constructions, of the legs of Donne's compasses. Or, as she herself put it in Italian:

> cor mio a cui si volge l'altro mio core / qual calamita al pòlo
>
> my heart to which my other heart turns, / like a magnet to the pole

In that characteristically 'intricate puzzle of notions and sounds',[59] the pole's submerged referent is the North: this speaker has a doubled heart.

Like the secret heart in *Cor Mio*, Christina's English-language poem with an Italian title, 'welding one whole of two divided parts', so England and Italy stand in parental relation to the Rossetti siblings and simultaneously in sibling relationship to them. As in the familial context the relation, not the gender, matters. In relation to each other, England and Italy – as familial, linguistic and literary forces – are discrete and different, but within the same order, like brother and sister. And at a scholarly level, these complex familial, linguistic and literary relations provide one way in, one key, to the verbal complexities of both Christina and Dante Gabriel's poetry, which prove the source of the richest critical rewards.

Notes

1 I use the term British to avoid the vulgar error of incorporating Scotland and Wales into England, but of course that was standard practice in the nineteenth century, and is partly unavoidable here.

2 See the opening chapter of my *Christina Rossetti: A Literary Biography* (London: Jonathan Cape, 1994), for a fuller exploration of this.

3 My spellings indicate the differences audible vocally when the names are read aloud.

4 CGR later spoke also of being trained in 'English composition'.

5 John Schad, *Victorians in Theory*, 1999, p. 8.

6 Rosy-Posy would be one of the less offensive appellations.

7 Some 1,600 London residents enumerated in 1851 Census declared themselves as being born in Italy. Though small, the Italian community was not homogenous.

8 'Charity' by William Underhill at the National Institute of Fine Arts, see *Illustrated London News*, 10.04.1858.

9 For instance, Disraeli's famous formulation of the nation as 'workshop of the world' in the House of Commons, 15.03.1838.

10 Reviewing Moore's *Life of Byron* in the *Edinburgh Review*, 53 (1831), p. 550.

11 William Holman Hunt, *Pre-Raphaelitism and the Pre-Raphaelite Brotherhood*, I, 1905; this remark seems to express something of Hunt's own feeling over Dante Gabriel Rossetti's lack of principle.

12 Iconographically, ruins were taken as Italy's emblem, standing for the long decay of a once-glorious past – or twice-glorious if the Renaissance were added to the Roman.

13 *Childe Harold's Pilgrimage*, canto iv.

14 Letter to John Hobhouse, as preface to canto iv, *Childe Harold's Pilgrimage*, 1818.

15 *Letters of Percy Bysshe Shelley*, ed Frederick L Jones, 1964, ii, p. 67.

16 WMR to George Scharf, 06.03.1895, *Selected Letters of William Michael Rossetti*, ed. RW Peattie, Pennsylvania State University Press, 1990, no. 507.

17 FG Stephens remarked on her 'very English form' in 'Dante Gabriel Rossetti', *Portfolio*, 1894, p. 7.

18 See Helen Rossetti Angeli, *Dante Gabriel Rossetti: His Friends and His Enemies*, 1949.

19 Gabriele Rossetti, *A Versified Autobiography*, ed. William Michael Rossetti, 1901,

20 V Tinkler-Villani, 'Exiles at Home: the case of the Rossettis', *Journal of Anglo-Italian Studies*, vol. 6 (2001), p. 232.

21 Alison Chapman, 'Father's Place, Mother's Space', in *The Culture of Christina Rossetti:*

Female Poetics and Victorian Contexts, ed. Mary Arseneau, Antony H Harrison and Lorraine Janzen Kooistra, Ohio, Athens, 1999, p. 236.

22 Joaquin Miller, 'Recollections of the Rossetti Dinner', *Overland Monthly*, February 1920, p. 138.

23 Sidney Colvin, *Memories and Notes*, 1921, p. 62.

24 WMR's allusions to DGR's 'national' characteristics are from *FLM*, I, p. 71.

25 Peattie, no. 600. The text is from WMR's copy, not that sent to the recipient, but the use of three words of Italian in the middle strongly indicates that the original was also in English. Angela Thirlwell also tells us that when his wife Lucy wrote postcards in Italian so the servants didn't read them, WMR expressed his preference for the 'native tongue', English. For further discussion of WMR's sense of identity, see also Angela Thirlwell, *William and Lucy: The Other Rossettis*, London, Yale Univesity Press, 2003, pp. 253–5.

26 And of course, honest. At his funeral an old friend chatted with William Michael Rossetti's son and daughters about his 'inflexible rectitude of conduct'; see Peattie no. 607, n. 1.

27 Peattie, no. 211. Napoleon, the greatest conqueror and ruler; Mazzini, 'the greatest of ideal statesmen, patriot'; and Garibaldi 'the greatest and most flawless personal hero'. Napoleon's being Corsican made him Italian rather than French.

28 DW, no. 1588. On this occasion DGR sent with his visitor, Rafaelle Giovagnoli, a letter of introduction courteously written in Italian.

29 'fisonomia tutta italiana' – see Jan Marsh, *Christina Rossetti*, 1994, p. 23.

30 William Michael Rossetti, *Dante Gabriel Rossetti: His Family Letters with a Memoir*, 1895, I, p. 54.

31 'If you wish to exchange two calms for two storms'; see John Woodhouse, 'The Rossetti siblings in the correspondence of their father', *Journal of Anglo–Italian Studies*, vol. 6 (2001), p. 209.

32 Harrison, no. 281.

33 *The Family Letters of Christina Georgina Rossetti*, ed. William Michael Rossetti, 1908, p. 184.

34 Harrison, no. 281.

35 Sonnets 21–22, 'Later Life: A Double Sonnet of Sonnets', originally published in *A Pageant and Other Poems*, 1881.

36 Harrison, no. 281.

37 *Time Flies*, entry for 22 August.

38 Sonnet 21, 'Later Life'.

39 *Time Flies*, entry for 4 August.

40 *Time Flies*, entry for 22 August.

41 William Michael Rossetti, *Some Reminiscences*, 1906, ii, p. 346. He was however aware that there was a great gulf between such an idea as a practical possibility and 'contemplating it in the mind's eye as alluring'.

42 *Time Flies*, entry for 5 January.

43 Schad 1999, p. 32.

44 In this context the Rossettis were not friends, but Italians themselves. WMR is recorded as attending a meeting of the Friends of Italy in 1852, however, when Mazzini was the speaker, and the connexion might repay more study considering the eminent figures involved in the society like Leigh Hunt and Landor. Another adherent was the painter Jane Benham Hay, a coeval and admirer of DGR, whose painting *England and Italy* at the Royal Academy in 1859 was an allegorical work showing a fair

English boy and an Italian ragamuffin. According to the artist, this illustrated 'the pure happiness of *our* children [and] the obstination of the oppressed and suffering poor of Italy.' Reviewers held the political point pictorially unproven, but it's a visual signal of British perceptions of the Italian struggle.

45 William Michael Rossetti, *Democratic Sonnets*, 1907.

46 Henceforth DGR ignored all events and positions, 'apart from a general conviction that there was no reason why Austrians should, as in the days of his youth, be lording it over Italians' (William Michael Rossetti, *Dante Gabriel Rossetti: FLM*, 1895, I, p. 411). CGR was more engaged – at least we may judge from her occasional political utterances in prose and verse that she was English enough to be roused by the massacre of Britons in India in 1857, but not so English as to applaud the killing of Egyptians by British guns in 1881. In fact, national feeling is irrelevant in her case: CGR was against massacres, by whomsoever, as in her rather unexpected poem on the Franco–Prussian War (1871), and her lost verses 'The Massacre of Perugia' in 1859.

47 At l. 373 *Dante at Verona* employs an anglicized version of this, but using proscript as a noun.

48 Incidentally, while WMR was writing thus, DGR was commemorating the battle of Trafalgar. In fact WMR's sonnets were internationalist; celebrating events around the world. But the Italian ones are especially fervent.

49 Dante Gabriel Rossetti, *Early Italian Poets*, 1861.

50 V Tinkler-Villani, 'Exiles at Home: the case of the Rossettis', *Journal of Anglo–Italian Studies*, vol. 6 (2001), p. 231.

51 Privately printed in *The Bouquet from Marylebone Gardens*, 1852.

52 WMR gives 1865 as date of composition for all. *Enrica* appeared as 'An English Drawing Room' in 1874 (actually December 1873) in a Routledge/Dalziel gift book, then as *Enrica 1865* in CGR's [Collected] *Poems* of 1875. *Italia!* and An *'immurata' sister* were published by CGR in *A Pageant and Other Poems*, 1881. *En route* appeared posthumously, edited by WMR in Christina Rossetti, *New Poems* 1896, where WMR took the title for three coherent stanzas from a manuscript with the same heading containing 'three pieces which seem to have little connection one with the other.' (*New Poems*, p. 384.)

53 CCG assisted Enrica Filopanti in unsuccessful searches for employment in language teaching in London. In Italy, her husband had believed that they were Dante and Beatrice reincarnated – possibly the germ of an idea that contributed in due course to the concept of *Monna Innominata* as a modern-voice sequence by Beatrice's contemporary.

54 *The Collected Poems of Christina Rossetti*, ed. William Michael Rossetti, 1908, p. 486.

55 To one critic, CGR is 'to some extent' herself the figure of Enrica, the Italian woman in England; see John Schad, *Victorians in Theory*, 1999, p. 8. Schad uses this as springboard for Irigaray-inspired assertions that the phrase reads as forbidden sexual desire between women, an avenue of his own.

56 See n. 52 above.

57 *New Poems*, 1896, p. 384.

58 *Mother Country* was first published on its own in *Macmillan's Magazine* in 1866, then included in the devotional section of combined volume *Poems* in 1875.

59 Valeria Tinkler-Villani, 'Christina Rossetti's Italian Poems' in *Beauty and the Beast*, ed. Peter Liebreghts and Wim Tigges, Rodopi, Amsterdam, 1996, p. 36.

2

WILLIAM MICHAEL AND LUCY ROSSETTI: OUTSIDER INSIDERS – THE TRUE COSMOPOLITANS

Angela Thirlwell

Even among the kindness of strangers, in the land of liberty, in the cosmopolitan city of London where he created a 'little Italy' around himself, Gabriele Rossetti the archetypal outsider lived in exile. He encouraged his dual-inheritance children born into a new mother country to:

> grow, grow up to patriot love;
> In you the blood and name of me is stored
> To England from Abruzzo transmigrate.
> Free you were born, and I was born a serf.[1]

From their earliest days the Rossetti children were conscious of their double cultural loyalties as they spoke Italian with their father and English with their mother: their cultural heroes were both Dante and Shakespeare.

The Anglo-Italian nature of the family was reinforced by its context within a wider cosmopolitan community in which exotic dissidents and *émigrés* gravitated to Gabriele Rossetti, a lodestar patriot in exile. In a paradoxical situation, the family was both integrated into and alien from English society. Visitors like young Holman Hunt felt a real *frisson* listening to tragic passions aired within the international buzz of the Rossetti home, such as he had never heard before, except on the stage. 'The father arose to receive me from a group of foreigners around the fire, all escaped revolutionists from the Continent [...] The conversation was in Italian, but occasionally merged into French [...] objects of the severest denunciations were Bomba, Pio Nono, and Metternich [...] Count Rosso and his memory; with these execrated names were uttered in different tones those of Mazzini, Garibaldi, and Louis Napoleon who had once been a visitor'.[2] Hunt's sense of himself as a stranger and his choice of language in the surrounding passage from his autobiography – 'refugees', 'excitement', 'gesticulate', 'sighs and groans', 'distress', 'alien company' – suggest how exotic, how non-British the Rossetti family was perceived to be within London society during the late 1840s and early 1850s.

Years later, Dante Gabriel's doctor, Thomas Gordon Hake, attributed his patient's genius to his mixed ancestry, but also alluded to the Rossetti status as outsiders. 'The family, one and all, are almost purely Italian. The father, a poet, was a Neapolitan; the mother was a Tuscan, with some Scotch blood. Rossetti may be regarded, not as English, but as one of those powerful leavens with which the genius of one country sometimes ferments that of another, to give it a new vitality'.[3] Dr Hake interpreted Italian-British duality as positive and creative but Olive Rossetti Agresti, William and Lucy's eldest daughter, felt this same duality was responsible for destructive and unresolved conflicts in the temperament of her aunt, Christina Rossetti. 'The fire was there, the passionate heart was there [...] the deep and tender family affections so characteristic of her Italian ancestry were there, but all under strict control, all mastered and repressed by the puritanical conventional strain inherited from the quarter of English blood that came to her from the Pierces [her maternal grandparents] whom my father remembered as severe and strict protestants of the Hell fire variety'.[4]

In light of their early exposure to European political debate and their Anglo-Italian ancestry, it is curious that only William Michael, the third of the four Rossettis, became in his maturity a true cosmopolitan and outward-looking internationalist. Cosmopolitanism is a contestable notion that resists stable definition. It implies a way of looking at the world that is the reverse of narrow nationalism. Political, social or aesthetic thinking may shift towards or away from cosmopolitanism at various stages of a life. It is more unusual to maintain a cosmopolitan outlook, as William Rossetti did, throughout a long lifetime. His position was underpinned not simply by theories or ideals, but by actions. From a biographer's perspective, Lucy and William – 'the other Rossettis' – present intriguing but contrasting models of Victorian cosmopolitanism, altogether different from their more famous relations. Whereas most of the Rossetti family of their generation might today have been Eurosceptics, William and Lucy were Europhiles 'before the word had been invented', as William said of his agnosticism.[5]

William's cultural and national identity was as divided as that of his siblings, an inevitable tension between emotional loyalties but one he resolved with grace throughout his long life. The blood in his veins, as he proudly told Walt Whitman, was three-quarters Italian.[6] In his youth, William looked Italianate and moody enough to have been continually in demand as a model for Pre-Raphaelite paintings, but his temperament was reserved, stoical and, externally at least, stereotypically English. But for William, the political land-scape was always wider than little England. He took an informed and radical interest in world events which he shared with Lucy, as in this letter to her on 12 September 1876 on the 'Turco-European' question:

I believe we may yet see the Turk chained & gagged in his own back yard, & his subjects kicking their heels about while he impotently scowls. England, I think, will be compelled to move – the government set on by the people (almost always better than their rulers) horrified at the loath-some Bulgarian business, & England will move other European powers – & they will checkmate Turkey.[7]

Although William fiercely identified with Italy in her struggle for unity and independence, counted Garibaldi as his 'greatest and most flawless personal hero',[8] and loved the land of his ancestors which he regarded, as he told the Italian Ambassador, as being his 'native country almost in equal degree with England'[9], he thought of himself as English. His natural sphere of operation was always England. In particular, he was a Londoner and never lived any-where else. From this secure base his political and social interests enlarged to transcend mere national issues. His lifelong cultural and intellectual commit-ments were English, Italian, American, French, Eastern European, Oriental, Antipodean and ultimately global.

Many of these allegiances are indicated in his fifty *Democratic Sonnets*, more significant for their politics than their poetry. Addressing a whole gamut of international issues, they offer a distillation of his macro-perspective. The hundred sonnets he had originally projected in 1881 indicated the inter-national scope of his political interests, and focused on public events and personalities of his own time. He arranged his subjects in national sections, in broadly chronological order, ranging from the reburial of Napoleon in 1841 to affairs in the Transvaal and Ireland in 1881.

Although Gabriel had initially encouraged William's poetic project, he soon realized he had ignited a potentially fatal fuse. 'Several of William's truest friends, no less than myself, are greatly alarmed at the tone taken in some of his Sonnets respecting 'Tyrannicide', 'Fenianism', and other incen-diary subjects,' he wrote on 12 April 1881 to the heavily pregnant Lucy, ten days before the birth of her twins, 'the very title *Democratic Sonnets* seems to me most objectionable when coming from one who depends on the government for his bread.'[10]

William replied to Gabriel the next day:

This is a country in which political and religious opinions are free, and in this very Office men of all shades of opinion are to be found. The present government is by no means a Tory or anti-democratic one. It contains (not to speak of such men as Gladstone, Forster, and Fawcett) 3 of the most determined democrats and anti-aristocrats in the country – Bright, Chamberlain, and the avowed republican Dilke. Democracy is not inconsistent with the English Monarchy: it co-exists with that at the present moment to a large extent, and is certain to advance further and further. However, I am not wedded to the mere title *Democratic Sonnets*, and if I see cause (which at present I don't) I will substitute another [...] Any idea of my undertaking to write verse about the public events of my own time, and yet failing to show that I sympathize with foreign republics, and detest oppression, retrogression, and obscurantism, whether abroad or at home, must be nugatory. To set me going is to set me going on my own path.

William considered he had previously written stronger stuff than anything in the sonnets, for instance on Robespierre and the execution of Charles I in his *Lives of the Poets* (1878), but 'nobody ever, official or reviewers so far as I know, raised any question about them.'[11]

Gabriel retired from the fray but not without some parting shots. 'I have said my say, which I felt to be my duty.'[12] Eventually William's hectic spate of poetic activity ground to a standstill. More than twenty-five years later, at the invitation of his 'half-nephew', young Ford Madox [Ford] Hueffer, William's sonnets were finally published in two volumes, at the democratic price of one shilling each, on 20 February 1907 in 'The Contemporary Poets Series'. If they had appeared when they were written in the early 1880s, Gabriel was right in thinking they could have caused a sensation and William's *Democratic Sonnets* might have been truly contemporary. By 1907 much of their political gunfire had been defused. The world had moved on and was already arming for the Great War that was to cause William deep dismay throughout his last years. But the *Democratic Sonnets* remain his political manifesto. The most con- spicuous factor of the sequence is rage at an apathetic world, against the old orders, tyranny and oppression. Yet his global agenda of human rights for all is compressed into one of the most traditional and concentrated of poetic forms – the sonnet and the sonnet sequence.

Why did William choose the sonnet form, whose traditional format could hardly be said to match his radical politics? All the sonnets are Petrarchan, rather than the more robust, homegrown, Shakespearean model. He wanted to exploit the sonnet's unique power, the control and concentration possible within fourteen lines and unforgiving metrics. Its formal discipline was a metaphor for the discipline of a revolutionary, and William had been aware of its potential since boyhood when he, Gabriel, and sometimes Christina, wrote *bouts-rimés* sonnets to order, to pre-set rhyme schemes and against the clock.

The *Democratic Sonnets* are agitprop poems against injustice, employing stark contrasts and swingeing social sarcasm. Bitter sonnets address the American Civil War, the Irish famine, the Crimean and Boer wars, the freeing of serfs in Russia, the unification of Italy, the Paris commune, the Fenians, as well as affairs in Poland, Austria and Hungary. This is poetry as polemic, more usually found in prose. William is at his best in the sonnets which condemn inequities meted out in Ireland or denounce slavery. He inveighs against English apathy towards events during the American Civil War in *England and America, 1861–1865*:

> Mourn, England. – "Wherefore mourn? Because my sons
> Across the Atlantic wring each other's throats,
> And corpses reckon thick as simmering motes
> In dusty sunbeams, and the roar of guns
> Drowns the bride's kiss"
>   […] – England, mourn
> Mourn for thyself if thou wilt not for these.
> Thou stood'st erect, the champion of the slave:
> And now thou floutest at the man who frees
> The black and fettered limbs, while blessings rave,
> Rave mid thy cheers, for slavery's cause outworn.[13]

Always a socialist and 'a democratic republican', William abhorred war and jingoism.[14] During the American Civil War his libertarian anti-slavery principles in England often made him feel 'singular and solitary in a roomful of company'.[15] At a dinner in 1866, William rebuked Whistler for giving an offensive impersonation of a fellow passenger on board ship home from Valparaiso. Whistler apparently had 'set himself to snub & insult a negro gentleman (he calls him the Marquis de Marmalade)', knocked his head against the ship's boiler and kicked him all through the ladies' cabin, merely 'because the poor man is a negro (his humorous account of the circumstances exhibited the most naïve & inveterate prejudice)', observed William.[16] He unhesitatingly asserted a whole range of liberal, minority views on racism, imperialism, republicanism and women's suffrage.

The *Democratic Sonnets* are arranged on the page to graphically underscore William's theme, the conflict between oppression and freedom throughout the contemporary world. A sonnet about outrageous treatment of the Irish is juxtaposed with one about Dickens: 'Friend of the friendless […] Illuminator of the darkest slum'. A deposed tyrant Louis Philippe, 'denounced from land to land', is placed adjacent to William's political ideal – *The Republic, 1848*:

> Republic, field unlimited of man,
> Equal, free-pasturing, and generous;
> Home of the homeless and calamitous;
> World-wide embrace unknowing of caste or clan.[17]

William deplored dictators, slavery, war and starvation. His ideals were those of Shelley and Whitman. Naturally he supported the 1871 Paris commune, lashing the festering carcass of imperialism:

> Shall the Republic be once more betrayed?
>   [...] shall the Corsican's
> Unlineal nephew foist again on France
> His festered carcass, or his changeling's grade
> Of empire purple-born? Rather than this,
> Parisians, Paris shall herself become
> Her own Republic. Here shall Freedom's cry
> At least shout forth, and roar the recreants dumb.
> Soar, Paris, if our France be Europe's hiss!
> Here live we free, or free with Paris die![18]

This sonnet brings the first volume to a crescendo of political outrage. William's cry from the heart is intensified by questions, exclamations, verbal repetitions and rhetorical devices which lead dramatically, and melodramatically, to the triumphant rise and fall of the final line where even martyrdom is exultant – 'Here live we free, or free with Paris die!' William sustains martyrdom's theme in the second volume, although his heroes are not religious zealots, but patriots who are prepared to die for their cause all over Europe and the New World. Sometimes he alters the format of juxtaposing two contrasting sonnets on opposite pages, and instead places two sonnets side by side for intensification. For instance, he locates *The Red Shirt, 1860–1867* adjacent to *Cavour, 1861*.

The sonnet to Garibaldi ends the Italian and most substantial section of the second volume. In the German section that follows, William's literary hero is the poet Heine because of his association with 'bright revolt'. Under the Austro-Hungarian heading he launches a bitter attack on Metternich, 'the despot's prop, the people's adversary', contorting his lines in response to the physical impact of stagger and stench, 'the garotte of tyranny', the 'kick which vibrates worldwide'. William invites Metternich, a 'name of nameless stench to Italy', to 'rot from off the earth'. He despises Metternich's 'impassive mask' and smooth diplomacy, and denounces Haynau, who implemented barbaric reprisals against insurgents in Hungary:

> He bared the backs of women, and he whipped
> Their naked flesh: women, Hungarians born,
> Whose crime was thrilling with their country torn
> By dual beak of Austria's eagle.[19]

In a play on words William conflates Haynau's very name into a ravening hyaena. In sections on Russia and America he raises the emotional register yet again to attack serfdom and slavery. Loathing kings, czars and Caesars, William concedes in choked onomatopoeic language that twenty-three million Russians 'the age-long-cankering collar quitted' when serfdom was abolished under Czar Alexander II. Similarly in the American section, his most heartfelt emotion is for *The Slaves Freed, 1865*:

> Black skin and darkened mind; sinews and thews
> Born to be worked and sold and worked again...
> Pulpit and law-court lash the negro down.[20]

William's heroes were the iconic John Brown, a martyr on the scale of Jesus Christ, and Abraham Lincoln, who signed the momentous edict of emancipation in 1865. When Booth's bullet assassinates Lincoln, 'America/Groans' with the author of *Democratic Sonnets*. In his final pair of sonnets, William surveys 'the Past' and tries to see 'a purpose in the ages' to suggest that 'through the old order gleams the new'. His imagery drawn from gradations of light is only partially optimistic, more suggestive of how little convinced this angry old man remained about the perfectibility of humankind worldwide.

❉

Lucy Madox Brown Rossetti's life may be considered, if not as a resolved paradox like William's, more as a description of two counter-arcs. Intellectually she moved from bohemianism to conservatism, reminiscent of her biographical subject, Mary Shelley.[21] Geographically, she moved quite literally from the Continent (born in Paris in 1843) to England for the years of her education, career, marriage, children, and back again to a wider Europe, where she restlessly trailed through her final decade in search of a cure for tuberculosis, dying finally on the Italian Riviera in 1894. She lies in San Remo today 'beside the murmurous Mediterranean' in a cosmopolitan cemetery, among Russians, Americans, Canadians, French, Italians, Scots, Germans, English and Poles, of all religions – or like herself, of none.

Lucy and William, the outsider-insiders in the Rossetti story, are examples of two opposing versions of Victorian cosmopolitanism, both of which confront issues of danger and risk-taking. Although he was always comfortable abroad and enjoyed the physicality of foreign travel even into old age, William's cosmopolitanism was essentially rooted in intellect, a matter of conscious, moral choice. For him, abroad was a hospitable place. Contemporary comments on Lucy stress the intellectuality of her conversation, the stringency of her mind. But ironically, invalidism and convalescence prescribed a cosmopolitanism of the body, a literal outlawing of her presence from England for long periods, only intensifying her sense of ostracism and isolation. Her cosmopolitanism was not a cerebral choice. It was imposed upon her by prevailing medical advice to the tubercular middle classes. For Lucy, abroad was a dangerous place and consequently aroused the most querulous aspects of her nature. William's position as a cosmopolitan of the mind, an insider abroad and an outsider at home, was easier to sustain than her enforced exile of the body.

Exile, however, also encompassed its logical correlative – liberty. In thrall to consumption, the unspeakable big 'C' of the nineteenth century, Lucy complained unfairly that 'London is very superior' to Pallanza, the little Italian town on Lake Maggiore.[22] She longed for home: 'you know I never wished to come'.[23] On the other hand, escape from the yellow fogs of home allowed her to breathe again, both physically and creatively. In Pau in 1888, uplifted by the 'the snow and cloud capped range of the Pyrenees', the light and balmy air infused her lungs, and so exalted her hopes that she resumed writing her life of Mary Shelley. Dramatic atmospheric conditions in Biarritz, where mountain meets ocean, liberated her still further so that she was able to express herself in paint again.[24]

During her twenties, Lucy had examined English literary subjects with foreign settings, which allowed her to deal with issues of exile and separation in her art, eerily prefiguring themes that were to engage her so painfully in later life. She copied her father Ford Madox Brown's watercolour *Jacopo Foscari in Prison*, 1870, which now hangs in the William Morris Gallery at Walthamstow, showing the doomed Foscari in a Venetian prison taking a final farewell from his wife.[25] The subject was familiar to Brown and Lucy from Byron's tragedy *The Two Foscari* (1821) and Verdi's opera *I due Foscari* of 1844. They also may have known Francesco Hayez's painting (1844) of the same subject, which gave a modern, political dimension to a tragic historical story.

Lucy's 1871 *Ferdinand and Miranda*, her first oil painting, was exhibited at the

Figure 1. 'The Fair Geraldine, or The Magic Mirror', Lucy Madox Brown
Rossetti's beguiling Romantic treatment of the theme of lovers, travel and
separation

Dudley Gallery 1872, inspired by Shakespeare's *Tempest.* The scene is set on a
magical island supposedly off the Italian coast, and shows Miranda, a political
refugee, playing chess – a metaphor for the game of love – with Ferdinand, a
shipwreck survivor from another country.[26] Lucy's *Romeo in the tomb of Juliet,*
choosing another Italianate Shakespearean setting, shows the ultimate closure
of the journey metaphor in death itself and the final separation of lovers.[27]

Lucy drew on Thomas Nashe's *The Unfortunate Traveller* (1594) for an ambitious watercolour, *The Fair Geraldine, or The Magic Mirror,* exhibited at the
Dudley Gallery in 1872 – perhaps her most beguiling Romantic treatment of
the theme of lovers, travel and separation (see Figure 1).[28]

When, in *The Unfortunate Traveller,* the poet and sonneteer the Earl of Surrey
fell in love with Lady Geraldine, he declared that 'her high exalted sunbeams

have set the Phoenix nest of my breast on fire'. But he was bound to travel to Italy, for which he asked Fair Geraldine's permission. While abroad, Surrey met the 'greatest conjuror in Christendom' and asked him to test Geraldine's fidelity by displaying her 'lively image […] in the glass' to see 'what at that instant she did and with whom she was talking.' The wizard 'showed her us without any more ado, sick weeping on her bed, and resolved all unto devout religion for the absence of her lord'.[29] Nashe's Geraldine was indeed faithful to her one true love, and the magic mirror reflected a tearful image of mythic female loyalty.

In her picture Lucy subtly changed the story and the image in the glass. As Cornelius Agrippa draws the curtain aside from a huge circular mirror, Geraldine is discovered, still faithful, but she is no longer lachrymose in bed. Instead she is resplendent in nature, seated in a garden of courtly love, reading by a lake. The book in her hands, absorbing her totally, is none other than *The Songs and Sonnets of the Earl of Surrey*. The poet kneels spellbound before the image of his constant mistress. Love may be changeable, suggested by the chameleon running down the top right hand side of the picture, life itself transmutable by death, indicated by the emblems of the turning globe, the skull and *Vanitas* book at the foot of the stairs, but fair Geraldine has remained ideally true to her poet-lover. Human love, suggests the artist, is perfectible, even in the face of physical separation. Wittily, Lucy incorporates not just one, but two 'pictures within her picture'. The magic mirror is the central focus, but at the top left a Tudor diamond-paned window opens across the rooftops of a timbered town, perhaps Wittenberg or the court of Emperor Charles V, both staging posts in the Earl of Surrey's cosmopolitan travels.

As the traveller knows, everything passes except love and art itself, in this case the symbolic book of Surrey's poetry, which makes a small bid for human immortality. Similarly, Lucy's own art achieved a kind of immortality, literally a rebirth in the town of her death, a sort of posthumous cosmopolitanism. For their millennial celebrations in 2000, San Remo hosted an international exhibition, *Arti Figurative tra l'800 e il '900 nel Ponente Ligure*, which prominently featured the work of Lucy Madox Brown Rossetti.

❋

William's cosmopolitanism was a driving factor in his influential art criticism and lifelong connoisseurship. His place in the contemporary British art world was pivotal, as an original Pre-Raphaelite 'Brother' and keeper of the Pre-Raphaelite Brotherhood (PRB) *Journal*. A prolific journalist, he acted as a cultural conduit, interpreting British art to a global audience and bringing foreign art, especially Oriental and French, to the attention of art lovers at home, aiming always to democratize and demystify the discussion of art. William contributed to transatlantic dialogue, writing 'Art News from London' for Stillman's New York *Crayon*, 1855–6. He co-organized the Exhibition of British Art, which visited New York, Philadelphia and Boston in 1857–8, giving Pre-Raphaelitism an international dimension and inciting debate. As a republic, America always occupied a symbolic, emotional locus in William's socio-political landscape.

One of the most attractive features of William's personality was his recognition and fostering of genius in other people. His selected edition of *Walt Whitman* (1868) excluded some poems entirely (in deference to 'a nervous age'), altered their arrangement and supplied titles to poems untitled by Whitman. For these editorial interventions he was subsequently attacked. Nevertheless, William gave Whitman his first British audience, by hailing his 'absolute and entire originality' and *Leaves of Grass* as 'the poem both of Personality and of Democracy; and [...] of American nationalism [...] *par excellence* the modern poem'.[30] Years later Theodore Watts-Dunton, Swinburne's guardian, predicted that William's admiration for Whitman would 'in 20 years hence destroy [his] reputation as a critic'.[31] Watts-Dunton was no literary forecaster. It was William's prophetic recognition of Whitman's genius within the context of largely hostile opinion that ensured his reputation for risk-taking and discerning criticism. He further extended his American interests by editing Longfellow, Lowell and Whittier for Moxon's Popular Poets series, as well as his own anthology of *American Poems*.

Within Europe, William's love of Italy was indelible, but true to his egalitarian principles he refused an Italian State honour in 1909. His knowledge of Italian was so scholarly that even his brother sought his advice on points of translation. He published his own blank verse translation of Dante's *Hell* in 1865. Encyclopaedia Britannica invited him to contribute many entries on Italian painters and, never having been a university man, he was honoured when Oxford asked him to examine Italian in 1882, and later to give the Taylorian Lecture on Leopardi in 1891, in the same European series as Mallarmé and Pater. William presented Leopardi's nihilism and profound pessimism without censure, providing an analytical, psycho-biographical explanation. For William, Leopardi's supreme unhappiness did not prevent him from being the greatest Italian poet since Petrarch. Interestingly, Gladstone had written an elegant anonymous article acknowledging Leopardi's genius in 1850, but for the politician the poet's consuming negativity and lack of Christianity ultimately weighed in the balance against his true originality.[32]

William continued to combine his Anglo-Italian cultural sympathies. He was elected to chair the jury at the first Venice Biennale in 1895 and, at over eighty, published *Dante and his Convito* (1910). In these later years, foreigners, not only Italians, gravitated to his London home, as they had gravitated to his father's half a century before. And as a final tribute to his father, he translated Gabriele's *Versified Autobiography* into English in 1901.

William wasn't just an Englishman Italianate. Aesthetically he was a Francophile too, frequently and favourably reviewing French art, from the Paris Exposition of 1855 to early Impressionism.[33] Alphonse Legros, the French artist, painted his portrait in 1861, which William liked enough to use as the frontispiece to his autobiography. William and Lucy maintained French friendships and both were at ease in the language; he reckoned he had visited Paris itself over forty times.

It was a pioneering taste for Orientalism, especially the art of Hokusai and Hiroshige, which so often took him to Paris to scour the print shops. Out of five hundred items in his personal art collection, William calculated that Japanese or Chinese works made up nearly a quarter. This early taste for 'Japonesque' as he called it, led to his full recognition of Whistler's new Oriental-influenced art, so that in spite of loyalty to his old friend Ruskin, William felt compelled to testify on Whistler's behalf in the famous libel trial of 1878. Although William never travelled to the East, he did get as far as Australia in 1897, and even hankered to bring home a wombat. He enjoyed Australian friendships and introduced Australia's adopted son Francis Adams' verse-play *Tiberius* in 1894.

Lucy and William were cross-cultural cosmopolitans politically as well as aesthetically. Sharing admiration for Whitman and Shelley, both were democratic republicans and socialists. In 1887 William signed a petition to spare the lives of seven Chicago anarchists condemned for terrorism. His subversive sympathies caused him and Lucy to allow their children to run *The Torch*, an international anarchist magazine admired by 'red' Emma Goldman, from a printing press in their basement.

Lucy's cosmopolitanism was aesthetic in the first instance and later a matter of medical emergency, unlike William's which was a cogent and conscious socio-political choice. Her pathology forced cosmopolitanism upon her so that as a sublimated substitute for her thwarted art, she frantically educated her young children to write Greek plays at five years old and to learn European languages, dead and alive.

In spite of her illness and constant domestic demands, she still yearned for intellectual pursuits and recognition in the intellectual world. Painting took up physical time, space and effort that she found increasingly difficult to grant herself. So when John Ingram, editor of the 'Eminent Women Series', asked William in January 1886 if he knew anyone qualified to write the life of Mary Shelley, William proposed Lucy.[34] She had coughed up blood during a devastating attack of bronchial pneumonia the previous winter and still coughed alarmingly, especially at night. Ingram's offer set her a new challenge and a new perspective. Lucy was drawn to Mary Shelley as a biographical subject both by chance and for other, subtler reasons. Initially, she simply responded to the commission. As soon as she began work, she became aware of its perfect symmetry.

William regarded his literary work on Shelley, the *Memoir* and successive editions of the *Works*, as well as many other selections, articles and lectures, almost in the nature of a sacred trust. Shelley's poetry, ideals, politics and atheism, all enmeshed with his tragic and romantic death in Italy, had been emotional elements in the friendship that 'melted into love' between Lucy and William when they visited his grave together in Rome in 1873.[35]

In a sense, Lucy wrote this biography to participate in William's literary life. As a parallel, she noted that Mary wrote *Frankenstein* for Shelley and read the chapters to him one by one.[36] Lucy read her chapters to William when he joined her in her winter exile in Biarritz early in 1889. Mary Shelley was not just a romantic extension of the poet; she was a misunderstood personality and a serious artist with whom Lucy could identify at an intimate level. As her research progressed, she admired Mary's intellectual grit more and more and subconsciously recognized a temperament similar to her own that veered from volatile to depressive.

In Lucy's mind, art was linked with Italy and she shared with Mary an intense visual appreciation of that country. Most of Mary's most searing life experiences had taken place in Italy, and for Lucy, too, it was inextricably connected with love and death. She and William fell in love there, but ironically, tuberculosis later made Italy a place both of Lucy's banishment and her autonomy. Lucy was able to draw on her own travels to convey Mary's reaction to Italian beauty, as here in Sorrento. 'She feels herself to be in Paradise; and who that has been in that wonderful country would not sympathise with her enthusiasm! To be carried up the heights to Ravello, and to see the glorious panorama around, she considered, surpassed all her previous most noble experiences.'[37] Lucy's response to the Neapolitan coastline is deeply felt but imprecise and oddly bleached of colour, as if the artist in her could only convey light and perspective with a brush. Mary, on the other hand, especially in *Frankenstein* (1818), is skilled at visual effects of landscape and seascape, in her element describing the elements, 'mountain cataracts, Alpine storms, water lashed into waves and foam by the wind', as Lucy accurately notes.[38]

Lucy wrote a substantial number of chapters in the French Pyrenees during winter 1888–9. She used her own fretful experience to empathize with Mary's 'passing depression […] that often comes when shut in by mountains away

Figure 2. **William at Lucy's grave, 1907**[44]

from home'.[39] When she decamped from Pau to Biarritz, she heard the tide surging and sighing incessantly on the beach. She only had to look at the Atlantic outside her window to word-paint electric storms Mary saw in Switzerland in 1816, 'lighting up lake and pine forests with the most vivid brilliancy, and then nothing but blackness with rolling thunder'.[40] Lucy experienced a thirty-hour hurricane at Biarritz, which perhaps informed her physical description of the storm that killed Shelley. 'For a time the sea seemed solidified and appeared as of lead, with an oily scum; the wind did not ruffle it. Then sounds of thunder, wind, and rain filled the air; these lasted with fury for twenty minutes; then a lull, and anxious looks among the boats which had rushed into the harbour for Shelley's bark. No glass could find it on

Figure 3. **The Hotel Cosmopolite, San Remo**

the horizon.'[41] This is one of Lucy's most effective sections of narrative, tense, precise and evocative.

In spite of her inexperience as a writer or literary critic, Lucy knew it was Mary's literary work, not merely her association with Shelley, that provided the *'raison d'être* for this biography'.[42] Mary's life was romantic, tragic and haunting, but its main significance lay in the originality of her writing, especially *Frankenstein*. Lucy's analysis of *Frankenstein* took the form of a detailed retelling of the story with pertinent commentary, unafraid to criticize Mary's awkward 'framed' structure, 'which might with advantage have been avoided'.[43]

Writing her biography of Mary Shelley enabled Lucy to cross more than territorial frontiers. Terminal illness was transcended, at least for a while, and she found fresh worlds of interest that she could actively share with William. Her cosmopolitanism of the body had taken her on a journey into the past and into Mary's creative mind.

When William returned to San Remo to revisit Lucy's grave in 1907, he did not stay at the Hotel Victoria[45] where she had died, as it had 'been converted into a Convent for some of the Nuns expatriated from France', although he was allowed to 'walk into the garden & see the outside of the death-room of dear Lucy'.[46] Nor did he choose the Royal or the De Londres, as he might have done in this Anglophile resort. Instead he chose the Hotel Cosmopolitain, as he called it, which still stands today, an emblematic reminder of William Michael Rossetti's citizenship of the world.

Notes

1 William Michael Rossetti, *Gabriele Rossetti: A Versified Autobiography* (London: Sands, 1901), p. 90.
2 W Holman Hunt, *Pre-Raphaelitism and the Pre-Raphaelite Brotherhood*, 2 vols (London: Macmillan, 1905), I, pp. 154–5.
3 T Gordon Hake, *Memoirs of Eighty Years* (London: Richard Bentley, 1892), p. 230.
4 Felicita Jurlaro, *Christina Georgina Rossetti* (London: Excalibur Press, 1990), p. 75.
5 William Michael Rossetti, *Some Reminiscences*, 2 vols (London: Brown, Langham, 1906), I, p. 122.
6 *Selected Letters of William Michael Rossetti*, ed. by Roger W Peattie (University Park: The Pennsylvania State University Press, 1990), p. 286 (William Michael Rossetti to Walt Whitman, 31 March 1872).
7 University of British Columbia, Rare Books and Special Collections, Angeli-Dennis Collection 7–6 (William Michael Rossetti to Lucy Madox Brown Rossetti, 12 September [18]76).
8 *Selected Letters of William Michael Rossetti*, p. 286 (William Michael Rossetti to Walt Whitman, 31 March 1872).
9 *Selected Letters of William Michael Rossetti*, p. 669 (William Michael Rossetti to Marchese Antonio di San Giuliano, 12 September 1909).
10 *Letters of Dante Gabriel Rossetti*, ed. by Oswald Doughty and JR Wahl, 4 vols (Oxford: Oxford University Press, 1967), IV, 1865.
11 *Selected Letters of William Michael Rossetti*, pp. 396–7.
12 *Letters of Dante Gabriel Rossetti*, IV, 1870.
13 William Michael Rossetti, *Democratic Sonnets*, 2 vols (London: Alston Rivers, 1907), I, p. xix.
14 *Selected Letters of William Michael Rossetti*, p. 186 (William Michael Rossetti to Walt Whitman, 8 December 1867).
15 William Michael Rossetti, 'English Opinion on the American War', *Atlantic Monthly*, 17 February 1866, pp. 129–30.
16 William Michael Rossetti, MS Diary, 2 November 1866, Bodleian, Ms.Facs.c.94.
17 William Michael Rossetti, *Democratic Sonnets*, 2 vols (London: Alston Rivers, 1907), I, p. xxvii.
18 William Michael Rossetti, *Democratic Sonnets*, I, p. xxxiv.
19 William Michael Rossetti, *Democratic Sonnets*, II, p. xxiii.
20 William Michael Rossetti, *Democratic Sonnets*, II, p. xxviii.
21 Lucy Madox Rossetti, *Mrs. Shelley* (London: WH Allen, 1890).
22 University of British Columbia, Rare Books and Special Collections, Angeli-Dennis Collection, 9–10 (Lucy Rossetti to William Michael Rossetti, 10 November 1893).
23 University of British Columbia, Rare Books and Special Collections, Angeli-Dennis Collection, 9–10 (Lucy Rossetti to William Michael Rossetti, 10 October 1893)
24 '3 Studies of Sea & Sky, watercolour, at Biarritz', William Michael Rossetti's 1908

Inventory Page 9 item 106 and page 26 item 476[2], University of British Columbia, Angeli-Dennis Collection, 18–4, and possibly 'Portrait of a French landlady', information from Mrs. Phyllis Marshall, The Stone Gallery, Burford, Oxon. 31 May 1997 – pictures unlocated.

25 Lucy Madox Brown's copy of *The Two Foscari*, The Fredeman Family Collection, Vancouver, British Columbia, Canada.

26 Private collection.

27 Wightwick Manor, Wolverhampton, National Trust.

28 Private collection.

29 Thomas Nashe, *The Unfortunate Traveller and Other Works*, ed. by JB Steane (London: Penguin Books, 1985), pp. 288–9, 299.

30 *Poems by Walt Whitman*, ed. by William Michael Rossetti (London: John Camden Hotten, 1868), p. 5.

31 William Michael Rossetti's MS. Diary, 21 May 1887, University of British Columbia, Rare Books and Special Collections, Angeli-Dennis Collection, 15–5, or Microfilm 950023, A.1.1.5.

32 William Ewart Gladstone, 'Works and Life of Giacomo Leopardi' published anonymously, *The Quarterly Review*, vol. lxxxvi, no. clxxii, March 1850, pp. 295–336.

33 See Julie L'Enfant, *William Rossetti's Art Criticism* (Lanham, Maryland: University Press of America, 1999), pp. 102–16.

34 University of British Columbia, Rare Books and Special Collections, Angeli-Dennis Collection, 22–4 (John Ingram to William Rossetti, 11 January 1886).

35 Lucy Madox Rossetti, *Mrs. Shelley* (London: WH Allen, 1890), p. 19.

36 ibid. p. 116.

37 ibid. pp. 229–30.

38 ibid. p. 218.

39 ibid. p. 216.

40 ibid. p. 97.

41 ibid. p. 169.

42 ibid. p. 186.

43 ibid. p. 102.

44 'Today, wh. happens to be my birthday, we returned to the Cemetery with the Photographer Scotto […] I want again to get a photogr. of the tombstone, but this time as part of a general view, with the trees tc – also myself standing behind the tombstone. The photogr. was taken, & has I believe come well.' William Michael Rossetti's unpublished MS Diary, Wednesday 25 September 1907, University of British Columbia, Rare Books and Special Collections, Angeli-Dennis Collection, 16–3, or Microfilm 950024, A.1.1.11.

45 Now a school.

46 William Michael Rossetti's MS Diary, 14–24 September 1907, University of British Columbia, Rare Books and Special Collections, Angeli-Dennis Collection, 16–3, or Microfilm 950024, A.1.1.11.

PART II

AESTHETICS IN A COMMERCIAL WORLD

3

THE TAXMAN AND THE AESTHETE: THE CANON ACCORDING TO WM ROSSETTI

Peter Mandler

One autumn morning just over a hundred years ago – it was the 2nd of November 1900 – a tall, gouty, bald and bearded old man, looking much like what he was, a retired civil servant in the Inland Revenue, boarded the 9.45 train at King's Cross bound for Holbeck in Yorkshire. At 1.30, having dined in the luncheon car, he changed at Holbeck for the branch line to Otley, where he arrived at 1.54 and was met by a conveyance which took him on to his final destination, Farnley Hall. Farnley's occupants and accoutrements were cloaked in black crape, for the head of the Fawkes family had died earlier that year, but the rest of the household – the widow, three daughters, and three sons, including the youngest two recently returned from the Boer War – were assembled to greet their official visitor, who confided to his diary that he was 'very kindly received', though his mission was a rather grim one and potentially very expensive to the Fawkeses.[1]

William Michael Rossetti had come to Yorkshire to decide whether the celebrated Farnley Turners – along with a miscellaneous collection of Old Masters, eighteenth-century portraits, snuffboxes, plate, Civil War swords and banners, and Oliver Cromwell's old felt hat – were part of the British national heritage. If they were, they would not be liable to estate duty at 8% of their market value, by the standards of the day a swingeingly high impost. Since 1896, the Treasury had been instructed to exempt from the new progressive estate duty any 'pictures, prints, books, manuscripts, works of art, scientific collections, or other things not yielding income as appear to the Treasury to be of national, scientific, or historic interest'. This was a responsibility the Treasury had been very reluctant to take on. How was it to judge whether specific works of art or other objects were of 'national or historic interest'? It was inclined to doubt whether works of art could have a 'national or historic' interest at all, much less that civil servants were qualified to pronounce upon it. But the politicians had so decreed, and obediently the Treasury had set up the machinery for evaluation and exemption. Fortunately, the man for the job was at hand. William Michael Rossetti had recently retired as Assistant Secretary of the Inland Revenue. As one of the premier art critics of Victorian London, he could be expected to know a real work of art from a fake, and a really important from a merely imposing one. As an Inland Revenue man, he could also be relied upon to be sparing in his largesse, bestowing national significance – and tax exemption – only where it was truly merited. And, his chiefs might have felt, as an extra added bonus, his democratic and republican sympathies were well known, so he was unlikely to be bowled over by toffs or too easily impressed by their possessions. [2]

At Farnley Rossetti showed all these faces. He didn't need to waste much time over the Turners – they were famous and beyond question, and in fact he had seen them already, when they were shown in London some years earlier with a view to a sale that never materialized.[3] He did look twice at a series of Rhine views that for a moment he thought might be copies, but concluded eventually that they were 'very rapid sketches in body-colour[...]without their being worked up by Turner into completed watercolours'.[4] All the Turners plus three Civil War swords belonging to Cromwell, Fairfax and Lambert, Cromwell's hat, and two snuffboxes, he decided were definitely deserving of exemption. Ten of the best Old Masters and portraits he included also, including a Magdalene allegedly by Velasquez which he thought more likely to be by Mabuse. A further half dozen he exempted on a generous interpretation, including a Rubens 'regarded in the Family as a work of conspicuous and undisputed excellence', though he doubted their taste and the picture's complete authenticity, and even a pretty dubious Caravaggio – 'I hardly suppose it is by Caravaggio, but it *might* be. A smallish picture, forcibly but rather rudely painted'. He rejected another half dozen which the family had offered up as by Correggio, Annibale Carraci and Guercino, in which he absolutely did not believe. Most of the others were small beer, but, adding insult to injury, he told the Treasury to bump up the valuations on all these non-exempt pictures by 15%, adding correspondingly to the duty payable. Like a good radical, he asked to try on Cromwell's hat – he was disappointed that it 'fit easily upon my own head, which is always reckoned on the whole a small one'; he took the opportunity to snatch some private conversation with the younger son, recently released from a South African prisoner-of-war camp, and was gratified to find they shared pro-Boer sympathies. The next morning he took an early train home. He would be back in the North in a few weeks, to see the pictures left by Ruskin (and again to increase the valuations). It was an interesting, varied responsibility, and he kept it up for six years; he was obviously just the right man for the job, but it was a decidedly odd job for the late Victorian Treasury to be doing in the first place. In this essay I hope to explain how the two, normally separate sides of Rossetti's life – the taxman and the aesthete – came together, and to explore briefly what might be the implications for the public status of art in *fin de siècle* Britain.

Rossetti was one of the lesser-known exemplars of that celebrated Victorian phenomenon, the intellectual who holds down a relatively undemanding day job in the civil service in order to support a true vocation in the world of arts and letters.[5] He went to work at the Inland Revenue as a junior clerk, in 1845, aged fifteen, simply to support the family. Over the next fifty years he crept up the Inland Revenue ladder, while simultaneously leading an almost completely separate life as amanuensis of the Pre-Raphaelite Brotherhood (PRB), guardian of his wayward brother and accomplished art and literary critic for the *Spectator*, the *Academy* and the *Athenaeum*. He almost never spoke about his professional life to his artistic and literary friends, rarely about art to his office associates. Although he thought briefly about bringing his professional and vocational lives into closer correspondence by applying for posts at the National Gallery or the British Museum, he was more concerned to keep up his income than to bridge a divide which had its advantages.[6] The only juncture at which the two worlds threatened to conflict came in 1881, when the preparation of Rossetti's *Democratic Sonnets* unfortunately coincided with a vacancy in the top-ranking Secretaryship of the Inland Revenue which Rossetti hoped to fill. His wife and brother begged him to reconsider publication. William admitted that the publication of politically radical (and, especially, republican) poems might hurt his chances of promotion, but beyond this he was – rightly – sanguine: 'This is a country in which political and religious opinions are free, and in this very Office men of all shades of opinion are to be found'. But he did postpone publication until much later, after his retirement. And he never won the final promotion, either.[7]

In 1888, rather unexpectedly, the two worlds came together at the instance not of Rossetti but of his employers. The Inland Revenue needed advice on the valuation of art collections for the purposes of assessing death duties. This was a new problem. For most of the nineteenth century tax rates had been low and most of the valuable country-house collections had been exempt because they had been treated as part of tax-exempt landed estates. In the 1880s tax rates had begun to climb, and many landowners began to break up their collections in part to meet tax liabilities. As these Old Master collections came onto the market, attracting rich French and German (and later American) buyers, art values rose shockingly and at the same time many of the unsold pictures lost their tax exemption. Thus the Inland Revenue had many more estates containing art collections to consider, at much higher values, with potentially a much higher tax liability. Rossetti, whose art expertise had hitherto gone totally unnoticed in the office, was now asked to pronounce upon the valuation of major collections submitted by executors after a death; usually this entailed only glancing over a list, but sometimes he had to go to a country or town house and inspect the collection in person.[8] After 1891, when Rossetti single-handedly earned the revenue £7,000 by revaluing the Wallace collection, he was paid extra for this work on a sliding scale depending on the size of the collection and the distance he had to travel.[9] This work continued – and indeed formed a useful income supplement – after Rossetti's retirement from the Inland Revenue in 1894. And from 1897 he was asked to take on an additional responsibility, the judgement about tax exemption that was at issue on his trip to Farnley Hall.

Tax exemption came about after Sir William Harcourt had introduced the new, progressive estate duty in 1894. When the Tories returned to power the following year, they came under intense pressure from landowners to provide some relief. In reality neither the revenue nor public opinion would brook any substantial relief. The provision for tax exemption for works of art of 'national, scientific or historic interest', which the Tories did enact in 1896, was only possible because it posed as a defence of the national heritage, a measure to prevent the sale and export of works of art that ought to remain on British soil. But this required the Treasury to decide what constituted the national heritage, and at first the Treasury was neither disposed nor equipped to make any such judgements. A few embarrassing attempts were made to employ the directors of the National Gallery and the National Portrait Gallery for this purpose, but those gentlemen proved too imprecise and too prone to strike cosy deals with the owners. It was far more efficient, and cheaper, to add exemption to Rossetti's existing responsibilities for valuation.[10]

The valuation work had involved all kinds of pictures, modern collections as well as Old Masters, but particularly the latter, because modern collections were more likely to be sold on the death of their owners and the valuation would be determined in the market. The exemption work was almost entirely focused on the historic; one of the complaints about the exemption clause was precisely that it favoured Old Masters over the productions of contemporary creativity. The criteria which Rossetti was instructed to apply were, first, whether the pictures were of a sufficient standard to qualify them for admittance to the national collections (the National Gallery and the National Portrait Gallery), or, second, whether as a collection they had historic interest as illustrating an important locality or family. Artistic interest alone was deliberately excluded. So the pictures in question were principally of two kinds –

Old Masters and family portraits. In this the Farnley Turners were exceptional, the flotsam and jetsam of Old Masters at Farnley more typical.

Rossetti was as qualified as anyone to pass judgements on Old Masters – which is not necessarily to say highly qualified. Opportunities for the systematic study of Old Masters were not plentiful in mid- or even late Victorian Britain. The National Gallery's collection was small though growing. The great private collections were only erratically accessible. Country house collections were often open to connoisseurs, but the kind of gentlemanly connoisseur who had time and leisure to travel the country looking in on private collections was a dying breed, while the new kind of quasi-professional connoisseur was unlikely to have opportunity or inclination for such an art-crawl.[11] The great private collections in London were often not as accessible as they once had been.[12] Special exhibitions for educational purposes were a new and promising means of disseminating art-historical and art-critical knowledge, and undoubtedly the celebrated 1857 Art Treasures Exhibition in Manchester set a valuable precedent. But the new municipal museums that grew up in the wake of the Manchester Exhibition's success were dependent on gifts and loans for building up their collections and exhibitions, and most of these came from aldermen and other municipal magnates whose collections were predominantly modern.[13] Without considerable travelling, therefore, the student of Old Masters was dependent upon books. Much of the relevant scholarship was in German or Italian. The illustrated art book was still in its infancy. And while Ruskin had galvanized the criticism of modern painting, the standard of art-historical criticism in the Victorian periodical press was not high.

In this thin field Rossetti did have, almost accidentally, some special qualifications. Mastery of Italian, and extensive familiarity with Italy and its own art treasures, were crucial assets. Rossetti's first visit to Italy came as late as September 1860, when he took his annual holiday from the Inland Revenue in Florence and Siena, visiting the Brownings. Thereafter he took frequent extended summer holidays on the Continent, with special though not exclusive attention to Italy. This relatively late blossoming of his Italian side coincided with a new interest in the history of art. In his early career as a critic, Rossetti was of course concerned principally to promote the claims of his brother and the other Pre-Raphaelites, for which purpose he had sometimes to disclaim any particular knowledge of or interest in Italian art, lest the misnomer 'Pre-Raphaelite' distract from the Brotherhood's mission of creating a new British art for their day. By the 1860s, however, Rossetti's career as a modern art critic was already nearly at an end; he collected his modern art criticism in what was as close as he could manage to a definitive statement, *Fine Art, Chiefly Contemporary*, in 1867.[14]

Thereafter, apart from a spell as a regular critic for the *Academy* from 1873 to 1878, he wrote little or no art criticism of any kind. But where his art criticism left off, his art history took up. From the mid-1870s to the late 1880s, much of his spare time was occupied (a good deal of it in the British Museum Reading Room) researching a series of articles for the 9th edition of the *Encyclopedia Britannica*, which appeared between 1876 and 1888. In all he covered almost 60 artists, mostly Italian, though (significantly for his Revenue work) also some British artists, including Lely, Kneller and Gainsborough. On the Italian side, he was assigned most of the major figures, including stars of the Grand Tour collections like Canaletto, Claude, the Carracci and Salvator Rosa, great masters of the High Renaissance like Titian and Tintoretto, and also figures from the newly fashionable early Italian school – Cimabue, Fra Angelico, Fra Filippo Lippi.[15] He was sorry to have missed out on Raphael and Michelangelo.[16]

This substantial series of articles – reprinted in the 10th edition and then again in the famous 11th edition, where some were revised and expanded by Rossetti's nephew Ford Madox Hueffer – represents a serious body of exposition upon the history of art, and one which must have been widely influential in shaping many people's ideas on the subject. They deserve closer scrutiny, but for present purposes, it is enough to indicate that they took Rossetti pretty deeply into the study of just the kind of art which he had to confront in the course of his valuation and exemption duties. Rossetti was characteristically modest about their value. 'My function was rather that of the "utility man" than of the desiderated expert bespeaking his own subjects', he wrote in his autobiography.[17] But how many Anglophone 'desiderated experts' were there in such subjects? Rossetti's articles rested on very wide reading in English and Italian scholarship. They showed a good awareness of the availability of examples of artists' work in private and public collections in Britain, as well as on the Continent. By 1894 he considered himself enough of an expert on Old Masters to offer to produce a corrected, annotated catalogue of the National Gallery's holdings, though he was unable to find a publisher for such a product.[18] And, as one might expect from a Rossetti, the *Britannica* articles were not shy of making judgements, either about the merits of specific artists, or about experts' and galleries' dubious identifications.

In the *Britannica* articles, Rossetti adumbrated a clearly Ruskinian taste. Titian and Tintoretto (called Tintoret by the Victorians) were supreme masters, but the early Italians got all due credit. Of course it had been his assignment in these articles to introduce great painters to those who might know little or nothing of them. Personally he remained more interested in modern art (though as he aged less approving of the contemporary avant-garde). In private, he was prepared to be pretty critical of otherwise sacred cows, and especially of the post-Raphaelite productions with which the great aristocratic collections were well stocked. On a comparatively rare visit to the National Gallery in April 1885, to see the celebrated Ansidei Madonna by Raphael for which the government had recently paid the Duke of Marlborough £70,000 to avert export, Rossetti had been unimpressed. 'It corresponds nearly enough with what I surmised of it from engravings. Colour fine; and taken as a whole certainly a work which raises the character of the Gallery. [But] I dislike the insipid face of the Virgin, and the odd pos-turing of the Baptist's legs, and I cannot but dissent from the idea of spending such a sum as £70,000 of public money for this'.[19] He had a similar reaction to the eighteenth-century portraits, which he found on the whole too smooth and glib. 'I think the very great vogue which Romney has had of late years is to a large extent factitious and silly', he wrote in June 1890 after a viewing at Christie's.[20] Even Gainsborough, who could be 'admirably pure and vital', often fell into a mere 'charming suavity of hand'.[21]

His personal predilections did not keep him from appreciating the current state of the market, and in his valuation work he routinely upgraded the fash-ionable Old Masters whom he loved – Titian, Velasquez, Rembrandt – and portraitists whom he did not, and he just as routinely downgraded the Grand Tour paintings, which in the previous generation had fetched the highest prices.[22] He was much more alert to both of these trends than were owners or appraisers, especially in the provinces; only appraisals by the major London auction houses were allowed to go unchecked, and if for large sums not even they were exempt. On certain occasions, Rossetti's valuations could be very far indeed from those of appraisers, though revaluations in both directions might in the end cancel themselves out, leaving the Revenue none the richer. For instance, Rossetti's valuation in 1894 of the Earl of Derby's collections entailed cutting down the prices of works by Giordano, Rosa and Caravaggio – all Grand Tour favourites – by as much as 60%, while at the same time six choice canvases by Van Dyck, Hals, Gainsborough, Romney and Koninck shot up from £1000 to £7280 – 'and, were they to run up a good deal higher than that, I should not be surprised', Rossetti granted to his superiors. His appraisal of the whole collection was only about £1000 higher overall than that of the original estimate by appraisers who 'have not a very accurate understanding of the value of pictures'.[23] Such appraisals required only a good judgement of the market. But Rossetti also had considerable licence to draw rather fine distinctions between good and bad examples of fashionable pictures in order to pronounce upon their national and historic interest, and also to make technical decisions about authenticity which might have linger-ing connoisseurial as well as financial implications.

In making these value judgements about portraits and Old Masters,

Rossetti exercised his discretion with great conscientiousness. In many cases he was the first trained outsider to have seen these pictures in centuries – certainly the first since Ruskin had reconstructed the canons of taste. The pictures were very often dark and filthy with age and dirt, and garlanded with preposterous attributions. As we saw at Farnley, Rossetti did not have a very high opinion of the typical landowner's taste in such things, and he rather enjoyed in his reports correcting them in their misattributions and commenting on their poor judgement. As he wrote in his memoirs, 'to judge from the quality of works collected and preserved – several fine things among a majority of others which are not only indifferent but even rubbishy – it would seem that next to none of the owners or inheritors have in their own minds a fixed and luminous criterion of taste. I have scarcely ever entered one of these mansions without feeling that, were the pictures mine, I would rearrange them so as to give due prominence to the good ones, and would get absolutely rid of a lot of inferior stuff. Sell them off for a mere bagatelle – give them away – anything rather than continue housing them'.[24] This is not to say that Rossetti's own evaluations were particularly luminous. But in their day they were firm and independent. 'I always perform on the rough & ready principle: form my own personal opinion, &, with occasional reference to books on my own shelves, stick to it', he explained to FG Stephens in 1901.[25] Eventually, of course, his judgements benefited from accumulated experience. It is not possible to be precise, but in the ten years of his peak activity as inspector of art Rossetti must have reported on well over 100 and perhaps as many as 200 collections.[26] He was therefore, by 1904, when he finally abandoned the work, one of the best informed men in Britain as to the contents of the nation's private art collections.

By referring to Rossetti as an inspector of art – never a title he held officially – I mean to point to the potential in the role he played and refined, a potential not realized by his successors. Other European countries had official art academies and departments. They had long traditions of purchasing works of art for public collections, and of evaluating works in private hands for public purposes such as conservation or export control. In Britain – liberal politically and fairly anaesthetic culturally – there was no such apparatus. Art came into public ownership almost exclusively by private donation. The status even of the national collections was only quasi-public and their trustees were mostly drawn from, or had developed close ties to, the private art-holding class. The public was not seen to have any claim over privately held art.

On the surface of it, the 1896 scheme of tax exemption might have marked the beginning of a change to a Continental-style system of shared ownership, where in exchange for tax exemption private owners would gradually cede rights to the public: restrictions on sale and export, the keeping up of conservation standards, the right of public access to view and enjoy the shared goods, ultimately perhaps outright public ownership. From this point of view Rossetti's post might indeed be seen as a fledgling inspectorate of art, analogous to the French inspectorate of moveable works of art for the Commission des Monuments Historiques. It could be seen, too, as only one of a cluster of related State interventions in Britain to preserve and take some responsibility for the cultural heritage – the establishment in 1869 of the Royal Commission on Historical Manuscripts, with its paid inspectors unearthing and cataloguing the private manuscript collections of the land; the Inspectorate of Ancient Monuments established in 1882, which both scheduled (that is, listed) and, by agreement, registered (that is, extended official protection to) ancient monuments; and, somewhat later, in 1908, the appointment of the Royal Commission on Historical Monuments, with a brief extended from ancient monuments alone to historic buildings, and again with a paid Inspectorate from 1910.

Possibly Rossetti saw himself in this light; but probably not. His personal concerns were much more for the fate of modern art than for the cultural heritage, and he would have been more interested in another French government programme, the *envoi* system whereby the State bought the productions of contemporary artists for public display.[27] Here, as noted above, he was in tune with a substantial body of opinion, including much of the best educated artistic opinion in Britain, which held that an undue emphasis upon the artistic 'heritage' might threaten to dampen contemporary creativity. Beyond this, however, it is important to remember that, while Rossetti was a democratic radical, he was a nineteenth-century *British* democratic radical, and he was no reflexive supporter of State action for anything, least of all State interference in free markets. His disapproval of the expenditure of £70,000 on a Raphael for the National Gallery, to which I have already alluded, is telling – and typical of radical (and a good deal of the mainstream) opinion of the day.

In any case, the role that Rossetti filled was neither intended as – nor did it turn out to be – the origins of a national art inspectorate. The 1896 tax exemption scheme, while cloaked in the language of heritage protection to ease its passage through Parliament, was purely and simply a scheme to relieve art holders of taxation. There was no *quid pro quo* for the public. It did not even impede export, as the result of tax exemption was to *reduce* the tax payable when an exempt work was later sold on the open market. Neither did the other, comparable schemes – inspection of historical manuscripts, monuments and buildings – develop into a public heritage inspectorate. They were all voluntary and were accepted by private owners only insofar as they offered benefits – advice and assistance with cataloguing and conservation – without fettering the rights of private ownership. This resistance to public claims on the cultural heritage was not, however, the position solely of private owners; it was shared, as I've already suggested, by many democratic radicals like Rossetti. It was not until after the Second World War – in an entirely different political atmosphere, dominated by a quite different kind of radicalism – that the rights of the public were asserted more forcibly, by imposing restrictions on the use and sale of protected property. In the sphere of works of art, restrictions were finally placed on the owners of tax-exempt items in 1950; more concerted efforts were made to bring tax-exempt items into public ownership; loose export controls were applied in 1953.

In the first half of the twentieth century, therefore, tax exemption remained what it had been designed to be, principally a tax dodge for the rich. When Rossetti retired from his valuation and exemption work in 1904, his responsibilities were divided up between the curators of the national collections. The Treasury had resisted this in 1896, because, they feared, curators and owners would collude together to exempt indiscriminately; they had been fortunate then to find in Rossetti such an independent and public-spirited alternative. After 1904, when the curators took over, the level of exemption did rise significantly – largely because the tax levels rose also and exemption became far more worthwhile. As a result, curators learned more about the contents of private collections, building up their expertise but also giving them a prospective view of future acquisitions. Apart from the curators from the Victoria and Albert Museum, however, they were not civil servants and did not think of themselves primarily as serving public purposes in this work – precisely the Treasury's fear. William Michael Rossetti had been *sui generis* – a taxman *and* an aesthete – capable of serving both masters, Art and the State. But it is far from clear whether, in turn-of-the-century Britain, there was really any call for his services.

Notes

1 The details of Rossetti's visit to Farnley, here and below, are reconstructed from his Report to the Inland Revenue in Public Record Office, IR62/19, 5 Nov. 1900, and from his manuscript diary entries for 1–3 Nov. 1900, in the Angeli-Dennis Collection, Special Collections, University of British Columbia [hereafter, WMR (William Michael Rossetti) Diary]. I am grateful to the Department of Special Collections, University of British Columbia, for supplying a microfilm copy of Rossetti's diaries.

2 I discuss the genesis of this tax exemption in greater detail in 'Art, Death and Taxes: The Taxation of Works of Art in Britain, 1796–1914', *Historical Research*, 74 (2001), 271–97.

3 WMR Diary, 25 Jun. 1890; WMR to the Inland Revenue, 27 Jul. 1900: PRO, IR62/19.

4 WMR Diary, 11 Nov. 1900.

5 At the time of writing there was no biography of WMR; the nearest was Stanley

Weintraub's *Four Rossettis* (London: WH Allen, 1978). But Angela Thirlwell's joint biography of WMR and his wife Lucy was published by Yale University Press towards the end of 2003.

6 On the National Gallery post, see WMR Diary, Jan. 1878 passim and 15 Feb. 1878.

7 Weintraub, *Four Rossettis*, pp. 232–4; WMR to Dante Gabriel Rossetti, 13 Apr. 1881: Roger W Peattie (ed.), *Selected Letters of William Michael Rossetti* (University Park, PA: Pennsylvania State University Press, 1990), p. 396; WMR Diary, 14, 17 Nov. 1881.

8 Previously the Legacy Office had used one of its own officials, MP Jackson, to value pictures in an informal way, but after his retirement in October 1887 the Treasury had refused to commission him to do this work formally; thus Rossetti was approached in January 1888, and his own role became increasingly formal thereafter. See [LN Guillemard], 'Memorandum of Death Duties (Picture, etc., Cases)', 1904, in PRO, IR74/1; also WMR Diary, 30 Jan. 1888.

9 PRO, T1/8641D/6447; WMR Diary, 17 Feb., 26 Feb.-1 Mar., 2 Mar. 1891, 9 Mar., 6 Apr. 1892.

10 See the to and-fro correspondence, 1896–7, in PRO, T1/9184C/15081.

11 Peter Mandler, *The Fall and Rise of the Stately Home* (New Haven and London: Yale University Press, 1997), ch. 5.

12 On the other hand, some newer collections were open for the first time later in the nineteenth century. For the complicated situation of private collections in London, see Giles Waterfield, 'The Town House as Gallery of Art', *London Journal* 20 (1995), pp. 47–66.

13 These developments are well summarised in Giles Waterfield, 'Art Galleries and the Public', in *Art Treasures of England: The Regional Collections* (London: Royal Academy of Arts, 1998), esp. pp. 28–44.

14 WMR's modern art criticism is amply discussed in Roger William Peattie, *William Michael Rossetti as Critic and Editor, Together with a Consideration of His Life and Character* (Ph.D., Univ. of London, 1966) and Julie L'Enfant, *William Rossetti's Art Criticism: The Search for Truth in Victorian Art* (Lanham, MD: University Press of America, 1998).

15 There is no discussion of these articles in either Peattie or L'Enfant, although Peattie includes a comprehensive listing in his bibliography.

16 William Michael Rossetti, *Some Reminiscences* (London: Brown, Langham, 1906), pp. 472–3.

17 Ibid.

18 L'Enfant, *William Rossetti's Art Criticism*, pp. 320–1.

19 WMR Diary, 6 Apr. 1885.

20 WMR Diary, 25 Jun. 1890.

21 WMR Diary, 30 Aug. 1867.

22 Though in upgrading a pair of Romney portraits in 1897, he granted that in the current inflated market they would probably sell for a higher sum still – which they did when auctioned off three years later. WMR Diary, 7 Jul. 1900.

23 WMR, Report, 19 May 1894, with itemized valuations: PRO, IR 59/153.

24 WMR, *Some Reminiscences*, pp. 548–9; see also WMR Diary, 30 Apr. 1883: 'the present race of the British aristocracy is singularly apathetic in questions of art'.

25 L'Enfant, *William Rossetti's Art Criticism*, pp. 128–9.

26 A certain amount can be inferred from Rossetti's earnings as a freelance inspector, although as they were made on a sliding scale according to distance and size of collection such inferences cannot be precise. It does not appear that Rossetti recorded all of

his valuations in his diary, omitting, one imagines, most of the paper valuations that required no visit and some that required only a dash into the West End.

27 For which see Daniel J Sherman, *Worthy Monuments: Art Museums and the Politics of Culture in Nineteenth-Century France* (Cambridge: Harvard University Press, 1989).

4

COPYRIGHT AND CONTROL: CHRISTINA ROSSETTI AND HER PUBLISHERS

Lorraine Janzen Kooistra

In April 1874 Christina Rossetti signed a book contract with Alexander Macmillan that stands out as an anomaly in the business practices of both author and publisher. She sold her copyright in *Speaking Likenesses* (then titled *Nowhere and Its Inhabitants*) for £35, thereby granting Macmillan complete ownership in her intellectual property and relinquishing her own present and future rights in its production and profits. In all other transactions for her general trade publications (though not for her religious works)[1] Rossetti insisted on retaining her copyright and, with it, her control over her work as both aesthetic object and commercial commodity. For his part, Macmillan was known to be a publisher who consistently advised authors to retain rights in their work.[2] Indeed, not long after signing this agreement with Christina, Macmillan made a presentation before the Copyright Commission of 1876 on the rights of authors in their own work,[3] and he continued to lobby for changes to British law that would ensure that 'property in books' would receive the same protection 'as property in land or in the funds'.[4] Given their evident concord on authorial ownership of creative work, why did Macmillan require the copyright as a condition for publishing *Speaking Likenesses*, and why did Rossetti agree to relinquish her rights?

To answer these questions it is necessary to examine the publishing history of the book that immediately preceded *Speaking Likenesses*, and that instigated Rossetti's brief defection from Macmillan: *Sing-Song: A Nursery Rhyme Book* (1872). Although Alexander Macmillan reputedly took great pride in the fact that 'no writer of note ever transferred [his or her] allegiance to another firm',[5] Christina Rossetti dramatically departed from the House of Macmillan in 1870 after a disagreement over her *Sing-Song* manuscript, only to renew their business relationship four years later with the publication of *Speaking Likenesses*. The forces behind Rossetti's departure and return centre on issues of copyright and control and are enmeshed in the power relations that developed between poet and publisher in the increasingly professional and international literary marketplace of the 1860s and 1870s.

Both Christina Rossetti and her brother, Dante Gabriel, published their first books of poetry in these decades of increased internationalism. British poets enjoyed readerships on both side of the Atlantic. Their books were published simultaneously (or as near as might be) in Britain and the United States, and were reviewed by the periodical presses of both countries. British publishing houses, in competition with a growing cadre of publishers for an expanding audience of book buyers, became more and more attuned to the conditions of the marketplace. In the manufacture of poetry, as of any other product, supply and demand ruled the day, and those with capital had the greatest control over the production and distribution of goods. Competitive capitalism frequently left the unprotected, unprofessionalized Victorian poet at a disadvantage. In the relationship between poets and publishers, as an *Athenaeum* writer commented in 1875, 'the balance of power [was] on the side of the publishers' because 'the publishers have the money, and the authors have not'. The writer emphasized that 'the heaviest weights in the scale are the London publishers'.[6]

Alexander Macmillan was certainly one of the most significant heavyweights in the world of Victorian publishing. In the early 1860s the ambitious publisher was just beginning to develop his London branch, coming up from Cambridge once a week to see to his business in the metropolis and to host his famous Tobacco Parliaments, attended by poets as popular as the Poet Laureate, Alfred Tennyson, and as unpublished as Dante Gabriel Rossetti, neither of whom Macmillan had in his stable of writers at the time. Dante Gabriel had hoped to convince Macmillan to publish his first book of poetry, *The Early Italian Poets* (1861), but his exorbitant demands – all expenses paid and 100 guineas down – were more than any publisher was willing to expend on a poet whose value had not been proven in the marketplace.[7] Ultimately, Smith and Elder brought out the book – but only after Ruskin had privately advanced a £100 subvention for expenses.[8] Christina's more modest expectations of an equal share in the profits after expenses had been paid were met in Macmillan's agreement to publish her first two volumes of poetry, *Goblin Market and Other Poems* (1862) and *The Prince's Progress and Other Poems* (1866). The half-profits system became their standard contract for all future publications except *Speaking Likenesses*.

The Rossettis also had dealings with other London publishers, the most significant being FS Ellis, a bookseller who had turned to publishing in the

1860s and whose list featured the Pre-Raphaelite poets. During the spring of 1870, as he was bringing out Dante Gabriel's very successful *Poems*, Ellis also published Christina's collection of short stories, *Commonplace*, and first agreed, then withdrew from his commitment to publish her third volume of poetry, *Sing-Song*. At issue for both Macmillan and Ellis in their rejection of the nursery rhymes was the cost of producing an expensive illustrated book. At issue for Christina Rossetti was controlling the production of the work she had conceived of as a composite of image and text, with an illustration on every page.

When Christina and Dante Gabriel Rossetti entered the poetry market in the early 1860s, they were well aware that the London publishers had the advantage when it came to publishing poetry, but the siblings found ways, both individually and together, to tip the scales a little more in their own favour. This was no easy feat, for poetry has never been an easy sell, then or now. While a Felicia Hemans, a Martin Tupper or an Alfred Tennyson might sell many volumes of their verses, the print runs for most Victorian poets were in the hundreds, not thousands, of copies, and the number of aspiring poets seeking publication greatly exceeded the number of readers who would buy their books. Macmillan's editor, David Masson, calculated that 'some 20,000 of her Majesty's subjects in these islands [. . .] write verse more or less respectably', while the numbers who actually bought and read poetry numbered in the thousands rather than the tens of thousands.[9]

Knowing that poetry could command only a very small corner of the market, the publisher had to determine, as Macmillan put it, 'the point where [poetic] utterance is so imbued with genius that it will command a sale'. A publisher's business, in his view, was 'to calculate what will commercially pay. Unless it will there is no reason why it should be printed'.[10] The business of poets, as the Rossettis saw it, was to ensure they had some control over the book as aesthetic object, to see that their work was advertised and reviewed appropriately, and to safeguard their financial interest in England and America. While both parties were concerned with personal profit and reputation, their individual interests did not always coincide. Thus poets and publishers became engaged in a struggle for power over the production and property right issues attendant on bringing books of poetry through the press.

In the 1860s – the 'Golden Age of Illustrated Books' – the one kind of poetic production that could reasonably be expected to command a sale, particularly during the rapidly expanding Christmas market that came to dominate the Victorian book trade, was the illustrated collection or anthology. Enterprising publishers understood that packaging sells the product, and that the physical appeal of a book embellished with wood engravings 'in the best style' could attract customers and increase sales, thus justifying the added expense. They protected their interests and limited their risks by bringing out illustrated editions only after the poetry had proven itself in the marketplace – as, for example, Jean Ingelow's *Poems* had when the Dalziels brought it out as one of their Fine Art Books in 1867, lavishly illustrated by Pinwell, North, Houghton, et al. First published in 1863 (in both England and America), *Poems* went through 30 editions and had clearly established itself as a commodity worth investing in by 1867.[11] The Dalziel Brothers, a firm of wood engravers that dominated the illustrated poetry market of the 1860s, brought out Ingelow's book as one volume in the handsome series of illustrated quartos they produced annually as Christmas gift books.[12] In 1861, the Rossettis found a way to break into the poetry market by convincing the cautious Alexander Macmillan to do what had never been done before: bring out a first collection of poetry by a virtually unknown poet in illustrated form.[13]

Macmillan was no fool. He knew that he had 'got a poet at last' in the person of Christina Rossetti when 'Up-Hill' was published to general applause in *Macmillan's Magazine*.[14] When Dante Gabriel offered to provide both frontispiece and illustrated title page for *Goblin Market and Other Poems* at no other charge than the same number of complimentary copies given the author,[15] Macmillan closed the deal. He no doubt calculated that the excellence of the verses themselves might be profitably augmented by the allure of illustrations by Dante Gabriel Rossetti, the mysterious painter whose work was never publicly exhibited. If he could bring out an illustrated first edition at no extra cost apart from the engraving fee, he might well score a publishing coup. He therefore decided to publish *Goblin Market* as 'an exceedingly pretty little volume' for the Christmas sales season of 1861.[16] 'Prettiness', he knew, was a saleable commodity. As he told his brother Daniel years before when they were embarking on their partnership, 'You don't know the influence of prettiness on even sensible people'.[17] Macmillan published both *Goblin Market and Other Poems* and *The Prince's Progress and Other Poems* as beautiful books in advance of their time, unified by the illustrated frontispieces, title pages and binding designs provided by Dante Gabriel Rossetti. It would not be until the *fin de siècle* that the promise of these books bore fruit, and first editions of poetry regularly came to be produced as well-designed aesthetic objects.

Both Rossettis gained by their visual/verbal collaboration on Christina's books. First of all, they individually enhanced their name and fame as poet and artist. Christina achieved her ambition of having her poetry published by a reputable publisher and reviewed in the periodical press, while Dante Gabriel was able to increase his reputation and influence as an illustrator. Secondly, the collaborative publications enabled them to develop their shared interest in combining poetry with pictures. As Jerome McGann has pointed out, Dante Gabriel's lack of success in bringing out his own poetry in illustrated form made his sister's books a crucial vehicle for developing his interest in 'the decorative possibilities of the book as physical object'.[18] Christina, meanwhile, though sharing some of her brother's bibliographic interests, was principally concerned with presenting her work within a hermeneutic framework that would encourage her readers to interpret all visual signs – linguistic, iconic, natural – as material symbols replete with spiritual meaning. Dante Gabriel's framing frontispieces and title pages, with their symbolic detail and allegoric import, provided just such an interpretative context for her poetry by requiring her readers to seek correspondences between visual sign and verbal signifier.

The same number of benefits did not accrue to the publisher, however. While Macmillan enhanced his reputation as a publisher of good literature in handsome editions, he also lost a good deal of his usual control over both aesthetic and commercial matters. Accustomed to giving very 'precise instructions to the designers who worked for him',[19] Macmillan was forced to give way to the Rossettis in all artistic matters. For *Goblin Market and Other Poems*, Macmillan suggested that Dante Gabriel produce 'a quaint woodcut initial – not elaborate and not sprawling down the page, but with a queer goblin, say, grinning at a sweet, patient woman face'. Instead, Dante Gabriel insisted on a frontispiece and title-page design, and initially selected 'A Birthday' as his subject for the former. When he later reverted to the title poem, 'Goblin Market', for both frontispiece and title page, he emphasized that he had done so to satisfy his own compositional requirements, not the publisher's.[20] The frontispiece and title-page designs for *The Prince's Progress and Other Poems* were also selected by the artist in consultation with the poet rather than the publisher. In fact, work had begun on the drawings while the poem was still in progress, long before Macmillan had seen the manuscript for Christina's new volume, let alone signed a contract for it.[21]

In addition to ceding aesthetic decisions to the two Rossettis, Macmillan also lost some commercial control over his firm's products. Working virtually as his sister's agent, Dante Gabriel even took such matters as prepublication advertising into his own hands, sending an advance notice on *The Prince's Progress* to the *Athenaeum* in March 1865:

> Miss Christina Rossetti will soon publish by Messrs. Macmillan, another volume of poems, of about the same bulk as that entitled 'Goblin Market' by the same lady. Like the latter, the new book will be illustrated by two designs by Mr. D.G. Rossetti. The proposed title is 'The Prince's Progress, and Other Poems'.[22]

As Jan Marsh points out, such unauthorized publicity was likely concocted by Dante Gabriel as a means of coercing the publisher to accept Christina's new book.[23] The notice was both high handed and premature. The actual

situation in March 1865 was that talks had just been opened between publisher and poet about bringing out a second volume, but Dante Gabriel had
not yet forwarded his sister's manuscript to Macmillan for consideration.
Thus, Macmillan had not even seen the manuscript yet, let alone agreed to
publish it, with or without illustrations. Moreover, the artist would not have
the announced illustrations ready for the engravers for another year. Indeed,
due to delays in preparing the woodblocks, neither *Goblin Market* nor *The
Prince's Progress* was ready for the Christmas sales season, thus effectively negat-
ing the publisher's marketing strategy and adversely affecting sales. *Goblin
Market and Other Poems*, published in March 1862, did not go into a second edition until 1865; *The Prince's Progress and Other Poems*, published in June 1866,
'left a deficit after all' copies had been sold, owing 'to [the] delay & expence
[*sic*] of the frontispiece', as Macmillan informed Christina during the *Sing-Song*
negotiations in January 1870.[24]

Christina's dealings with Macmillan over the *Sing-Song* manuscript show
the publisher eager to reassert his control over the book as both a commercial
commodity and an aesthetic object. Evidently eager to re-establish his pre-
dominance by a display of his professional knowledge of the market,
Macmillan opened negotiations by questioning the nursery rhymes' chances
for a positive reception:

> The little Rhymes are somewhat perplexing. They are many of them
> very beautiful, some very appropriate to childhood, all of course have
> merit of a high order. But the public taste in England? That is the
> question.

He then emphasized the extraordinary outlay he would be responsible for if
each of the 121 rhymes were accompanied, as the poet wished, with a head-
piece illustration. Finally, having done his best to undermine his author's
confidence, Macmillan offered to publish *Sing-Song* on condition that Christina
sell him the copyright for £35 and give him absolute control over the work: 'I
should like to publish [the nursery rhymes], and if I do I would like to have
them myself to deal with as I saw fit'. He was willing to negotiate for a limited-
term copyright, the rights reverting to the poet after three years; but he was
adamant that he needed complete control over the book during the period of
its production and initial distribution.[25]

Christina, however, was equally insistent that she retain some degree of
artistic control over her book, particularly with regard to the illustrations that
were so important to her conception of the nursery rhymes as a whole. She
had carefully prepared a fair-copy manuscript for her publisher, with her own
pencil sketches illustrating each verse, as a guide to the layout and design her
book required.[26] Each of her sing-songs, like William Blake's *Songs of Innocence*

and Experience, was to work as an image/text composite, with the pictures engaging dialogically with the text. Selling her copyright to Macmillan would result in an unacceptable loss of control over her work. Christina therefore retrieved her manuscript from her erstwhile publisher and immediately sent it off to FS Ellis, who was then about to bring out her brother's first volume of original poems. In response Macmillan wrote, not without some acerbity, that he would 'be very glad indeed to see your Poems more successful & profitable to you in the hands of another publisher than they have been in ours. You will perhaps not wonder that I don't think the fault has been wholly ours'.[27] The Rossettis, however, saw the situation differently. As Dante Gabriel explained to Swinburne, Christina 'resolved to leave Macmillan after a degree of meanness in his proposals which was really highly laughable. Ellis will pay much better – indeed I believe as well as can be managed'.[28]

Glad to include Christina among the Pre-Raphaelite authors he was beginning to represent, Ellis did indeed offer her better terms than those she had enjoyed at Macmillan's: a 'fourth part of the publishing price' on every copy sold, to be paid to the poet with every new issue of 500 copies[29] – the same 25% royalties he had given Dante Gabriel. He also set about immediately to publish her short story collection, *Commonplace*, and even began to look into bringing out a combined edition of *Goblin Market* and *The Prince's Progress*, something Macmillan had balked at in the face of slow sales and low profits. To his chagrin, however, Ellis discovered that Christina's work was not as saleable a commodity as her brother's. Although Dante Gabriel's *Poems* sold 1,000 copies within two weeks of publication and went into multiple editions, *Commonplace* did not sell well. This made the publisher think again about bringing out another work by Christina, and a costly illustrated one at that, and he gradually began to withdraw his commitment to publish *Sing-Song*.

Once again, it was the prohibitive cost of the 121 illustrations that gave the publisher his leverage against the poet. Perhaps with more goodwill than business acumen, Ellis had agreed to substitute his selected illustrator, Charles Fairfax Murray, for the Rossettis' choice, their friend Alice Boyd, a painter with no experience in book illustration.[30] He may have calculated that by hiring a 'lady amateur' he would be saving some outlay. A desire to cut the costs of a lavishly illustrated edition certainly lay behind his decision to use the graphotype reproduction process rather than the usual wood-engraving. Although hailed in 1867 as an innovative process costing 'just half the price of wood-engraving', graphotype had been largely abandoned as a viable option by the early 1870s. Problems included the rapid degeneration of the plates (they were usable only for about a month), the blurred impressions that often resulted, and the difficulty artists had in drawing their composition exactly as it was to be reproduced, for once a line was drawn, it could not 'be altered or erased, as in a wood-block'.[31] Ellis's inexperience in bringing out illustrated books no doubt influenced his selection of an experimental and unsuccessful reproduction process that had little to recommend it apart from reduced expenditure.

When the first proofs of Alice's drawings were pulled from the graphotype plates in late May, it was clear to all – publisher, artist, and poet – that the unsatisfactory impressions could not be used in the printed book. It was equally clear that the whole publishing project was now in jeopardy. As Alice wrote to Ellis, "I fancy [. . .] Miss Rossetti's little book cannot be published as woodcuts of course would be so very costly'.[32] The publisher in turn presented Christina with some 'melancholy statistics' about the costs of illustrated editions and his expenses to date, leading Christina to propose that Ellis 'put a stop to all further outlay on the rhymes, until you can judge whether my name is marketable'.[33] Production in fact had ceased for nine months before Ellis made his final decision not to publish *Sing-Song*. In February 1871 the publisher wrote Christina to say that he could not 'see his way to getting illustrations suitable to his position as connected with the best artists', offering her £35 'by way of compensation for the delay' – ironically, the same amount Macmillan had offered for the copyright a year before.[34]

It was at this point that *Sing-Song* became essentially a joint international publication, taken on by an American publisher but produced by London printers and engravers. Having tried two London publishers without success, Christina turned to her only other publishing connection, Roberts Brothers of Boston. She had originally planned to send her verses 'to my Boston publishers' if Macmillan turned down the manuscript, but the arrangements with Ellis put these plans on hold.[35] The American firm had brought out a combined illustrated edition of her first two volumes in 1866, at the same time that Macmillan published *The Prince's Progress*, and indeed with the aid of the London firm's sheets and woodblocks.[36] Christina had been introduced to Thomas Niles, managing editor at Roberts Brothers, through Jean Ingelow. Under the guidance of Niles, who opened a London office to facilitate the business, Roberts Brothers was in the process of creating a comfortable corner in the book trade by bringing out American editions of British poets. In the days before international copyright this was advantageous to the poets themselves because it gave them American as well as British rights to the work; many, like Christina Rossetti, were happy to accept the small 10% royalty Roberts Brothers offered in exchange for such security. Nevertheless, there were complications. The present state of British copyright law required that the world premiere must be the British edition if British copyright were to be secured; this meant that the production sequence had to be on a tight, and carefully coordinated, transatlantic schedule.[37]

The foundation of Roberts Brothers' success in this line was established in 1863, when the firm introduced Jean Ingelow's poetry to an appreciative American readership.[38] Moreover, the firm followed up its initial success with the first edition (manifested in its successive reprints) with an equally successful new edition in 1867. Aware of the current vogue for illustrated editions of poetry on both sides of the Atlantic, Niles approached the Dalziel Brothers' engraving firm in London about collaborating in a joint Anglo-American venture. Thus it was the American publisher who introduced the British poet, Jean Ingelow, to the London engravers, an action that resulted in the Dalziels subsequently producing Ingelow's *Poems* as one of their illustrated gift books.[39] It was also the American publisher who introduced Christina Rossetti's nursery rhymes to the Dalziels, thus causing *Sing-Song* to be produced as another of their Fine Art Books. While *Sing-Song* bears the Routledge imprint, in actuality Routledge was no more than a distributor for the Dalziels, having no dealings at all in either contractual matters or the details of physical production.[40]

When Christina opened negotiations with Roberts Brothers in February 1871 about the American publication of *Sing-Song*, it was on the understanding that the American firm would take the necessary steps with one of the London publishers to ensure her British copyright.[41] Before committing to the publication, however, Niles brought her illustrated manuscript to the Dalziels for a costing of the 121 woodcuts. The Dalziels were so taken with the nursery rhymes that they decided to 'speculate in the book' themselves with regard to the English edition.[42] In April the Dalziels made an offer of £25 on the first 1,000 copies, which Christina agreed to, 'if you will first inform me whom you intend employing to design the illustrations and if of course the name pleases me'.[43] After more than a year shopping around her manuscript, she was determined not to relinquish artistic control at this late stage. In June she closed with Roberts Brothers' separate offer of 10% after expenses. Her prospects of profit, as William Michael wrote in his Diary, seemed 'remote and meagre',[44] but she had at least gained her objective of retaining some power over the process of production. And, with the help of her family – especially her two brothers – she exercised this right vigorously, despite her increasing ill health as she succumbed to the debilitating effects of Graves' disease. Although the Dalziels had originally planned to bring out the book, like most in their Fine Art series, as one illustrated by many hands (they proposed Zwecker, Sulman and Fraser), they acceded to the Rossettis' counter-proposal that their Pre-Raphaelite associate, Arthur Hughes, alone design the cuts.[45]

As a gifted children's book artist, Hughes was a perfect choice for illustrator, well able to follow the poet's suggestive manuscript sketches in order to realize the visual/verbal dialogue she had envisioned for her nursery rhymes. When *Sing-Song* was at last published in November 1871, Dante Gabriel declared the book charming in both image and text. Although he had not been able to provide the binding design and illustrations for his sister's third volume of poetry as he had for her first two, Dante Gabriel continued to support her publishing career in whatever way he could. To ensure that *Sing-Song* got the reception it deserved, he did some of the same behind-the-scenes orchestration of reviews that he had arranged for his own *Poems* eighteen months earlier. In this case, he wrote Westland Marston asking for 'sympathetic nurture' of the book in the *Athenaeum*, adding in a postscript 'that the drawings in it by Arthur Hughes are to my mind beyond all praise'.[46]

From preproduction negotiations through production to reception, the Rossetti siblings managed to ensure personal control over all matters of importance to them – except, of course, the unpredictable market. The *Sing-Song* that resulted was a biblio-aesthetic tour de force in which picture and poem were integrated into a composite whole. Reviewers immediately recognized it as a remarkable book, and critical assessment has remained high in the 130 years since. However, despite the fact that the international release of her book gave Christina every reason to hope *Sing-Song* might be a commercial success, and perhaps even bring her the elusive popularity that had thus far not accompanied her high critical reputation,[47] her nursery rhymes enjoyed only modest sales, bringing neither poet nor publisher significant profit. By April of 1872, the American edition 'had not yet covered its expenses – one obstacle being that it reached the country too late' for the all-important Christmas sales season.[48] And in the final analysis it is capital that confers power. Lacking the ability to bring her publishers sufficient profit, Rossetti lost ground in the balance of power.

When she approached Roberts Brothers in January 1873 with her next manuscript, a collection of stories for children, the firm was no longer interested in acting as her primary agent – though they were, of course, happy to revert to their old procedure of bringing out American editions of her British publications. It took Christina another year before she was able to swallow her pride enough to turn to her 'first publisher Mr. Macmillan'.[49] Perhaps she spent the interval seeking other publishing possibilities, though there is no evidence for this. What is clear is that in February 1874, four years after her departure from Macmillan, Christina once again asked the publisher to consider one of her manuscripts. Her anxiety is evident in her awkward and apologetic querying letter:

> Dear Mr Macmillan
> I have tried to write a little prose story, such as might I think do for a child's Xmas volume, & if you would allow me to send it you to be looked at you would truly oblige me.

As a strategic reminder that her work had, at last, brought the firm and herself some profit, Christina then refers to a statement she had recently received from Macmillan's firm, indicating that the second edition of *Goblin Market and Other Poems* had nearly sold out, and was finally showing a small profit. [50]

Eager to entice his errant author back to the Macmillan fold, the publisher wrote at once to say he would be very interested in seeing the manuscript, and even hinted that he was thinking about bringing out *Goblin Market* and *The Prince's Progress* in a combined edition – a proposal that had proved a stumbling block during their last negotiations in 1870.[51] At the same time, Macmillan needed to reassert his power over the poet. He kept her waiting for his decision for two months, and when he finally accepted the manuscript, his terms were chastening. Rather than their old system of half-profits, the publisher repeated the terms he had offered for *Sing-Song* – the same £35 for the copyright that had driven her away in the first place. Once again the issue was the cost of illustrations: Macmillan was simply not willing to undertake the expense unless he had full control over production.[52] Anxious to bring out her book for the Christmas market, and with no other options on the immediate horizon, Christina capitulated and sold the copyright.[53]

While neither Macmillan nor Rossetti favoured the sale of authorial copyright in general, such an agreement was in fact a common contract in the Victorian publishing industry. Some authors found selling their copyright appealing because it meant that they received a guaranteed price for their work, regardless of sales. However, this could work to their disadvantage, too. If the book proved a great success, the publisher might make 'so large a profit over the years that the author felt aggrieved'.[54] The possibility of this may have been partly behind Christina's attempt to effect a renegotiation of the contract when one thousand copies of *Speaking Likenesses* had sold within two months of publication:

> Well, at this point of partial success, perhaps I may fairly suggest that if after all you should prefer our returning to our old system of half profits – the profits at this moment being for aught I know *0*. – I shall be most happy to fall back on those familiar terms, & run the risk of something or nothing as the case may be. I may get *more*, I know, by some incalculable contingency; but I count on no such result: I may equally get *less*, or get *nothing*. In short, if you [. . .] leave present terms to stand, I shall like my £35: or if you change to halves, I shall like them perhaps on the whole better.

Rossetti clearly prized ownership of her intellectual property over financial profit. Her attempt to exchange the old system of half-profits for the agreed-on sale of the copyright, however, proved unsuccessful.[55]

The consequences of selling her copyright in *Speaking Likenesses* gave Christina an unpleasant lesson in what could happen when she relinquished control over her creative work. While she was able to secure her chosen artist, Arthur Hughes, as the commissioned illustrator for this book, she had no further control over either the number or nature of the pictures he produced.[56] All correspondence relating to the artwork was conducted between the publisher and the illustrator. Thus, unlike the collaborative relationship Christina and Hughes had enjoyed in the production of *Sing-Song*, with the artist using the poet's manuscript sketches as a guide for his own designs, the relation between author and illustrator in the production of *Speaking Likenesses* was a distant one. For the first time since she had begun bringing out her work in illustrated form in 1862, Christina had no direct contact with her artist and lost all aesthetic control over her work. While this situation may or may not have adversely affected the pictures – Christina seems to have been happy with them, although Hughes was not[57] – it certainly had a negative effect on the book as a whole. With the power of production completely in the hands of the publisher, Christina was forced to accept a presentation that was distasteful to her – clumsy wording on the title page, inaccurate captions, and, most woeful of all, misleading descriptors for her stories and characters to make them appear part of the fairy genre then in vogue.[58]

After this dismal experience in what could happen when she relinquished control, Christina Rossetti became more resolute than ever that she retain her authorial rights in her trade publications. When Macmillan tried once again to purchase her copyright for her new volume of poetry, *A Pageant and Other Poems*, in 1881, Christina refused 'to sign the proposed Form,' stating unequivocally that 'copyright is my hobby: with it I cannot part'.[59] In *The Rossetti–Macmillan Letters*, Lona Mosk Packer wonders why the poet should have written on this point so strongly: 'Although Christina "invariably reserved copyright", it would seem that Macmillan was the last man against whom she would need to protect herself. Since 1862 he had been advising his authors not to part with copyright'.[60] However, as this account of the business relations of Christina Rossetti and Alexander Macmillan between 1862 and 1881 makes clear, the issue of copyright had long been a vexed issue between publisher and poet. Macmillan's loss of control over matters of production and marketing in the publication of her first two illustrated volumes of poetry led him to insist on absolute control in the bringing out of future illustrated works by her. Meanwhile, Christina's loss of control over the book as aesthetic object in the publication of *Speaking Likenesses* convinced her that she must retain her copyright in all future transactions. The final skirmish came with Macmillan's proposal to purchase the copyright to *A Pageant and Other Poems*, which Christina Rossetti so famously refused. But the battle lines were barely drawn before Macmillan retreated; his risk, after all, would not be great, as *A Pageant* was not to be illustrated. Having realigned the balance of power a little more equitably between poet and publisher, at least from his perspective, Macmillan graciously returned to his usual position on matters of copyright. In this and all further transactions with the House of Macmillan, Christina retained the rights to her own intellectual property.

Notes

I would like to thank the Social Sciences and Humanities Research Council of Canada and Nipissing University, whose support made the research for this chapter possible.

1 Rossetti routinely sold the copyright for her devotional works to the Society for Promoting Christian Knowledge (SPCK). See Lorraine Janzen Kooistra, *Christina Rossetti and Illustration: A Publishing History* (Athens: Ohio University Press, 2002), chapter 4.

2 GL Graves, *Life and Letters of Alexander Macmillan* (London: Macmillan, 1910), p. 390.

3 Grant Allen, 'The Ethics of Copyright', *Macmillan's Magazine*, 43 (1880), pp. 15–34.

4 Quoted in Graves, p. 320.

5 Graves, p. 390.

6 Chas E Pascoe, 'International Copyright with America', *Athenaeum*, no. 2489 (10 July, 1875), p. 52.

7 Jan Marsh, *Dante Gabriel Rossetti: Poet and Painter* (London: Weidenfeld & Nicolson, 1999), p. 191.

8 Dante Gabriel Rossetti, *The Letters of Dante Gabriel Rossetti*, ed. by Oswald Doughty and John Robert Wahl, 4 vols (Oxford: Clarendon Press, 1965–7), vol. ii, p. 409.

9 Graves, p. 170.

10 Graves, p. 194.

11 Maureen Peters, *Jean Ingelow: Victorian Poetess* (Totowa, NJ: Rowman and Littlefield, 1972), p. 64.

12 FA Mumby, *The House of Routledge 1834–1934* (London: George Routledge & Sons, 1934), pp. 72–3.

13 As Paul Goldman notes, Christina Rossetti's *Goblin Market* and *The Prince's Progress* are the exception to the rule that Victorian 'illustrated editions were reprints of works which had already proved good sellers in unillustrated form'. *Victorian Illustrated Books 1860–1870: The Heyday of Wood-Engraving* (London: British Museum Press, 1994), p. 26.

14 *Letters of Dante Gabriel Rossetti*, vol. ii, p. 389.

15 Both Christina and Dante Gabriel received six complimentary copies from Macmillan on publication. See Christina Rossetti, *Letters of Christina Rossetti*, ed. Antony H Harrison, 4 vols. (Charlottesville and London: University Press of Virginia, 1997–), vol. i, p. 161; and an undated letter from Dante Gabriel Rossetti to Alexander Macmillan in the Berg Collection of the New York Public Library.

16 George A Macmillan, ed., *Letters of Alexander Macmillan* (Printed for Private Circulation, 1908), p. 95.

17 Graves, p. 67.

18 Jerome J McGann, *Dante Gabriel Rossetti and The Game That Must Be Lost* (New Haven & London: Yale University Press, 2000), p. 69.

19 Charles Morgan, *The House of Macmillan (1843–1943)* (London: Macmillan, 1943), p. 64.

20 Dante Gabriel Rossetti to Alexander Macmillan, Monday [Oct.–Dec. 1861?], Berg Collection of the New York Public Library. See also WE Fredeman, '"Woodman, Spare that Block": The Published, Unpublished, and Projected Illustrations and Book Designs of Dante Gabriel Rossetti', *Journal of Pre-Raphaelite Studies*, n.s. 5 (Spring 1996), p. 15.

21 Janzen Kooistra, chapter 2.

22 *Letters of Christina Rossetti*, vol. i, p. 237, n. 4.

23 Marsh, pp. 298–9.

24 Alexander Macmillan to Christina Rossetti, 17 February 1870, folio 691 in General Letter Books (8 September 1869–23 May 1870), Macmillan Papers, The British Library Department of Manuscripts, Add. MS 55390.

25 Alexander Macmillan to Christina Rossetti, 15 February 1870, folio 672 in General Letter Books (8 Sept. 1869–23 May 1870), Macmillan Papers, The British Library Department of Manuscripts, Add. MS 55390.

26 Now housed in The British Library Department of Manuscripts, Ashley MS 1371.

27 Alexander Macmillan to Christina Rossetti, 21 February 1870, folio 702 in General Letter Books (8 Sept. 1869–23 May 1870), Macmillan Papers, The British Library Department of Manuscripts, Add. MS 55390.

28 *Letters of Dante Gabriel Rossetti*, vol. ii, p. 797.

29 *Letters of Christina Rossetti*, vol. i, p. 342.

30 *Letters of Christina Rossetti*, vol. i, pp. 343–4.

31 J Carpenter, 'Concerning the Graphotype', *Once a Week* (16 Feb. 1867), pp. 181, 183.

32 See 4 letters from Alice Boyd to FS Ellis, dated 24 May–15 June 1870, Ellis Papers, UCLA Library Special Collection no. 425, box 2, folder 4. I am grateful to Andrew Stauffer for drawing my attention to this important series of letters.

33 *Letters of Christina Rossetti*, vol. i, pp. 358, 356.

34 William Michael Rossetti, *The Diary of William Michael Rossetti 1870–1873*, ed. by Odette Bornand (Oxford: Clarendon Press, 1977), p. 43.

35 *Letters of Christina Rossetti*, vol. i, p. 339.

36 The use of the woodblocks caught Dante Gabriel by surprise. See his letter to Macmillan of 30 January 1866 in Lona Mosk Packer, ed., *The Rossetti–Macmillan Letters* (Berkeley: University of California Press, 1963), p. 61. Christina was also disappointed with the edition, which, by using the first proof sheets, was 'mis-printed entire!', *Letters of Christina Rossetti*, vol. i, pp. 271–2.

37 Simon Nowell-Smith, *International Copyright Law and the Publisher in the Reign of Queen Victoria* (Oxford: Clarendon Press, 1968), p. 65.

38 Packer, pp. 58–9.

39 Dalziel, *The Brothers Dalziel: A Record of Fifty Years' Work, 1840–1890* (London: Methuen, 1901), p. 234.

40 There is no entry for *Sing-Song* in the Routledge Publication Book #9 (1866–1889), vol. 4, which gives details of print and binding orders, paper costs, reprinting dates and advertising. The book is advertised, however, in the Routledge catalogue for 1872. Routledge Archive no. 215, The Archives of Routledge and Kegan Paul, University College, London.

41 *The Diary of William Michael Rossetti*, p. 44.

42 *Ibid.*, pp. 51, 56, 58.

43 *Letters of Christina Rossetti*, vol. i, p. 369.

44 *The Diary of William Michael Rossetti*, p. 72.

45 *Letters of Christina Rossetti*, vol. i, pp. 369–70; and *The Diary of William Michael Rossetti*, p. 63. During this period of ill health, William carried out business transactions on Christina's behalf. William did, of course, consult fully with Christina before making any proposals to the Dalziels.

46 Dante Gabriel Rossetti to Westland Marston, 21 November 1871. Unpublished letter in The Christina Rossetti Collection of Mary Louise and Frederick E Maser, Bryn Mawr College. Marston's review was published (anonymously) in the *Athenaeum* on 6 January 1872.

47 See the letter from Roberts Brothers to William Michael, printed in *Letters of Dante Gabriel Rossetti*, vol. iii, p. 924, n. 4.

48 *The Diary of William Michael Rossetti*, p. 185.

49 *Letters of Christina Rossetti*, vol. i, pp. 418–19.

50 *Letters of Christina Rossetti*, vol. ii, pp. 6–7.

51 *Ibid.*, p. 7.

52 Alexander Macmillan to Christina Rossetti, 18 April 1874 in the Letter Book for 1874, Macmillan Papers, The British Library Department of Manuscripts, Add. MS 55395.

53 *Letters of Christina Rossetti*, vol. ii, pp. 9–10.

54 Nowell-Smith, p. 51.

55 *Letters of Christina Rossetti*, vol. ii, pp. 38–9.

56 *Ibid.*, p. 15.

57 In sending a presentation copy to Dante Gabriel on the publication of *Speaking Likenesses*, Christina wrote 'I hope Mr Hughes will meet with your approval, even if you skip my text' (*Letters of Christina Rossetti*, vol. ii, p. 29). Hughes, however, did not give his own work full approval. On hearing of Christina's death in 1894 he wrote: 'I like to think I did the "Sing Song" [. . .] and regret dreadfully that I did not make better drawings to the *Speaking Likenesses*'. Quoted in Leonard Roberts, ed., *Arthur Hughes: His Life and Works. A Catalogue Raisonné* (Woodbridge, Suffolk: Antique Collectors' Club, 1997), p. 27.

58 *Letters of Christina Rossetti*, vol. ii, pp. 30–1. See also Janzen Kooistra, Chapter 3.

59 *Letters of Christina Rossetti*, vol. ii, p. 269.

60 Packer, p. 134. See also *Ibid.*, n. 1.

5

RECOLLECTIONS OF PB SHELLEY: WILLIAM MICHAEL ROSSETTI, POLITICAL COMMITMENT AND LITERARY CAPITAL

Michelle Hawley

In 1917, Richard Garnett observed of William Michael Rossetti that 'perhaps no man of his day ha[d] been more constantly before the public as a man of letters.'[1] Indeed, a quick review of his many and various contributions suffices to demonstrate Garnett's point. During the brief period 1871–3, covered in William Michael Rossetti's diaries, he introduced Whitman to England, helped establish Blake's and Shelley's reputations, defended Swinburne's *Poems and Ballads* and edited numerous volumes of *Moxon's* series of Popular Poets. He edited both Dante Gabriel Rossetti's and Christina Rossetti's work, helped to manage their careers, and provided emotional and financial support for the Rossetti family.

Despite his centrality in English letters and his significance within the Rossetti household and pre-Raphaelite circle, William Michael Rossetti remains a shadowy figure. The critical consensus is that 'the third Rossetti' was a 'distressed pedant' producing 'barren superfluity' and of interest primarily for his supporting position in an all-star cast of Pre-Raphaelite poets and painters.[2] Indeed, William Michael is a marginal figure for a variety of reasons. His literary and political interests do not map neatly onto prevailing narratives of nineteenth-century aesthetics or Pre-Raphaelitism. Typical of these narratives is the line taken by Peter Burger, who argues that by the late nineteenth-century art 'abandoned' its political content 'in the name of aesthetic autonomy.'[3] Or as Terry Eagleton laments, 'aesthetics is born at the moment of art's effective demise as a political force, flourishes on the corpse of its social relevance'.[4] Such a narrative seems to aptly describe the changing political orientation of the Pre-Raphaelite Brotherhood: in 1848, the brotherhood appeared radical, anti-institutional and inter-national; but by 1890, it had become associated with commodity culture, English art and its attendant insularity. The so-called Fleshly School Controversy, which erupted in 1871 when Robert Buchanan condemned the Rossetti circle for its coterie and elitism, underlines the extent to which many perceived that aesthetics was increasingly retreating into an autonomous sphere.

A brief survey of William Michael Rossetti's work, however, complicates such stories. A political radical, he supported the North in the American Civil War, considered himself to be a republican and sympathized with the Paris Commune in 1871. Over the course of thirty years, he worked on a series of *Democratic Sonnets* which he withheld from publication after his family expressed concern that their political radicalism might jeopardize his government post. Not only have his politics failed to interest literary critics but his poetry has provoked little interest because its virtues have seemed to lie primarily in the novelty of its political sentiments. As his most sympathetic critic, Walter Arinshtein, noted in his extensive consideration of Rossetti's *Democratic Sonnets*, 'the sequence of poems is less of interest for literary than historical reasons; namely, they are unusual in that they express radical sentiments rarely found in poetry between the eve of Chartism and the dawn of socialism'.[5]

Although William Michael's political interests seem to diverge from the central tendencies of Pre-Raphaelitism, a closer look at his editorial work on Shelley reveals that his political poetry is informed by one of the central problems of Pre-Raphaelite aestheticism, namely the difficulties of carrying out the romantic project in the late nineteenth century. In particular, Pre-Raphaelitism registers a felt tension between the romantic idealism of its subjects on the one hand and a heightened awareness of art's commodification on the other. As Jerome McGann has explained in a significant essay on Dante Gabriel Rossetti's poetry and painting, Rossetti explored the significance of imaginative work in an image of mechanical reproduction, in an age where ' the best that has been known and thought in the world' is seen to be quite literally a product, the output of what we now call the 'culture' of the 'consciousness' industries.[6] Similarly, William Michael's work on Shelley registers a felt tension between the political idealism he admired in Shelleyan romanticism and his participation in the emerging Shelley industry, whose object was to produce cultural capital and profit from the new market for collectible first editions. William Michael stood at, and indeed helped to create, a crossroads where the popular and radical romanticism of the early nineteenth century was reinvented as a cultural commodity and institutionalized as English romantic literature.

This essay will show how William Michael shaped a textual field that accommodated his seemingly divergent commitments to political radicalism

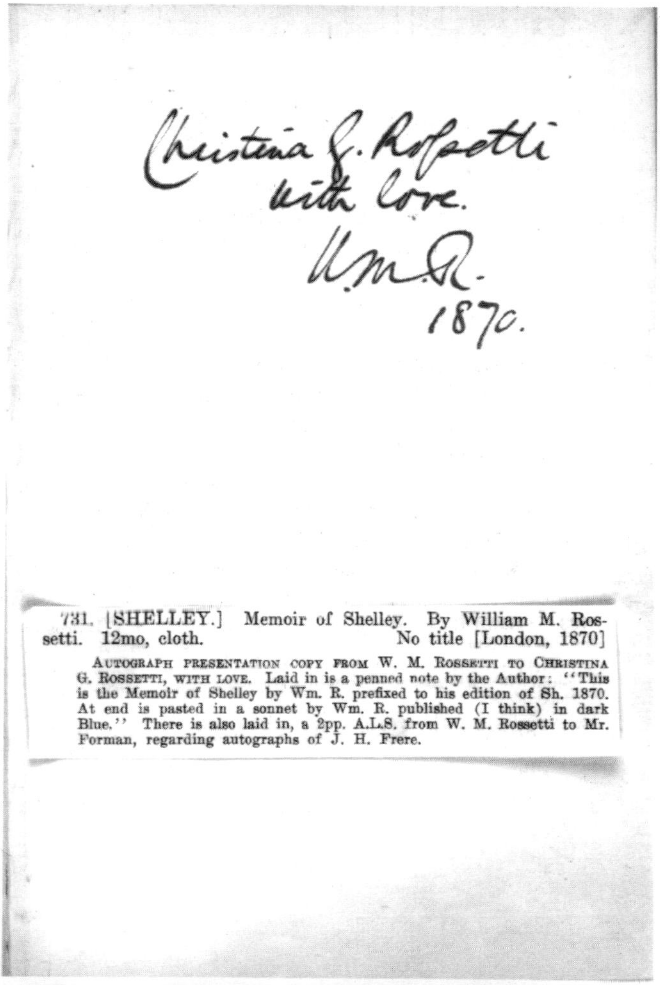
Christina G. Rossetti
with love.
W.M.R.
1870.

731. [SHELLEY.] Memoir of Shelley. By William M. Rossetti. 12mo, cloth. No title [London, 1870]

AUTOGRAPH PRESENTATION COPY FROM W. M. ROSSETTI TO CHRISTINA G. ROSSETTI, WITH LOVE. Laid in is a penned note by the Author: "This is the Memoir of Shelley by Wm. R. prefixed to his edition of Sh. 1870. At end is pasted in a sonnet by Wm. R. published (I think) in dark Blue." There is also laid in, a 2pp. A.L.S. from W. M. Rossetti to Mr. Forman, regarding autographs of J. H. Frere.

Figure 4.* Dedication to Christina Rossetti, from William Michael's 1870 *Memoir of Shelley

and to the aestheticization of romanticism. In order to map out the contours of this textual field, I will track several moments in the life of a particular copy of William Michael's *Memoirs of Shelley*, developing a story about how it participates in two opposing movements of a dialectic. The *Memoir*, published in 1870, was a reprint of William Michael's preface to the 1870 edition of *Moxon's Shelley*. This edition was first given to Christina Rossetti by William Michael (see Figure 4). It then passed into the library of William Buxton Forman, book collector, editor and forger of romantic and Victorian texts;

The figure that you here see put
Was for H. Buxton Forman cut,
Amid his household gods to bide
And relics culled from far and wide.
This book is his on whom you look,
For Scott his graving tackle took

And etched the man to watch therein.
That none by guile the book might win.
Then note far! of great and small
The world holds books enough for all.
Of roughly handling this beware,
And put it in its place with care.

Figure 5. **Bookplate from William Michael Rossetti's** *Memoir of Shelley*

and finally ended up in the collections of Henry Huntington. On the inside
front cover, Buxton Forman had pasted his own private library bookplate (see
Figure 5).

On the last page, he had affixed a copy of William Michael Rossetti's
sonnet, 'Shelley's Heart'. The first section examines 'Shelley's Heart' as a
speculation on the afterlife of romanticism in the last third of the nineteenth

century. The second section focuses on how Rossetti's editing of Shelley and collecting of Shelleyana participated in the process by which romantic writers became cultural capital. That is to say, they were detached and abstracted from their political context and circulated as signs of national identity, literary taste and bourgeois individualism. The third section explores how Shelley signified a repoliticized romanticism for Rossetti and English republicanism in 1870. The final section concludes by linking William Michael's aesthetics to the issues that sparked the Fleshly School controversy in 1871.

1. Shelley's Heart

The theme and location of 'Shelley's Heart', pasted into the last page of Buxton Forman's edition of the *Memoir*, present in microcosm the historical and aesthetic problem that, as we shall see, plays itself out in the longer history of the *Memoir* as a whole. One of the first sonnets Rossetti had written for his projected cycle of *Democratic Sonnets*, 'Shelley's Heart', speculates on the after-life of Shelleyan romanticism.[7] Since the *Democratic Sonnets* were not published in his lifetime, however, 'Shelley's Heart' stands alone, a fragment collected and framed within Buxton Forman's collection, where its original political undertones are buried and muted. The poem itself might be said to reflect on the status of its own reception, on the dangers of removing Shelley's heart from its poetic corpus:

> Trelawny's hand, which held'st the sacred heart,
> The heart of Shelley, and hast felt the fire
> Wherein the drossier framework of that lyre
> Of heaven and earth was molten—but its part
> Immortal echoes always, and shall dart
> Pangs of keen love to human souls, and dire
> Ecstatic sorrow of joy, as higher and higher
> They mount to know thee, Shelley, what thou art—
> Trelawny's hand, did then the outward burn
> As once the inward? O cor cordium,
> Which wast a spirit of love, and now a clot,
> What other other flame was wont to come
> Lambent from thee to fainter hearts, and turn—
> Red like thy death-pyre's heat—their lukewarmth hot!

The situation of the macabre poem is the legendary occasion when Edward Trelawny, friend and memoirist of Shelley and Byron, was rumoured to have snatched Shelley's heart from the 'funeral pyre'. The afterlife of Shelley's heart is no less grotesque; Trelawny eventually gave it to Mary Shelley, who kept it as a bookmark in *Adonais*.[8] Not surprisingly, when Rossetti submitted the poem to *The Fortnightly Review*, John Morley rejected it for reasons which Rossetti takes issue with in his diary: 'Morley wouldn't stand my Shelley sonnet. Professes to think it "very perfect" in execution but "terribly physical" in idea. On confess this objection… does not particularly impress me'.[9] Indeed, much of William Michael's early poetry seemed to dwell on what Morley describes as the 'terribly physical'. 'Mrs. Holmes Grey', for instance, tells the story of a physician's wife who leaves her husband to pursue another man. When Mrs. Holmes Grey is rejected, she dies of apoplexy, leaving her husband to spin out fantasies of revenge. At the end of the poem, Rossetti dwells on the lurid aspects of Mr. Gray's revenge fantasies and on the morbid and detailed descriptions of his wife's corpse in an open coffin. The 'ultra-realistic' style of 'Mrs. Holmes Grey' borders on 'the point of grotesqueness'; Rossetti's use of the physical remains of 'Mrs. Holmes Grey' thus helps make 'Mrs. Holmes Grey' into what Roll-Hansen and Fredeman have identified as a 'key poem' for Pre-Raphaelitism more generally.[10]

Rossetti's contemplation of the 'terribly physical' in 'Shelley's Heart' is similarly central to his aesthetic agenda. Where 'Mrs. Holmes Grey' reflects on the fate of romanticism in the age of realism, 'Shelley's Heart' reflects on the relics of romanticism, unflinchingly considering the material artifacts that convey and/or compromise its legacy. In more general terms, Rossetti's sonnet reflects on the contradictions that structure his commitment to radical romanticism amidst an age of aestheticism in which literary value was increasingly subject to the pressures of the literary marketplace and late-nineteenth-century capitalism. In considering the afterlife of Shelley's heart, the sonnet poses a Shelleyan question about the possibility of poetic incarnation. The formal organization of the poem highlights questions about incarnation as it moves from the material realm in the first stanza, which meditates on the physical remains of Shelley and on Trelawny's sensations as he retrieves the heart, to the second, which speculates on the possibility of transcendence. Linking the two separate realms and stanzas is the enjambment in line 4, 'its part/ Immortal echoes always, and shall dart'. The syntax carries the reader over the line break between the stanzas, enacting a leap of faith from the material realm towards the moment of transcendent immortality and metaphoric transformation. However, the hyperbaton 'part/immortal' creates an awkward pause after 'part', perhaps suggesting hesitation, indicating that a lack of faith belies the leap of faith. There are other moments of poetic clumsiness that might alternately be read as appropriate to the theme of the poem. For instance, the substitution of a dactyl for an iamb in the last meter of the final line, 'lukewarm hot', makes for an awkward crescendo and rhymes with 'clot', perhaps the most unromantic word in the poem. Whether intentional or not, these moments certainly foreground the gulf between Rossetti's poetic aspiration and the fumbling, fallen, human world in which poetry is composed and read.

On one level, 'Shelley's Heart' rehearses a Shelleyan question about the possibility of 'poetic incarnation', considering the survival of poetic inspiration in something that has been separated from its origins. As the poet in 'Shelley's Heart' 'ascends higher and higher' in his quest to know 'Shelley, what thou art', he retraces Shelley's own analogical quest to represent the ideal in 'Ode To a Skylark', 'what thou art we know not'. However, where 'To a Skylark' performs an idealist reflection on how poetry falls short of its aspirations because it is subject to the limits of language and human consciousness, 'Shelley's Heart' might be seen as a materialist reflection on the afterlife of romantic poetry in a Victorian culture of things.

2. Collections

William Michael was an avid collector of all things related to Shelley, many of which he received from the very Trelawny who is the subject of his address in 'Shelley's heart'. In his *Reminiscences* he catalogues his Shelley collection with unabashed relish:

> [Trelawny] gave me his own copy of the privately printed Queen Mab, a strange and precious relic, a fragment of Shelley's charred skull, which he had picked out of the funeral-furnace. I put it into a very simple locket; and he, liking this arrangement got me to bespeak a similar locket for another fragment of the skull which he retained.... He bestowed upon me the sofa which Shelley had procured for himself in Pisa... the poet must probably have passed the very last night of his life. It is in beechwood (or, as some say, in Italian walnut-wood) – a very roomy couch, of simple yet rather tasteful construction. The pedigree of the sofa, after Shelley's sudden death, is as follows: Mrs. Shelley, Leigh Hunt, Charles Armitage Brown (the friend of Keats), Baron Kirkup, was... informed by [Trelawny] that he had better resign the sofa, lest it should at the last get totally overlooked as so much antiquated and unprized upholstery of one defunct.... So it did... and the Shelley sofa, one of my most valued possessions, faces me as I write these words.[11]

Collecting Shelley is a theme to which Rossetti repeatedly returns. His complaint that the widow of Simoncini will not part with Shelley's Spyglass for under £40 is a typical indication of the attention Rossetti pays to an object's status as an item in a collector's market. Not surprisingly, scholars who have emphasized the importance of William Michael's role in establishing Shelley's reputation have tended to see his Shelley collection as something of an embarrassment. For example, Diderek Roll-Hansen states: 'He has an important place in the revival of interest in Shelley... although more and more he tended to antiquarianism and the collection of Shelley relics (Shelley's sofa, a piece of Shelley's skull).'[12] Unable to reconcile William Michael's genuine interest in Shelley's poetry with his mania for relics, Roll-Hansen constructs a narrative of a 'fall' into antiquarianism. However, one of the problems with such accounting for his collection in terms of a declension from his true literary interests is that Rossetti's collecting of Shelley was, from the beginning, deeply intertwined with his 'real' interest in Shelley.

Moreover, 'Shelley's Heart' might be read as a sonnet that reflects on Rossetti's passion for collecting, suggesting an intimate and dialectical relationship between his antiquarianism and his political utopianism. The grotesque realism of 'Shelley's Heart', with its emphasis on the 'terribly physical', seems to draw attention to the way in which Shelleyan romanticism had become a relic in the hands of Shelley's collectors. 'Shelley's Heart' thus seems uncannily to prophesy its own fate: the sonnet would become one of the many Shelley 'relics culled from far and wide' pictured on the label that Buxton Forman fixed to his private collection of nineteenth-century Romantic and Victorian texts.

Furthermore, Rossetti's role as a man of letters and his contributions to Shelley scholarship need to be considered in the context of changes taking place within the nineteenth-century book-collecting market. As Norman Feltes has demonstrated, during the last third of the nineteenth century, although literature laid ideological claim to autonomy, literary value was determined increasingly by the market in book collecting and by changes in publishing more generally.[13] At that time, Victorian publishing underwent a transition into a late-capitalist monopoly mode of production as a separation emerged between the author, bookseller and publisher. This transformation affected both the concept of literary value and the book-collecting market. Beginning in the 1870s, both book collecting and literary value became increasingly associated 'not only with the traditional but also with the very recent, not only the exceptional, but also the personal, not only the best, but also the accessible'. Rossetti's editing of Shelley dovetailed with the conditions that underwrote a new craze for collecting first editions of nineteenth-century poets. John Carter's classic *Taste and Technique in Book Collecting* credits Buxton Forman's bibliographical book, *A Shelley Library*, for revolutionizing book collecting.[14] However, it is interesting to note that this book probably owes much in conception to a book that William Michael Rossetti worked on between

1872 and 1879. Rossetti wanted to 'collect into one body all the accessible letters of Shelley, intermixed, in right chronological order, with all the passages
in his poetry and prose which relate to himself. These writings, thus ordered
and efficiently annotated would in effect form a quasi-autobiography'.[15]
Rossetti's book, *Cor Cordium,* never found a publisher. But the enterprising
Buxton Forman, to whom Rossetti sold it, turned it to more profitable ends.
Indeed, much of Rossetti's scholarship was exploited by Buxton Forman and
his partner Thomas J Wise, who capitalized on William's generosity. One
example of this is the Hitchener correspondence, which Rossetti had obtained
authorization to include in *Cor Cordium.* Rossetti unsuspectingly lent it to
Thomas J Wise, who later pirated the correspondence for his own profits.[16]

The material conditions of publication which authorized *Rossetti's Memoir of
Shelley* in the first place thus contributed to the process by which romantic
writings were *detached* and *abstracted* from their social and political contexts and
circulated as so many signs of national identity, literary taste and bourgeois
individualism by the end of the nineteenth century.

3. Utopianism

However, for William Michael Rossetti, the desire to collect is not just about
the will towards mastery that accompanies possessive individualism (and
that is a recurring theme in so much Victorian poetry from Browning's
'Porphyria's Lover' to Dante Gabriel's 'Jenny'). 'Shelley's Heart' contains a
utopian impulse. Like Shelley's final question in 'Ode to the West Wind' - 'if
Winter comes can spring be far behind?' - Rossetti's question, 'What other
flame was wont to come Lambent from thee to fainter hearts, and turn-Red
like thy death-pyre's heat—their lukewarmth hot!', longs for renewal. The
utopian impulse behind William Michael's collection of Shelleyana is perhaps
best understood in terms provided by Walter Benjamin's reflections on his
own collection of children's books in his essay 'Unpacking My Library': 'To a
true collector the acquisition of an old book is its rebirth. This is the childlike
element which in a collector mingles with the element of old age... To renew
the old world - that is the collector's deepest desire when he is driven to
acquire new things'.[17] Benjamin continues to describe the impulse behind
collecting:

> There is in the life of a collector a dialectical tension between the poles of
> disorder and order. Naturally, his existence is tied to many other things
> as well: to a very mysterious relationship to[...] also to a relationship to
> objects which does not emphasize their function, utilitarian value – that
> is, their usefulness, but studies and loves them as the scene, the stage, of

their fate. The most profound enchantment for the collector is the lock-
ing of individual items within a magic circle in which they are fixed as
the final thrill, the thrill of acquisition, passes over them.[18]

For Benjamin collecting is driven by a utopian impulse, the significance of
which can not be reduced to the exchange or use value of the collected
objects. So too for William Michael Rossetti, whose fascination with Shelley
was linked to his desire for political renewal. Although his *Memoir of Shelley* was
bound to wind up in the collector's market and amidst the relics at the
Huntington Library, it was, at the time of its publication, directed at least partially towards another audience.

When the *Memoir* was initially published in 1870, it coincided with the
high point of republicanism in England and reflected Rossetti's literary commitment to political radicalism. When his friend Keningale Robert Cook
proposed starting a republican newspaper in 1871, Rossetti replied enthusias-
tically:

> Among my personal friends the following are all more or less decided
> republicans and likely to respond in one form or another – Swinburne,
> Morris, W.B. Scott, Allingham, Huffer, Mathilde Blind, Nettleship – also
> (artists who write little or not at all) Madox Brown and Burne Jones...
> As for myself, I am, always have been, and am confident of always
> remaining a republican – and ultra republican, siding with the Paris
> Commune etc.... I should certainly feel more satisfaction in writing in a
> republican journal, of good literary standing, than in any other; and
> might probably, if invited to do so, find opportunities from time to
> time.[19]

For Rossetti and for others who were directly involved with the republican
movement, literary and political issues were closely connected. Poetry played
a symbolic role in radical republican circles, where Shelley's name was a vir-
tual synonym for utopian politics.[20] *The Republican*, a short-lived radical paper,
announced 'Our statesmen have dull, prosaic eyes, and never look with them
beyond the next day, or indeed the next moment. How much need there is of
what may be named Shelleyism in the public life of nations! Let a transcendental poetry envelope and interfuse the world, and swiftly would social and
political existence be quickened and transfigured thereby'.[21] Here, rather
than employing the adjective 'poetic' to describe radical politics, the
Republican deploys the term of 'poetry' to designate radical politics. Political
opposition is related not just in terms of, but *as* aesthetic difference: 'poetry',
or 'Shelleyism', stands against the 'prose' of liberal statesmen. For the writer,

poetry's power resides in its ability to transform time, or 'quicken political existence', to break through the continuum of the present into the future. The explicit contrast between the politics of prose and of poetry carries with it an implicit Shelleyan contrast between their configuration of temporal reality. Shelley saw poets as 'legislators' and 'prophets' because they '[beheld] the future in the present'. While a story is 'a catalogue of detached facts, which have no other bond of connexion than time, place, circumstance, cause and effect... a certain combination of events which can never recur again', a poem 'is universal' and 'for ever develops new and wonderful applications'.[22]

Republicans valued poetry's ability to challenge the boundaries between the private and public spheres, and to valorize a model of active political citizenship. Clearly, William Michael Rossetti recognized the significance of Shelley to republicans. He was a regular reader of Charles Bradlaugh's *National Reformer*, the self-styled 'official' organ of the republican movement. It was through a discussion about Shelley in the pages of *The National Reformer* that he came to know James Thomson (BV), whose work he would help promote. After Thomson had favourably reviewed Rossetti's *Moxon's Shelley*, Rossetti replied to Thomson and the readers of the *National Reformer*, stating 'anything about Shelley is, I dare say, interesting to your readers as much as to myself'.[23]

As it happened, Rossetti's reply appeared on March 26, 1871 (the date the Paris Commune was declared) in an edition which contained an enthusiastic review of Swinburne's Shelleyan *Songs Before Sunrise*. Given their shared political and literary interests, it is not surprising that the two men struck up a regular correspondence, most often concerning editorial questions pertaining to Shelley. When Rossetti first invites Thomson to visit him in Euston Square on 21 April 1873, he sought to entice B.V. not with the promise to discuss politics or poetry, but rather to see his collection of Shelley relics.

> I have for instance a piece of his blackened skull, given me by Trelawny, who picked it out of the furnace, and the regard in which I hold this relic makes me understand the feelings of a Roman Catholic in parallel cases... Also I am doing with much diligence another Shelley Job I have long contemplated – collection (with elucidatory notes, etc.) of every scrap of his poetry or prose personal to himself – principally letters, as far as prose is concerned.[24]

Rossetti's letter revisits the scene of 'Shelley's Heart', perhaps offering an implicit parallel between Trelawny's salvaging of Shelley's corporeal fragment and his own collection of the fragments of Shelley's textual corpus for his projected *Cor Cordium*.

Rossetti's letter to Thomson, with its reference to Roman Catholicism, conveys an invitation not only to see Shelley's skull but also to participate in a ritual experience. His expressed Catholic sentiments link William's collection of Shelley relics with Dante Gabriel's own collection of art at Tudor House, where he lived after the death of Elizabeth Siddal in 1862. As Elizabeth Helsinger has shown in her discussion of the social and aesthetic experiments of the Pre-Raphaelites in the 1860s, at the Tudor House 'artistic and exotic objects acquired again an "aura" of mysterious power lost in the crowded displays at the Crystal Palace, the Royal Academy, or the cluttered drawing rooms of an acquisitive bourgeoisie'. Although the Tudor House was not like William Morris's Red House, 'an experiment in collaborative work and play' that anticipated socialist experiments, it did nonetheless express an aesthetic resistance to the Victorian market for art. As Helsinger explains, 'to collect Rossetti's work was to join a self-selected circle of those who rejected the tasteless excesses of these displays to create in their own houses a ritual space for the contemplation of art, re-sacralizing the aesthetic in defiance of mass consumption'.[25] Similarly, when William Michael invited Thomson to see Shelley's skull, he symbolically imagined a ritual space from whence he could reanimate the past for the purposes of the present.

In his introduction to the *Memoir of Shelley*, Rossetti acknowledges the continued relevance of Shelley's revolutionary politics: 'These were years of revolution: and indeed what years, since the great disintegration of 1789–93 have not been so? And how many more are we not destined to see until the work of those mighty days shall be in some approximate degree openly accepted and firmly constituted.' For Rossetti, the poetry of Shelley had only just begun to fulfil its revolutionary promise. Against the commonly held view, popularized by Thomas Medwin, that Shelley's political leanings were fundamentally aristocratic and constitutional, Rossetti insists that Shelley had nothing good to say about the British constitution and cared little about historical tradition. Writing in *The Fortnightly Review* in 1871, Rossetti develops more fully his understated intimation that Shelley's politics are of the revolutionary and continental variety. 'Shelley in 1812–13: an unpublished poem and other particulars etc' discusses the significance of several documents he had discovered in the Office of Public Records, including a poem called 'The Devils Walk' and a manifesto entitled 'Declaration of Rights'. Rossetti explains that 'The Declaration of Rights' was posted and passed out by Daniel Hill, a servant of Shelley, who claimed that a mysterious man dressed in black paid him to post the papers. Rossetti reprints the declaration and then pursues a detailed comparison between Shelley's document and 'similar documents in the history of the French Revolution—the one adopted by the Constituent Assembly in August 1789, and the other proposed in April, 1793, by

Robespierre'.[26] Rossetti's emphasis on Shelley's continentalism is an inter-esting irony given the importance of William Michael Rossetti's work in establishing Shelley within a tradition of *English* poets.

4. The Fleshly School

Finally, I wish to consider the *Memoir* in relationship to the Fleshly School Controversy that erupted after the publication of Dante Gabriel Rossetti's volume of poems.[27] It is not generally known that William Michael's edition of Shelley fell under attack from the same quarters as Dante Gabriel Rossetti's *Poems*, namely Robert Buchanan. Buchanan's anonymous review in *The Athaneum* in 1870 savaged William Michael's *Memoir* and editorial decisions, in terms that could have come straight out of his attack on 'The Fleshly School'.[28] In the article, William Michael is described as 'deficient in qualifications', 'pretentious' and 'lacking in originality'. Where Shelley should be treated with impartiality, Rossetti's memoir is 'fanatical'. Condemned for its sensationalism, Rossetti's memoir is deemed morally corrupt and is criti-cized for reading sexual innuendos between the lines of Shelley's letters. Rossetti is charged with portraying the 'lofty' Shelley as an insincere plagiar-ist. Last but not least, Rossetti's prose comes under attack. He is 'guilty of gross violation of taste in conception and phraseology... mistaking slang for wit and coarseness for strength'. Some of the phrases singled out by Buchanan include: 'cut up for'; 'went in for'; and 'the vomit of creation who wrote a review of Queen Mab'. In both this review and in his critique of 'The Fleshly School', Buchanan expresses anxiety about the Rossetti brothers' transgres-sions of the boundaries between high culture and mass culture, the ideal and the sensational, the literary and the pornographic that circulates on 'holywell street'.

While William Michael Rossetti's critical writings have since been recog-nized for both the breadth and depth of their achievement, modern critics still continue to wince when it comes to his prose. However, his propensity for combining technical and academic language with neologisms and slang might be seen as a critical proposal very much in keeping with the aesthetic agenda he puts forth in his critical writings. William Michael's championing of Whitman and Joaquin Cincinnatus Miller signals his interest in the radical linguistic and stylistic challenges to English literariness and in the social challenges embedded therein. Indeed, Rossetti celebrated American poetry and American poets for the same reasons that, he felt, most Englishmen disliked America and sided with the South in the civil war. 'The Majority of the English are conservative—many political liberals are social conservatives and think the southerners are "better gentlemen".'[29] Similarly, he chastises the British public for disliking Lincoln because he rose from the populace. When Rossetti defends Whitman against his English critics, he recognizes that the American poet might offend English literary sensibilities for similar reasons. While he admits that Whitman 'uses a large number of words detestable to the literary sense, sometimes actually misapplied, and at best fitted for a Yankee stump orator', he goes on to acknowledge that therein lies much of Whitman's democratic power. For Rossetti, Whitman is the poet of democracy and the future. Whitman's 'defects are prominent enough indeed, yet only like so many scraps and debris rolled on in the rush of the torrent'.[30]

Rossetti takes bohemian delight in celebrating the great American poetry of Miller, a writer who has not read Whitman, Byron, Poe or Burns, who 'has a bullet imbedded in his right arm', and who is rumoured to have born a child out of wedlock to a Comanche Indian woman. He also seems to take great pleasure in introducing Miller to literary circles, where people are alternately attracted and repelled by his 'coarse and uncivilized' manner.[31] Reviewing Miller's *Pacific Poems* and *Songs of the Sierras* in the *Academy*, he praises 'this… truly remarkable book', comparing his 'strange, outlandish, and romantic' writings, characterized by 'excitement' and 'ambition', to those of Byron, Swinburne and Victor Hugo.[32]

To close these reflections on the tensions within William Michael's radical romantic aestheticism, we might recall a well-known fact that the first use of the phrase associated with aestheticism, 'Art for Art's sake', appeared in Swinburne's book on Blake. It is often forgotten, however, that in the same book, Swinburne celebrated Blake, along with Whitman, for his republicanism and democratic politics. When William Michael Rossetti writes a pamphlet defending Swinburne's *Poems and Ballads* against charges of obscenity, he celebrated Swinburne as a poet who refused to have 'his literary liberty abridged', a phrase that captures both Rossetti's and Swinburne's commitment to aestheticism and political radicalism.[33] After describing Swinburne as the most Shelleyan of poets, he describes Swinburne's dominant characteristics: 'his poetry is literary poetry of the intensest kind… his is a poetry for poetry students. He is radically indifferent, and indeed hostile, to what most persons care for; and he poetizes, for the greater part, from a point of view which they will neither adopt nor understand… It should be added, however, that he is far the reverse of tardy in national or political… in these matters he might be described as fanatical.'[34]

Notes

1 Odette Bornand, 'Introduction', *William Michael Rossetti's Diaries, 1870–1873* (Oxford: Clarendon Press, 1993), p. xxii.

2 Diderik Roll-Hansen, 'The Third Rossetti Reconsidered', in *The Journal of Pre-Raphaelite Studies*, iv, no. 1, 1983 (1–11).

3 Peter Burger, *Theory of the Avant-Garde*, trans. Michael Shaw (Minneapolis: University of Minnesota Press, 1985), p. 2.

4 Terry Eagleton, *Ideology of the Aesthetic* (London: Blackwell, 1990).

5 Leonid Arinshstein and William E Fredeman, 'William Michael Rossetti's "Democratic Sonnets", in *Victorian Studies*, 9:3 (1971), 241–74. William E Fredeman, 'William Michael Rossetti and the Wise-Forman Conspiracy: A Footnote to a Sequel', *The Book Collector*, 36:1 (1987), pp. 55–71.

6 Jerome McGann, Rossetti or the Truth Betrayed', in *Towards a Literature of Knowledge* (Chicago: University of Chicago Press, 1989), p. 71.

7 William Michael Rossetti, 'Editing Shelley, Etc.; Trelawny' in *Some Reminisces* of *William Michael* Rossetti, 2 vols (New York: AMS, 1906), pp. 358–97. In this chapter Rossetti describes his most significant editorial work on Shelley. This includes the first edition of *Moxon's Shelley*, which appeared in 1870 and was followed by a 2-volume edition for Moxon's Popular Poets series. The Memoir was then reprinted in Moxon's *Lives of the Famous Poets*. In *The Fortnightly Review*, January 1871, Rossetti published an article to be discussed in section 3, 'Shelley in 1812–13, an Unpublished Poem and other Particulars'. He delivered two lectures on *Shelley's Life and Writings*, del. 1875 which were republished in 1878 in *The Atheneum*. In 1885, he became president of the Shelley Society, where he delivered 3 lectures on *Prometheus Unbound*, 2 later lectures on Shelley and Leopardi, and one lecture on Shelley at the Lake of Geneva, article on Shelley in The Encyclopeadia Britannica, 1886 (see fully annotated edition of *Adonais* – 385).

8 Mary Shelley, *The Journals of Mary Shelley*, volume 2, ed. by Paul Feldman and Diana Scott-Kilvert (Baltimore: Johns Hopkins University Press, 1995) p. 444, fn. 2; p. 435, fn. 1.

9 William Michael Rossetti, *The Diary of William Michael Rossetti 1870–1873*, ed. by Odette Bornand (Oxford: Clarendon Press, 1977), p. 242.

10 William Fredeman, 'A Key Poem of the Pre-Raphaelite Movement: W.M. Rossetti's "Mrs. Holmes Grey"', in *Nineteenth-Century Literary Perspectives*, ed. by Clyde de L Ryals (Durham: Duke University Press, 1974); and Roll-Hansen, p. 7.

11 William Michael Rossetti, *Some Reminiscences*, 2 vols (New York: AMS Press, 1970), p. 375.

12 Roll-Hansen, 'The Third Rossetti', p. 10.

13 NN Feltes, *Literary Capital and the Late Victorian Novel* (Madison: University of Wisconsin Press, 1993) pp. 37–40.

14 John Carter, *Taste & Technique in Book-Collecting: A Study of Recent Developments in Great Britain and the United States* (Cambridge, Cambridge University Press, 1949). Carter explains that Forman's *A Shelley Library* was an important innovation because it was 'not a mere hand-list but a fully annotated and richly informative study of Shelley's original editions. Published by the Shelley Society in 1886 and subtitled 'an essay in bibliography', it marked a radical advance, not only in its detailed technical treatment of a single author's first editions but also in its forethought for the collector's wants' (p. 24).

15 William Michael Rossetti, *Some Reminiscences*, p. 368.

16 William E Fredeman, 'W.M. Rossetti and the Wise-Forman Conspiracy', in *The Book Collector*, 36:1 (Spring 1987), 55–71. Fredeman clears Rossetti of the charge that he was a co-conspirator with Wise and Foreman. Tracking Rossetti's manuscripts, he shows that 'Wise is unscrupulous early in their acquaintance, he embarrassed Rossetti by printing without the authorization of their owner Shelley's Letters to Elizabeth Hitchner, the manuscripts of which W had foolishly allowed him to transcribe. Wise used William as a golden goose from whom he could inveigle an endless supply of manuscripts, private printings and memorabilia, both to enhance his own collection and to build a stock' (p. 64). For more on Wise and Forman, see John Carter and James Pollard, *An Enquiry into the Nature of Certain 19th Century Pamphlets* (London, 1934).

17 Benjamin, 'Unpacking My Library', *Illuminations* (New York: Shocken, 1968), p. 61.

18 Walter Benjamin, 'Unpacking My Library', p. 60.

19 WMR to Keningale Robert Cook, 9 July 1871, in *Selected Letters of William Michael Rossetti*, ed. by Roger W Peattie (University Park: Pennsylvania State University Press, 1990), p. 275.

20 On Shelley's radical poetic legacy see Anne F Janowitz, *Lyric and Labour in the Romantic Tradition* (Cambridge: Cambridge University Press, 1998); for a good discussion of Swinburne and republican poetry in 1870, see Stephanie Kuduk, ' "A Sword of a Song": Swinburne's Republican Aesthetics in *Songs before Sunrise'* in *Victorian Studies*, 43 (Winter 2001), 253–78. Important historical studies of republicanism include Royden Harrison, *Before the Socialists* (London: 1965); Edward Royle, *Radicals, Secularists, Republicans: Popular Freethought in Britain 1866–1915* (Manchester: Manchester University Press, 1980); FA D'Arcy, 'Charles Bradlaugh and the Republican Movement', in *Historical Journal*, 25 (1982), 367–83; and Antony Taylor, 'Republicanism Reappraised: Anti-Monarchism and the English radical tradition, 1850–1872' in *Re-reading the Constitution: New narratives in the Political History of England's Long Nineteenth Century* (Cambridge: Cambridge University Press, 1996), pp. 154–78.

21 'Obstruction, Destruction, Construction', *The Republican*, May 1, 1871.

22 PB Shelley, 'A Defense of Poetry', *Shelley's Poetry and Prose*, ed. by Donald Reiman and Sharon Powers (New York: WW Norton, 1977), p. 485.

23 WM Rossetti, *The National Reformer*, March 26, 1871.

24 WMR to James Thomson, 21 April 1873, in *Selected Letters*.

25 Elizabeth K Helsinger, 'Pre-Raphaelite Arts: Aesthetic and Social Experimentation in the 1860s' in *Ideas from the National Humanities Center*, 5:2 (1998).

26 William Michael Rossetti, 'Shelley in 1812–1813: An Unpublished Poem and other Particulars', in *The Fortnightly Review*, 9 (January1871), 67–83.

27 For a good discussion of the controversy, see Christopher Murray, 'D.G. Rossetti, A.C. Swinburne and R.W. Buchanan: The Fleshly School Revisited', 2 (Spring 1965), 174–207.

28 (Anonymous – really Buchanan) '*The Poetic Works of P.B. Shelley. A Revised Text with Notes and a Memoir. By W.M. Rossetti*' reviewed in *The Athaneum* (29 January 1870), 154–5. Murray identifies Buchanan as the reviewer in 'The Fleshly School Revisited'.

29 William Michael Rossetti, 'English Opinion on the American War', in *The Atlantic Monthly*, (February 1866), 29–49.

30 William Michael Rossetti, 'Walt Whitman's Poems' in *The Chronicle* 1 (6 July 1867) 352–4. For more on Rossetti and Whitman, see especially Julianne Ramsay 'A British view to an American War: Whitman's "Drum-Taps" Cluster and the Editorial

Influence of William Michael Rossetti', in *The Walt Whitman Quarterly Review*, 14 (Spring 1997), 166–81. Ramsay argues that Rossetti's editing and anthologization of Whitman influenced the structure of the 'Drums Taps' Cluster in *Leaves of Grass*.

31 *Diary*, May 18, 1871.

32 William Michael Rossetti, 'Songs of the Sierras', in *The Academy* (June, 1871), 300–3.

33 William Michael Rossetti, *Swinburne's Poems and Ballads: A Criticism* (London: Hotten, 1866). For a good discussion of Rossetti's defence of Swinburne, see Roger Peattie, 'William Michael Rossetti and the Defense of Swinburne's *Poems and Ballads* in *Harvard Library Bulletin* 19 (1971), 356–75.

34 Rossetti, *Swinburne's Poems*, p. 42.

PART III

FAITH IN AN AGE OF SCIENCE

6

PEWS, PERIODICALS AND POLITICS: THE ROSSETTI WOMEN AS HIGH CHURCH CONTROVERSIALISTS

Mary Arseneau

In the course of his two-volume *Reminiscences*, William Michael Rossetti refers in passing to the 'day-by-day humdrum of the female members of the family',[1] thus dismissing in a phrase the matters domestic, devotional and charitable which consumed the daily energies of the Rossetti women. While this 'day-by-day humdrum' is largely undocumented, careful attention to epistolary references, unpublished sources and forgotten publications does provide insight into at least one of its aspects – Frances, Maria and Christina Rossetti's lively shared commitment to Anglo-Catholicism, its politics and publications. Somewhat paradoxically, it was within the confines of the conservative, traditional and authoritarian Anglo-Catholic church that the Rossetti women expressed their most egalitarian and reform-minded ideals. Often assumed to be conservative and conventional, the Rossetti women complicate this supposition in their public involvement with the 'free and open Church' movement. The Rossetti women's commitment to the abolition of the pew-rent system can be documented over a period of several decades, and in outlining it we can expand our understanding of Christina Rossetti's activism, already known to include anti-vivisection, protection of minors and aid to sexually exploited women. It is in this neglected corner of Rossetti scholarship, particularly in Maria and Christina's writings on church politics published in High Church periodicals, that we find some of their most incisive and urgently stated cultural critique.

As John Shelton Reed has asserted, Anglo-Catholicism was a 'counter-cultural' movement: 'many of the practices the movement championed were symbolic affronts to the central values of Victorian middle-class culture, and

[…] a few were actual threats to those values'.[2] Following the drama and controversy surrounding the Tractarian period of 1833–45, the years of the Anglo-Catholic revival and its Ritualist emphasis were in their own way equally turbulent. During this period, much of the public outcry against Anglo-Catholicism was levelled at innovations in ceremonial and decorative practices in worship, for instance: frequent celebration of the eucharist; auricular confession; the mixed chalice; clergymen preaching in the surplice; candles and flowers on the altar; and the movement toward free and open seating. Maria and Christina Rossetti were particularly committed to reform on this last question, and showed themselves willing to enter public debate on pew rents.

The campaign against pew rents in the Church of England 'became a mark of Tractarian tendencies as early as the 1830s'.[3] The 'free and open Church' movement agitated for the abolition of the pew system that allowed worshippers to pay for appropriated seating – that is, a private pew for the use of the subscriber only, advantageously positioned for viewing and hearing the service, and at a discreet distance from the 'free seats' occupied by working-class members of the congregation. Under the pew-rent system, not only was the congregation segregated by class, but there were also often not enough seats to accommodate worshippers who were unable to pay for their seating. The system, reformers argued, alienated the poor who could not afford a rented pew and thus felt as if they did not belong to the worshipping community. Parishes were often in the grip of financial exigency: when a church was not endowed, it relied heavily on the income generated by pew rents; thus 'the system tended to be financially necessary just where it was socially undesirable'. Ironically, in very poor parishes or districts, so heavy was the reliance on income generated by pew rents that there were sometimes no seats available for working-class worshippers.[4] In *Church and People in an Industrial City*, ER Wickham remarks on 'a mountain of evidence showing clearly that the appropriation and renting of seats worked against the best interests of the Church by excluding the working people, and destroying the proper influence of the incumbent over the people whom he could neither invite to church, nor blame for not coming'.[5]

In outlining the Rossetti women's position on pew rents through a period of five decades, we can reconstruct a partial history of their High Church activism. Before 1839, Frances had a disagreement with Dr. Penfold, rector at Trinity Church, Marylebone Road, over pew rent.[6] We know few details of this conflict, but Frances's transcription into her commonplace book of a poem expressing outrage at the injustice prevailing in the Church of England provides evidence of her sympathies with the individual unable to pay for appropriated seating and her indignation at the 'scandal/ That desecrates our age'. While 'the obsequious beadle' welcomes the rich lady, a working-class woman 'On whose wan face was graven/ Life's hardest discipline,' finds that there is no place for her:

> The few free seats were crowded
> Where she could rest and pray;
>
> . . .
>
> 'God's house holds no poor sinners,'
> She sigh'd, and crept away.[7]

Class and social privilege, Frances clearly thought, should carry no weight in 'God's house'.

That Christina and Maria were themselves deeply involved in the issue of pew rents becomes apparent in their respective cognate prose pieces on the subject. Christina's 'Some Pros and Cons. About Pews' was first published in July 1867 in *The Churchman's Shilling Magazine and Family Treasury*.[8] The story seems specifically to have arisen out of the Rev. Henry W Burrows's initiative to abolish pew rents in the Rossettis' parish – Christ Church, Albany Street. Christina Rossetti is propagandizing, taking the debate to an audience beyond her own parish apparently in an effort to instigate and support reform further afield. The publication of 'Some Pros and Cons' possibly also shows the influence of Christina's friend the Rev. Dr Richard Frederick Littledale, a prominent Anglo-Catholic controversialist whom she met in 1864, and who became her close friend, confessor and spiritual advisor. A public advocate of open churches, Littledale may be supposed to have by word and example urged Christina into the fray.[9]

In 1865 Burrows circulated a paper to the inhabitants of the district and members of the congregation stating his reasons for putting an end to the objectionable practice of pew rents, 'and then called a public meeting of parishioners and pew-renters, before whom he laid the matter, earnestly pleading that our Father's House should be open to receive all His children equally'.[10] In his own history, *The Half-Century of Christ Church, St. Pancras, Albany Street*, Burrows states that he was following the example set by Mr Wroth at St. Philip's, Clerkenwell (which in 1859 became 'the first church in London with rented pews to abandon the system').[11] The two main obstacles to the open-church movement were financial considerations and the personal sensibilities of the pew-renters. Burrows, the father of a large family whose income was generated by pew rents, himself acknowledged that 'it was difficult to give up profitable pew-rents and throw oneself on the offertory'.[12] The twelve reasons he offers in support of his proposition are statements of principle, first and foremost the principle that 'the Services of the Church are the natural inherent right of all the baptised in the parish, as such, and equally'.[13] It was agreed that the district and congregation should be invited to express their opinion on Burrows's initiative. Along with others in the parish and district, the Rossetti women would have been issued with voting papers.[14] While a majority voted in favour of the change, it would seem that a modicum of resistance remained, for in the event Burrows recounts that the 'transition to the new system was made easier by the concession that pew-renters residing in the parish might retain their sittings, though no longer paying for them'.[15] Burrows's biographer clarifies this concession further, stating that while parishioners had the option of retaining the same number of seats in the open bench which replaced their former pew, Burrows in fact successfully persuaded a 'large number' of seat-holders to resign their seats completely. The change was celebrated as a success: the poor 'flocked into the Church', and members of all classes in the congregation embraced the church with increased zeal.[16] By the time Burrows left Christ Church in 1878, 'out of more than 1100 seatings, less than twenty remained appropriated'.[17]

With the exception of reference to 'family feelings' (which Burrows concludes are as important to the poor as they are to the rich), matters of personal feeling which generated so much of the resistance to open seating are barely touched upon in Burrows's list: Christina's short story, meanwhile, offers a more complete picture of the responses of individual types, of conflicting values and of the debate that ensued. The genesis of Christina's story in parish politics has always been acknowledged, but the existence of a remarkably similar story by Maria has thus far, I believe, escaped scholarly notice. In an 1885 letter to Henry Buxton Forman, Christina lists among Maria's works 'a Dialogue paper on Free and Unappropriated Church Sittings in a high-Church monthly entitled "New and Old"'.[18] Published in 1873 in the first number of *New and Old': for Seed-Time and Harvest. A Parochial Magazine for all Readers*, Maria's 'Pews: A Colloquy. "One with Another"',[19] is a brief prose piece – a dialogue among men and women, lay and clergy, who discuss pew rents over luncheon at a Mrs Brooke's house. Indeed, Maria's 'Pews: A Colloquy' is so strikingly similar to Christina's 'Pros and Cons' that they would appear to have been written in consultation with each other or in response to a common impetus. Both present their arguments against pew rents by means of a debate among characters, some of whom express the most frequent objections to reform, only to have these objections reasonably answered by supporters of free seating. In Maria's 'Dialogue paper', for instance, the general fear that lost pew-rent revenues would lead to financial instability for a parish is answered by her 'good old widow lady' Mrs Brooke, who points out that the danger can be avoided if 'each actual seat-holder [would] offer annually a sum equal to his abolished pew-rent'. Decreased personal comfort in worship, as former pew holders find themselves seated next to those less respectable or clean than themselves, is acknowledged as a small sacrifice richly compensated by the knowledge that it makes the church truly open to all.

At one point in Maria's discussion, Mr Berridge, 'a gentleman connected with the press', enters with his completely secular perspective. In his exaggerated presumption that his values and point of view are beyond dispute, Maria quietly signals another set of values: *'Don't we see'*, Mr Berridge declares, 'that wherever any character stamps itself strongly on the State, it stamps itself on the Church too? Where a property qualification is required to give a man a vote in political affairs, *isn't it obvious* that money will also affect his position as a Churchman? *Who can doubt it?*' (my emphasis). Maria's implicit critique cuts two ways. First, in overstating and thus exposing the assumption that the State should dictate the character of the Church at all, she recalls not only the earliest battlecry of the Oxford Movement, John Keble's 1833 sermon on 'National Apostasy' in which he denounced Parliament's interference in Church governance, but also William Dodsworth's impassioned sermons at Christ Church during the Gorham controversy in 1850.[20] But perhaps Maria's critique also suggests that influence might ideally flow from the Church to the State, for the abolition of pew rents provides a model of equality that the political order had yet to achieve.

Christina's short story, later revised and republished as 'Pros and Cons' in her prose collection *Commonplace, and Other Short Stories* (1870), is similar to Maria's in addressing individual responses to loss of privilege. Christina's story has a lighter touch, more humour, and begins *in medias res* at a tea in the Rectory: '"But my dear doctor," cried Mrs. Plume, "you never can seriously mean it"'.[21] Christina's characters are social types whose specific objections are forecast by their names, for example, Mr Sale, whose economic bias inclines him to consider only the loss of income generated by pew rents, and Mr Home, who argues for appropriated seating on the grounds of 'the sacredness of family affection'.[22] In the earlier periodical version of the story, the Rector answers the objection that church seating is a 'petty question of appearance' compared to worldwide atrocities including slavery, suttee and genocide: 'But whilst the negro writhes beneath the lash of an inhuman master, whilst the Indian widow burns herself in a soul-destroying superstition, whilst the bushman, dwindling before our face, lives and dies as the beasts that perish, shall we divert our attention from such matters of life and death to fix it on a petty question of appearance'?[23] 'Stretch full hands to remote spots', the Rector encourages his parishioners, but not at the expense of attending to inequities closer to home.[24]

Dr Goodman urges his parishioners to reject 'the system of worldly

England' and the inequities inscribed in it – specifically, the reverence of class distinction and economic privilege articulated by Mr Stone, the 'warmest man in the parish', who speaks with 'his fat hands in his fat pockets': 'The tendency of the day is to level social distinctions and to elevate unduly the lower orders. In this parish at least let us combine to keep up wise barriers between class and class, and to maintain that fundamental principle practically bowed to all over our happy England, that what you can pay for you can purchase'.[25] The social justice of this 'fundamental principle' is suspect, and the Rector's ensuing rejection of worldly systems amounts to a rejection of the dominant values of Victorian culture:[26]

> 'What Mr. Stone has alleged may be the system of worldly England; though many a man professing far less than we do would repudiate so monstrous a principle; but as Churchmen we can have nothing to do with it. God's gifts are bought without money and without price. "Ho, every one," cries His invitation. I, therefore, as His most unworthy ambassador, protest that in His house I will no longer buy and sell as in a market.'[27]

Christina Rossetti's rejection of the commercial paradigm as a 'monstrous' principle is explicit here and resonates throughout her writing.[28]

Both Maria and Christina's stories are unabashedly didactic and persuasive, specifically designed to enlighten and influence the readership of *The Churchman's Shilling Magazine* and '*New and Old*', both High-Church monthlies. Significantly, both Maria's and Christina's discussion of pews appeared in the first volumes of their respective periodicals. We might therefore surmise that Maria and Christina were in close enough contact with their editors either to hear about a new magazine before its first appearance or to have their work personally solicited.[29] What might have attracted the Rossettis' support? The publication of Maria's 'Pews: A Colloquy' in the first issue of '*New and Old*', and Christina's repeated appearances in the first two volumes of *The Churchman's Shilling Magazine* (she appeared in five separate monthly issues between April and November 1867, with 'The Waves of this Troublesome World' parts 1 and 2, 'Some Pros and Cons. About Pews', 'Dante, an English Classic' and 'A Safe Investment') suggest a principled commitment to High Church periodicals espousing Anglo-Catholic beliefs and aimed at a lay audience. Both periodicals were aimed at a High Church readership and had very specific mission statements. '*New and Old*', edited by the Rev. Charles Gutch and first published in January 1873, states in the first number its aim to 'amuse and please, for we are by no means among the number of those who dislike harmless mirth; but our great aim will be to edify'.[30] *The Churchman's*

Shilling Magazine, edited by the Rev. Robert H Baynes, first acknowledges the 'immense popularity' of periodical literature, emphasizing the moral influence wielded by such publications whose 'power for good or evil [is] far greater than perhaps is commonly allowed'. Baynes hopes to fill a specific niche: 'Of periodicals having to do with the general literature of the day there is no lack; but of those having any direct or definite connection with the Church of England and its authorised teaching, there are but few, and those few are for the most part of so entirely theological a nature as to render them unsuitable for general reading'.[31] The Rossettis' commitment to '*New and Old*' continued with a household subscription to the periodical and the appearance of Christina's own work in later issues.[32] Within a few years, Rossetti would take her tale of religious controversy over pews and two other religious tales published in *The Churchman's Shilling Magazine*, 'The Waves of this Troublesome World' and 'A Safe Investment', to a more general audience in *Commonplace, and Other Short Stories* (1870).

The sisters shared another religious publisher in common, the Society for the Promotion of Christian Knowledge, or SPCK. Maria's *Letters to my Bible Class on thirty-nine Sundays*, a series of epistolary lessons in scripture and personal conduct, was written in 1860 for the parish's Young Women's Friendly Society,[33] and published by the SPCK in 1872. In this instance, *Letters to my Bible Class* may have been instrumental in directing Christina toward the second (and less studied) phase of her career in which she concentrated on devotional prose, an enterprise in which Christina clearly aligns her writing and her values with her sister's: 'I have just sold a little book (its copyright) for £40 to the S.P.C.K.,' she told William Michael, adding that the SPCK 'is the same Society as published Maria's 'Letters to my Bible Class' in old days'.[34] Christina devoted much of her energy in the last twenty years of her life to religious writing, and the SPCK would publish six of her books between 1879 and 1892. Christina also contributed to the SPCK's *The Dawn of Day*, an illustrated monthly, two sketches that shed light on the material, educational and catechetical aspects of the Rossetti and Polidori women's outreach to the poor. These two sketches – in which, incidentally, Maria is described as a 'pew-opener'[35] – are minor in literary terms; nevertheless, they offer a glimpse of largely unrecorded and forgotten work undertaken by the women of the Rossetti circle. Moreover, their disappearance for a time from bibliographies of Christina's work indicates something important about the patterns of neglect in the biographical and critical history.

In addition to illuminating the Rossetti women's commitment to Anglo-Catholic politics and publications, I would also argue that the 'free and open Church' debate brings into focus a coherent economy that makes sense of all of Christina Rossetti's 'works', charitable, devotional and literary. Maria and

Christina depict church politics as a site of colliding economic paradigms, and they level harsh criticism at the market forces that determine Britain's national character and underwrite its inequitable social arrangements – Mr Stone's revered 'fundamental principle practically bowed to all over our happy England, that what you can pay for you can purchase'. In their position papers on pew rents, Maria and Christina Rossetti not only emphatically distinguish between the values and jurisdictions of Church and State, they also champion an alternative economic model.[36]

A fuller statement on the contrast between the secular economy and the Christian economy of salvation can be found in 'A Safe Investment', another of Christina's contributions to *The Churchman's Shilling Magazine*.[37] This short story recounts in apocalyptic mode a series of catastrophes by which investments in financial, industrial and commercial enterprise all meet with reversal. Gas works, banks, ships and cisterns are exploded, bankrupted, sunk and fractured in a sequence of calamities:

> Every tale was diverse, yet, in fact, every one was the same. Each speaker had sunk all that he had in some plausible investment, the investment had burst like a bubble, and now one and all in desperate sorrow could but bewail their ruin as without remedy. They had no eyes, no thought, no sympathy, save each man for himself; none stretched a helping hand to his neighbour, or spoke a word of comfort, or cared who sank or who swam in this desolation which had come like a flood.[38]

One woman, an island of calm, cheerfulness and hospitality in the midst of general despair and ruin describes the 'safe investment' of the title. Instructed early in life that 'riches do certainly make to themselves wings and fly away', she has instead invested in 'an everlasting habitation', and laid up 'treasure where neither moth nor rust doth corrupt'.[39] The principles of this divine economy are expressed in financial terms – 'invest', 'riches', 'gold', 'treasure', 'deposits', 'debtor', 'prospered', 'account', 'interest' – but this economy operates by a distinct set of rules, counter to those governing secular economies, rules based on trust, community, selflessness and open-handed generosity to those in need. She adds, 'And as I know whom I have trusted, and am persuaded that He will keep that which I commit to Him, I gladly spend and am spent, being a succourer of many, and looking for the recompense of the reward'.[40] The acquisition of economic capital is supplanted by the accumulation of spiritual capital, and focus shifts from worldly wealth in the present to a heavenly reward in the future.

In fact, the term 'economy' – in its many senses – suggestively and usefully clusters various central concerns in Christina Rossetti's writings, expressing a coherent 'thought style',[11] a constellation of values shared by the Rossetti women. 'Economy', etymologically rooted in household management, evokes the private, female, domestic sphere that the Rossetti women inhabited. Central to their economy is charity, which begins with economy or thrift at home and extends outwards in good works. Their economy is characterized by fasting, giving, saving – it is future-oriented and involves patience, waiting for salvation as the future reward. This 'thought style' could be characterized as radical conservatism, a philosophy profoundly at odds with mainstream bourgeois and capitalist Victorian values. It is deeply committed to conservation and protection of the vulnerable, as evidenced in a dedication to anti-vivisection, the protection of minors, and reclaiming 'fallen' women. In its theological sense, economy embraces the doctrine of reserve, the judicious disclosure of spiritual truths, and the sacramental system. Poetically, economy imbues the linguistic reserve that Christina exercises, her conciseness, and also the symbolic capital her language accrues as imagery circulates among devotional and non-devotional poems.

Christina and Maria Rossetti's translation of the language of economic capital to spiritual capital has an important Biblical source in the Parable of the Unprofitable Servant who fails to invest wisely the talent entrusted to him.[42] Maria alludes to this parable in 'Pews: A Colloquy', where the open church advocate Mr Brooke argues that those who enjoy social status and wealth are like 'the servant to whom ten talents have been committed, and of whom the increase of ten will be required'. '"But why cannot he act upon this as well in a pew as in an open sitting?"', Mrs Wells asks:

'As well in a distinguished and exclusive place secured by money, as in an undistinguished one held by the tenure of a common Christianity, I suppose you mean; for that is the gist of the question,' replied the Priest. 'My answer is – Because no steward's sense of accountableness is increased by spending his master's money on his own comfort. Because no man's trust in riches is diminished by finding there is nothing even in God's sanctuary which they will not buy.'[43]

Maria eschews earthly economies in favour of spiritual economies. Meanwhile, in 'A Prayer for Use of Talents' in *Called to Be Saints*, Christina exploits not only the contrast between earthly riches and 'heavenly treasure'; she also elaborates what is latent in the parable, an analogy between economic capital and personal capital, playing on the double meaning of 'talent' as both a monetary unit and a special ability or aptitude. Enjoined by God with 'spending, labouring, influencing others, as those who must give account not of their own souls only, but of their brother's also', the individual must make a return on the 'talents' with which he is entrusted. Christina's sense that her talent, her artistic and intellectual gifts, must be used 'labouring' and 'influencing others'; her conviction of 'one's own responsibility in use of an influential talent'[44] motivates much of the later part of her career. Her brother Dante Gabriel, for his part, expressed concern that she risked her reputation as a poet in publishing devotional writings with a religious press. Christina responded – 'I don't think harm will accrue from my S.P.C.K. books, even to my standing; if it did, I should still be glad to throw my grain of dust into the religious scale'.[45]

In publishing with the SPCK Christina followed Maria's lead, for it was she who first published with them. By the time Christina was publishing with the SPCK, her interests as a writer had more in common with Maria than they did with her brothers and the Pre-Raphaelite Movement. Finally, the male Rossettis did not participate in the Rossetti women's 'thought style' as I have outlined it here, an observation that might lead scholars and students of Christina Rossetti to conclude that it is more instructive to contextualize Rossetti's development and aims as a writer within this female and religiously minded circle than within the androcentric Pre-Raphaelite Brotherhood. For Christina, in the long run, sisterhood was more important than brotherhood, and the Anglo-Catholic identity more significant than the Pre-Raphaelite aesthetic. Something of this contest of allegiances and clash of values is captured in Max Beerbohm's humorous cartoon in which Dante Gabriel berates Christina for resisting his recreation of her appearance within a Pre-Raphaelite aesthetic: 'What is the use, Christina, of having a heart like a singing bird and a water-shoot and all the rest of it, if you insist on getting yourself up like a pew-opener?'[46]

Appendix

PEWS: A COLLOQUY.
"One with Another."
Maria F Rossetti

Mrs. Brooke, a good old widow lady who lived alone in a quiet street at the West End of London, had one day quite a succession of visitors at her luncheon table; and every one of them had a different reason for talking about pews. The first comer was her much younger friend Mrs. Wells, who was cordially welcomed with–

"My dear Mrs. Wells! just at the right moment: here's luncheon, the best friend of chat."

"Thank you," replied Mrs. Wells, "I shall really be glad of some; I have been a long business round, beginning at S. Timothy's Church."

Mrs. B. "Church does not sound much like business."

Mrs. W. "No, but this was strictly a business transaction; I have been taking a pew there."

Mrs. B. "Then are you giving up your pew at S. Titus's?"

Mrs. W. "I beg your pardon; my pew is giving up me."

Mrs. B. "Oh, the Churchwardens have given you notice to quit?"

Mrs. W. "No, but Mr. Sutton has sent my husband a circular, announcing his intention of doing away in three months' time with pews, rents, charities, appropriation, income, and Curates."

Mrs. B. "Pray, my dear friend, was that in the circular?"

Mrs. W. "No, the Offertory was in the circular; but we all know what Curates and charities come of an income that comes – or doesn't come – of the Offertory. Empty purses make empty bags."

Mrs. B. "But surely the present congregation have that matter in their own hands; why should not each actual seat-holder offer annually a sum equal to his abolished pew-rent?

Mrs. W. "Yes, if the present seat-holders continue to attend; but you see they won't; we, for two, won't."

Mrs. B. "May I ask why?"

Mrs. W. "Because we don't choose to go to Church in such a wretched way – we really can't attend to our prayers when our neighbours are unpleasant sort of people. Why, it is not six months since we changed our pew because a sitting in it was taken by a gentleman who lived at some distance, and who used to come into Church panting and puffing."

Mrs. B. "Then it seems pew-doors don't quite shut out neighbours you object to."

Mrs. W. "No, but with plenty of unlet seats all round you can change as often as you are made uncomfortable."

Mrs. B. "Ah, to be sure; I had not thought of that. Perhaps, with a little explanation from you, even Mr. Sutton might come to understand the nature of an ideal congregation. Could you not tell him that it consists of, 1. First class pew-renters in the nave, very select indeed; puffing and panting, among other things, are disqualifications. 2. Second class pew-renters, consisting of persons disqualified for the nave, but otherwise respectable, occupying nook-and-corner pews. 3. Empty pews, affording free circulation to first class molested by second class who do not know their place. 4. Poor non-renters, all in Sunday clothes, on unmistakeable free-seats."

But here – "My dear mother, what obtuse Mr. Sutton has shown himself incapable of apprehending so fundamental a truth?" – broke in a manly voice at the further end of the room. The speaker had entered unperceived. He was Mrs. Brooke's second son, about forty years of age, a devoted Priest labouring night and day in a Mission recently established in one of the poorest districts of London.

"Begin your luncheon, John," returned his mother, "and I'll tell you. He is the clergyman of S. Titus', Mrs. Wells's parish; and he is about to sacrifice the best interests of a highly respectable congregation by setting on foot a crusade against pews."

"A crusade – yes in truth, for it bears the stamp of the Cross" – began the Priest; but he was interrupted by a third entrance – Mr. Berridge, a gentleman connected with the press, the son of Mrs. Brooke's once dearest schoolfriend: regarded with special love for his dead mother's sake. He too was welcomed to the table; and there discoursed of pews.

"Thank you, I haven't a minute to spare, but I'll take a mouthful – the fact is, in two hours' time I must be ready with an article for the *Main Chance Journal* – a pamphlet has just come out on the subject of free Churches, and I have to review it, and cut it up pretty well too. Don't we see that wherever any character stamps itself strongly on the State, it stamps itself on the Church too? Where a property qualification is required to give a man a vote in political affairs, isn't it obvious that money will also affect his position as a Churchman? Who can doubt it?"

"Not I, assuredly," quietly responded Mr. Brooke. "The possession of money does most materially affect his position."

"Well, then," triumphantly rejoined Mr. Berridge, "you who thus truly estimate the importance of money, will scarcely refuse to recognize that importance by allowing it to secure for its owners such places in Church as shall harmonize with an influential position."

"Really, Mr. Brooke," put in the delighted Mrs. Wells, "I had scarcely hoped you, who have not a single pew in your Church, would find anything at all to say on my side. Then you don't find the plan answer after all?"

"Pardon me," was the rejoinder; "I find it answer just on the very ground that wealth does affect a Christian's religious position; that – considering the power and influence which accompany it in this life – it constitutes him the servant to whom ten talents have been committed, and of whom the increase of ten will be required."

A pause ensued. Then – "But why cannot he act upon this as well in a pew as in an open sitting?" asked Mrs. Wells.

"As well in a distinguished and exclusive place secured by money, as in an undistinguished one held by the tenure of a common Christianity, I suppose you mean; for that is the gist of the question," replied the Priest. "My answer is – Because no steward's sense of accountableness is increased by spending his master's money on his own comfort. Because no man's trust in riches is diminished by finding there is nothing even in God's sanctuary which they will not buy."

"But, John," interposed his mother, "you have not touched upon what my dear friend feels as her chief difficulty. She finds that she really can pray more quietly and attentively in a fixed sitting, and with neighbours of her own choice, than in a chance place, and with chance neighbours. I think you must admit the difficulty to be a real one."

"I do admit it, mother – no doubt a trial and a sacrifice is involved. But where is it said in the Gospel that the rich may compound sacrifices for money? Where do we read that our Lord shunned any one because he was dirty? or that under a burning sky, in a country where water is scarcer and insects rifer than in our own, crowds of some thousands were all clean? And what word of our Lord teaches that we may trench upon brotherly charity to secure quietness and conscious recollectedness?"

Here Mr. Berridge disappeared with a friendly nod to his hostess. Mrs. Wells replied with a sigh; "I do believe we shall have to stay at S. Titus' after all: my husband will be glad, for it was only to please me he was going to leave. But I really cannot always manage kneeling without a proper hassock; and carrying one's books every day to Church is fatiguing; and constant shifting puts an end to all the sweet and pious associations which cluster round an accustomed place."

"My dear Mrs. Wells," said Mr. Brooke, "will you bear with my answering these objections, as Mr. Sutton, being your parish Priest, would be bound to answer them if stated to him?"

"Certainly I will," was the reply; "indeed, if you can prove them unfounded, I will engage not to start them again to him or any one else."

"Then first, as to kneeling – hassocks or an equivalent are always provided in free Churches. Secondly, as to the books: was it really not you whom I one day met in a back street with some half-dozen tradesmen's books in one hand, and a bag of apparently heavier matter in the other?"

"You might meet me there most days," said Mrs. Wells, "for that back street is my district; the bag is always stocked with tracts for lending, and books for reading to the blind and sick, of whom I have several to visit; and on Tuesdays I pay my weekly bills as I go along."

"Then are you not ashamed to make difficulties with regard to Church which are not difficulties with regard to anything else? Would not five minutes' meditation on our Lord bearing His Cross put an end for ever to the book objection?"

Mrs. Wells coloured. "But you speak as if I had proposed giving up Church on this account."

"I beg your pardon; you don't propose giving up Church, that would be a loss to your own soul; but you do wish to perpetuate a system which keeps your brethren from profiting by the same means of saving theirs. Only do what God calls you to, trusting in Him; then your pious associations will extend over the whole Church: you will see your difficulties vanish, and compensations for what sacrifice you make spring up on every side."

Notes

1   *Some Reminiscences of William Michael Rossetti*, 2 vols (London: Brown, Langham, 1906), i, p. 271.
2   John Shelton Reed, *Glorious Battle: The Cultural Politics of Victorian Anglo-Catholicism* (Nashville and London: Vanderbilt University Press, 1996), p. xxii. Reed notes that the separation of sexes during worship (closely associated with the Ritualist movement) and the promotion of auricular confession were particularly seen as threats to patriarchal authority (pp. 193–201).
3   Reed, *Glorious Battle*, p. 137.
4   KS Inglis, *Churches and the Working Classes in Victorian England* (London: Routledge and Kegan Paul, 1963), pp. 51, 49–50.
5   ER Wickham, *Church and People in an Industrial City* (London: Lutterworth Press, 1957), p. 116.
6   *Some Reminiscences*, i, p. 126.
7   The quoted lines are from the poem 'London Churches' by R Monckton Milnes, *Hood's Magazine and Comic Miscellany*, 2 (July 1844), pp. 77–8.
8   'Some Pros and Cons. About Pews', *Churchman's Shilling Magazine and Family Treasury*, 1 (1867), pp. 496–500. Reprinted as 'Pros and Cons' in *Commonplace, and Other Short Stories* (London: Macmillan, 1870), pp. 257–67 and in *Selected Prose of Christina Rossetti*, ed. by David A Kent and PG Stanwood (New York: St. Martin's Press, 1998), pp. 112–16. Further references will be to this modern edition and will be cited parenthetically.
9   Christina Rossetti's letters to Emily Newton reveal a shared interest in church politics, in particular the abolition of pew rents (*Letters of Christina Rossetti*, ed. by Antony H Harrison, 4 vols [Charlottesville and London: University Press of Virginia, 1997–] i, pp. 251, 261).
10 E Wordsworth, *Henry William Burrows: Memorials*, with Introduction by the Lord Bishop of Salisbury (London: Kegan Paul, 1894), p. 156.
11 Inglis, p. 50. By the 1870s 'free and open' churches were common (Reed, *Glorious Battle*, p. 139).
12 Henry W Burrows, *The Half-Century of Christ Church, St. Pancras, Albany Street* (London: Skeffington, 1887), p. 42.
13 Burrows, *The Half-Century of Christ Church*, p. 43.
14 Burrows states that seat-holders and 'all inhabitants of the better houses through the district' (*The Half-Century of Christ Church*, pp. 46–7) were invited to vote on the issue; meanwhile, Wordsworth indicates that the vote was more inclusive, that all parishioners along with all seat-holders had a vote, and in both categories the majority voted in favour of abandoning the pew-rent system (*The Half-Century of Christ Church*, p. 156).
15 Burrows, *The Half-Century of Christ Church*, p. 47.

16 Burrows, *The Half-Century of Christ Church*, p. 49; Wordsworth, *Henry William Burrows: Memorials*, pp. 157–8.
17 Wordsworth, *Henry William Burrows: Memorials*, p. 157.
18 (*Letters of Christina Rossetti*, iii, p. 282). Christina's letter to Forman mentions another short periodical publication, 'a set of queries on a Life of Sir Hudson Lowe in "Notes and Queries"'. Interestingly, there is a Burrows connection to the *Notes and Queries* piece on Sir Hudson Lowe: Burrows himself was the son of Colonel Montagu Burrows, who '[i]n 1815 succeeded Sir Hudson Lowe in his command of a division of the British army in South France, when that officer was summoned to take charge of Napoleon at St. Helena' (Wordsworth, *Henry William Burrows: Memorials*, pp. 3–4).
19 Maria F Rossetti, 'Pews: A Colloquy. "One with Another"', *'New and Old': for Seed-Time and Harvest. A Parochial Magazine for all Readers*, 1 (January 1873), pp. 113–16. Because this text is newly identified and is not readily available, the full text is reprinted in the appendix at the end of this chapter.
20 The Gorham controversy began with the Bishop of Exeter's examination of the doctrine of the Rev. George Cornelius Gorham, proposed for the living of Brampford Speke. The Bishop, finding Gorham's position on baptismal regeneration unacceptable, refused to instate him in his living. The case was taken to the Judicial Committee of the Privy Council, a secular authority, who decided that Gorham was allowed to teach that Baptism's sacramental grace depends on the qualification of the recipient, that regeneration in baptism is not unconditional. Thus, the Gorham Judgement permitted an individual clergyman to deny the doctrine of baptism as set forth in the *Book of Common Prayer*; moreover, the archbishops' and bishops' acceptance of the judgement appeared a tacit acknowledgment of the State's right to make rulings on matters of doctrine (Thomas Jay Williams and Allan Walter Campbell, *The Park Village Sisterhood* [London: SPCK, 1965], p. 78). Dodsworth himself, along with other prominent Anglican clergy, became part of a second wave of conversion to Rome launched by this controversy. Before his conversion, however, Dodsworth preached from the pulpit of Christ Church impassioned sermons denouncing the judgement of the Judicial Committee of the Privy Council.
21 *Selected Prose of Christina Rossetti*, p. 112.
22 *Selected Prose of Christina Rossetti*, p. 115.
23 'Some Pros and Cons', *Churchman's Shilling Magazine*, p. 496.
24 *Selected Prose of Christina Rossetti*, p. 113.
25 *Selected Prose of Christina Rossetti*, pp. 115–16.
26 Notably, 'Pros and Cons' avoids debating a Ritualist innovation usually perceived as an overt threat to patriarchal authority, 'the division of the sexes in distinct aisles' which the Rector (and implicitly Christina Rossetti) declares 'a question by itself, and one which I am not now discussing' (*Selected Prose of Christina Rossetti*, p. 115). The historical link between the movement toward free seating and division of the sexes is clear. A survey conducted by the London Free and Open Church Association, published in 1876, reveals that the sexes were divided in roughly a third of the 'Free and Open' churches in London that responded. Conversely, of the London churches with appropriated seating and with weekly offertory responding to same survey, none divided the sexes (London Free and Open Church Association, *Free and Open Churches: Facts and Opinions from Five Hundred Parishes in Town and Country*, 2nd ed. [London, 1876]).
27 *Selected Prose of Christina Rossetti*, p. 116.
28 Christina Rossetti was consistent with the tendencies of the Oxford Movement in

distinguishing between the jurisdictions of Church and State. Howard W Fulweiler states, 'The broader significance of the Oxford Movement for contemporary students of Western culture lies in its making explicit and conscious the English evolution from a "single society" to a pluralistic society. After the work of Locke, Hobbes, Bacon, Butler, and Hume had prepared the way, the Oxford Movement in the fourth decade of the nineteenth century signalled the end of the earlier participative system of social organization in which Church and State were at once mutually inclusive and coextensive. Ironically, the Movement's call for a revival of supernaturalism made it clear that belief in supernaturalism itself was a matter of human volition, of conscious choice, was not a given. Being a member of a divine society was henceforth to be quite separate from being a citizen of the State' ('The Oxford Movement: 1833–45' in *Victorian Prose: A Guide to Research*, ed. by David J DeLaura [New York: MLA, 1973], pp. 361–86 [p. 364]).

29   Robert Hall Baynes, editor of *The Churchman's Shilling Magazine*, had approached Rossetti first in 1864 via Alexander Macmillan, asking for permission to include 'From House to Home' in an anthology he was compiling 'to promote a charitable object' (*Letters of Christina Rossetti*, i, p. 206 and i, p. 211).

30   'The New Year', *'New and Old': for Seed-Time and Harvest. A Parochial Magazine for all Readers*, 1 (January 1873), p. 1–3 (p. 2). The article is unsigned but is presumably by the editor. Rossetti was also well pleased by the periodical's commitment to 'the good cause' of anti-vivisection (*Letters of Christina Rossetti*, ii, pp. 216–17).

31   *Churchman's Shilling Magazine*, 1 (March 1867), p. iii.

32   For further discussion of Rossetti's publications in *'New and Old'* see Diane D'Amico, 'Christina Rossetti's "Helpmeet"', *Victorian Newsletter*, 85 (Spring 1994), pp. 25–9; and Mary Arseneau and Jan Marsh, 'Intertextuality and Intratextuality: The Full Text of Christina Rossetti's "Harmony on First Corinthians XIII" Rediscovered', *Victorian Newsletter*, 88 (Fall 1995), pp. 17–26.

33   Burrows's history details the work of this society (*The Half-Century of Christ Church*, pp. 33–4).

34   *Letters of Christina Rossetti*, ii, p. 204.

35   *Selected Prose of Christina Rossetti*, p. 156.

36   Kathryn Burlinson makes a similar claim, stating that Rossetti's 'treatment of a whole range of nineteenth-century ideologies marks her out as a passionate and singular critic of bourgeois culture: Victorian capitalism, materialism, consumerism, and commodity culture are reviled' (*Christina Rossetti*: Writers and their Work [Plymouth: Northcote, 1998], p. 32).

37   'A Safe Investment', *Churchman's Shilling Magazine*, 2 (November 1967), pp. 287–92; reprinted in *Commonplace*, pp. 241–53. Further references will be to *Commonplace*.

38   'A Safe Investment', pp. 249–50.

39   'A Safe Investment', pp. 251–2.

40   'A Safe Investment', p. 235.

41   The term is from Mary Douglas's *Thought Styles: Critical Essays on Good Taste* (London: Sage Publications, 1996).

42   Matt. 25: 14–30, variant version in Luke 19: 12–27. Two servants, entrusted by their master with five and two talents respectively, invest shrewdly and please their master in returning the talents doubled. The master praises their good stewardship and rewards them 'I will make thee ruler over many things: enter thou into the joy of the lord' (Matt. 25:21 and 25:23). The third servant, who has hidden his talent in the earth and can

present no profit, is called wicked and slothful. His one talent is taken from him and given to the first servant. The unprofitable servant is then cast into 'outer darkness'.
43 Maria F Rossetti 'Pews: A Colloquy', pp. 114–5.
44 *Letters of Christina Rossetti*, ii, 243–4.
45 *Letters of Christina Rossetti*, ii, 257.
46 Max Beerbohm, *Rossetti and His Circle*, ed. with an introduction by N John Hall (New Haven and London: Yale University Press, 1987), no. 12.

7

'A SORT OF AESTHETICO-CATHOLIC REVIVAL': CHRISTINA ROSSETTI AND THE LONDON RITUALIST SCENE

Emma Mason

On Christmas Eve of 1865 Benjamin Jowett wrote to a friend: 'If you walked abroad you would be greatly astonished at the change which has come over the churches of London; there is a sort of aesthetico-Catholic revival going on.'[1] Jowett's shocked reaction to the aesthetic change that had taken place within the Church of England in the 1860s paralleled responses within the popular press, *John Bull*, the *Edinburgh Review* and *The Patriot* all warning their readers of the impending invasion of Roman Catholicism into Britain. The Evangelical-driven *London Quarterly Review* concluded that the nation was simply seeing the 'abundant fruit' of the Romanizing plot 'laid in Oxford thirty years ago.'[2] What is being commented upon here is the spread of ritualism, born into the Victorian consciousness by the Oxford Movement as the *London Quarterly Review* notes, and evocative of striking liturgical and decorative changes within the church space. In its most basic sense, ritual was, as Jowett thought, an aesthetic movement, evinced within churches by the appearance of altar lights, candles, veils, flowers and the burning of incense. On a more complex level, ritualism signified a return to the medieval church, with its implications of ascetic practices and disciplined worship, as well as a profound regard for the visible part of devotion.

Ritualism is widely commented upon in studies of Anglo-Catholicism and the Oxford Movement, but few note the poetics that arose from ritualism during the nineteenth century, GB Tennyson's *Victorian Devotional Poetry* being the striking exception.[3] Recognizing the genre of nineteenth-century ritual poetics opens up, not only the verse of little-known writers such as Adelaide Anne Procter and Isaac Williams, but also the work of Christina Rossetti, marked as it is by an at times intense ritual quality. By locating Rossetti within a ritualist scene especially prominent in London from the 1860s onward, the reader is able to address the critically underdeveloped subject of ritual imagery in her verse. Viewing Christina Rossetti within this ritualist context underlines her position in Victorian Anglo-Catholicism while illuminating her personal beliefs, connections with Tractarian preachers and personal poetic methodology. What follows begins by discussing how ritualism signified itself within the church space and then moves on to indicate how Christina's own church, Christ Church, Albany Street in London, might be understood as a ritualist institution. The poet's own reception of ritualist aesthetics and practice derived from the Oxford Movement clergyman, Edward Pusey, pivotal in the foundation of Christ Church and preaching there to the great impress of its laity. Pusey's reestablishment of confession and conventual sisterhoods within Anglicanism profoundly moved Christina, as her short story *Maude* (1850) reveals, and certainly the preacher's ominous presence on Albany Street affected the poet's Tractarian self-fashioning. While such fashioning may have contributed to her much-debated adolescent breakdown, an idea taken up here, it also aroused a fascination with regard to ritualism that infused Christina's devotional poetry and consequently laid bare her intense Anglo-Catholic faith.

In 1843, Christina began to attend Christ Church, Albany Street, at that time presided over by the priest William Dodsworth. Dodsworth was a close associate of Edward Pusey, who himself was a key figure in the movement from which Victorian Anglo-Catholicism later emerged. This was the Oxford Movement, also known as Tractarianism and founded in the 1830s by a group of University-based clergymen intent on reinstating High Church principles within the Church of England. Looking back to a Laudian and medieval Catholicism, rather than an Italianate Roman Catholicism, the Movement remained associated with Rome because of its reassertion of the supernatural authority of the church, as well as its reestablishment of practices such as confession. Moreover, it sought to promote visible devotion, that is, conveying one's faith through adorning and decorating the church, through a form of medieval ceremonial.[4] In the mid-nineteenth century, the Movement effected a return to visible devotion which impacted on churches in Oxford and elsewhere, particularly in London. For some, such a shift was rebarbative, the seventh Earl of Shaftesbury reporting after his 1866 visit to the ritualist St Albans in Holborn that:

Such a scene of theatrical gymnastics, of singing, screaming, genuflections, such a series of strange movements of the priests, their backs almost always to the people, as I never saw before even in a Romish

Temple. Clouds upon clouds of incense, the censer frequently refreshed by the High Priest, who kissed the spoon, as he dug out the sacred powder, and swung it about at the end of a silver chain [. . .] The Communicants went up to the tune of soft music, as though it had been a melodrama, and one was astonished, at the close, that there was no fall of the curtain.[5]

This kind of adornment formed the basis of Tractarian worship for many believers, and formed a fundamental aspect of Christ Church, built as part of Bishop Charles James Blomfield's scheme to construct fifty new churches in London, and funded in part by Pusey.[6] Consecrated in 1837, Christ Church appeared, according to its second incumbent, Henry William Burrows, amidst 'a time of fervour and revival of church principles, and it is not too much to say that Christ Church became the leading church in the movement'.[7]

Burrows is an important figure in examining the ritualistic qualities of Christ Church due to his role as historian to the building, manifested in his book *The Half-Century of Christ Church*, published in 1887. The study traces the development of Christ Church and outlines both its considerable involvement in local education and poor relief, as well as its ritualism. Burrows confesses that, from the inception of Christ Church, 'a section of the religious world' was 'alarmed by the first tokens of the approach which had not then taken the name of Ritualism, but was voted downright Romanism'.[8] His declaration that 'the arrangements inside were not what we should now consider very ritualistic,' however, betrays not only what heights ritualism had reached in the 1880s, but also Burrows' need to detach Christ Church historically from what many considered Popery.[9] Burrows would have been acutely sensitive about these matters, taking over from Dodsworth in 1851 because the latter had scandalously removed to the Roman Catholic church. How then can we understand Christ Church as a ritualistic institution if its only surviving record attempts to render it otherwise? First, Burrows himself discloses the ritualism within Christ Church by regularly referring to it even after he has tried to undermine its presence. He consistently remarks upon the amount of money spent on decorating the church, highlights the copy of 'Raffaelle's Transfiguration' on the altar, notes the elaborate renovation of the organ, chronicles the donation of an ornate font and its later embellishment, and draws attention to the splendour of its jewelled communion plate, oak pews, marble floors and stained windows.[10]

A more detailed picture of the ritualism inherent to Christ Church may be found in an 1844 manuscript drawn up for the private use of Mr Delane, the Editor of *The Times*, and entitled *The Principal Clergy of London* (1844). The manuscript, now held in the Bodleian Library, classifies clergymen on a scale listing over twenty kinds of religious position within the Church of England: at the top are those deemed 'As near Roman as possible' and at the bottom those 'On the verge of Dissent.'[11] Second from top come the 'Decided Tractarians,' a classification in which Dodsworth is listed and his Church thus deemed ritualistic. The manuscript renders Christ Church as a place 'illuminated with the Back Light: [and] everything arranged to produce "effect"', and then refers the reader to its description of 'St Paul, Knightsbridge' for further information. St Paul's was presided over by the infamous WJE Bennett, forced out of his cure at St Barnabas, Pimlico for extreme ritualism.[12] Of Bennett's, and by implication Dodsworth's, Church, the manuscript states:

> The service in this church approaches [. . .] v. nearly to that of a R. C. Cathedral [...] All the responses are chanted – the litany by the intendent himself: – there are boy choristers in white gowns to assist: – the Altar is as nearly a 'High Altar' as possible [... and] there are constant genuflexions [sic] + bowings toward it. The sermon is of course preached in a surplice[13]

Christ Church, then, was defined by its ritualism and it is no wonder that Sara Coleridge, a member of the congregation along with Rossetti, noted its strong Tractarian element and presence of what she called 'thoroughgoing "Puseyites"'.[14]

The word 'Puseyite' signified a particular kind of excessively ritualist believer, and was derived from Pusey because many considered his own extreme faith too close to Romanism. In a short piece entitled 'What is Puseyism?' the preacher himself declared that the 'class of views' designated by his name indicated six main ideas: high thoughts of the two Sacraments; a high estimate of Episcopacy as God's ordinance; an emphasis upon the visible Church; a strong regard for ordinances, daily public prayers, fasts and feasts and so on; reverence for and deference to the Ancient Church; and a love of the visible, ritualistic part of devotion.[15] Of the latter, Pusey stressed that the 'decoration of the church' acted powerfully and 'insensibly on the mind', provoking his critics to attack him as an ethereal, extreme and thus dangerous member of the Church.[16] In his notorious *Secret History of the Oxford Movement* (1898), for example, Walter Walsh accused Pusey, with some grounds, of wearing hair shirts, entering into severe fasting schemes, acting as a secret agent for Rome and encouraging numerous secret religious societies.[17] Pusey was condemned by publications such as *Punch*, figured as a moth drawn to a Roman Catholic candle in one issue, and attacked within popular fiction like *Barchester Towers* (1857), wherein Mr Slope expresses a furious hostility towards Pusey's followers. Slope 'trembles in agony at the iniquities of the Puseyites', with their satanic 'black silk waistcoats' and prayer books, 'printed with red letters, and ornamented with a cross on the back.'[18] An extreme ascetic, Pusey was attracted to the discipline and ritual imposed in church, and Burrows states that he was particularly impressed with the 'exceptional zeal of some members of the congregation' at Christ Church itself.[19] Pusey chose Christ Church as the site of the first Anglican Sisterhood and often preached there to great effect as Sara Coleridge observed, declaring: 'He is certainly, to my feelings, more impressive than anyone else in the pulpit [. . .] While listening to him, you do not seem to see and hear a *preacher*, but to have visible before you a most earnest and devout spirit, striving to carry out in this world a high religious theory.'[20] As Jan Marsh suggests, if the matured Mrs Coleridge was affected as deeply as these comments bear out, the young and sensitive Rossetti may have been overawed and bewildered by Pusey's fervour.[21]

Pusey's influence over Christina Rossetti's sense of herself as a Tractarian is fundamental to an understanding of her interest in ritualism and may even have contributed to her 'breakdown' in 1845 due to religious mania. Arguably, Rossetti became a Puseyite of sorts, always dressing in black like the women of Pusey's Sisterhood and fasting to mimic the clergyman's ascetic lifestyle.[22] In her commentary on the apocalypse, *The Face of the Deep* (1892), Christina bemoaned the lack of discipline in Church, lamenting that: 'Sunday is being diverted by some to business, by others to pleasure [. . .] Our solemn feasts languish, and our fasts where are they?'[23] While some members of Christ Church thought Pusey and his Sisterhood to be a sign of disguised Roman Catholicism, Christina was clearly enamoured by them. As an associate of the St Mary Magdalene House of Charity, Highgate, Rossetti became a kind of part-time sister, and yet felt unable to join a real sisterhood, haunted as she was by her own unworthiness before God.[24] This sense of unworthiness may itself have been derived from Pusey, who wrote to Keble that he felt 'scarred all over and seamed with sin, so that I am a monster to myself; I loathe myself; I can feel of myself only like one covered with leprosy from head to foot; guarded as I have been, there is no one with whom I do not compare myself, and find myself worse than they.'[25]

There is a noticeable similarity in tone between Pusey's sorrowful disclosure and the contents of a letter written by Christina to a dying Dante Gabriel, increasingly concerned with his past actions and conduct towards the end of his life. She writes: 'I want to assure you that, however harassed by memory or anxiety you may be, I have (more or less) heretofore gone through the same ordeal. I have borne myself till I became unbearable to myself, and then I have found help in confession and absolution and spiritual counsel, and relief inexpressible.'[26] Further, as Marsh recognizes, Christina's short story, *Maude*, expresses a similar sensation of unworthiness, the narrative following the spiritual breakdown of a fifteen-year-old girl whose demise is signalled by her refusal to take communion on account of her sins.[27] As Christina intimates in the poem, 'After Communion', to receive the body and blood of Christ is a process which moulds the soul into a waiting room for Christ's 'flame' to reside, until it explodes within heaven.[28] The believer's personal relationship with Christ is tightened here: his role as Lord becoming God, Friend now Lover and King Spouse, a bond underlined by the 'banner' of 'love' which frames their union, a clear reference to the Song of Solomon.[29] Alarmed, then, by the prospect of such an intense alliance with God, the spiritually disturbed Maude refuses to receive communion. She declares: 'I will not profane Holy Things; I will not add this to all the rest. I have gone over and over again, thinking I should come right in time, and I do not come right [. . .] Some day I may be fit again to approach the Holy Altar, but till then I will at least refrain from dishonouring it.' Maude finally breaks down, 'leaning upon the table and weeping bitterly' in remorse.[30]

Maude, while not directly autobiographical, remains reflective of Christina's own childhood, in particular her 1845 'breakdown' noted by nearly all of her biographers as transforming her from a whimsical and impetuous little girl, to a controlled, introspective and apprehensive young woman. At fifteen, she suffered an illness manifesting symptoms of dark depression, weight loss, great fatigue and violent outbursts, including an occasion on which she tore open her arm with a pair of scissors. Having seen many different physicians who failed to diagnose her, the distinguished Dr Charles Hare was consulted, observing that between the ages of sixteen and eighteen, Christina was 'more or less out of her mind (suffering, in fact, from a form of insanity, I believe a kind of religious mania).'[31] Her poetry of this time, morbid, morose and melancholy, attests more to a writer aware of Victorian poetic style than one in the throes of nervous breakdown, and while its themes are less obviously religious, it remains obsessed with God and faith.[32] Christina's biographers, however, seem cautious in attributing religious mania to her, Kathleen Jones declaring that her illness was unlikely to have been caused by 'excessive religious zeal', attributing it to Christina's prudent escape from 'domestic and social duties.'[33] Lona Mosk Packer's notoriously ungrounded assertion that Christina engaged in a tragic love-affair sidelines her religious breakdown, and Marsh's inference that her father forced her into 'some sexual activity at the age of twelve or thirteen' merely gestures that this may have made her 'vulnerable to the teaching of Pusey and Dodsworth.'[34]

Framed by her obsessively devout Tractarian faith, Christina Rossetti's adolescent breakdown can instead be attributed to her religious feelings which caused her to feel extreme emotions of guilt and unworthiness that she was unable to intellectualize until her later life. Dr Hare's assessment was probably correct in attributing religious mania to her, an explanation reliant on recognizing the poet as a fervent Tractarian. Rossetti was not alone in her predicament, faith consuming the juvenile poet as it did many young middle-class women in the nineteenth century. One recalls Florence Nightingale's religious breakdown at seventeen and the fictional Lucy Snowe's disturbing fixation on Catholicism in *Villette*, driven to 'the church and confessional' because of a 'cruel sense of desolation' that 'pained [her] mind.'[35] Pusey had defended the practice of confession to Manning precisely because of its healing effects upon a fourteen-year-old girl whose spiritual depression was lifted by the magical outcome of her penitential revelations.[36] Similarly, Rossetti's tortured and manic state subsided, and Marsh contends that by moving away from Pusey's direction, 'she endeavoured to create and share with others a contemplative understanding of the divine order.'[37] Rossetti continued to assume the 'lowest place' psychologically, intensifying her stringent faith, and yet seems to have developed happy relationships with both friends and family, undermining the conception of her as a desolate and lonely soul.[38] Both Janet Camp Troxell and Antony Harrison have recognized a satirical, confident and witty writer in Rossetti's letters: Troxell pointing out her 'vivid humour,' and Harrison noting her will to self-promotion, one which balances her usual avowal of unworthiness.[39]

Rossetti suffered while she remained a Puseyite, but partly because she had chosen to fashion herself that way, and attendance at the ritualist Christ Church would have required her to assume a sombre High Church demeanour. At the same time, it is clear that she was gratified through her position within a Tractarian establishment, aesthetically appreciative of the medieval adornment so apparent in Christ Church, and invested in its accentuation of sin and the practice of confession as a way of relieving such contrition. Pusey himself had revived confession as early as 1838 and vehemently defended it in his pamphlet, *The Entire Absolution of the Penitent* (1846), arguing that confession must be regularly and systematically instituted in the Church of England, and maintaining that this view was endorsed by some of the Reformers and Caroline Divines.[40] Yet Pusey's endorsement of confession served only to reaffirm his mysterious and depraved identity for some, the practice viewed by critics as a kind of secret privilege for Tractarians to indulge in Roman practice. EA Knox described it as 'a rite stigmatised as papistical' and so 'all the more alluring,' the 'thrill of mystery and of persecution for the faith' adding 'to the joy of unburdening the conscience'; while Charles James Blomfield, Bishop of London, declared that confession was 'the source of unspeakable abominations.'[41] Such horrors were thought to have the potential to damage two dominant nineteenth-century institutions: first, the Church of England, threatened by the spread of Catholic mannerisms;

and secondly, the Victorian family unit, which, it was feared, would be intruded into by the questioning priest.[42] Confessing one's sins to God through the medium of a human agent in the space of a confessional box threatened Victorian sensibility because it forced one to broadcast sin outside of the family to a priest portrayed as perversely eager to listen.

Several of Rossetti's poems illustrate the value which she placed on confession, her series of poems on St Peter, for example, movingly portraying the desire to 'confess in ecstasy,' as her sonnet, 'Have I not striven' underlines the importance of 'Confessing' to 'angels and to men'.[43] Rossetti's interest in confession affirmed the fears of many anti-Catholic critics that the practice was particularly alluring to women, cajoled into betraying personal secrets to predatory male confessors. As Charles Maurice Davies alleged in *Philip Paternoster* (1858): 'It would be a fatal day for England if ever England's wives and daughters were led to deem the confessional a more sacred place than the home.'[44] Women tended to outnumber men not only in receiving confession but also in ritualist congregations, and the Anglo-Catholic John Chambers expressed serious concern about 'the scoffing censure that our churches are filled and our Altars crowded with women.' One young curate even despaired that ritualism was a conspiring 'female movement,' wherein women could usurp the places of clerics.[45] Much of what signalled a ritualist church, its luxurious floral displays, embroidered kneelers and hangings and other such refined furnishings, was created by women, and Rossetti seems to have enjoyed the aesthetic ornamentation of her own parish. As she wrote to Caroline Gemmer in 1870: 'This Xmas at Christ Church we had a new and to me most delightful decoration, a large red cross reared on high in the Chancel arch; I hope it may reappear at Easter, though perhaps in different colours.'[46]

With its display of ritual and Catholic mystery, then, Christ Church offered the poet a realm in which she could think about God in a manner transcendent of mere piety, with Pusey and Dodsworth as her spiritual guides. Moreover, as Sara Coleridge claimed, the religious atmosphere at Christ Church produced 'a flavour of combined learning and piety, and of literary and artistic refinement', encouraging its members to appreciate God, not only with theological writings, but through literature. As Burrows notes, the efforts of women like Rossetti's sister, Maria, in forging a pedagogical climate within Christ Church led to its eventual establishment of a commercial school for girls and boys in the early 1850s. The religious instruction offered here was primarily aesthetic, spoken poetical and artistic renderings of scripture appealing to the imagination in believers, many of whom remained illiterate.[47] Poetry was especially valued by the Tractarians as the best genre through which to communicate God's truths, Newman writing that it paralleled faith in its provision of 'the evidence of things not seen', and Keble declaring it 'a channel of supernatural knowledge.'[48] Rossetti's poetry is lined with ritual imagery, both outwardly in its allusions to crucifixes, candles, incense and so on; and implicitly, using such symbolism to connote an intense adoration of Christ. Her devotional collection *Verses* (1893) reads like a handbook of ritualist ceremony, mysteriously connoting such practises to lure the reader into an aesthetic as well as a spiritual atmosphere. It is as if Rossetti forges the poem as a church space in the manner of Herbert in *The Temple* (1633) or Isaac Williams in *The Cathedral* (1838), decorating its interior to invite contemplation on deeper religious secrets.

Many of the poems in *Verses* in fact do not describe a ritual ceremony to the reader but instead position him or her as a worshipper within a ritual church. In this sense, Rossetti uses the poem as what Walter Pater referred to as a 'religious "retreat" ', one in which the reader can contemplate theology and belief.[49] For Pater, the 'perfect poem' is precisely that which has 'no uncharacteristic or tarnished or vulgar decoration', but remains aesthetically pleasing because of its 'necessary' ornament.[50] Rossetti's use of ritualism complements this definition because its aesthetic and ornamental sense adheres only to a strict and genuinely expressed set of religious beliefs that may be contemplated through ritual design. In her poem 'You who looked on passed ages as a glass', Christina even deems ritualism a 'hush of nature' in which to 'think on Rome [. . .] Not as it is now but as it once was'.[51] She thus decorates her poems to recall an ancient ritualist service, making countless references to flowers, incense, chancels, veils and candles as well as to more specific objects.[52] 'Advent Sunday', for example, invokes the 'lighted lamps and garlands' that illuminated the church where 'Light in all eyes' describes the 'mitred priests' who led the service. 'Christmas Carols' refers to the prayer bells, while 'Lift up thine eyes to seek the invisible' describes the 'golden harps' and 'The joy of Saints' the golden censers. Incense again appears in 'Thy lovely saints do bring Thee love', smothering the worshippers within a fog that renders them all equal before God. Precious stones in Rossetti's poetry are also customary, rubies, diamonds, pearls and other gemstones set into the structure of poems such as '"His Banner over me was Love" ', 'Whence death has vanished like a shifting sand' and '"Beautiful for situation" '. Such imagery creates a luminous atmosphere within these devotional poems, which is enhanced further by constant references to seraphs and cherubs who float around a grandly crowned and robed Christ.[53]

Christ himself is often rendered through a distinctly ritualized depiction, the crucifixion focused on as a kind of Eucharistic rite. For Rossetti, the image of the crucifix was a bloody and Gothic symbol of sacrifice, pain and Christ's savage murder, often illuminated in ritualist churches to imbue them with a spectral splendour. As she contended in *The Face of the Deep*: 'the Cross is the nucleus of heaven'.[54] Rossetti's poems on the crucifixion provoke the reader to always observe its ritual overtones, the narrator's response shifted to the fore to create a relationship between Christ and the believer like that forged between priest and worshipper within the church. Her narrators confront the crucifix by identifying with Christ's pain rather than glorifying in its brutality, quietly contemplating what he died for within the ritual space of the poem. The narrator of 'Good Friday', for example, is frozen by the terror of what she perceives when confronted by the crucifix:

> Am I a stone and not a sheep
> That I can stand, O Christ, beneath Thy Cross
> To number drop by drop Thy Blood's slow loss,
> And yet not weep?[55]

The image of Christ's steady loss of blood is sombre and sets a gory example for the believer, whom, Rossetti states in 'Thy Servant will go and fight with this Philistine', should consistently seek death to convince God she is truly penitent: 'never stint[ing]/ Body or breath or blood' and always demonstrating 'proof in grace,' prepared to 'Die for thy Lord, as once for thee thy Lord'.[56] The bloody image of the crucifix, then, focuses the believer's attention on how she should present herself before God.

Rossetti may have derived her ritual emphasis on Christ's blood from Williams' sonnets, inspired, according to Tennyson, by a 'Continental Catholic piety' which would have appealed to the Anglo-Italian poet.[57] Williams' focus on the crucifixion in his collections *The Cathedral* (1838) and *The Altar* (1847) presents a narrator embroiled within the Gothic horror of Christ's physical suffering and reliving Christ's death as a sensual experience.[58] As the narrator of 'The Cross Dripping Blood' states:

> Blood from His Hands is falling, drop by drop,
> And from his Temples; now in streams they roll –
> Haste downward to the earth as to their goal;
> Now hang on His pale Body, and there stop,
> Or on the wood below; till from the top
> Unto the base the blood-stains mark the whole.[59]

The narrator graphically confirms the butchery of crucifixion by depicting a faded and beaten Christ whose blood dribbles down his body, dangling off his frame and then soaking the cross on which he hangs. Rossetti recalls such horror in 'Palm Sunday,' for example, intently thinking on Christ as one

'Compassed with thorns and bleeding everywhere'.[60] So too in 'Despised and Rejected' does she envision Christ as a repudiated messiah, rejected by the narrator and forced into a metaphoric crucifixion wherein he sobs: 'My Feet bleed, see My Face/ See My Hands bleed that bring thee grace,/ My Heart doth bleed for thee'.[61] Fashioned as a beaten and bloodstained martyr, Christ evokes a bloodiness enactive of the ritualized communion of Anglo-Catholic ceremony, one Rossetti further reinforces in her Eucharistic images of the saints.

Christina's reverence for saintly ethereal beings is most obvious in her hagiographic *Called To Be Saints: The Minor Festivals Devotionally Studied* (1881), a discussion of the black-letter Saints.[62] Within this study, the poet betrayed a ritual admiration for the saints frowned upon by the conventional 'Protestant' tradition in the Church of England. In the twenty-second of the *Thirty-Nine Articles*, for example, the invocation of saints is rejected as a form of vain idolatry which takes the 'form of a grotesque polytheism' in its obscuration of God, obstructing the believer's personal 'mediation' with Christ at the same time.[63] The saints remained central to Tractarian worship and those poems wherein Rossetti invokes them read like a ritual litany of the saints.

The poet safeguarded her portraits of the saints from anti-Papists, however, by overtly declaring Christ's supremacy over them in order to dissociate herself from 'Romanist' idolatry. Christ is championed as 'better than Thy saints' in 'The Chiefest among ten thousand'; and in 'Half Dead', the saintly trainee 'Christs' merely emulating their Lord, praying to 'grow more like Thee day by day'.[64] Yet such generic salutes do not detract from the intensity of Rossetti's poems about saints, wherein they either rescue Christ from a bloody predicament or rise spectre-like before the believer complete with the gashes and cuts of a martyr. The saints in 'Before the Throne, and before the Lamb' enunciate 'the voice of an unclouded thundering' as Christ rises before them, expressing their misery at the pain he has suffered and enclosing him within their ranks.[65] The saints form a circle around Christ to demarcate a sacred ground in which the cleansing of souls may take place, beginning by laundering his blood-drenched garments with the white glare that shines from their purity. Christ's once muddy clothes are newly depicted as a 'raiment [of] white' that the saints have 'slowly spun' from 'blood-steeped linen,' and in turn, their own luminosity sparkles more intensely than before.

The saints of 'All Saints: Martyrs' also radiate a shining and fiery glow as they enter into 'New Jerusalem,' revitalized by Christ who grants them eternal life 'for evermore'.[66] Lavishly rendered by Rossetti as 'All luminous and lovely in their gore,' the saints here mirror Williams' depiction of Christ as a 'bleeding spectacle', and this intensifies the Gothic overtones of Catholic sainthood in the poem.[67] The same passionate and inflamed image of sainthood appears in the sonnet 'All Saints', as the saints drift 'like a stream of incense launched on flame' from 'death to life above'. Catapulted on such a divine explosion, the saints spread their incense-filled haze around so that heaven begins to resemble the intense interiors of Christ Church or St Albans.[68] It is here, in the midst of a metaphorical ritual ceremonial, that 'God makes glad His Saints', both 'Numbered and treasured by the Almighty Hand' like stars or 'grains of sand'.[69] The representation of the saints as tiny fractions of a larger body in 'All Saints' connotes to Rossetti's reader that she too will be joined with this final heavenly mass once absolved in paradise, envisioning sainthood as the ultimate goal of all believers. Ritual almost becomes a signifier of heaven on earth here and as such might be understood as a kind of halfway house between the two realms, rendering the medievalized church space a premonition of paradise.

By mapping the language of Rossetti's devotional verse onto a ritual context, then, we can begin to recreate Tractarian ceremonial as the poet would have witnessed it at Christ Church. This is important not only because it adds a further aesthetic dimension to Rossetti's still undervalued religious poetry, but also because it renders such poetry as a kind of historical document. *Verses* can thus be read as a companion piece to Burrows' history of Christ Church, both writers serving to conjure the atmosphere of a place of worship central to both mid nineteenth-century ritualism and Victorian Anglo-Catholicism. Moreover, these poems, touched as they are by the services Rossetti attended at Christ Church, illuminate the deep experience of standing before preachers such as Pusey and Dodsworth. By tracing a kind of ritual poetics in *Verses*, the reader is enabled to reconstruct Rossetti's interest in the ritualist scene so prevalent in Victorian London and in doing so, more clearly perceive her status as a religious commentator as well as poet.

Notes

1 In Paul Thureau-Dangin, *The English Catholic Revival in the Nineteenth-Century*, 2 vols (New York: EP Dutton and Co., n.d.), in John Shelton Reed, *Glorious Battle: The Cultural Politics of Victorian Anglo-Catholicism* (Nashville and London: Vanderbilt University Press, 1996), pp.60–1.

2 Shelton Reed, *Glorious Battle*, p. 60.

3 GB Tennyson, *Victorian Devotional Poetry: The Tractarian Mode* (Massachusetts: Harvard University Press, 1981).

4 See Owen Chadwick, *The Mind of the Oxford Movement* (London: Adam and Charles Black, 1960), p. 51.

5 In Edwin Hodder, *The Life and Work of the Seventh Earl of Shaftesbury, K. G.* (London: Cassell, 1886), in Shelton Reed, *Glorious Battle*, p. 61; see also Geoffrey Rowell, *The Vision Glorious: Themes and Personalities of the Catholic Revival in Anglicanism* (Oxford: Oxford University Press, 1983), p. 129.

6   Pusey contributed £1000 in cash, see Henry William Burrows, *The Half-Century of Christ Church, Albany Street, St. Pancras* (London: Skeffington and Son, 1887), p. 9; further references to Burrows's *Half-Century* appear in the text.

7   Burrows, *Christ Church*, p. 14.

8   Burrows, *Christ Church*, pp. 10–11.

9   Burrows, *Christ Church*, p. 11.

10 Burrows, *Christ Church*, pp. 21, 31, 47, 50, 66.

11 'The Principal Clergy of London: Classified According to their opinions on the Great Church questions of the day', 1844, Bodleian Library, MS Add c.290; the classification scale is written at the beginning of the manuscript and appears as follows: As near Roman as possible – Decided Tractarians – All Strong Tractarians – Strong Tractarians – Tractarians – A leaning toward the Tractarian party – Supposed leaning toward the Tractarian party – Moderates openly attached to neither party but supposed to incline rather towards the *High* than the *Low* Church – [. . .] Moderates; – all of the old 'High and Dry' School – Moderates: – Supposed to be rather inclined to *High* Church – Moderates: – supposed to be inclined to *Low* Church – Moderates: – inclined to the Evangelical party – Evangelical moderates – Evangelical moderates but a stage in advance of the last four – Evangelicals – Strong Evangelicals – Very Decided Evangelicals – Very Low Church 'After the Tractarian Heresy' – Decidedly Low Church [. . .] – extremely low Church prepared to take any step against Tractarianism – On the verge of Dissent, pp. 3–4; further references to the manuscript are given after quotations in the text.

12 Rossetti may have met Bennett at Frome, a small country town by Longleat House where her Aunt Charlotte was Governess to Lady Bath who in turn had employed Bennett after he had been sacked from St Barnabus.

13 'Principal Clergy of London', p. 7.

14 Burrows, *Christ Church*, p. 67.

15 Henry Parry Liddon, *Life of Edward Bouverie Pusey: Doctor of Divinity, Canon of Christ Church Regius Professor of Hebrew in the University of Oxford*, ed. Rev. JO Johnson and Rev. Robert J Wilson, 4 vols (London: Longmans, Green and Co, 1894), ii, p. 140.

16 Liddon, *Life of Edward Bouverie Pusey*, ii, p. 140.

17 Walter Walsh, *The Secret History of the Oxford Movement* [Third Edition] (London: Swan Sonnenschein and Co., 1898), pp. 36ff.

18 'The Puseyite Moth and Roman Candle,' *Punch* (1850), in Shelton Reed, *Glorious Battle*, p. xiii; and Anthony Trollope, *Barchester Towers* [1857], ed. John Sutherland (Oxford: Oxford University Press, 1998), p. 28.

19 Burrows, *Christ Church*, p. 16.

20 Sara Coleridge, *Life and Letters of Sara Coleridge*, 2 vols (1873), in Jan Marsh, *Christina Rossetti: A Literary Biography* (London: Pimlico, 1995), p. 57.

21 Marsh, *Christina Rossetti*, p. 57.

22 Liddon, *Life of Edward Bouverie Pusey*, iii, p. 26.

23 Christina Rossetti, *The Face of the Deep* (London: SPCK), 1892), p. 243.

24 Elaine Showalter, ed., *Christina Rossetti: Maude; Dinah Mulock Craik: On Sisterhoods, a Woman's Thoughts about Women* (London: William Pickering, 1993), p. xiii; see also, Diane D'Amico, '"Equal Before God": Christina Rossetti and the Fallen Women of Highgate Penitentiary,' *Gender and Discourse in Victorian Literature and Art*, ed. Antony H Harrison and Beverly Taylor (Dekalb: Northern Illinois University Press, 1992), pp. 67–83.

25 Edward Bouverie Pusey, letter to John Keble, n.d., in Liddon, *Life of Edward Bouverie Pusey*, iii, p. 96.

26 Christina Rossetti, letter to Dante Gabriel Rossetti, 2 December 1881, in Marsh, *Christina Rossetti*, p. 60.

27 Christina Rossetti, *Maude* (1849–50), in *Poems and Prose*, ed. Jan Marsh (London: Everyman, 1994), pp. 251–74. It is of note that Rossetti wrote a sequel to *Maude* entitled *Corrispondenza Famigliare (Family Correspondence)*, an unfinished epistolary novel written in Italian and first published in *The Bouquet* (1852).

28 'After Communion', in Poems Added in *Goblin Market, The Prince's Progress and Other Poems* (1875), in *Complete Poems of Christina Rossetti*, i, pp. 191–230.

29 op. cit., ll. 1–5.

30 *Maude*, p. 267.

31 James A Kohl traces Hare's note to the blank pages of Godfrey Bilchett's copy of MacKenzie Bell's *Christina Rossetti: A Biographical and Critical Study* (1898), in 'A Medical Comment on Christina Rossetti,' *Notes and Queries*, 15:213:11 (1968), 423–4 (p. 423); see also Marsh, *Christina Rossetti*, pp. 52–3.

32 Undoubtedly Rossetti was physically ill at this time, and her family history displayed distinct cases of mental illness, most notably her uncle John Polidori, author of *The Vampyre* (1819) and physician to Byron, who committed suicide in 1821. Rossetti's failing health, however, should not be overstated. Frances Thomas reminds us of the young poet's cheery letters to her brothers at this time, in *Christina Rossetti: A Biography* (London: Virago Press, 1992), p. 53; and Kathleen Jones remarks upon Rossetti's supposed hysteria as a convenient escape from the world, reminding us of Dora Greenwell's comment that ill health established a 'little cave to run into' which had 'many social immunities' for Rossetti, in Kathleen Jones, *Learning Not to be First: The Life of Christina Rossetti* (Oxford: Oxford University Press, 1992), pp. 20–1.

33 Jones, *Learning*, pp. 18, 21.

34 LM Packer, *Christina Rossetti* (Cambridge: Cambridge University Press, 1963); Marsh, *Christina Rossetti*, p. 260.

35 Charlotte Brontë, *Villette* [1853] (New York: Oxford University Press, 1990), p. 231; see also Susan David Bernstein, *Confessional Subjects: Revelations of Gender and Power in Victorian Literature and Culture* (Chapel Hill and London: The University of North Carolina Press, 1997), p. 58.

36 In Keith Denison, 'Dr Pusey as Confessor and Spiritual Counsellor,' *Pusey Rediscovered*, ed. Perry Butler (London: SPCK, 1983), in Marsh, *Christina Rossetti*, p. 63.

37 Marsh, *Christina Rossetti*, p. 452.

38 When Rossetti's niece, Helen Rossetti, burst into a sudden temper, Rossetti claims to have been reminded of herself as a child, and there is no suggestion that William's daughter was an abused and agonised melancholic. Rossetti told Helen: 'You must not imagine that your Aunt was always the calm and sedate person you now behold. I, too, had a very passionate temper [and] on one occasion, being rebuked by my dear Mother for some fault, I seized upon a pair of scissors, and ripped up my arm to vent my wrath,' in Marsh, *Christina Rossetti*, p. 50; atrocious behaviour indeed, but a not unheard of eruption in the life of a sensitive girl.

39 Janet Camp Troxell, *Three Rossettis: Unpublished Letters from Dante Gabriel, Christina and William* (Massachusetts: Harvard University Press, 1937), p.148; Antony H Harrison, 'Epistolary Relations: The Correspondence of Christina Rossetti and Dante Gabriel Rossetti,' *The Journal of Pre-Raphaelite Studies*, 4 (1995), 91–101 (p. 95); see also *The Letters*

of Christina Rossetti, ed. Antony H Harrison, 4 vols (Charlottesville and London: The University Press of Virginia, 1997–).

40 EB Pusey, *The Entire Absolution of the Penitent* (1846), in Peter Benedict Nockles, *The Oxford Movement in Context: Anglican High Churchmanship 1760–1857* (Cambridge: Cambridge University Press, 1994), pp. 249–50.

41 EA Knox, *The Tractarian Movement: 1833–1845* (London: Putnam, 1934), in Shelton Reed, *Glorious Battle*, p. 49; CJ Blomfield, *A Charge to the Clergy of London* [1842], in James Bentley, *Ritualism and Politics in Victorian Britain: The Attempt to Legislate for Belief* (Oxford: Oxford University Press, 1978), p. 30; Walsh also attacked Pusey in this context by reciting the story of Miss Cusack, also known as the Nun of Kenmare, who, after receiving confession from Pusey, wrote: 'I believe that the secrecy, and concealment, and devices which had to be used to get an audience with the Doctor, for the purpose of Confessing had a little, if it had not a good deal, to do with his success', see NF Cusack, *The Story of my Life* (1891), in Walsh, *Secret History* (1898), p. 87.

42 Bentley, *Ritualism*, pp. 30–1.

43 All Rossetti poems are from *Verses* (1893), in *The Complete Poems of Christina Rossetti: A Variorum Edition*, 3 vols, ed. RW Crump (Baton Rouge and London: Louisiana State University Press, 1986), pp. 179–335, unless otherwise indicated.

44 Charles Maurice Davies, *Philip Paternoster* (1858), in Bernstein, *Confessional Subjects*, p. 47.

45 John Charles Chambers, 'Private Confession and Absolution' (1867), in Shelton Reed, *Glorious Battle*, p. 187.

46 Christina Rossetti, letter to Caroline Gemmer, 4 February 1870, Harrison, *The Letters of Christina Rossetti*, i, p. 340.

47 Burrows, *Christ Church*, pp. 34, 36.

48 John Henry Newman, 'Sermons, chiefly on the Theory of Religious Belief,' in Chadwick, *Mind of the Oxford Movement*, pp. 71–3; Keble, Keble, 'Tract 89: On the Mysticism attributed to the Early Fathers of the Church' *Tracts for the Times by members of the University of Oxford*, 6 vols (London: JGF and J Rivington, 1841), p. 185.

49 Walter Pater, *Appreciations: With an Essay on Style* (London: Macmillan, 1890), p. 14.

50 Pater, *Appreciations*, p. 15.

51 In Christina Rossetti, *Unpublished Poems* (n.d.), in *Complete Poems of Christina Rossetti*, iii, pp. 115–301; even as Rossetti rejects Italianate Catholicism, she remains respectful of the latter's tradition and followers, her sonnet 'Cardinal Newman' venerating the newly converted Catholic as a 'Champion of the Cross' (l. 1).

52 References to flowers in *Verses* are numerous, but see, for example, 'Thy lilies drink the dew', 'Who hath despised the day of small things,' 'Where shall I find a white rose blowing?' and 'Consider the Lilies of the field'; on incense see 'All Saints' and 'Thy lovely saints do bring Thee love'; on veils, see 'Sooner or later: yet at last', 'St Bartholomew' and 'Are they not all Ministering Spirits?' and 'Earth has clear call of daily bells' for a reference to the chancel.

53 See, for example, 'This near-at-hand land breeds pain by measure.'

54 *The Face of the Deep*, p. 504.

55 'Good Friday', in *The Prince's Progress and Other Poems* (1866), in *Complete Poems of Christina Rossetti*, i, pp. 95–187.

56 'Thy Servant will go and fight with this Philistine', in *Verses* (1893), ll. 12–14.

57 Tennyson, *Victorian Devotional Poetry*, p. 168.

58 Isaac Williams, *The Cathedral or the Catholic and Apostolic Church in England* (Oxford: John

Henry Parker; London: JGF and J Rivington, 1838); *The Altar: Or, Meditations in Verse on the Great Christian Sacrifice (With numerous illustrations)* (London: James Burns, 1847); further references to these editions are given after quotations in the text, stating the Section number in which they appear, and where necessary, are signified by the titles *Cathedral* and *Altar*.

59 'The Cross Dripping Blood', in *Altar*, xxii, ll. 1–6.

60 'Palm Sunday', l. 5.

61 'Despised and Rejected', in *The Prince's Progress and Other Poems*, ll. 45–7.

62 The 'black letter saints' are lesser, non-scriptural figures, distinct from the major saints who are marked by red letters in the Book of Common Prayer Calendar.

63 Reverend E Tyrrell Green, *The Thirty Nine Articles and The Age of the Reformation: An Historical and Doctrinal Exposition in the Light of Contemporary Documents* (London: Wells Gardner, Darton and Co., 1896), pp. 146, 160–1.

64 'Half Dead' (*Verses*), l. 12; 'The Chiefest among ten   thousand' (*Verses*), l. 6.

65 'Before the Throne and before the Lamb' (*Verses*), l. 2.

66 'All Saints: Martyrs' (*Verses*), ll. 2, 5.

67 'All Saints: Martyrs' (*Verses*), l. 3, 'The Holy Land' (*Cathedral*), xxvi.

68 'All Saints' (*Verses*), ll. 9–10.

69 'All Saints' (*Verses*), ll. 14, 1–2.

8

IN THE FOOTSTEPS OF HIS FATHER? DANTEAN ALLEGORY IN GABRIELE ROSSETTI AND DANTE GABRIEL ROSSETTI

Valeria Tinkler-Villani

In this chapter, I follow some of the of cultural forces at play in England in the nineteenth century, with Gabriele Rossetti and some of his children as the focal point. Gabriele's was an enforced exile, meaning that he suddenly arrived on the English scene from a very different environment – in this case, early nineteenth-century Neapolitan society, with its political turbulence that existed both openly on the streets and hidden in secret societies. Author of patriotic songs against the Bourbon rulers in Naples and a member of the secret society of the Carbonari,[1] Gabriele had been a successful librettist, an activity he continued in England, where he also taught Italian (at Kings College, London, between 1831 and 1843). Although his Dante studies were recondite and a matter for the expert scholar, the controversy they aroused would presumably have received attention proportionate to his general presence on the English cultural scene.

The boldness of Gabriele's interpretation of Dante was a violent intrusion into early Victorian culture – what Charles Lyell, the famous geologist and son of the Charles Lyell who was Rossetti's patron, would have called a 'catastrophist' rather than a 'uniformitarian' process. Gabriele's career highlights developments in a significant relationship in the culture of nineteenth-century England, that between the creative writer and the scientist.

I first trace some aspects of Gabriele Rossetti's presence on the English cultural scene, then move to a brief survey of certain ideas in his Dante studies, and finally discuss Dante Gabriel's possible response to the issues his father raised. I also look at the varying attitudes towards allegory during this period, and show how these were indicative of significant changes in cultural practice in nineteenth-century England.

In his autobiography in verse, *La Vita Mia – Il Testamento*, Gabriele Rossetti entrusts the defence of his own work to his four children: all four will, he says, 'confound the unbelieving enemies'.[2] Gabriele is referring to the views defined by his son, William Michael Rossetti, as the 'allegorical, non-natural, or abstruse interpretations which our father put upon Dante and the Italian Mediaeval and Renaissance writers'. In Gabriele's view, the writings of Dante and other writers, as William Michael put it, 'have an esoteric significance and value highly different and divergent from their exoteric meaning'.[3] Rossetti senior's dubious scholarship cost him his job at King's College, London – thereby forcing his wife and daughters to attempt to set up a school – and also cost him his reputation and health. Although the Rossetti children were keen to distance themselves from their father's views on allegory, the burden of inheritance Gabriele placed upon his four children needed to be answered, even if by the rejection of these views or by an opposing stress on literality.

The two less celebrated Rossetti children were very directly engaged with Dante. In the introduction to her *Shadow of Dante* (1871), Maria Francesca indirectly acknowledges the grounds for complex interpretations such as Gabriele's, for she admits that Dante's poetry 'is elliptical – it is recondite'.[4] But her own aim and method are 'faithful literality', a phrase she repeats twice.[5] This explains why she went on to use William Michael's translation for quotations from the *Inferno* and Longfellow's translation for the other *cantiche*: they are 'line-for-line blank verse translations'. She further acknowledges her obligations first to her 'late dear Father', and then, among others, to Charles Bagot Cayley.

William Michael, too, stresses that 'The aim of this translation of Dante [his version of *Inferno*, 1865] may be summed up in one word – Literality'.[6] He distinguishes between translating the form of the poem (which entails preserving rhyme, metre and so on) and the substance, which requires literality. There is a greater unifying concept, which he calls 'fidelity'. By respecting both form and substance, fidelity is true to 'the spirit' of a poem, although to focus on only one of these aims (form or substance) will allow the translator to reproduce at least part of the spirit of the original.

In this respect, William Michael's attitude differs from that of other translations of Dante. He comments that Cary not only discards the form but also only 'gives Dante's substance with moderate literality', and therefore 'does not, to my [William Michael's] judgement, come *very* close to the spirit'. Carlyle, on the contrary, 'gives the substance, and its spirit', his prose translation, totally neglectful of form, being the epitome of literality. A more successful attempt, in William Michael's view, is the translation by Charles Bagot Cayley, who 'gives substance, form, and spirit, as far as the mutual concessions inevitable to the very arduous threefold attempt will allow', his translation being in terza rima. William Michael states that he himself follows the example of Pollock, who steers a middle course: 'unconditional literality' in matter, accompanied by some retention of rhythm by using blank verse'. In his introduction William Michael carefully avoids expressing 'adherence or dissent from [sic] the various theories and interpretations' that have been promoted – including, clearly, his father's – and repeatedly stresses that for him to 'take him [Dante] literally is enough'; he will only focus on 'the *primary* meaning' [his emphasis].

The Cayley acknowledged by Maria and praised by William is none other than the family friend and (presumed) beloved of Christina – and, more importantly in this context, the pupil of Gabriele. These personal relationships might have blinded the Rossettis' judgements, since Cayley's terza rima is a very painful affair:

> Upon the journey of our life midway,
>   I found myself within a darksome wood,
> As from the right path I had gone astray.
> Ah! But to speak hereof is drearihood;[7]

Nevertheless, Cayley handsomely acknowledges Gabriele Rossetti's work in his translation of the *Commedia* (*Hell* in 1851, followed by the other *cantiche* in the same decade), confirming that Gabriele's presence on the English scene was enhanced through his teaching.

A third aspect of Gabriele's influence is well illustrated by the case of Charles Lyell and his son:

> The two remarkable works of Professor Rossetti, 'Il comento analitico della Divina Comedia' and 'Lo spirito antipapale di Dante' gave occasion to the following translations.[8]

These are the very first sentences of the preface to the elder Charles Lyell's versions of Dante's shorter lyrics, *The Canzoniere of Dante Alighieri, Including the Poems of the Vita Nuova and Convito* (1835). In the preface, Lyell also distances himself from the recondite interpretations Rossetti had placed on the *Commedia*. In Lyell's translations of Dante's shorter poems, the reader 'is presented merely with the literal sense of the text; for the allegorical and mystical sense he is referred to the writings of the single commentator who has attempted and hazarded their explanation'.[9]

In the second edition of the same work (1842), Lyell added an essay that condemns Rossetti's method and rejects the subjectivity inherent in allegory, which is 'like a mirror of irregular surface; it can reflect the object faithfully in one point of view, and can distort it in various ways at the pleasure of the holder'.[10]

This stricter censure could be partly due to the influence on Charles Lyell of his son, the celebrated geologist Charles Lyell. According to Brian P Dolan, Charles Lyell the younger was assuming a 'new-fangled professional image' as a professor at King's College London (which he joined in 1831), supported by Charles Babbage. Both Lyell and Babbage were involved in the then current arguments concerning sound or unsound methodologies in the sciences, the reform of scientific practices and, in particular, the reform of the most correct ways of representing scientific knowledge.[11] Discussions on competing approaches to scientific study and scientific writing were rampant at that time: for example, personally observed records and calculations were set against travellers' reports or historical documentation, and reliance on mechanical calculations with complete erasure of the human factor – as in the construction of Babbage's calculating machine, which even printed out its own calculations – was set against belief in established theories whose proofs one subsequently pursues.

Charles Lyell junior's opposition to Rossetti and to allegory could be part of this development in the culture of the time, involving the role and method of the scholar and scientist. A letter by Lyell to his father (London, April 1828) is illuminating in this and other respects. He describes a pleasant evening:

> The party – Sir Walter Scott, Cooper [sic](the American novelist) ... Mr and Mrs Lockhart, Scott's son and unmarried daughter .... Lady Davy ... was talking well of Manzoni's new celebrated novel, 'I promessi sposi', so I got her afterwards upon Dante; and she said, 'I bought Rossetti,' and read some, but left off for fear I should feel obliged to give way to his theories. I am a devoted admirer of Dante, and should never forgive the man who lessened him in my estimation. There was too much politics perhaps before, but an allegory in every word is horrid. I admire Johnson for saying after all his labours the honest truth, that a person had best read Shakespeare after all, quite through, before he looked at a single note, and I advise all to read Dante as I have done, three times, and as I mean to do a fourth, before they read Rossetti.[12]

Apart from confirming the spread of Gabriele's fame in England, this extract also clarifies the nature of Lyell's opposition: his rejection of too much 'allegory', and support for a contrasting systematic method of direct analysis based on personal observation – a scientific method.

The claims to literality and the attacks on allegory seem quite extraordinary if we consider that Dante had himself clearly stated in the *Commedia* that his poetry conveyed significance hidden under a veil – 'sotto il velame de li versi strani'[13] – and had even provided a key to his four allegorical layers in the letter to Can Grande. It seems almost a logical impossibility to claim fidelity in the case of an art which declares that it is presenting the most encompassing and far-reaching truths, and that the only way to do this is in a referentially indirect mode. A physicist would not call his models and calculations allegories, but such models and calculations might construct a representation of the universe which is as theoretical as an allegory. The clarity of representation of mathematical formulae is in the service of something that is only a possible model of reality; so it is – sometimes – with allegory. Allegory is a poetic structure in which abstraction and particulars meet.[14]

Gabriele's presence on the English cultural scene was more varied than is often realized. He wrote some philosophical or religious poems, though they were in Italian and would be rendered into English only later (by William Michael). He also wrote libretti, particularly in the period between 1828 and 1831. *Medora e Corrado, cantata melodrammatica, con cori, tratta dal corsaro di Byron* was one of those certainly performed in London. As for *La Schiava di Bagdad*, 'a semi-serious opera', it was published in the Millar's Italian and English Theatre series. The preface informs us that HN Millar, 'being aware of the interest now universally felt in the Italian opera, and the language in which it is performed', devised a series which presented to 'amateurs and the Public in general' libretti of Italian operas with the Italian original and an English version on facing pages; in this case, the texts were 'revised by Signor Rossetti'.[15] Rossetti's fame, therefore, would have spread by various means, some more private and some more popular than Dante studies.

The kind of verse Rossetti produced for these libretti is the kind he also used in some of his religious verse. He uses the baroque language expressing pathetic feeling (as in Neapolitan opera) and a heavily stressed metre with a very strict pattern. Metastasio is definitely a model for both:

So ben ch'e mio quel core
Or che mi dici addio;
Ma chi sa poi s'e mio
Quando ritorni a me?[16]

[I know that heart is mine
Now that you're saying goodbye;
But will it still be mine
When you return to me?]

If Dante Gabriel did not scrutinize his father's work, Christina might well have done so. She certainly used the same language and metre in some of her poems in *Il Rosseggiar dell'Oriente*.[17]

But it is Rossetti's Dante studies which are the crux of the matter. Although in recent years some scholars have expressed the hope that more sympathetic scholarship will produce a contextual assessment of Rossetti's studies, little has in fact been done in this direction. In the present context, I must limit my comments here to one or two aspects of Rossetti's work.

Rossetti's theories were based on one principle: that much medieval poetry was part of a political sectarian system which used sectarian language.[18] He believed that medieval love poets used an allegorical system based on Love, and that they had adopted arcane signs and coded language. In his own day, the Carbonari (of whom he was a member) followed a similar practice, hiding their aims under religious emblems.[19] Indeed, Rossetti saw a direct line between the Carbonari and the sectarian Ghibelline movement of Dante's age, of which the *Commedia* was the highest codification. Even if we see Rossetti's meta-interpretation as at best highly subjective and at worst insane, we can still learn from his view of the language of stilnovista poetry as sectarian language. It is a language which is arcane and coded and which hides, by way of allegory, narratives very different from what appear. In such sectarian language each word could be a sign, a single symbol, whose apparent, conceptual meaning fits into the general narrative, but whose real significance, inherent in the word itself, could depend on the physical position in which the word is placed in the coded text, and is, indeed, almost a gesture pointing to a parallel world.

Gabriele claimed the existence of such sectarian language, and in doing so became an object of ridicule. This was partly, no doubt, because in England at that time reform and open struggle between 'the two nations' were the large issues, and there was no framework which would allow people to even begin to understand the secret dealings of a sectarian political system. A second reason might also be the fall into disrepute of the methodology Rossetti followed: he started with a conviction, then built a theory, and finally searched for proof. Thirdly, his political focus would also form an obstacle to understanding. There is, however, a major strength in Gabriele's studies: his learning – mainly his knowledge of Dante's work and his ability to link passages not only from all the *cantiche*, but also from Dante's other works. For example, he points out how in his Epistle V to Henry VII, Dante refers to Virgil's Eclogue V, 6, thus linking Dante's use of Virgil with his political ideals. Gabriele reminds us that in the Middle Ages this eclogue was regarded as having been 'written for Augustus and interpreted for Jesus Christ', and concludes that 'Dante's Jesus Christ is merged with his Augustus'.[20]

Gabriele's handling of the figure of Beatrice is a good illustration of his views and method. He shares the traditional view that Beatrice was an allegorical figure corresponding to Philosophy in the *Convivio* and Theology in the *Commedia*. But if Dante's programme was a political one and the *Commedia* a Ghibelline text, and if Beatrice in the *Commedia* is Dante's final goal, she cannot but be the figure of the emperor.[21] This would be confirmed by Dante's use of the eagle as a symbol of the Roman empire and as an image with which to compare Beatrice (albeit in Canto I of Paradiso). Gabriele builds his system on such correspondences, some of which were also observed by later commentators.

In 1958, Charles S Singleton hinged his own interpretation of the *Commedia* in the *Journey to Beatrice* on one major crux: 'the analogy Beatrice-Christ'.[22] His reading turns on revelation and theology: although he quotes the very same passage from the *De Monarchia* in connection with Canto 33 as Rossetti,[23] he interprets any political statement as an image of a theological one. Mark Musa in 1981 carries the argument forward by seeing Beatrice as a figure now of Divine Revelation, now of Salvation, Matilda being directly '*figura Christi*'.[24] In all the various translations and commentaries, the many imperial emblems or political concepts, such as the eagle and the reference to the Roman empire,[25] are glossed, but they are seen as additional detail rather than as part of a structure of meaning. The prophecy of the coming of an emperor in *Purgatorio* XXXIII is footnoted by all, and most point out the correspondence between this prophecy and the analogous prophecy in the very first canto of *Inferno*. Today, such a network of images is seen as mere historical reference to fourteenth-century Florence, and is extraneous to the predominant view of the *Commedia* as a philosophical or theological divine poem. Gabriele, on the other hand, is not blind to readings other than political ones, and recognizes that Dante crosses complex images to express one single idea: for example, Dante 'considers one and the same object – the Roman Emperor – now as the Virgin Mary, now as the figure of the Saviour'.[26] Gabriele, therefore, anticipates a view close to Singleton's by more than a hundred years.

My aim here is not to vindicate Gabriele's views, but to stress that the readers of his day were in no way able to understand his views, and that this caused an even larger ripple in the culture of the time. The violence of the intrusion – the discrepancy between Gabriele's perspective and the cultural-historical paradigm predominant in England in the nineteenth century – caused the violence, and eventually the scale, of the response.

The twentieth century has been no more sympathetic to Gabriele Rossetti than the nineteenth. Umberto Eco, one of the few scholars to refer to him,

uses his Dante studies as examples of overinterpretation, or what he calls
'paranoid readings'. Eco points out how Gabriele isolates individual words
out of context, attributing a very specific meaning to general words, as when
he attempts to isolate in the *Commedia* evidence of the presence of Rosicrucian
codes concerned with the Passion. Gabriele, Eco reports, needs to find the
symbols of the cross, the rose and the pelican; since he cannot find them all
together, he is content to find any bird anywhere. Eco jeers at Gabriele's identification of the pelican with Beatrice: it is 'a poetic blunder for Dante to represent his beloved by the awkward features of a birded pelican'. Oddly, the
semiotician sees Beatrice as merely Dante's beloved, and the sign 'pelican' as
an equation between a bird's and a woman's face. He then concludes his
treatment of Gabriele:

> In all, in his desperate and rather pathetic fowling, Rossetti finds in the
> divine poem seven fowls and eleven birds and ascribes them all to the
> pelican family: but they are all far from the rose.[27]

However, in an analogical, not a referential relationship, if Beatrice is Jesus
Christ she might well be figured as a pelican. Moreover, it is a sign of
Gabriele's committed devotion to Dante's work to search the total poem for a
few birds (without the assistance of a computer). Above all, what Gabriele
does is sift a mass of imaged evidence, attempting to move to levels of abstraction in search of spiritual meaning. This rigid focus on single words and their
recondite significance, ridiculed by Eco, is useful when considering some
aspects of Dante Gabriel Rossetti's art.

If he did not scrutinize his father's work, Dante Gabriel must nevertheless
have breathed in some traces of his father's views of sectarian language.
Dante Gabriel's use of allegory has been discussed in various ways, both in his
poems and paintings. His 'For an Allegorical Dance of Women, by Andrea
Mantegna (In the Louvre)' has traditionally been seen as a rejection of allegory: according to David Riede, this poem firmly states that 'art communi-
cates by sensation rather than by abstract allegorical thought'.[28] In a more
recent, very different reading of the same poem, Jerome McGann stresses
how 'the explanatory power rises, paradoxically, from the distance separating
the equivalent forms' of poem and painting, words and images.[29] What I want
to stress in this context is a reversal in the poem. There is a complete shift
away from forms of personal, individual ways of knowing ('Scarcely, I think',
and 'I believe') – including physical sensation, which is limited ('he/ Just felt
their hair'), and also including calculations and scientific reporting ('nor gave
ear to trace/ How many feet') – to an impersonal, distanced object ('it') which
contains meaning. Thus, in spite of limited sensation, absence of accuracy,

and excess of 'blind assuredness of thought to know the dancers', the result is a true artistic object: a poem (describing also the painting), erasing the person of the artist. Authorial intention, romantic lyric, sense perception, theoretical approaches, conceptual explanations – all disappear in the resolution of the poem:

.... It is bitter glad
Even unto tears. Its meaning filleth it,
A secret of the wells of Life: to wit:–
The earth's each pulse shall keep the sense it had
With all, though the mind's labour run to nought.[30]

It would be a mistake, I think, to assume as Riede does that the phrase 'the mind's labour' describes allegory. This phrase refers only to the dry 'blind fixedness of thought', which is one extreme of intellectual labour – the theoretical thrust, totally severed from perception ('blind'). Similarly, in 'the sense it had/ With all', 'sense' does not signify physical sensation only. Language has offered the poet the perfect word to signify sensation merged with significance. Allegory here, as I see it, is 'the pulse' *joined to* 'the sense it had/ With all'. Allegory joins the particular, 'each', with the general 'all'. Allegory points us to the 'secret of the wells of Life'. The circularity of 'Its meaning filleth it' is the result of an interplay of equivalent forms, particular and general, the object and its sense. The meaning, however, continues to be 'secret', and that is precisely the strength of allegory: that it contains a mass of evidence, an array of icons – as well as movement and colour – within an identifiable but unstable pattern, and thus becomes a guide to spiritual or conceptual meaning. Later, WB Yeats would spell out in a rhetorical question the attempt to distinguish the dancer from the dance; Dante Gabriel's solution is inherent in language and poetry as physical and conceptual, thanks to his special use of allegory. Dante Gabriel does not reject his father's inheritance out of hand, but transforms it into his own art.

Dante Gabriel might have felt he was picking up his father's sword when he produced *The Early Italian Poets together with Dante's Vita Nuova*, later called *Dante and his Circle* (1861, 1874). These translations from Dante's lyrics could be called a rewriting of Lyell's *Il Canzoniere di Dante Alighieri*; for, in spite of the title, Lyell had also translated three poems by Cino da Pistoia, five by Dante da Majano, two by Guido Cavalcanti and two by Michelangelo Buonarroti. Dante Gabriel translated more poems by these poets, and also some by Cecco Angiolieri and a few others. But the striking differences between the translations of Lyell and Dante Gabriel only highlight the complexity of Dante Gabriel's vision. I will use, as an example, one of Dante's most famous lyrics from the *Rime petrose*, or stony rhymes: the *seconda petrosa*, the sestina 'Al poco giorno'. This is the third stanza:

> Quand'ella ha in testa una ghirlanda d'erba,
> trae da la mente nostra ogn'altra donna;
> perch'è si mischia il crespo giallo e 'l verde
> sì bel, ch'Amor lì viene a stare a l'ombra,
> che m'ha serrato intra piccioli colli
> più forte assai che la calcina petra.

The sestina uses six fixed rhyming words: here, erba ('grass'), 'donna' (lady), 'verde' (green), 'ombra' (shade), 'colli' (hills) and 'petra' (stone, or – with a capital letter – the female version of the name Peter).

Lyell's literality in respect of the matter of the poem in this case involves a complete disregard for the form. If he was fully faithful to the matter, he could still (in William Michael's terms) retain some of the spirit of the poem. But Lyell's literality means fidelity to the possible meaning of the images suggested by the words rather than to the power of the words themselves; he omits 'ombra', places the words wherever they best fit the syntax, and searches for the appropriate word to suit the context in which it is found:

> When of *wild flowers* a garland crowns her head,
> she draws each other *lady* from our mind:
> the *green* she mingles with her golden curls
> so beauteously, that Love admiring stands,
> and I, who stand fast locked 'midst gentle *hills*,
> am fixed more firmly than the lime*stone* cliff.

'Grass' is rendered in this stanza with 'wild flowers'. Elsewhere, in combination with healing, it is translated as 'herb' ('and herb is none can heal the wound she gives'). When collocated with strong nouns denoting large objects, it is rendered with a phrase: 'nor hill, nor rampart strong, nor *verdant bough*'. In other positions the word 'grass' is retained, as in the cryptic closure of Dante's poem, to which I will return later:

> [when] darkest shades descend upon the hills
> the youthful lady in her arbour green
> dispels them like a diamond in the grass.[31]

Dante Gabriel Rossetti's version of the poem is entitled 'Sestina, Of the Lady Pietra degli Scrovigni',[32] and this is his version of the third stanza also quoted from Lyell:

> When on her hair she sets a crown of *grass*
> The thought has no more room for other *lady*;

Because she weaves the yellow with the *green*
So well that Love sits down there in the *shade,–*
Love who has shut me in among low *hills*
Faster than between walls of granite-*stone.*

Dante Gabriel announces the specificity of his approach by referring by name
to the figure usually known simply as a stony lady, an allegorical 'Pietra'. As
for the rest of the poem, instead of producing interpretations, Dante Gabriel
is absolutely strict in reproducing the words of the original. Dante Gabriel's
principle aim as a translator is to produce 'a good poem', and the only way to
do this successfully is to aim primarily not at 'literality', but at 'fidelity'. It is
only in exceptional cases that the translator is fortunate enough to be able to
combine literality with fidelity.[33] In his version, Dante Gabriel does not compromise on word order or synonyms. In this sense the sestina is the ideal
medium to observe the poet's impulse, since here the words stand on their
own, abstracted from any context to do with usage. To crown oneself with
grass might appear, in everyday terms, impossible. It might also seem a poetic
blunder on the speaker's part – to imagine his beloved with grass on her head.
But in Dante Gabriel, as in Dante, it is not the stuff, the green matter, the
signified that celebrates the lady; instead, it is the intrinsic power of the word
'grass', in its printed form, which allows it to crown the lady Pietra. The translation is a chemical experiment with words, pure words, as the elements.

Such an experiment is especially crucial in the case of translation. For if
words are concrete elements, with the addition of a high charge of figural
abstraction, then two things are possible: either the transmission of meaning
can more easily be successful (for neither usage nor situation are relevant –
only the existence of a word and the existence of its figural charge), or
the translation will theorize the difficulties of transmission. Dante Gabriel's
poetry insists on the material basis of a figural abstraction (the material basis
being not only the historicity, but also the printed word and the form of a
poem). It is not just a question of limiting translation to strictly observing the
form of the original; through absolute fidelity to the form, Dante Gabriel is
also being faithful to the spirit of the original – in form *and* in the referential
power of the words on the page.

In their *Time and the Crystal*, Robert Durling and Ronald Martinez apply
medieval knowledge of gems and use in poetry of the complex concept of time
to the *Rime petrose*, unearthing remarkable interpretations. One of the most
striking is the reading of the last line of the *seconda petrosa*:

Quantunque I colli fanno più nera ombra,
sotto un bel verde la giovane donna
la fa sparer, com'uom petra sott'erba.

The traditional reading of these lines is followed in Lyell's version, cited above, and Dante Gabriel's:

> How dark soe'er the hills throw out their shade,
> Under her summer-green the beautiful lady
> Covers it, like a stone cover'd in grass.

It is the simile in the last line that has remained a scholarly crux throughout the centuries: the black shadows produced by the hills are hidden by the young woman under beautiful greenery, 'just as a man hides a stone under grass' – which is rather odd of this man. Not surprisingly, both Lyell and Dante Gabriel omit him. In addition, Lyell translates '*petra*' ('stone') as 'diamond', thus losing the direct identification of the woman with the stone. For a full understanding of Durling and Martinez's interpretation, I must refer the reader to their volume. It may suffice here to say that the meaning, according to their research, is dependent on an awareness that the simple words 'petra' and 'erba' correspond to the power of gems and of medicinal herbs. The authors put forward the view that the two words, in this final line, signify 'the heliotrope', which is both a stone and a plant ('heliotropium' and 'heliotropia') respectively. The line does not suggest that a man hides a stone under grass, but that, as medieval lapidaries state, 'if [the gem] is joined to an herb of the same name, it draws whoever bears it from human sight'.[34] It is the man, therefore, who becomes invisible, creating a correspondence between human being and cosmos. The original order of the words and even the exact prepositions are crucial to the meaning. The general structure and meaning of the sestina support this detail, for, referring to the sun, the two heliotropes conclude the movement of the sestina, which follows the complex mimesis of solar motion; the final line also clinches the articulated correspondence between woman and stone. The interpretation proposed, accompanied as it is by a full exposition of medieval learning, of Dante's own use of lapidaries and of his transformation of Arnaut's use of them, is fully convincing. This study reveals a Dante that is as distinct from Cary's Dante, or Longfellow's Dante, or Eliot's Dante as these all are different from Gabriele Rossetti's. Though 'fowling' for a pelican might have been misguided in motive and aim, Gabriele's approach and way of thinking were close to Dante's poetic practice and form of mind, as we are now discovering. In spite of his 'fidelity', even Dante Gabriel failed here – but then, Dante's conceptual framework is very bold and recondite.

Gabriele's views were shaped by a culture very far removed from that of his host country. Although his actual scholarship was not accepted, the extreme opposition between it and the predominant model was such that his fame and the controversy his work aroused contributed to much of the astonishing flowering of Dante studies in England in the nineteenth century and after. In a general sense, I suggest that Gabriele Rossetti's work hit England in a catastrophic shift, like the earthquakes whose effects were studied by Lyell's son. Literature, it would seem, moves in a catastrophic as well as a gradualist way. The contrast between Gabriele Rossetti's life and work and the cultural forces at play in nineteenth-century England sheds light on issues such as right interpretation, hidden power of language and deep systems of significance. On an individual level, his father's views also explain some of the ways in which Dante Gabriel's art works, including his explorations, in poetry and painting, of ways of knowing and of representing objects and mind in art. Placed in this context, Dante Gabriel's dialectic between the conceptual and the physical reveal the complex, innovative, programmatic nature of his art, an art that makes use of a sectarian language with recondite workings.

Notes

1　The name '*Carbonari*' means sellers of coal, and many of the society's secret codes were based on the terminology used by the sellers of coal guild.

2　Gabriele Rossetti, *La Vita Mia – Il Testamento* (Lanciano: R Carabba, 1910), p. 125 – 'confondere gl'increduli nemici'; unless otherwise specified, translations from the Italian are my own.

3　William Michael Rossetti, 'Preface' to Dante Gabriel Rossetti, *Dante and his Circle, with the Italian Poets Preceding him* (London: Ellis and Elvey, 1892), p. vii. Gabriele's views are found in *L'Inferno di Dante, con un Comento analitico* (1826); *Sullo Spirito Antipapale che produsse la Riforma* (1832); *Il Mistero dell'Amor Platonico del Medio Evo* (1840); and *La Beatrice di Dante* (1842).

4　Maria Francesca Rossetti, *A Shadow of Dante* (London: Rivingtons, 1871), pp. 3, 6.

5　See also my 'Exiles at Home: the Case of the Rossettis', in *Journal of Anglo-Italian Studies*, vol. 6, 2001, esp. pp. 228–9.

6　'Preface' to *The Comedy of Dante Allighieri*, Part 1, *The Hell* (London and Cambridge: Macmillan & Co, 1865), p. i.

7　CB Cayley, *The Vision of Hell* (London: Longman, Brown, Green, & Longman), 1851, p. 1.

8　'Preface' to *The Canzoniere of Dante Alighieri, Including the Poems of the Vita Nuova and Convito*, trans. by Charles Lyell (London: John Murray, 1835), p. vii.

9　Op. cit., pp. viii–ix.

10　'On the Antipapal Spirit of Dante Alighieri', in *The Poems of the Vita Nuova and Convito of Dante Alighieri*, transl by Charles Lyell (London: CF Molini, 1842), p. lxxxii.

11　Brian P Dolan, 'Representing Novelty: Charles Babbage, Charles Lyell, and Experiments in Early Victorian Geology', in *History of Science* , vol. 36 (1998), p. 299.

12　*Life, Letters and Journals of Sir Charles Lyell*, edited by his sister-in-law, Mrs Lyell, in 2 vols (London: John Murray, 1881), i, pp. 180–1.

13　*Inferno*, Canto ix.

14　For a discussion of allegory in the nineteenth century, see Ch. 8 of Theresa M Kelly, *Reinventing Allegory* (Cambridge: CUP, 1997), pp. 217–48.

15 *La Schiava di Bagdad (The Slave of Baghdad)*, a semi-serious opera in two acts (London: HN Millar, n.d).

16 *Medora e Corrado, Cantata melodrammatica, con cori, tratta dal Corsaro di Byron*, poesia di Gabriele Rossetti (Londra: Joseph Mallet, n.d. [1832]), p. 12.

17 See my 'Christina Rossetti's Italian Poems', in *Beauty and the Beast*, eds Peter Liebregts and Wim Tigges (Amsterdam & Atlanta, GA: Rodopi, 1996), pp. 31–42.

18 *Comento Analitico al* Purgatorio *di Dante Alighieri*, ed. by Pompeo Giannantonio (Firenze: Leo S Olschki, 1967), pp. 456 ff.

19 Op. cit., pp. 458–9.

20 p. 214.

21 p. 371.

22 *Journey to Beatrice* (Baltimore and London: John Hopkins, 1955 rpt 1977), pp. 73–85. Singleton insists Beatrice is not Christ, and not even a figure of Christ, which is the Griffin; but that she operates similarly to Christ; Singleton calls her arrival 'the advent of Beatrice', and he points out that immediately after Dante comes face to face with her, she proceeds to judge the state of Dante's soul (pp. 73–85).

23 *Comento*, p. 363.

24 *The Divine Comedy*, vol. ii: *Purgatory*, trans. by Mark Musa (Penguin, 1981), pp. 338, 339 (notes to Canto 33, esp. to ll. 80–1 and ll. 95–6).

25 *Purgatorio* xxxiii, ll. 37–9, l. 43.

26 'E più tardi ne avremo una pruova di novella; poiché scorgeremo ch'ei considera l'unico oggetto, l'Imperadore de' Romani, ora come madonna, ora come il figurato Salvatore', p. 374.

27 See Eco's Tanner Lectures delivered at Cambridge, and the second of two articles based on these lectures, 'Some Paranoid Readings', in *Times Literary Supplement* 4552 (1990), pp. 604, 706.

28 David G Riede, *Dante Gabriel Rossetti and the Limits of Victorian Vision* (Ithaca and London: Cornell University Press, 1983), p. 100.

29 Jerome McGann, *Dante Gabriel Rossetti and the Game that Must be Lost* (New Haven & London: Yale University Press, 2000), p. 25.

30 *The Poetical Works of Dante Gabriel Rossetti*, ed. by William Michael Rossetti (London: Ellis and Elvey, 1905), p. 346.

31 *The Canzoniere of Dante Alighieri* (1835), pp. 312, 313.

32 This is the title used in *The Works*, xii (1911); my text below is from 'To the Dim Light', *The Portable Dante* (New York: Viking, 1947 rpt 1978), pp. 625–6.

33 'Preface to the first edition' (1861), *Dante and his Circle*, p. xiii.

34 Robert M Durling and Ronald L Martinez, *Time and the Crystal: Studies in Dante's* Rime Petrose (Berkeley et al: University of California Press, 1990), p. 116; see for this discussion Chapter 3 *passim*, 'The Sun and the Heliotrope', pp. 109–37, which contains quotes from a number of luminaries and lapidaries, mainly from the works of Joan Evans.

9

MYSTIC, MADWOMAN OR METAPHYSICIAN?: THE ANALOGICAL THEODICY OF CHRISTINA ROSSETTI

Maria Keaton

Of all the commonly anthologized woman poets of the nineteenth century, two stand out through the distinction of having their work criticized in detailed relation to their lives: Emily Dickinson and Christina Rossetti. A sense of fascination with the unusual lives of these two poets seems to permeate most analysis of their poetry as well. For Christina Rossetti in particular, this fascination (which has informed most critical judgements of her work) has had a double-sided emphasis, and the sides stand in an opposition to each other that is hard to escape. Many of her critics present her as an interesting psychological case, writing from a background of a repressed life. The other view, taken by some of her popular biographers, is of Christina as a mystic, a devout Christian whose life of faith gives her work something of an exemplar's authority. In both cases, however, it is Christina's life that becomes the bridge between the twentieth-century audience attempting to understand the works of the poet, and the stances the poet takes as a writer. Where Christina's poetry is difficult to understand, ideas about her biography and its possible connection to her writing are used to explain how the confusions may have come about. In this paper, I will write about some work of Christina's that seems to be an anomaly in terms of her biography: her poems for children, *Sing-Song*, are written with a maternal attention to the world of childhood by someone who never experienced motherhood personally. Without a direct biographical connection between this facet of Christina's poetry and life, analysis of this part of her poetry is difficult to explain by bracketing it with her life experience, particularly in view of its apparent emphasis on explaining the world to those younger than the speaker. Given this, I will look closely at some of the poems in *Sing-Song* according to the theological stance Christina seems to be taking within the poems. As it stands, *Sing-Song* appears to say more about its author's metaphysical ideas than about her response to her life experiences; in particular, she uses these deceptively simple lyrics to express her understanding of the Anglo-Catholic doctrines of Analogy and Reserve.

Both the popular writers who treat Christina as a sort of Christian Everywoman whose poetry and life reflect a devotional struggle, and the academics who see her writing as a response to several psychological traumas that occasioned quite another kind of conflict, find in her work a great deal of material upon which to reflect. Mary Hinderlie, writing for a fairly well-educated but not necessarily scholarly audience in the *Christmas* annual for Augsburg Publishing house, calls Christina 'the last of the singers of David's line' and points out that 'the fullness of her human warmth is why she appeals as a religious poet. Her lines throb with the urgency of a heart [...] honest in its admission of sin'.[1] The emphasis here is on Christina as fused with her devotional poetry; she is not separated from her work.

Later in the twentieth century, Christina's poetry is perceived as being interlinked with her life in quite a different way. In common with several other critics, Frances Thomas explains Christina's *Monna Innominata* sequence as her way of dealing with her inability to accept Charles Bagot Cayley's offer of marriage.[2] But Thomas values Christina's religious grounds for refusing to accept Bagot Cayley as a husband quite differently from the way Hinderlie celebrated Christina's 'religious poetry'. Thomas writes, 'The world of nineteenth-century high religion was not our world: within its overheated and protected enclosure, souls grew into exotic and tortured shapes'.[3] Having made the point that religion could serve to produce the kind of angst that often finds a creative outlet, Thomas returns to this theme throughout her biographical writing. She refers at one point to 'the folds of religion [that] settled around [Christina] and turned slowly into stone', and says that during the time of this 'hardening' of Christina's faith, her poems continued to 'retain their predominantly melancholy cast'.[4] Even more specifically than Hinderlie, Thomas relates a strain in Christina's poetry to the impact of Anglo-Catholicism on Christina's personal life.

It is worth commenting on some of the implications of viewing Christina's work through the filter of her biography. Thomas's work in particular takes for granted that Christina's form of Anglo-Catholicism was responsible for both a personal and poetic melancholia. This assumption calls for further exploration, for two reasons: first, it relates the angst Christina may have felt towards her religious observances; secondly, the speaker in all the poems is considered to be Christina herself, rather than a poetic persona. The second part of this criticism applies to Hinderlie's assumptions in her treatment of Christina's work as '*her* human warmth' and '*honest* in [...] admission of sin'. Because Christina Rossetti the individual is assumed to have lived a life of repression and trauma of one sort or another, her poetry likewise becomes part of, in Gilbert and Gubar's famous phrase, 'the aesthetics of renunciation'.[5] It is true that renunciation, with its attendant themes of loss, absence and repentance is part of the philosophy of her poetry, but explaining her poetry solely in those terms forecloses on her work's complexity. Keane notes that the 'biographical emphasis' on Christina's work has been explored throughout the nineteenth and twentieth centuries and suggests that one way to develop scholarship on Christina Rossetti would be to 'study [...] the writer's poetic craftsmanship' and begin a 're-evaluation' of her entire poetic output.[6]

The sheer volume of Christina's poetry makes this re-evaluation a substantial challenge. There is the added difficulty of stylistic progression – or lack of it – over time within Christina's work: Keane somewhat wryly notes that she 'had achieved her mature style by twenty'.[7] Though Christina's work exhibits some variation over time, the techniques of her poetry are often recursive, making her work difficult to consider in any unitary way. An assessment of her work in its entirety cannot be done without devoting years to the project, but aspects of her technique may be related to small samplings of her work, and thus an assessment of this kind can be built up bit by bit.

Such a workable sampling may be found in Christina's book of lyrics for children, *Sing-Song*, a book which Jan Marsh has seen as a recreation of the author's own childhood,[8] but which also seems to have a kind of teaching function, relating moral ideas to natural symbols. While I will be considering Christina's work in relation to her Anglo-Catholicism, I will not be examining the effect of Christina's personality on her poetry, as Thomas and Hinderlie have done. Rather, I will look at the workings of two of the theological doctrines that John Keble explained in his *Tracts for the Times*, and which Christina appears to have drawn on in both *Sing-Song* and some of her later devotional works.

These doctrines of Analogy and Reserve inform *Sing-Song*, and one of Rossetti's adult devotional books, *Time Flies*, in remarkably similar ways. Both books share a concern with the cycle of time, as a kind of picturing of the divinely ordained cycle of eternity.[9] This concern with earthly chronology and its reflection of the cycles of Christianity would alone link these books to the Tractarian doctrine of Analogy; in a more basic way, their existence as devotional and creative works means that they fulfil one of the Analogic functions, because the desire to create writing which praises God parallels the desire to create a world which would be full of praise to Him.[10] Of course, in

Keble's view, the human creative imagination is a picture of the ultimate Creator's, and not to be confused with the Person Himself; still, the creative imagination of the human poet is to be prized, because it leads to seeking out metaphors in the world (all of which suggest the presence of the Ultimate, because it is itself a metaphor for God's activity).[11]

The most basic definition of Analogy, in fact, has to do with metaphor and symbol. Simply put, Analogy is the doctrine that everything visible is a symbol of some attribute of God, and that each symbol has the capacity to teach human beings something about Him. As John Keble put it in his essay 'Sacred Poetry', 'every scene in nature [is] an occasion [...] a topic—of devotion'.[12] Furthermore, the doctrine of Analogy is not only nature-related; Keble casts the net much wider for Analogic topics when he writes in Tract 89 that 'external things [...] [are] fraught with imaginative associations [...] parabolical lessons of conduct [...] symbolic language in which GOD speaks to us of a world out of sight'.[13] Keble uses a verse from St. Paul's Epistle to the Romans to justify this view of the visible world; 'The invisible things of Him are understood by things which are made'.[14] The Incarnation is the crux of this doctrine; it represents the fusion of the natural and the supernatural, of 'symbol' and 'event'.[15]

If this doctrine of Analogy sounds like Shakespeare's idea that a truly good person can find 'sermons in stones [...] books in running brooks, and good in everything',[16] it should – because in many ways, the doctrine of Analogy is a return to the doctrines of design and typology so prevalent in the sixteenth and seventeenth centuries. Two of the greatest Metaphysical poets, Donne and Herbert, used analogies from the visible world – and ordinary, everyday scenes at that – to explain spiritual realities in their poetry. Perhaps the first piece of evidence in the case for Christina Rossetti as a poet of Analogy are the comparisons made by critics between Christina and Donne, or Christina and Herbert. Hinderlie observes that 'she reminds one [...] of John Donne [...] who mingled love subjects with the religious'.[17] Though the biographical reminder comes through in Hinderlie's comparison, there is also some notion of Analogy at work; the poetry of strictly human love may help to explain the relationship between the soul and God. In a much longer comparison of Rossetti and Herbert, Diane D'Amico gets to the core of how both poets used Analogy; 'Rossetti follows Herbert's pattern of focusing on a single point in each stanza [...] embodied in a central image.'[18] The crucial equation of symbol to point is what gives Christina Rossetti's poetry its strongest claim to Analogy as explained by Keble.

Unlike Herbert or Donne, however, Christina left a legacy of poetry that was not strictly for adults, yet used Analogy in sophisticated ways. Her book of nursery rhymes, *Sing-Song*, was published in 1871 and was 'Dedicated/

Without permission/ To the baby who suggested' it.[19] The dedication, and the outward simplicity of the poems, suggests a juvenile audience; yet what is full of word-music and easy to understand for children may carry meaningful appeal for adults as well.

The critical response to this book has been varied. Frances Thomas writes of the 'poignant simplicity' of 'these poems, written by a middle-aged spinster' which have 'the logic of childhood', using 'simple analogies'.[20] Other critics, however, have commented on the structure and technique of this deceptively simple work. Because, according to Smulders, there are 'three [...] simultaneous temporal sequences' which form one 'narrative from cradle to grave' within it,[21] she posits for *Sing-Song* an 'architectural refinement' and a 'fullness of meaning' which make it 'not unadapted for mature reflection'.[22]

The reflections of such a mature audience may include an interpretation of the theodicy expressed in some of the short lyrics that compose the *Sing-Song* cycle. Some of the analogies expressed in *Sing-Song*, true to the definition of Analogy as a doctrine, reflect truth in extremely simple symbols, but it does not follow that the analogies are all themselves simple. Indeed, *Sing-Song* follows another Tractarian doctrine, that of Reserve, far more closely than *Time Flies*, Christina Rossetti's adult devotional book. Tennyson notes that the doctrine of Reserve tends to make analogies more complex rather than less, because it states that while all visible things symbolize the spiritual, the symbols are not (and should not be) explained beyond our ability to understand them.[23] Therefore, clear explanations of what the earthly symbol means in spiritual or theological terms are not given in what is purported to be a book for children. Not only does this make sense in terms of the artist's appreciation of the audience (children, after all, are much less likely to enjoy a 'preachy' text than one which relies on word-music and interesting imagery) but also as a complicating factor which makes the analogies more interesting for an adult audience to tease out. While some emblems are made immediately clear, as in the poem that begins, 'What are heavy? sea-sand and sorrow'[24] and in another that begins 'Hope is like a harebell trembling from its birth',[25] many others are left to the adult imagination.

Among the many fascinating poems which are uninterpreted for children but which serve as an interesting portrayal of theological ideas for adults are three which appear to conceptualize the roles of the Persons of the Trinity in ways both complex and condensed. The first, 'Brown and Furry/ Caterpillar in a hurry',[26] is a very accurate and naturalistic portrayal of a caterpillar's life and its metamorphosis into a butterfly – but two things seem to set this poem apart from naturalism. The first is a subtle word choice in the sixth line, 'The *chosen* spot' (emphasis mine). This could mean simply that the caterpillar has chosen the spot to walk on, but choice is not a quality often associated with caterpillars. However, the word 'chosen' is a nexus of woven theological meanings; the chosen people are those among whom God has chosen to send His Son, and the 'chosen spot' might refer to earth, or Israel. Within the context of the powerful closing couplet of the poem, the second clue that the poem has a meaning which lies beneath its surface, the analogy to Christ becomes more evident. A caterpillar does not literally 'die' within the cocoon, nor does it really 'live again' as a butterfly, but by using those words in the last two lines of the poem, Christina evokes the ancient tradition of the butterfly as a symbol of the resurrected Christ.[27] The second poem, 'A white hen sitting', is even more casual and mundane, and thus even more subtle. Once again, the closing lines hold the meaning, and once again, multiple meanings could be derived from the poem. On its surface, it is merely the picture of the maternal care a 'white hen' gives her chicks; she shelters them under her wings from a sort of unholy trinity of an owl, a hawk and a bat.[28] But a working knowledge of Psalm 91 connects this word picture with an image of the care given by God. Psalm 91.4 says of God that 'He shall cover thee with his feathers, and under his wings shalt thou trust.' Even the wording connects with the line of Christina's poem '[...] chicks beneath their mother's wing'.[29] Another point of contact between Psalm 91 and the poem again devolves on a subtle choice. Two of the creatures Christina uses to represent hazards are night fliers, while the hawk is most active during the day. Psalm 91.5 and 6 doubly emphasize a contrast between night time and daytime dangers; 'the terror by night [...] the arrow that flieth by day' and 'the pestilence that walketh in darkness [...] the destruction that wasteth at noonday'.[30] The last of the poems that explain the Persons of the Trinity through natural analogies is one of the most familiar of the *Sing-Song* poems, but has apparently been given little consideration as a theological poem. 'Who has seen the wind?' is a realistic treatment of both the wind's invisibility and its powerful, visible effects. Yet it connects with a tradition of the representation of the Holy Spirit as old as Scripture itself. On Pentecost, the effects of the Holy Spirit's power began with 'a sound as of a rushing mighty *wind*'.[31] In the gospel of John, Christ explains the Holy Spirit's work in terms of a divine wind; of particular interest because of its direct connection to Christina's poem is Christ's point that one cannot tell 'whence' the wind 'cometh', or 'whither it goeth.'[32] The same Greek word, *pneuma*, is used to mean both spirit and wind in the New Testament. In the Old Testament, 'the trees of the wood' are portrayed as natural objects which 'sing out at the presence of the Lord' – surely a reference to the sound made by their motion in the wind.[33] In Christina's poem, the effect of the wind upon the trees is again given a religious significance by a word choice close to the end of the poem, 'When the trees *bow down* their *heads*'.[34] The image of collective head-bowing, while it works perfectly to describe the windswept trees, also pictures the kind of communal prayer immediately recognizable to an audience familiar with church liturgies. A lesson is taken from nature in the best Analogical style here. Bowing the head is a reverential gesture; the trees bow their heads in reverence at the wind, which though invisible has powerful effects. If the trees can bow to the wind, surely humans can reverentially bow their heads to the powerful effect of the invisible Holy Spirit – the *pneuma* of their experience.

These three poems prove that Christina Rossetti's metaphysical wit, even as exercised in 'children's poetry', was subtle and complicated. That the inclusion of such delicate symbolism was deliberate is partially shown by two emblematic poems from *Sing-Song* whose images are explicated in Christina's book of devotions for adults, *Time Flies*. The first poem is one I have mentioned before, 'Hope is like a hare-bell'.[35] Though the equation of love with the rose seems simple enough, as does the mention that this flower has 'thorns' but is greater than either the lily or the hare-bell, the emblems of Faith and Hope,[36] Christina does not explain why the thorny flower, with all its potential for injuring its possessors, is superior to those which could not cause as much pain. Her use of Reserve is self-evident in the poem. In the adult devotional book, however, she explains what has been left unexplained in the children's poem; the thorns serve as a 'guard' for the rose, and as beautifiers for it.[37] Rossetti adds, 'If only we are such as love [God] [...]our [...]thorns are ordained for good'.[38] Here, apparent in two of her texts, is Christina's deliberate use of Analogy as part of her metaphysics. A second poem from *Sing-Song* has an equally apposite correlative in *Time Flies*. The poem 'Hopping frog, hop here and be seen' in the book of children's poetry[39] is an unusual nature poem, in that the speaker apostrophizes two animals usually treated as ugly and negligible, and both celebrates their good qualities and assures them of her kindness. A frog and a toad are rarely considered noteworthy enough for nature poetry, but Christina points out the beauty of the frog – 'Your cap is laced and your coat is green' and the 'harmless' nature of the toad.[40] The kindness is assured in the last line of each quatrain; for the frog, the speaker says '[...]we'll let each other alone'. The toad merits an even gentler response; 'You won't hurt me, and I won't hurt you'.[41] The poem shows sensitivity to the natural world, but no meaning is attributed to it – until, once again, the imagery is explicated in *Time Flies*. Christina writes in that text's entry for July 6 of having 'frightened' a frog when she touched it and of having been 'frightened' by another one, both incidents having occurred when she was a child.[42] Though she points out that, in earthly terms, it is foolish to be frightened of a frog, she takes the little animals as 'types' of the 'smallest, weakest, most grotesque, *wronged* creature' that might 'rise up in the Judgment to condemn us', presumably for the injuries done to it, 'and so frighten us effectually' (italics Christina's).[43] In that context, avoiding doing harm to a frog or a toad becomes a lesson on what is eternally significant; again, the smallest visible thing has become an analogy for spiritual benefit. Indeed, in another devotional taken from *Time Flies*, her words might have been those of Keble himself; 'to him 'that hath ears to hear' any good creature of God may convey a message.'[44] The inner quotation is from Matthew 11.17, and the whole expression of this theme is Keblesque in its combination of Biblical language with this interpretation of church doctrine. As Kent and Stanwood put it in their introduction to their anthology of Christina's prose, 'Rossetti hoped to help [her audience] read the text of everyday life' for what 'she refers to as 'spiritual lessons' and 'heavenly meanings''.[45] The task Christina took on in helping readers of everyday life to see the spiritual nature of that life connects nursery rhyme to devotion book, and the same kind of Analogic metaphysics is vital to both.

In conclusion, although the poems of *Sing-Song* can be taken as quite simple lyrics, 'nursery rhyme[...]which any child can enjoy', to quote Christina's friend Ellen Proctor,[46] it seems that their simplicity, like that of the poems of Emily Dickinson, is deceptive. A metaphysician who had a deep understanding of the Anglo-Catholic doctrines of Analogy and Reserve composed them; an artist skilled in choosing words to represent the finest shades of meaning wrote them. In connecting the nursery rhymes of *Sing-Song* to the doctrines of Analogy and Reserve, and to the systems of thought expressed in *Time Flies*, I have worked to do something of what Christina Rossetti did: evoke the power of the unseen.

Notes

1 Mary Hinderlie, 'Christina Rossetti', *Christmas*, 18 (1948), pp. 63–7 (pp. 67, 64).
2 Frances Thomas, *Christina Rossetti* (Hanley Swan, Worcs: The Self Publishing Group, 1992), pp. 216–19.
3 Thomas, *Christina Rossetti*, p. 219.
4 Thomas, *Christina Rossetti*, p. 302.
5 Sandra M Gilbert and Susan Gubar, 'Christina Rossetti', in *The Norton Anthology of English Literature*, ed. by MH Abrams and others, 4th edn (New York: Norton, 1993), pp. 1472–3 (p. 1473).
6 Robert N Keane, 'Christina Rossetti: A Reconsideration', *Nineteenth-Century Women Writers of the English Speaking World* (Westport, CT: Greenwood, 1986), pp. 99–106 (pp. 100, 101).
7 Keane, 'Christina Rossetti: A Reconsideration', p. 101.
8 Jan Marsh, *Christina Rossetti: A Writer's Life* (New York: Penguin, 1994), pp. 1–23.
9 Sharon Smulders, 'Sound, Sense and Structure in Christina Rossetti's *Sing-Song*', *Children's Literature*, 22 (1994), pp. 3–26 (pp. 3–4).

10 GB Tennyson, *Victorian Devotional Poetry: The Tractarian Mode* (Cambridge, MA: Harvard University Press, 1981), p. 62.

11 Tennyson, *Victorian Devotional Poetry*, pp. 62–3.

12 p. 31.

13 p. 54.

14 Romans 1.20, in Tennyson, *Victorian Devotional Poetry*, pp. 54, 66.

15 Mary Arseneau, 'Incarnation and Interpretation: Christina Rossetti, the Oxford Movement, and Goblin Market', *Victorian Poetry*, 31 (1993), pp. 79–93 (p. 81).

16 William Shakespeare, 'As You Like It,' *The Riverside Shakespeare*, ed. by G Blakemore Evans, (Boston: Houghton Mifflin, 1974), II.1.17.

17 Hinderlie, 'Christina Rossetti', p. 64.

18 Diane D'Amico, 'Reading and Re-Reading George Herbert and Christina Rossetti', *John Donne Journal*, 4 (1985), pp. 269–89 (p. 227).

19 Christina Rossetti, *Sing-Song* (London: Routledge, 1872; repr. Ann Arbor, MI: University Microfilms, 1966), dedication page.

20 Thomas, *Christina Rossetti*, pp. 269–70.

21 Smulders, 'Sound, Sense and Structure in Christina Rossetti's *Sing-Song*', p. 3.

22 Smulders, 'Sound, Sense and Structure in Christina Rossetti's *Sing-Song*', pp. 21–3.

23 Tennyson, *Victorian Devotional Poetry*, p. 44.

24 Christina Rossetti, *Sing-Song*, p. 34.

25 Christina Rossetti, *Sing-Song*, p. 17.

26 Christina Rossetti, *Sing-Song*, p. 39

27 Christina Rossetti, *Sing-Song*, p. 39.

28 Christina Rossetti, *Sing-Song*, p. 83.

29 Christina Rossetti, *Sing-Song*, p. 85.

30 Psalm 91.5, 91.6.

31 Acts 2.2.

32 John 3.8.

33 I Chronicles 16.33.

34 Christina Rossetti, *Sing-Song*, p. 93, line 7.

35 Christina Rossetti, *Sing-Song*, p. 17.

36 Christina Rossetti, *Sing-Song*, p. 17, l. 6.

37 All excerpts cited here from Rossetti's *Time Flies: A Reading Diary* (London: SPCK, 1885) are reprinted in *Selected Prose of Christina Rossetti*, ed. by David A Kent and PG Stanwood (New York: St. Martin's Press, 1998), pp. 297–330. Kent and Stanwood do not reprint the work in its entirety, but selections from it.

38 *Time Flies: A Reading Diary*, p. 324.

39 Christina Rossetti, *Sing-Song*, p. 56.

40 Christina Rossetti, *Sing-Song*, p. 56, ll. 3, 7.

41 Christina Rossetti, *Sing-Song*, p. 56, ll. 4–8.

42 Christina Rossetti's *Time Flies: A Reading Diary*, p. 317.

43 Christina Rossetti's *Time Flies: A Reading Diary*, p. 317.

44 Another of the *Time Flies* entries excerpted in *Selected Prose of Christina Rossetti*, the meditation for March 31 from which this quotation is taken clearly connects natural objects with their Analogic function as 'message' carriers (Christina Rossetti's *Time Flies: A Reading Diary*, p. 307).

45 David Kent and PG Stanwood, 'Introduction,' in *Selected Prose of Christina Rossetti*, ed. by David Kent and PG Stanwood (New York: St. Martin's Press, 1998), pp. 1–13 (p. 12).

The inner quotations from Christina here are also taken from *Time Flies*, and reflect, once again, her use of Analogy.

46 Ellen Proctor, *A Brief Memoir of Christina Rossetti* (London: SPCK, 1895), p. 33.

10

CHRISTINA ROSSETTI'S CHALLENGE TO VICTORIAN MENTALITY: THE PARODIC, UNCONVENTIONAL PATTERN OF 'MY DREAM'

Mariaconcetta Costantini

This essay looks at the 'transgressive elements' in which Christina Rossetti's poetry abounds, through a consideration of some of her linguistic and structural deviations from the canon. In the last few decades, her contribution to the 'modernization' of Victorian poetry has been widely acknowledged by scholars, who have praised her innovative devices, thereby atoning for the limiting views held by previous critics. Previously considered a 'religious' poet who withdrew from reality and looked back on the seventeenth century,[1] Christina has gained recognition as a conscious experimenter with new modes of representation which infringed on traditional norms and paved the way for the poetic 'revolution' of the twentieth century.[2]

The divergence between these critical assessments of her works can be explained to a great extent by the uneven strategies she adopted to circumvent censorship. As a female Victorian artist, Christina faced difficulties in gaining a voice and asserting her point of view freely. Excluded from the men-only meetings of the Pre-Raphaelite Brotherhood and subjected to the solicitous judgements of her brothers, who repeatedly tried to purge her poems of queerness and stylistic idiosyncracies,[3] she had to devise appropriate means of expression, which conveyed provocative messages without offending against contemporary moral standards. What some critics interpreted as a low-key or nostalgic poetic attitude was, mainly, a device she adopted to criticize established currents of ideology in subdued and apparently harmless tones.

Despite her religious preoccupations, Christina felt the inadequacy of many literary and social conventions, and constantly defied them in her verse. If it is true that she often hid her rebellious tension under a seemingly conventional structure, it is equally the case that her peculiar combination of irony, grotesqueness and wordplay testifies to her wish to challenge orthodoxy. In 'Goblin Market', for instance, she chose a traditional fairytale pattern to reduce the impact of disruptive issues and linguistic innovations, which contravened the poetic norms and the behavioural code of her age. This strategy of concealment proved quite effective. Most Victorian readers enthused about the poem, while only a few voiced concern about its 'immorality'.[4]

Christina's unconventional ideas derived from her clear perception of the limits and flaws of the dominant literary and cultural traditions that moulded the Victorian frame of mind. In confronting the canon both diachronically and synchronically, she felt the need to revise what she perceived as cliché, by experimenting with new forms of expression which might render more truthfully life's complexity. The intertextual references to the Troubadour and the Italian tradition, as well as the parodic use of Romantic *topoi* and the daring stylistic innovations of her poems, display her open-minded attitude to literature and the world about her. In the Preface to the sonnet sequence *Monna Innominata*, for instance, she argues against stereotypes of Medieval love poetry. Apart from questioning the desirability of Beatrice's and Laura's condition – '[they] have alike paid the exceptional penalty of exceptional honour, and have come down to use resplendent with charms, but (at least, to my apprehension) scant of attractiveness' – she reverses the roles of the Troubadour poet and his beloved 'donna innominata' by suggesting the possibility of a female (and more genuine) speaker-lover: 'Had such a lady spoken for herself, the portrait left us might have appeared more tender, if less dignified, than any drawn even by a devoted friend.'[5] *Monna Innominata* is the fictional love song of an unnamed lady, who, in being granted a voice, accomplishes even more than the wished-for figure mentioned in the Preface. In addition to acquiring a new status (from a silent object of desire, she becomes a sentimental and artistic subject), the female speaker modifies traditional love discourse, since she parodies or reverses some of its basic clichés: the sacredness of love memories is replaced by easy forgetfulness; the hierarchical relationship of lover and beloved is turned into a bond of 'happy equals';[6] and earthly love is diminished by an eroticized passion for God.

Christina's poetry adopts similar strategies to reconfigure a number of Romantic paradigms. It suffices to think of her revision of the Keatsian figures of the demon-lover, the femme fatale and the ill-starred lovers in some love lyrics ('Love from the North', 'The Convent Threshold'), or of her anti-metaphorical representation of birds and other natural creatures in 'Maiden-Song', 'A Green Cornfield' and 'Winter Rain'. To the Romantics' figurative language, Rossetti opposes a 'purer' and more referential idiom purged of those ideological markers that had gained validation and currency through continued poetic usage.[7]

The metaliterary awareness of her works was enhanced by the disquieting effects of scientific thinking on traditional beliefs. Like most Victorians, Christina could neither ignore the dreary implications of the theory of evolution, nor avoid meditating on the new worldview depicted by geologists and astronomers. Scarce though they are, Christina's reflections on science reveal her view of life as a set of multiple, contradictory and unfathomable truths. In a passage from *Seek and Find*, for instance, she conveys an idea of multiplicity and disorientation by focusing on two thorny scientific problems: that of the marginality of the Earth and the solar system in the universe; and the more general awareness of the risks deriving from fast-developing knowledge.

> There is something awe-striking, over-whelming, in contemplation of the stars. Their number, magnitudes, distances, orbits, we know not: any multitude our unaided eyes discern is but an instalment of that vaster multitude which the telescope reveals. [...] Knowledge runs apace: and our globe which once seemed large is now but a small planet among planets, while not one of our group of planets is large as compared with its central sun; and the sun itself may be no more than a sub-centre, it and all its system coursing but as satellites and sub-satellites around a general centre; and this again,— what of this? Is even this remote centre truly central, or is it no more than yet another sub-centre revolving around some point of overruling attraction, and swaying with it the harmonious encircling dance of its attendant worlds?[8]

The 'Chinese box' image of a 'centre' continually displaced into a 'sub-centre' renders well the crisis of anthropocentrism, which the diffusion of scientific ideas was contributing to accelerate.[9] The smaller the Earth appears in the vastness of the cosmos, the more insignificant man proves, since his astronomical discoveries do nothing but confirm his limited knowledge of reality. This paradox is most evident in the second part of the above excerpt. The hermeneutic anxiety conveyed by the question 'what of this?' is followed by the search for *one* truth, which the final option resolutely denies ('Is even this remote centre truly central, or is it no more than yet another sub-centre [...]?'). What is interesting to note here is that Christina uses an inductive method of observation, analysis and argumentation. To a fideistic attitude, she prefers a rational approach, which evidences her interest in the new methods of investigation of reality. Despite its limitations, reason is for her a better means of exploration than faith, whose dogmas were being undermined by scientific progress.

A similar approach characterizes some poems that pivot on the contrast *semiotic vs. actual*. In 'Symbols' (1849),[10] she expresses her disillusionment with two emblems of beauty and vitality, the rosebud and the birds' eggs, which fail to accomplish their traditional promises. Placed in an overwhelmingly fragile environment, they are suddenly (and incomprehensibly) turned into symbols of mortality. The text is as follows:

'Symbols'

I watched a rosebud very long
   Brought on by dew and sun and shower,
   Waiting to see the perfect flower:
Then, when I thought it should be strong,
   It opened at the matin hour   5
     And fell at evensong.

I watched a nest from day to day,
   A green nest full of pleasant shade,
   Wherein three speckled eggs were laid:
But when they should have hatched in May,   10
   The two old birds had grown afraid
     Or tired, and flew away.

Then in my wrath I broke the bough
   That I had tended so with care,
   Hoping its scent should fill the air;   15
I crushed the eggs, not heeding how
   Their ancient promise had been fair:
     I would have vengeance now.

But the dead branch spoke from the sod,
   And the eggs answered me again: 20
   Because we failed dost thou complain?
Is thy wrath just? And what if God,
   Who waiteth for thy fruits in vain,
     Should also take the rod?

The references to sight in the first two stanzas (the anaphoric verb 'I watched' (ll. 1, 7) and the syntagm 'Waiting to see', l. 3) enhance the tension between expectation and disappointment, since the wished-for events of blossoming and hatching never take place. Instead of fulfilling the speaker's hopes, the perceived bud and eggs record his or her frustration, and reveal the unbridge-able gap between reality and imagination. Not even the final stanza, which suggests an analogical comparison between earthly and divine things, pro-vides an explanation of the abortive deeds narrated in the poem. The under-lying question 'Why?', which the speaker never asks but continually suggests, is only made more obsessive by the poem's final queries. Death and destruc-tion are taken for granted in a world in which perfection is an unattainable aim.

By highlighting the antithesis of sight and vision, Rossetti states the primacy of scientific observation over idealism:[11] the abstract meaning of the 'symbols' is replaced by their referential value, which can only be captured by adopting scientific approaches. This does not mean that the observed phenomena can be fully explained. Christina's description of the failure to bear progeny is as enigmatic as the failures later examined by Darwin, whose optimistic idea of evolutionism did not entail the possibility of foretelling the future in detail.[12] In addition to its astounding realism, 'Symbols' bears witness to Christina's attempts to revise poetic and linguistic stereotypes. The stress she lays on the concreteness of the rosebud and the eggs reverses their traditional meta-phorical connotations, which the poetic canon had encoded and preserved for centuries.

Another telling example of her revisionist stance is the poem 'My Dream' (1855).[13] In its obscure, eccentric verse, Christina uses different textual strate-gies to oppose the dominant Victorian ethos. First, she merges literary allu-sions spanning centuries and, in parodying them, shows how simple allegory legitimizes cultural prejudice. Secondly, she indulges in the description of a cannibalistic feast that cancels any hope of a teleological design, showing how the primacy of civilized values is threatened by the competition for survival. Thirdly, she employs odd dialogic techniques which both entice and frustrate the reader's curiosity. These latter devices create a sense of hermeneutic con-fusion, which is a testimony to her wish to replace closeness with elusiveness, certainty with doubt, uniformity with diversity.

The title of the poem is already an index of its subversive meaning. The possessive 'My' emphasizes the speaker's own viewpoint, which will prove difficult to transmit and share, while the term 'dream' evokes a long tradition of oneiric literature dating back to Menippean satire. More precisely, 'My Dream' can be placed in the tradition of the 'dream of crisis', which according to Bakhtin flourishes in times of decadence and opens up unforeseen possibili-ties of regeneration.[14] To make the dream-form more disruptive, Christina does not limit herself to representing some disturbing fantasies. She also insists on the mysteriousness of her oneiric experience, which is deliberately left unsolved. In so doing, she reinforces the provocative effects of the poem, which can be read on many levels: religious, because of the lay and morbid nature of the 'enigma' described in the text; ontological, since the idea of a single truth is overtly undermined; intertextual, because of the parodic montage of many allusions to literary and scientific works; and linguistic, as testified by the plurisemantic quality and the puzzling dialogism of the verse.

Considered as a whole, 'My Dream' infringes on the interpretative guidelines of the age by questioning different kinds of authority and asserting the need for pluralism and open-endedness. Christina challenges the idea of the *telos*, as well as linguistic and poetic monologism,[15] since she denies any allegorical or clear-cut solution to her obscure dream. From this standpoint it is hardly surprising that some Victorian readers responded unfavourably to the poem. Among them, it is worth mentioning William Michael Rossetti who, in the 1904 edition of Christina's *Poetical Works*, expresses considerable irritation and perplexity:

> [...] the odd freakishness which flecked the extreme and almost excessive seriousness of her thought [...]. It looks like the narration of a true dream; and nothing seems as if it could account for so eccentric a train of notions, except that she in fact dreamed them. And yet she did not; for, in a copy of her collected edition of 1875, I find that she has marked the piece 'not a real dream'. As it was not a real dream, and she chose nevertheless to give it verbal form, one seeks for a meaning in it, and I for one cannot find any that bears development. She certainly liked the poem, and in this I and others quite agreed with her; I possess a little bit of paper, containing three illustrations of her own to *The Dream*, and bearing the date 16 March '55.[16]

In the first part of the quotation, William Michael highlights three puzzling aporias: the 'odd freakishness' of his sister's thought, which is in sheer contrast with her 'extreme [...] seriousness'; the problem of ascertaining whether Christina told a 'true dream', which she firmly denied; and the dilemma of searching for a meaning that is continually deferred. Unable to solve these riddles, he gets entangled in an even more complex question: that of the aesthetic enjoyment of the poem. Despite its obscurity, which deprives the reader of the Barthesian *plaisir*, 'My Dream' stimulates a response of *jouissance*.[17] William Michael himself admits feeling a strong relish for the poem, which seems to attract him exactly because it violates intelligibility. The adverb 'quite' that he uses to describe his surrender, emphasizes the contrast between the allure of the text and the interpretative standstill that the author textualizes to baffle contemporary readers' logical and moral expectations ('and she chose nevertheless to give it verbal form').

In order to trace the different strategies of displacement that bewildered Christina's readership, let us now examine the poem in detail:

'My Dream'

Hear now a curious dream I dreamed last night,
Each word whereof is weighed and sifted truth

I stood beside Euphrates while it swelled
Like overflowing Jordan in its youth:
It waxed and coloured sensibly to sight,   5
Till out of myriad pregnant waves there welled
Young crocodiles, a gaunt blunt-featured crew,
Fresh-hatched perhaps and daubed with birthday dew.
The rest if I should tell, I fear my friend,
My closest friend, would deem the facts untrue;   10
And therefore it were wisely left untold;
Yet if you will, why, hear it to the end.

Each crocodile was girt with massive gold
And polished stones that with their wearers grew:
But one there was who waxed beyond the rest,   15
Wore kinglier girdle and a kingly crown,
Whilst crowns and orbs and sceptres starred his breast
All gleamed compact and green with scale on scale,
But special burnishment adorned his mail
And special terror weighed upon his frown;   20
His punier brethren quaked before his tail,
Broad as a rafter, potent as a flail.
So he grew lord and master of his kin:
But who shall tell the tale of all their woes?
An execrable appetite arose,   25
He battened on them, crunched, and sucked them in.
He knew no law, he feared no binding law,
But ground them with inexorable jaw:
The luscious fat distilled upon his chin,
Exuded from his nostrils and his eyes,   30
While still like hungry death he fed his maw;
Till every minor crocodile being dead
And buried too, himself gorged to the full.
He slept with breath oppressed and unstrung claw.

Oh marvel passing strange which next I saw: 35
In sleep he dwindled to the common size,
And all the empire faded from his coat.

Then from far off a wingèd vessel came,
Swift as a swallow, subtle as a flame:
I know not what it bore of freight or host,   40
But white it was as an avenging ghost.
It levelled strong Euphrates in its course;
Supreme yet weightless as an idle mote
It seemed to tame the waters without force
Till not a murmur swelled or billow beat: 45
Lo, as the purple shadow swept the sands,
The prudent crocodile rose on his feet
And shed appropriate tears and wrung his hands

What can it mean? you ask. I answer not
For meaning, but myself must echo, What?   50
And tell it as I saw it on the spot.

The dream is about a lurid cannibalistic banquet, which takes place against a Biblical background. After becoming the king of his tribe, an enormous crocodile develops an 'execrable appetite' and starts to devour his smaller fellow beings. In describing the horrible deed, the speaker insists on its fiercest and most disgusting details and, to make his tale utterly shocking, announces that it is 'weighed and sifted truth'.

The conclusion of the poem is even more disorienting. A vessel arrives on the scene and seems to frighten the crocodile, who cries and wrings his hands in a mood of repentance. Yet, the apparent re-establishment of order is questioned by two textual elements: the adjective 'prudent' (l. 47), which attaches an ironic colouring to the crocodile's remorse, and the final questions asked by the poetic voice. By declaring his inability to interpret the dream ('What can it mean?', 'What?'), this latter conveys a sense of hermeneutic impasse. Instead of a clear moral, which might illuminate the crocodile's behaviour, he introduces two upsetting notions: the aporia of a conduct based on hypocrisy and 'prudence', and the parodic allusion to a traditional genre, the beast fable, whose basic rules are ostensibly violated.

To understand this point better, we need to investigate the richly intertextual pattern of the poem. In addition to the classical beast fable, which is evoked by the crocodile's anthropomorphic demeanour, Rossetti refers to a wide range of texts and genres, such as the Christian parable, the medieval romance, the allegorical romance, George Herbert's poem 'Jordan (1)' and Coleridge's 'Rime of the Ancient Mariner'. All these archetypes are combined in a palimpsestic structure, whose chief purpose appears to be to parody dominant discourses and ideologies. The absence of a moral, for example, creates a visible gap between 'My Dream' and two kinds of narratives based on exemplary events: the fable and the parable. Far from unveiling an edifying truth, the poem closes with the speaker's doubts, which make the crocodile's repentance quite improbable. Equally disturbing is the parody of the two forms of romance. If the heroism of chivalric poems is replaced by the baseness of the crocodile, who, despite his 'kingly' appearance, contravenes the medieval code of honour, the triumph of Vice over Virtue (implied by the unpunished act of cannibalism) reverses the ethical implications of traditional allegories.

Less evident is the parallelism with 'Jordan (1)'. The reference to the 'overflowing' Biblical river (l. 4) is not the only connection between 'My Dream' and the poem written by Herbert, whom Christina overtly admired. If we pay due attention to the text, it becomes clear that the 'truth' mentioned in line 2 introduces the question of verity in artistic creation. The same issue is dealt with in the opening lines of 'Jordan (1)': 'Who says that fictions only and false hair/ Become a verse? Is there in truth no beauty?'[18] Yet, there is a consistent difference between the two poems. While Herbert uses the antithesis sincerity/artificiality to maintain the superiority of religion over literature, Christina investigates the limits of allegory from a lay perspective. The result of her experiment is the overturning of ready-made associations and meanings. To the 'illusion' of a monologic worldview produced by a figurative language, she opposes the 'truthfulness' of an incomprehensible reality, in which allegory is replaced by polysemy.

Another piece of her intertextual jigsaw is 'The Rime of the Ancient Mariner'. The naval vocabulary ('crew', 'vessel'), the idea of betraying one's fellows' trust, the arrival of the ghostly vessel, the repentance theme, and the image of the crocodile wringing his hands – which is strongly reminiscent of that of the mariner's 'skinny hands'[19] – are all references to Coleridge's poem, which is subjected to criticism and revision. Yet by comparison with Coleridge, who writes a sustained albeit complex allegory, Christina confuses roles and symbolic values. The result is a semantic and ontological confusion, which triggers off a series of tricky questions. What exactly is the relationship between men and crocodiles? Does the animal world mirror human society, or is the latter more vicious and brutal than the former? And what is the real function of the vessel?

The first important element to consider is the presence of proto-evolutionary ideas.[20] The personification of the savage crocodile enables Rossetti to trace a parallelism between men and beasts, who share the same instinct of aggressiveness. Because of this instinct, which plays a crucial role in intraspecific selection, strong men are destined to prevail over their weaker fellows in precisely the same way that the huge crocodile thrives on his 'punier brethren' (l. 21). Whereas Coleridge conceives nature as a model of 'civilized' behaviour and invites transgressive people to adapt to it, Christina emphasizes the beastly features of human beings, who are subjected to the same ruthless laws that govern the lives of other animals. The scientific undertones of the poem are confirmed by the choice of crocodiles as the main characters. Early Victorian scientists were particularly interested in reptiles, which, together with fish, provided an important link between 'lower' and 'higher' species. Echoes of their arguments, which involved Darwin himself, can be found in religious and literary works published throughout the nineteenth century.[21] In these works, as with Rossetti's anthropomorphic crocodile, the classification of species often becomes a pretext to draw effective metaphors of mankind, to capture the evil and the contradictions of human beings by 'downgrading' them to the rank of 'lower' creatures with which they share primeval instincts.

The possibility of interpreting 'My Dream' as an evolutionary text validates the idea that Christina was launching a poetic attack on hegemonic culture. The image of a fierce struggle for life, in which brute instincts are victorious over higher values,[22] impairs some main tenets of Victorian ideology, namely, the middle-class concepts of morality and civilization, and their literary representation in the form of allegories based on a strict Manichean order. Not even the crocodile's shrinking to the common size and his 'appropriate tears' (l. 48) are convincing symptoms of contrition. Rather than offering an orthodox solution, Rossetti closes the poem suddenly and ambiguously, thus encouraging multiple readings of the many textual riddles.

A further index of subversion is the crude description of the banquet. The disgusting physical details, the various images of eating and dismembering, the nexuses life-death and killing-feeding, have much in common with the corporeal grotesqueness of popular culture, which Bakhtin considers as a 'triumphant and festive' emblem of collective renewal.[23] If allegory entails a spiritual transfiguration of worldly things, the bodily excess of 'My Dream' moves the focus from Heaven to Earth, from a spiritual essence to a belly that partakes in the natural cycles of death and regeneration. By granting the primacy of corporeal needs, which are portrayed in all their contradictions, Rossetti disputes the sacredness of a behavioural code based on the sheer opposition Good/Evil and, consequently, weakens the notion of authority asserted by that code.

In this respect, the speaker's dream fulfils an important metapoetic function, since Christina employs the rebellious energy of popular culture against

Victorian mentality. Through parody and polysemy, she exposes the complicity of art in maintaining the status quo, deconstructs long-standing forms of poetic support to the establishment, and creates an alternative 'open-ended' text, whose manifold gaps must be filled in by the reader. It is no coincidence, therefore, that in the first and last lines the speaker addresses his questions to a mysterious 'you', who is stimulated to interpret the oneiric vision. The reference to a hidden and dangerous meaning, which is ultimately denied by the question 'What?', shows the artist's unwillingness to transmit a clear message. In so doing, Rossetti highlights the process of deciphering stories, of looking for a hermeneutic truth which is neither evident nor unquestionable, but which rather splits into manifold, controversial truths.

In the recesses of her Victorian house, Christina opened up to different kinds of stimuli, and constantly crossed the borders of prudence. The choice of an 'irrational' form like the dream-poem enabled her to escape the strictures of her cultural milieu without suffering censorship. But her artistic project was carefully considered and accomplished. Behind her playfulness and relish for odd fantasies, we can trace a deliberate attempt to unveil the dangers of dominant ideologies, and declare the relativity and inscrutability of the world.

Notes

1 After Modernism and before the turning point of the 1970s, Christina Rossetti's fortune declined for a few decades. In that span of time, critics tended to define her as a 'minor' poet, who did not deserve to be included in the canon. Among her detractors, it is worth mentioning David Daiches, who in his 4-volume *A Critical History of English Literature* devotes less than one page to an analysis of her works. Apart from insisting on the inhibiting effects of her faith, he stresses the retrospective quality of her religious imagination and the limits of her poetic language: 'Her temper was hardly Victorian, and she availed herself of few of the Victorian poet's professional tricks. She might have done better in the seventeenth century, when her strong religious feeling might have found itself less at odds with the world she lived in and less restrictive of the total personality'. David Daiches, *A Critical History of English Literature*, 4 vols (London: Secker and Warburg, 1960), vol. iv, p. 1021.

2 To prove Christina's 'modernity', scholars have not only emphasized her innovative themes, metres and syntax. They have also referred to the admiration she won among late Victorians and Modernists before the decline of her fortunes that came to an end only in recent times. In 1893, for instance, Edmund Gosse praised the formal accomplishments of her poems, while two decades later Ford Madox Ford recognized her poetic greatness, thus showing that the linguistic strategies she employed somehow appealed to his Modernist tastes. Cf. Antony H Harrison, *Christina Rossetti in Context* (Brighton: The Harvester Press, 1988), pp. 39–40.

3 Although the question of her exclusion from the Brotherhood is still open to controversy, there are strong arguments for it. Cf. Jerome Bump, 'Christina Rossetti and the Pre-Raphaelite Brotherhood' in *The Achievement of Christina Rossetti*, ed. by David Kent

(Ithaca and London: Cornell University Press, 1987), pp. 322–45. On many occasions, Christina's brothers raised objections to her poems. Dante Gabriel, for instance, protested on the rhythmical irregularities of 'Goblin Market', which he defined 'metrical jerks' (quoted in Jerome Bump, 'Hopkins, Rossetti, and Pre-Raphaelitism' in *The Victorian Newsletter*, 57, Spring 1980, pp. 1–6 (p. 5). He also disapproved of her decision to publish 'Winter: My Secret' and 'Under the Rose', which he thought were respectively too personal and too vulgar. The latter poem, in his opinion, was inadequate for publication because it dealt too explicitly with the theme of illegitimacy. See Kathleen Jones, *Learning Not to Be the First. The Life of Christina Rossetti* (Adlestrop: The Windrush Press, 1991), pp. 109, 123–4. For the objections raised by William Michael against 'My Dream' see n. 15.

4   Apart from John Ruskin's complaint about the prosodic irregularity of 'Goblin Market', there are some negative evaluations of the poem, which stress its outrageous and obscure meaning. Alice Meynell, for instance, highlighted the 'hardly intelligible' moral of the poem, while a contemporary reviewer was indignant at its underlying suggestion that cheating the devil is better than resisting him. Cf. *Letters of Dante Gabriel Rossetti*, ed. by Oswald Doughty and John R Wahl, 4 vols (Oxford: Clarendon Press, 1967), vol. 2, p. 391; Angela Leighton, *Victorian Women Poets. Writing Against the Heart* (London and New York: Harvester Wheatsheaf, 1992), p. 137; and FA Rudd, 'Christina Rossetti' in *Catholic World*, 4 (1866), p. 845.

5   Christina Rossetti, *The Complete Poems*, ed. by Rebecca W Crump, notes and introduction by Betty S Flowers (Harmondsworth: Penguin, 2001), p. 294.

6   Christina Rossetti, *The Complete Poems*, ed. Crump, p. 297 (Sonnet 7, l. 3).

7   Cf. Mariaconcetta Costantini, *Poesia e sovversione. Christina Rossetti, Gerard Manley Hopkins* (Pescara: Edizioni Tracce, 2000), pp. 61–4, 150–4.

8   Christina Rossetti, *Seek and Find: A Double Series of Short Studies of the Benedicite* (London: SPCK, 1879), pp. 35–6.

9   Astronomical theories were the subject of much debate among the Victorians, who gained access to ideas formulated both in England and on the Continent through large-circulation books and treatises. A telling example is the nebular hypothesis illustrated in *Vestiges of the Natural History of Creation*, an ambitious synthesis of the latest scientific findings, which was published anonymously in 1844. In the first chapter, the author (Robert Chambers) quotes authoritative astronomers of the previous decades (Herschel, Laplace, Mossotti, etc.) to support his arguments for the nebular hypothesis and contributes to the ongoing debate on human knowledge by posing controversial questions about cosmical laws: 'What is that? Whence have come all these beautiful regulations?' *Vestiges*, 6th ed. (London: John Churchill, 1847), pp. 25–6. These questions, and the initial description of the smallness of the Earth in the solar system ('The mind fails to form an exact notion of a portion of space so immense; [...]', *Ibid.*, p. 2), are surprisingly akin to Christina's epistemological reflections. Although there is no evidence that she read *Vestiges*, she must have been familiar to the main themes of a book that was a great sensation at the time. For more details about the circulation of Chambers's work and the controversy it aroused, see James A Secord, *Victorian Sensation. The Extraordinary Publication, Reception, and Secret Authorship of* Vestiges of the Natural History of Creation (Chicago and London: The University of Chicago Press, 2000).

10   Christina Rossetti, *The Complete Poems*, ed. Crump, pp. 69–70.

11   In this regard, Rossetti is in line with most Victorian revivalists of Baconianism, who

believed in the possibility of attaining full knowledge through induction. Apart from Harriet Martineau and other enthusiasts for the analytical method used by the inquirer into nature, there were also theologians, such as the Reverend Thomas Chalmers, who thought that 'a truly inductive spirit' would provide a 'reliable testimony' of Scripture. Cf. James A. Secord, *Victorian Sensation*, cit., pp. 272–4, 478 and passim.

12 In the conclusion of the second edition of *The Origin of Species*, Darwin writes that 'of the species now living very few will transmit progeny of any kind to a far distant futurity'. In the following lines, however, he tries to temper the negativity of his statement by suggesting that 'the common and widely-spread species, belonging to the larger and dominant groups, [...] will ultimately prevail and procreate new and dominant species'. Charles Darwin, *The Origin of Species*, ed. by Gillian Beer (Oxford and New York: Oxford University Press, 1996), p. 395.

13 Christina Rossetti, *The Complete Poems*, ed. Crump, pp. 33–4.

14 Cf. Mikhail Bakhtin, *Problems of Dostoevsky's Poetics* (Minneapolis: University of Minnesota Press, 1993).

15 'Monologism, at its extreme, denies the existence outside itself of another consciousness with equal rights and equal responsibilities, another *I* with equal rights (*thou*). With a monologic approach (at its extreme or pure form) *another person* remains wholly and merely an *object* of consciousness, and not another consciousness. No response is expected from it that could change everything in the world of my consciousness. Monologue is finalised and deaf to the other's response, does not expect it and does not acknowledge in it any *decisive force*. Monologue manages without the other [...]. Monologue pretends to be the *ultimate word*. It closes down the represented world and represented person'. *Ibid.*, pp. 292–3.

16 *The Poetical Works of Christina Georgina Rossetti*, ed. by William Michael Rossetti (London: Macmillan, 1904), p. 479.

17 Cf. Roland Barthes, *The Pleasure of the Text* (New York: Hill and Wang, 1974).

18 George Herbert, *The Complete English Poems*, ed. by John Tobin (Harmondsworth: Penguin, 1991), p. 50.

19 *The Poems of Samuel Taylor Coleridge*, ed. by Sir AT Quiller-Couch (London: Oxford University Press, 1958), pp. 281–300 (ll. 9, 225).

20 In 1855 most Victorians were already familiar with the concept of transmutation. Ideas had started to circulate much earlier than the publication of *The Origin of Species*. It suffices to think of the 'great sensation' created by *Vestiges of the Natural History of Creation*, which sold almost forty thousand copies: 'As readable as a romance, based on the latest findings of science, *Vestiges* was an evolutionary epic that ranged from the formation of the solar system to reflections on the destiny of the human race. [...] Readers included aristocrats and handloom weavers; science writers and the wives of cotton manufacturers; evangelicals and militant freethinkers; [...]'. James A Secord, *Victorian Sensation*, cit., pp. 1–2. The idea of a relentless struggle for survival had been anticipated by Malthus, whose economic arguments had made a strong impression on public opinion. See also n. 21.

21 An example of this long controversy is Darwin's rejection of the genealogical system of classification constructed by the author of *Vestiges*. The notes he wrote in the margin of the sixth edition show that he did not only disagree with the idea of a fish passing into a reptile, but also questioned the accuracy of terms like 'lower' and 'higher'. Cf. Secord, *Victorian Sensation*, cit., p. 433. To realise how deeply Victorian artists were aware of these scientific questions, let us consider a brief passage from Hopkins' Sermons, in

which the poet reflects on the symbolism of the serpent (and the dragon) to ascertain the metaphysical attributes of the devil: 'Now among the vertebrates the reptiles go near to combine the qualities of the other classes in themselves and are, I think, taken by the Evolutionists as nearest the original vertebrate stem and as the point of departure for the rest. In this way clearly dragons are represented as gathering up the attributes of many creatures: [...] The dragon then symbolises one who aiming at every perfection ends by being a monster, a 'fright''. Gerard Manley Hopkins, 'Creation and Redemption. The Great Sacrifice' (1881) in *The Sermons and Devotional Writings of Gerard Manley Hopkins*, ed. by Christopher Devlin, SJ (London, New York and Toronto: Oxford University Press, 1959), p. 199.

22 Malthus' descriptions of the 'natural checks' that prevented population increase contributed to inspire such images, which are recurrent in Victorian poetry. It suffices to think of Tennyson's reflections on the conflict between natural and humanitarian values, which in Stanza 55 of 'In Memoriam' are epitomized by the two personified entities at strife: 'Are God and Nature then at strife,/ That Nature lends such evil dreams?/ So careful of the type she seems,/ So careless of the single life' (ll. 5–8).

23 Mikhail Bakhtin, *Rabelais and His World*, trans. by Hélène Iswolky (Bloomington: Indiana University Press, 1984), pp. 278–303.

PART IV

RADICAL POETICS

11

DG ROSSETTI AND THE ART OF THE INNER STANDING-POINT

Jerome McGann

Perhaps the most monumental moment in Dante Gabriel Rossetti's artistic career came in 1859–60 when he painted *Bocca Baciata*. This small oil picture of Fanny Cornforth signalled a line of work that would dominate the remainder of his life: the female portrait in oil, often imaginatively reconceived in legendary, mythological or literary terms. These pictures would also regularly grow in size and/or imposing presence, from works like *Fazio's Mistress* to *Venus Verticordia*, *Lady Lilith*, *Monna Vanna*, *Proserpine*, *Astarte Syriaca*.

Everyone knows about this turn to Venetian models – to Veronese and Titian perhaps especially – and away from his early pre-Raphaelite ideas, which were grounded in what Holman Hunt later deprecated as 'the childlike immaturities and limitations of the German and Italian quattrocentrists'. (Hunt had his own ideas about what was important in those primitive masters.) Like Hunt, most have observed Rossetti's turn with dismay. While Hunt admired the technical brilliance of *Bocca Baciata*, he deplored what he saw as its sensuality and 'epicurianism'. Ruskin would have precisely the same reaction as he observed the proliferation of Dante Gabriel's Venetian studies. Much later, as post-impressionism was turning to modernism, Roger Fry's influential 1916 essay 'Rossetti's Water-colours of 1857' set the terms for how Rossetti's work would be read for the remainder of the twentieth century. The marvellous drawings of the mid-1950s thereafter came to define for art historians whatever was important and interesting in Rossetti's pictorial work.

In all this well-known tale, however, one odd but crucial matter stands out: the fact that Dante Gabriel's turn to Venice has not been satisfactorily explained. Why veer away from the evident triumphs of the 1950s water-colours and their companion works – for example, the Tennyson illustrations and the remarkable drawings of Elizabeth Siddal, 'stamped with immortality' as Madox Brown said? The usual explanations are (1) that Rossetti wanted to work in what was perceived as a major medium (oil) and a major genre (portraiture), and (2) that he wanted to make more money from his art work. While both of these judgements are borne out in Rossetti's letters, they leave entirely unexplained the procedural and aesthetic relation between his work before and after 1860. Or I should say, they have left us only with Fry's explanation of the relation: that Dante Gabriel simply had no resources to go beyond his brilliant works on paper. (I point out in passing that Fry's view is little more than a modernist reprise on the Victorian judgements initially laid down by Ruskin and Hunt – and later, it should be noted, by Robert Buchanan when he reviewed Rossetti's literary work.)

I want to present a very different rationale for what was involved in Rossetti's 1860 'Venetian' turn. This explanation requires a comprehensive reflection on Rossetti's work, literary as well as pictorial. Rossetti was after all painter *and* poet. His poetry and fiction are intimately bound up with his pictorial and craft work, most especially his work in graphics and book design. This related set of interests signals his broadly based cultural concern with the function and place of art 'at the present time'.

The 1850s art work is clearly a disciplined critique of the conventions of realist illusionism, as Fry himself pointed out. Dante Gabriel's artistic argument is matched by most of his early literary works: that is to say, by 'The Blessed Damozel', 'Hand and Soul', 'St. Luke the Painter', the various sonnets for pictures, and the whole project of his Italian translations. The argument is complemented by a few other important works, like *Found, Mary Magdalene at the Door of Simon the Pharisee*, 'The Burden of Nineveh' and 'Jenny,' where Rossetti sought to develop his critique of realist illusion from within the illusionist forms themselves. Among these works 'Jenny' is crucial, as we shall see. It brought Rossetti to a point where he could articulate in a clear way an exact relation between realist forms (representations, images) and false social consciousness. It should be remembered, in this context, that Rossetti only completed this important poem in 1859–60, at the same time he was undertaking *Bocca Baciata*. The relation between the two works is defined by Fanny Cornforth, the prostitute he met in 1858 who would become his lover, his housekeeper and one of his closest friends. She is the central figure in both the poem and the painting, a relation unnoticed by most critics but one bearing great significance. It helps to explain how and why the watershed of 1859–60 turned Rossetti into the Victorian equivalent – bourgeois and sentimental – of Baudelaire's ironized and aristocratical 'Painter of Modern Life.'

❋

I will begin by recollecting a key set of Rossettian ideas, attitudes and procedures. Like many of his contemporaries, and most of his pre-Raphaelite
colleagues, Dante Gabriel approached his work in a critically self-conscious –
even a programmatic – way. Despite his well-known argument that 'fundamental brainwork' must control any aesthetic practice, the image of Rossetti
as careless and indulgent blew legend-laden through the trees of modernism
and its groves of academe. Whistler and Ford Madox Ford, who both admired
him, helped to found such views when they represented Dante Gabriel after
his death as unreflective, undisciplined, even lazy – 'an amateur in two arts', as
Whistler famously remarked. No one who has examined these matters attentively thinks such things any longer, I'm glad to say, and a growing number
of interested persons are beginning to see exactly *why* this imagination of
Rossetti was an important ideological feature of modernism's self-conception,
especially in England.

Nonetheless, when you compare Dante Gabriel with (say) Swinburne,
Morris or even Hunt, you can easily conclude that Rossetti had little interest
in writing critically or reflexively about art or literature, either in general or in
personal ways. His non-fiction corpus is small and, with some few (but crucial)
exceptions, it does not compel study or attention.

We may begin to shed some light on this odd and even paradoxical situation by recalling a key passage in Rossetti's essay 'The Stealthy School of
Criticism'.[1] He is defending his dramatic monologue 'Jenny' from the harsh
criticisms it had received from Robert Buchanan. The entire passage is so
important that we shall have to examine it in detail.

From the time of its first conception, Rossetti says, he was aware of the
difficulties the poem might pose for readers – even for careful readers who
'might still hold that the thought in it had better have dispensed with the situation which serves it for framework'. Rossetti is thinking here specifically of
readers like Ruskin, who were repelled by Rossetti's 'framework'. These readers led Dante Gabriel 'to consider how far a treatment from without might
here be possible', that is to say, whether it might be better to take up the
subject of prostitution in Victorian England in expository critical prose. That
Rossetti seems to have considered doing so is in itself remarkable and helps to
explain why he reckoned 'Jenny', when he finished his intermediate version in
1859, 'the most serious thing I have written' (as he told Allingham in
November 1859). Without explaining why he rejected the option of a prose
essay on Victorian prostitution, Rossetti goes on to discuss what is involved
when 'the thought in' his poem is cast in an imaginative rather than an expository 'framework'.

But the motive powers of art reverse the requirement of science, and
demand first of all an inner standing-point. The heart of such a mystery

as this must be plucked from the very world in which it beats or bleeds; and the beauty and pity, the self-questionings and all-questionings which it brings with it, can come with full force only from the mouth of one alive to its whole appeal, such as the speaker put forward in the poem – that is, of a young and thoughtful man of the world. To such a speaker, many half-cynical revulsions of feeling and reverie, and a recurrent presence of the impressions of beauty (however artificial) which first brought him within such a circle of influence, would be inevitable features of the dramatic relations portrayed.

This text needs careful glossing. One wants to note, for example, that Rossetti represents his 'speaker' in ambivalent terms (he is 'half-cynical', his aesthetic sense is inclined to the 'artificial', he is riven by 'self-questionings and all-questionings'). The phrase 'a young and thoughtful man of the world' sums up the speaker's problematic character as Rossetti sees him, for each term in that phrase is freighted with equivocal meanings. 'The dramatic relations portrayed' in the poem exhibit the young man's character – that is to say, the complex of social and psychological determinants that 'brought him within such a circle of influence' as the poem displays for us. Also notable, in this context, are the neutral tones, so to speak, that characterize Rossetti's commentary. Rossetti is evidently concerned to speak about the young man in cool and meticulous terms: to note that he is 'thoughtful', for instance, without at the same time implying that this thoughtfulness is an unequivocally positive virtue; or, by contrast, to note his taste for the 'artificial' without allowing that term to bear exclusively negative overtones, as it would in the orbit of romantic nature ideology. But of course Rossetti, like Blake, is anything but a poet and artist of nature. Both are urbanites.

Of greatest importance is Rossetti's reference to the '*inner* standing-point' as one of 'the motive powers of art'.[2] Rossetti had introduced the theory of the '*inner* standing-point' some years before, in an unpublished note to his pastiche poem 'Ave' (then titled 'Mater pulchrae delectionis'). The idea of art at an '*inner* standing-point' clearly represents a theoretical reflection on the dramatic monologue, and especially on Robert Browning's use of the form, which Rossetti much admired. Rossetti's thoughts on this genre, however, are quite different from Browning's – both in 1847–8, when he wrote 'Ave' as one of his 'Songs for the Art Catholic', and in 1859 and 1871, when his focus of attention was on 'Jenny'. Rossetti's comment is arguing that an '*inner* standing-point' is not simply a feature of a particular genre or poetic form, it is a foundational requirement of 'art'. Not just writing, not just poetry, but 'art' in general.

Let's briefly reconsider Dante Gabriel's thinking in 1847–8. Like those other two urban artists Poe and Baudelaire, Rossetti at the time was much involved with projects that cultivated escaping from the contemporary world. 'Ave' and the 'Songs of the Art Catholic' were magical texts written to open a passage whereby Rossetti could plunge into a lost land of his heart's desire. To manage this feat he elaborates various kinds of '*inner* standing-point' procedures. He composes pastiche works like 'Ave' and 'Mary's Girlhood', quasi-pastiche works like 'The Blessed Damozel', conjuring prose tales like 'Hand and Soul' and 'St Agnes of Intercession', and the ventriloquizing translations from Dante and other early Italian poets. In each case the crucial move does not abstract Rossetti away from his texts – which is Browning's object and great achievement – it involves Rossetti in his own poem's dramatic action. 'Ave' is a special kind of dramatic monologue where an '*inner* standing-point' is constructed and then occupied simultaneously by the writing/composing Victorian poet Rossetti and his imaginary Catholic antitype from the fourteenth-century. Behind Rossetti lie Browning's dramatic monologues, before him loom Yeats's masks.

When a poetics of the inner standing-point is undertaken in a poem of contemporary life such as 'Jenny', the results are very different from those gained when Dante Gabriel wrote 'Ave'. The world of 'Jenny' is no lost spiritual dreamland, it is an all-too-present nightmare. Readers to this day argue about whether the 'young and thoughtful man of the world' is offered for our judgement or our sympathy and about Rossetti's relation to his imaginative figure. Their ambivalences reflect Rossetti's own description, as we have seen, and they recall as well Ruskin's comments on the poem.

> The character of the speaker himself is too doubtful. He seems, even to me, anomalous. He reasons and feels entirely like a wise and just man, yet is occasionally drunk and brutal: no affection for the girl shows itself – his throwing the money into her hair is disorderly, and he is altogether a disorderly person. The right feeling is unnatural to him, and does not therefore truly touch us. I don't mean that an entirely right-minded person never keeps a mistress: but, if he does, he either loves her – or, not loving her, would blame himself, and be horror-struck for himself no less than for her, in such a moralizing fit.[3]

Remarkably, the passage simply puts in negative terms what Dante Gabriel himself said of the poem. Ruskin brings a truncated 'treatment from without' to both Rossetti's poem and the subject it takes up. He is uncomfortable with a work that presents its volatile materials in the equivocal ways fostered by an art executed at an inner standing-point.

'Jenny''s subsequent reception history, with its wildly varying interpretations, replicates the poem's textual condition at its originary historical moment. Treated 'from without', the poem appears replete with what Ruskin calls 'doubtful' events, feelings, ideas. Ruskin's brief commentary locates a few of the most striking from the indefinite number of others that might as well have been chosen. The 'young and thoughtful man of the world' objectifies this pervasive structure of doubtfulness within the 'framework' of the poem. But the poem itself *incarnates* that structure in the sense that it troubles every effort to judge or understand either the poem or its subject 'from without'. Biographically inflected readings of the poem – they are common – under-score this situation. The more explicit of these readings range between praise for Rossetti's enlightened or brave undertaking in the poem to sharp criticism of his sexist and pornographic illusions. Sometimes the biographical interest comes less explicitly – for example, when DMR Bentley discovers a moral resolution at the end of the poem.[4] Dante Gabriel's theory of the inner standing-point involves a major rewriting of the sympathetic contract poetry and art make with both their subjects and their readers. Romantic sympathy in its most authoritative cultural form displays – as Keats famously put the matter – 'the holiness of the heart's affections'. In this view, because the artist is imagined to have clearest access to that holy place, the artistic act becomes a moral and spiritual standard. Arnold would authorize this set of attitudes when he argued that poetry would replace religion for persons living in the modern world. His sonnet 'Shakespeare' represents this set of ideas about the transcendental status of poetry:

> Other abide our question. Thou art free.
> We ask and ask, thou smilest and art still,
> Outtopping knowledge.

That is the romance – really, the romanticism – of an art conceived as some still point of a turning world. Rossetti's aesthetic move called such a view into radical question. Or perhaps one should say, Rossetti exposed the bad faith on which it had come to rest, for the authority of Arnold's sonnet is pure illu-sion, as Arnold himself showed in other of his poems, especially a devastating work like 'The Buried Life.' In Rossetti's wonderful story 'Hand and Soul', the exposure comes when Chiaro dell Erma, Rossetti's surrogate, poses this question for himself and his art: 'May one be a devil without knowing it?' If the heart and its affections are that problematic, the ground of sympathy will only be gained through what Tennyson called, in one of *In Memoriam*'s wittiest and wickedest moments, 'honest doubt'.

So in reading 'Jenny' we want to see and to say that the poet sympathizes with the young and thoughtful man of the world precisely in that young man's contradictions. When Rossetti takes up his subject at an inner standing-point, he locates his poem at exactly the same point. The move puts the reader in an equivalently equivocal and difficult position, for the poem's sympathetic contract is written in doubtful and ambivalent characters. The contract must be entered on those uncertain terms. In this idea of art, the only understanding one will value is a questionable understanding, the only feelings to be trusted are doubtful and uncertain. To enter the poem is to enter a space for studying problems, of which the study-space itself is perhaps the primary one.

Rossetti's poem thus offers itself as a demonstration of these ideas about poetry and art. Although his comments in 'The Stealthy School of Criticism' emphasize the poem's programmatic character, the poem itself makes the strongest argument for these ideas – as it should, given Rossetti's theory. Rossetti indexes his procedure by representing the young man as a literary and bookish person. In the context of a dramatic monologue set in contemporary Victorian London, this move forces the poem to turn its reflecting mirror on itself. The contemporary reader, as the reactions of both Buchanan and Ruskin show, is left in a similarly equivocal position, for the reader is necessarily, by literary contract, the active agent of the reflexive operations solicited in the poem.

From our much later vantage, Dante Gabriel's approach to the 'motive powers' of artistic method inevitably brings to mind quantum field models and the names Heisenberg and Godel. I point this out not to hype Rossetti's work but to seize an analogy, familiar to us, for seeing the precise character of what is involved in Rossetti's theory, for seeing how 'undecidability' emerges in this kind of aesthetic space. When your judgements are located within the same field you are trying to describe, the very act of making a judgement sets precise limits upon it and calls out its asymmetries.

Does this young and thoughtful man of the world 'know [Jenny's] dreams', as he says he does in the poem? The answer is 'yes' – precisely as his words declare. The problem is that his words are, as we say, ambiguous – *not* because he is represented as deceitful (though he may be), but because we are kept by the poem from a determinate and objective understanding of what they mean. The reader reads from within the poem's 'framework', as Rossetti calls it. How shrewd and effective, for example, is Rossetti's choice of the word 'we' in that marvellous line 'Ah Jenny, yes, we know your dreams'.

Let me point out that Rossetti's inner standing-point does not exert its authority over Victorian readers alone. This procedural rule – perhaps it is even an aesthetic law, as Rossetti says – operates on any reading occasion, as the first-person plural pronoun in that cunning line indicates. Rossetti's critics come to his poem and tell what they see, tell what they think about the young man's representations of Jenny's dreams – as if they were saying, 'Ah, Rossetti, yes, we know *your* dreams.' What they declare – what we later readers say we know – are representations of representations. Although criticism and critics often covet definitive judgements, not least of all moral and value judgements, Rossetti's poetic method undermines that obscure object of desire. A poem like 'Jenny' is a dangerous critical mirror that turns the reader's eye back upon himself.

Approaching Rossetti's work in this context, we can better appreciate why he cast so many of his critical writings in imaginative rather than expository forms. Works like 'Hand and Soul' and 'Old and New Art' develop elaborate theoretical and historically self-conscious commentaries on art, poetry and general aesthetics. The central function of the famous 'double work of art' is itself a critical and hermeneutic one, as are Rossetti's two books of translations from 'early Italian' poetry. That case of the translations is particularly illuminating because the argument is not made in linguistic/semantic terms. The argument is graphical – really, bibliographical. *Dante and his Circle* (1874) is often referred to as the 'second edition' of *The Early Italian Poets* (1861), and while this description is technically correct, it obscures the sharp critical differences between the two books. Rossetti revised his translations very little at the linear level, but he did reorganize the 1861 book so as to produce in 1874 a clarified 'reading' of the material. While Dante is the focal point in both books, the 1874 volume reverses the 1861 order of its two large blocks of material. 1861 takes the reader on a journey through twelfth- and thirteenth-century writings to their culmination in Dante and the poets of the *stil novo* style. Dante comes into this book at what appears the historical apex of everything else. In 1874, by contrast, the 'Circle' of Dante named in the title is conceived in ideal rather than historical terms. Dante comes first in the book because Dante is the idea that gives intelligibility to everything and everyone else.

Casting programmatic ideas in bibliographical forms is a regular feature of Rossetti's work, as his famous and highly influential series of book-cover designs will remind us. He was meticulously attentive to the physical appearance of his literary works. As I've discussed these matters elsewhere, I will focus here on some neglected features of Rossetti's aestheticism, including some of its important theoretical implications. He writes poems to explicate pictures, and vice versa – his own poems, his own pictures, or poems by others (Poe, Tennyson and Allingham, for example) or paintings by various European artists: from unknown German fifteenth-century masters to Ingres and Holst and Burne-Jones. His 'Early Italian' translations are the same kind of work – the transmigration of one body of poetry into another verse body. For Rossetti, that the translation be poetical and imaginative is crucial. It is the index and vehicle of an inner standing-point.

Dante's thirteenth-century autobiographical account of his emergence as a missioned and programmatic poet – his *Vita Nuova* – is literally (*literally*) reborn in Rossetti's nineteenth-century 'New Life' translation. Rossetti's implicit argument – I should perhaps say 'instantiated argument' – is that the essential *meaning* of Dante's work is not semantic or even cognitive, it is vital. A treatment 'from without' will therefore miss the point. To explain the meaning of the *Vita Nuova*, Rossetti has to show that Dante's work possesses a distinct nineteenth-century form of life. So Rossetti must frame an argument for the work's meaning that will demonstrate that meaning, rather in the way one demonstrates mathematical propositions.

The key move is to show rather than to tell. Insofar as 'telling' may be involved, it comes as part of the demonstrative process. Dante's work sets the model for Rossetti's replication by placing imaginative texts – prose as well as poetical – at the centre of his work. The *Vita Nuova*'s prose narrative is a self-conscious reimagination of an unknown spiritual life he had been living, and the poems that organize this prose relation define and emblemize the growth of Dante's spiritual realization. They literally demonstrate the truth of his argument. But this great scheme of imaginative writing does have its own scholarly and technical exegeses. To his doubled imaginative account Dante appends a series of brief prose explications of his poems, the *divisiones*, that are meant to aid readers in a quest to discover through the autobiography a path to a new spiritual life of their own.

These *divisiones* are the only texts in the *Vita Nuova* that stand 'without' the work in any way at all. The *Vita Nuova* is so massively constructed at an 'inner standing-point', in fact, that these *explications de texte* get drawn into the action. But they are clearly placed in a subordinate relation. Their function is to show that the poems' incarnate spiritual meanings can be stated and described in cognitive and rational terms. They signal the fact that different individuals, including the author of the poems himself, will be able to see and recast the formal structure of the works in different ways and at different times. As such, these *divisiones* forecast acts of reimagination like Rossetti's nineteenth-century translations.

What we want most to see, however, is that Rossetti approaches the task of critical analysis and interpretation in performative rather than cognitive terms. Or perhaps I should say that he understands 'cognition' as an event that unfolds most effectively at an inner standing-point.

An interesting interpretive shift comes when the critical re-performance occurs in a different aesthetic medium – that is to say, in Rossetti's elaborate scene of doubled works. The standing-point remains 'inner' because the procedure remains aesthetic rather than intellectual. In these kinds of work, however, the effort is to introduce a dramatic instantiation of how 'objectivity' functions when the dominant space is inwardly organized. The pair of sonnets for *The Girlhood of Mary Virgin* is Rossetti's first effort to explore this situation by using imaginative texts to comment upon a pictorial work. Deploying a pastiche style in the sonnets, Rossetti fashions a set of critical explanations that elucidate the picture from within its own mythological space. The whole nexus of aesthetic materials, pictorial as well as textual, works up a theoretical argument – a representational argument, showing rather than telling – about the optimal form in which theory and cognition should operate.

One of the most striking implications of this argument is that presumptively unenlightened cultural work, like Mariolatry and primitivist aesthetic methods, possess great authority and power – particularly in historical moments like nineteenth-century Europe, dominated as they are by their ideologies of realism and progress. The argument, needless to say, is distinctively a 'preRaphaelite' argument, though also idiosyncratically Rossettian. It is exactly the same argument Rossetti makes in his story 'Hand and Soul', which is, among other things, a trenchant critique of Vasari's *Lives of the Painters*. It is a critique, of course, executed at an inner standing-point. It is also no debunking of Vasari. For Rossetti knows very well that Vasari was himself an active artist and that his *Lives* was cast in its own inner standing-point. How imaginative – not to say how fanciful and even fantastic – that great work actually *is* we now know very well thanks to the work of scholars like Paul Barolsky.[5]

When Rossetti uses texts to elucidate pictorial works his general method is to collapse or mitigate the illusion that texts and linguistic forms are simply vehicles for ideas. Within that illusion is concealed another (equally pernicious): that graphical representations are not ideated forms and, in the final view of the matter, cannot develop theoretical inquiries or intellectual arguments. When this illusion operates in purely textual space it obscures the crucial fact that the cognitive functions of textuality operate equally through bibliographical as through linguistic codes. Typefaces and page or book design instantiate ideas, a process Morris wittily called 'a thing to mind': that is to say, one is called to a reflective awareness of how material forms expose their cognitive features.

The critical and expository power of graphic forms gets most fully exposed, however, when pictures are made to elucidate texts. The nineteenth-century illustrated book, with which Rossetti's work is intimately connected, exhibits a remarkable array of graphical procedures for textual commentary and exegesis. Most of Rossetti's early drawings are literary, and he quickly began to turn these images into stunning examples of theoretical and conceptual art. Perhaps the first unmistakable masterpiece comes in 1846 – Rossetti had just turned eighteen – with his illustration of Poe, *The Raven: Angel Footfalls*. The textual focus of the image is stanza 14 of the poem, which runs thus:

Then methought the air grew denser, perfumed from an unseen censer
Swung by Seraphim whose footfalls tinkled on the tufted floor.
'Wretch,' I cried, 'thy God hath lent thee – by these angels he hath sent
    thee
Respite – respite and nepenthe, from thy memories of Lenore!
Quaff, oh quaff this kind nepenthe and forget this lost Lenore!'
Quoth the Raven, 'Nevermore.'

Rossetti drew this picture several times during 1846 and 1847. The first version (June 1846) shows 'A man reading... placed on the mantelpiece'.[6] When
Rossetti reconceived the picture in 1847 he made a striking reversal of one of
its key elements: the troop of angelic spirits in the second conception emerges
from behind the seated man and move past him toward the left of the picture
plane. In the first conception they had followed the same diagonal route but
in the opposite direction.

All kinds of interpretations could be developed for each of these two visual
conceptions. In the second picture, for example, the spirits appear a kind of
phantasmal emergence from a space that seems pictorially defined as a locus
of art and literature, as well as a locus of haunted memory. In the first they
appear out of the picture plane that separates the drawing from the observ-
able world, and they seem headed back to the space of art and memory: the
space populated by the bookcase, the literary sculptures and the hovering
figure of the dead Lenore – herself, of course, a purely mythical *figura* who, in
the second drawing, will be transfigured into a painting on the rear wall.
Those two textual representations frame the general terms in which a host of
more particular exegeses might easily be developed.

The chief point is to see, however, that the drawings are fully aware of their
power to think and rethink the subject addressed by the picture – that is to
say, are fully aware that Poe's poem can be explored intellectually through a
graphical treatment. Indeed, the very choice of subject indicates an intention
on Rossetti's part to take up in a general way the theoretical pretensions and
possibilities of artistic practice. Poe had famously used his own poem as the
focus of his remarkable theoretical essay 'The Philosophy of Composition' –
used it in fact so that, next to the prose essay, the poem seems the far more
theoretical of the two works. Rossetti's picture comes to make an argument on
behalf of the theoretical authority of pictorial expression *vis-à-vis* a paradigmatic instance of theoretical expression executed in textual form.

As in this early drawing, Rossetti laboured over his texts and his pictures all
his life. In many cases he would pick up a certain subject – say *Proserpine* or
Beata Beatrix or *The Damsel of the San Grael* – and develop multiple recastings for
his ideas, rethinking the image and its treatment in a sequence of apparently

obsessive variations that might extend over many years. That procedure was replicated at the micro level of his working process: his manuscripts and proofs display masses of revisions, additions and corrections to the smallest textual elements. The same kind of meticulous process is apparent in all of the pictorial work, as we may remember from the notorious example of his illustration of 1855, *The Maids of Elfin-Mere*, which he executed for Allingham's haunting ballad published in his collection *The Music Master*. Rossetti spent months reworking this tiny drawing (9 x 8.5 inches), making himself a nightmare for the Dalziel brothers who were charged with translating it into wood block. The smallest detail might precipitate a crisis at either the drawing or the printing stage. The completed illustration was recognized from the first as a masterpiece and is still so regarded, although Rossetti himself saw it as a failure and tore the image out of his copy of Allingham's book.

That story is often told either to illustrate Rossetti's difficult and imperious character or to demonstrate his technical incompetence and his lack of understanding of wood-block engraving. That Rossetti was demanding, not least of all upon himself, is past doubt, but the modernist legends of his technical problems always have to be scrutinized carefully. In this case they *are* pure legend, for we know that Rossetti understood wood-block engraving very well indeed. But I do not retell this story to clarify these kinds of misconceptions – others like Rodney Engen have done that.[7] The event is relevant to my argument about the theory and method of Rossettian art at an inner standing-point. Every smallest detail in a Rossetti picture is a struggle for ideational clarity, and the struggle is often most clearly displayed in Rossetti's works on paper. Think again about the great Tennyson illustrations – not only their masses of tiny, 'irrelevant' details, but their strange conceptual stances, often introducing figures and actions that have no explicit source in the text they depend from. Like those early sonnets for *The Girlhood of Mary Virgin*, what these images represent are acts of interpretation. They hold up a mirror not to Tennyson's poems but to Rossetti reading those poems. They are dramatic images of his mind thinking about the poems – just as his translations are dramatic images of his mind thinking about early Italian poetry and culture, in particular Dante.

❋

This thinking of course takes place in high Victorian England. Its artistic execution therefore necessarily reflects the world Rossetti is himself reflecting in and upon. With poems like 'Jenny' or pictures like *The Raven: Angel Footfalls* and the other illustrations to contemporary writing, we easily discern that Rossetti's world is his subject of attention. When the work focuses on

medieval, Arthurian and religious materials, however, we have to recall that
these subjects at the time were centres of ideological debate and controversy.
In such works Rossetti is negotiating his period's great cultural commodities.
His aesthetic and critical point of view is the inner standing-point.

Such is the general context for revisiting the pivotal moment in Rossetti's
career: 1859–60, when he made his definitive move to oil portraiture. With
Bocca Baciata Rossetti shifts the general context of his work from fourteenth-
and fifteenth-century Florence to sixteenth-century Venice. A text from
Boccaccio replaces the texts of Dante that had been Rossetti's preoccupation.
Most dramatic of all are a related pair of stylistic changes. First of all,
Rossetti's energetic dry brush watercolour yields to his pursuit of a highly
finished oil surface. Second, he turns from his delicate 1850s pen drawings of
Elizabeth Siddal to the oil portrait of Fanny Cornforth that inaugurated a
long series of erotic and often disturbing representations of women.

In the title of this new painting Rossetti gave a clear, if characteristically
oblique, signal of his purposes and ideas. The title quotes from the final sen-
tence of Boccaccio's tale of Alatiel and her numerous lovers. According to the
ironic moral Boccaccio appends to his tale, 'the kissed mouth loses none of its
freshness, but renews itself, like the moon.' That is to say, Alatiel's promiscuity
not only has brought no negative moral judgement against her, it has invigor-
ated her beauty and her character.

Like many of his contemporaries, Rossetti became preoccupied with the
figura of the Magdalene and of the 'fallen woman' in general. Choosing
Boccaccio's story to take up a subject he explored repeatedly in the 1850s,
Rossetti makes a painting that has much in common with 'Jenny', which he
was revising into its finished form at the same time. For Alatiel's erotic adven-
tures are triggered and then sustained by what Rossetti in his poem calls 'the
hatefulness of man'

> Who spares not to end what he began.
> Whose acts are ill and his speech ill,
> Who having used you at his will,
> Thrusts you aside as when I dine
> I serve the dishes and the wine.

Like Jenny, Alatiel's story is an index of a pattern of erotically deformed social
behaviours. Rossetti unfolds a contemporary version of this pattern and, as
these lines once again show, he implicates his poetic surrogate in his Victorian
story.

In Boccaccio, Alatiel's triumph over her various perils becomes a trope for
Boccaccio's tale-telling skills. Cleverness, wit and a brilliant comic dexterity
are the story's notable features. Boccaccio has little interest in investigating

social issues, erotic Puritanism, and the artist's relation to these kinds of problems. But those are exactly the matters that preoccupy Rossetti.

As with 'Jenny', however, Rossetti addresses the subject of *Bocca Baciata* at a diagonal, so to speak. Some fine decoding is needed to see that Rossetti's own life and work are the central subjects of both poem and picture. But we read these works weakly if we take them merely at their encrypted levels. Rossetti's inner standing-point seeks no refuge in his obliquity; he thrusts his procedure forward, as the title of the painting makes abundantly clear. Encryption and obliquity measure a form of aesthetic failure being represented in these works, and Rossetti uses Victorian sexual taboos as an objective correlative for the aesthetic issues with which he is concerned.

Like Baudelaire, Rossetti's social critique is indirect. Both examine the order of representations rather than the social and political orders mirrored in the representations. In this focus on the culture industries both Baudelaire and Rossetti define themselves squarely within the tradition of romantic social critique. Both then make a significant departure from that tradition: they use their own work to exemplify their arguments. What is hypocritical in Baudelaire and oblique in Rossetti signals a culpable and duplicitous aestheticism that their own work is forced to illustrate. The focus is on the illusion that artistic work transcends – either by a path of beauty or a path of truth – both coarse reality and ideological false consciousness. According to the argument Baudelaire and Rossetti are both making, this illusion will survive any representational attack that exempts itself from the argument, either explicitly or implicitly.

Rossetti's move to Venetian models is thus a coded way of representing himself, his work and his contemporary world. Sometimes the code will be encrypted in biographical terms: so Fazio's Mistress is Rossetti's friend and mistress, Fanny Cornforth, and Astarte Syriaca is, like Proserpine, Jane Morris. The codes are so masterfully complex that even their keys shift and mutate: is the Jane Morris of *Astarte Syriaca* the same as the Jane Morris of *Mnemosyne* or *La Donna della Finestra*? How do we decode *Lady Lilith*?

Other codes intervene, however, and complicate the task of deciphering the pictures. The title of *Bocca Baciata* defines one of Rossetti's characteristic moves: to mask a portrait with a literary or mythical allusion, or perhaps with some kind of poetical wordplay – as in *Veronica Veronese* – or with both, as in *Monna Vanna*. Playing throughout are the shifting and finally unreliable patterns of encryption that interpellate the viewer to equivalent acts of decoding. These are paintings conscious of the bad faith that they depend upon and reflect – the 'hypocrite spectateur.' The pictures *have* no illusions because they are through and through conscious of their own illusionism: images that beget fresh images in a continuum of pure simulacra.

What ties this world of mirrors to a knowable world is its agented contemporality. These pictures make us see that meanings are not inherent secrets, they are the practical outcomes of certain acts executed by particular persons: the artist Rossetti, first of all, and then the artist's implicated audiences. Encryption is thus made a second-order pictorial sign of the meaning-making action of artist and audience, both of whom occupy an inner standing-point in the aesthetic space.

Once that general artistic procedure is recognized, the programmatic character of the pictures unfolds itself. Ruskin recoiled from Rossetti's new Venetian pictures because they involved a very different view of Venetian art and its cultural significance for the Victorian world from the one argued by Ruskin in the final volume of *Modern Painters*. Like Rossetti, Ruskin was intent on contradicting the common and deprecating view of Venetian art. 'Put the idea from you at once', Ruskin intones, 'that Titian must have been a sensualist, and Veronese an unbeliever'.[8] The sensuality of Venetian art was an emblem of a 'wholly realist, universal, and manly' idea: 'that sensual passion in man was, not only a fact, but a divine fact' and that man, 'the perfect animal,' emblemized the perfection of his spiritual nature and his divine origin.[9] Ruskin sealed his argument with a new reading of Titian's painting of the Magdalene in the Pitti Palace – a picture he had reviled as 'disgusting' in the second volume of *Modern Painters*. 'Truly she is' disgusting, Ruskin writes in his recantation: 'A stout, red-faced woman, dull, and coarse of feature, with much of the animal in even her expression of repentance'.[10] But now he sees 'Titian's meaning' in this repellent representation: 'that it was possible for plain women to love no less vividly than beautiful ones; and for stout persons to repent'.[11]

Rossetti's argument about Venetian art has none of Ruskin's insipid and slightly ludicrous moralism. Like Ruskin, Rossetti finds in Venetian art images of himself and of his ideas about the world. These ideas involve, however, worldly rather than divine allegories. Most significant here is Rossetti's concentration on a signal feature of Venetian art that Ruskin finesses: the importance of rich draperies, clothing, floral decoration, jewellery and the profuse ornamental accoutrements of social wealth. Ruskin does not say so explicitly, but for him these are read as emblems of the 'manly realism' he wants to promote. For Rossetti, however, they are signs of contradiction. When he calls these Venetian forms back into his nineteenth-century imitations, his women come dressed to kill.

Everyone who looks at Rossetti's Venetian-inspired portraits reports their sinister and troubling character. The faces range from the coarse and vulgar to the beautiful and even majestic. In all cases, however, their ornamental paraphernalia seems laid upon them from without, as it does in Klimt. They seem to have been dressed up for the occasion: specifically, for the occasion of beauty, for their appearance in an artistic display. And in this respect we suddenly perceive the intimate relation – the complicity, in fact – between the discourse of high art and commodity fetishism.

No picture unfolds that revelation more splendidly and completely than *Monna Vanna*, that complex portrait whose ambiguous title sums up its fascinating and terrible set of contradictions. This is a Madonna, 'my' donna. Her name is 'Vanna', the nickname of Cavalcanti's favourite mistress, whom he often betrayed. Her full name was Giovanna, the lady of spring, but in its shortened form, and in the nineteenth-century, her name is also Vanity. But this is *my* lady Vanity. The lady is not a portrait of an actual person, she is the portrait of a fetish – more particularly, a commodity fetish. This figure is in fact Jenny herself now returned to us stripped of the sentimental illusions with which that young and thoughtful man of the world had first draped her. It is, paradoxically, a nude portrait, the Victorian bride stripped bare to her naked ornamental form.

Ah yes, Rossetti, we know your dreams. That is to say, this recurrent nightmare you display for us. It is the nightmare of an artistic practice that has discovered its self-alienation and then decided to represent the truth of that condition. As he pursues this paradoxical and self-destructive ideal, the surfaces of the pictures grow increasingly dead and finished. The contrast with the 1850s works on paper could not be, in this respect, more striking. And yet the continuity with those works also 'lies apparent', as Rossetti wrote of a lover in *The House of Life*. The subjects of the watercolours are not manly realist subjects, they are ideological subjects: the real social powers and presences that hide and disguise themselves in aesthetic and cultural forms (and most especially the forms propagated through art and religion). In the later oil portrait work Rossetti continues to paint the 'real presence' of these commodified forms. The difference is, however, that Rossetti does not represent this later work as a struggle of discovery, as he did in the watercolours. In the late oil portraits the illusion is a finished rather than a dynamic surface. A dead surface whose arresting power lies exactly there. *Consumeratum est*.

Notes

1 All Rossetti texts here are drawn from my online *The Complete Writings and Pictures of Dante Gabriel Rossetti: A Hypermedia Research Archive* (http://jefferson.village.virginia.edu/rossetti). The texts quoted are, unless otherwise indicated, the 'Reading Texts' supplied in the edition.

2 The best treatment of this matter is in Robert N Keane's 'Rossetti's Jenny: Moral Ambiguity and the 'Inner Standing Point'', *Papers on Language and Literature*, 9 (1973), 271–80.

3 See *Ruskin. Rossetti. Pre-Raphaelitism Papers 1854 to 1862*. Arranged and edited by William Michael Rossetti (George Allen: London, 1899), p. 234.

4 Robin Sheets gathers all but one of the key commentaries on the poem in her notes to her essay 'Pornography and Art: The Case of Jenny,' *Critical Inquiry*, 14 (1988), 315–34. Her argument with the traditions of criticism on the poem is seriously compromised by neglecting to take up Keane's important essay (see above, note 2).

5 See for example *Michelangelo's Nose: a Myth and its Maker* (Penn State UP: University Park, 1990) and *Why Mona Lisa Smiles and other tales by Vasari* (Penn State UP: University Park, 1991).

6 Virginia Surtees, *Dante Gabriel Rossetti. The Paintings and Drawings. A Catalogue Raisonné*. (Oxford UP: Oxford and London, 1971) I, p. 4.

7 See Rodney K Engen, *Pre-Raphaelite prints : the graphic art of Millais, Holman Hunt, Rossetti and their followers* (London : Lund Humphries, 1995).

8 *Modern Painters*, p. 244.

9 *Modern Painters*, p 252.

10 *Modern Painters*, vol. 2, pp. 251–2.

11 *Modern Painters*, vol. 2, pp. 252.

12

MAUNDERING MEDIEVALISM: DANTE GABRIEL ROSSETTI AND WILLIAM MORRIS'S POETRY

Clive Wilmer

William Morris's first book of poetry, *The Defence of Guenevere and Other Poems*, was published in 1858. It was dedicated

TO MY FRIEND
DANTE GABRIEL ROSSETTI
PAINTER[1]

Some biographical facts should be noted here. First, Dante Gabriel is not described as 'painter *and poet*', so there is a suggestion of the two men working in different, if complementary, fields. This is probably because in 1858 Dante Gabriel's verse was still unknown to the public. His translations, *The Early Italian Poets*, were not to appear till 1861, and his own poems not until 1870. Though Morris already knew and admired much of this work, he was, in publishing his own book of poetry, establishing his primacy in that art. It was a primacy that Rossetti was from the outset engagingly keen to acknowledge. Looking back in a letter of 1869, he writes of the 'estimate of [Morris] which I have long entertained, as being – all things considered – the greatest literary identity of our time'.[2] So Rossetti was no doubt happy to be described – in 1858 – as simply a painter.

Secondly, Morris describes him as 'my friend'. This was indeed the case, but we should remember that Morris was only 24 at the time and Rossetti six years his senior – a significant difference at that stage in their lives. In 1856 when they first met, moreover, Rossetti was already known as an artist, while Morris had only just graduated from Oxford. Morris at that time was working at architecture – he was articled to the practice of GE Street, one of the

Figure 6. 'La Belle Iseult', by William Morris

leading lights of the Gothic Revival – and Rossetti persuaded Morris to try his hand at painting. Under the painter's tutelage, Morris completed his rather stiff but by no means incompetent painting of *La Belle Iseult*, a picture with conventions derived from Rossetti which is nonetheless, with its nervous tension and touch of realism, very much Morris's own.[3]

That was in 1857. A little earlier in the same year, Rossetti had led a boisterous band of painters in an attempt to fresco what is now the library of the Oxford Union. The attempt ended in disaster when in less than six months the paintings began to peel off the walls. Morris's contribution to the venture –

How Sir Palomydes Loved La Belle Iseult with Exceeding Great Love out of Measure and how she Loved him not again but rather Sir Tristram – was especially ham-fisted and provoked Rossetti's laughter. Nevertheless, the work gave Morris the opportunity to make an attempt at decorating the ceiling, which, as Paul Thompson has said, helped him discover his talent for pattern-making.[4]

Furthermore, the subject of the painting, a sexual triangle, haunted Morris throughout his life. It was not just the stories of Iseult and Guenevere that obsessed him; he was also to reflect on the Trojan cycle and, above all, on that of Sigurd and Brynhild.[5] One feels it can be no accident that the obsession first became apparent just as Jane Burden entered the two men's lives. Jane was one of the 'stunners' whom Rossetti had invited to model for the painters at the Union. It seems extraordinary that almost at once Morris asked her to model for – of all subjects – *La Belle Iseult*, and that soon afterwards he asked her to marry him. It is even more extraordinary that between his proposal and their 1859 wedding, he published his apology for Arthur's adulterous queen, the title poem of *The Defence of Guenevere*. When exactly Rossetti began his love affair with Jane we shall probably never know, but it does seem that, from the start, Morris was unconsciously playing the betrayed husband. Rossetti was similarly preoccupied with adultery, betrayal and sexual guilt. In the same period he wrote both 'The Bride's Prelude' and certain triangular sonnets from *The House of Life*. Not long before meeting Morris, he had embarked on a series of watercolours that deal with the Lancelot/Guenevere subject, as well as the watercolour triptych, *Paolo and Francesca da Rimini* (1855).[6] (In Dante's *Inferno*, it will be remembered, this adulterous pair are led to their first kiss while reading the Old French romance of *Lancelot du Lac*.[7])

In the year of the Oxford Union adventure, Morris also became acquainted with John Ruskin, whose work he had admired since 1853. That year had seen the publication of volumes 2 and 3 of Ruskin's great work *The Stones of Venice*, and Morris and Edward Burne-Jones, then undergraduates, had read the whole book together. They had been particularly struck by the central chapter of volume 2, 'The Nature of Gothic', which had led them to the northern French cathedrals and inspired Morris with the dream of becoming an architect. The same chapter can be regarded as the main inspiration behind the firm of Morris, Marshall, Faulkner and Company, as the source of Morris's opposition to the destruction of ancient buildings through what was called 'restoration', and as the intellectual foundation to his habit of relating aesthetic questions to social ones. But Ruskin and Morris, though they spoke of one another with respect and affection, never became close friends. We may think of Dante Gabriel Rossetti and Ruskin as Morris's twin masters, but for many years the former as the intimate companion exerted the greater influence and urged Morris towards Aestheticism. It is nevertheless possible to say that Morris's career is divided between them. Morris made a considerable effort to tolerate Dante Gabriel's affair with his wife, but at some time in the early 1870s his affection for the painter seems to have ceased. It was precisely then that politics started moving to the centre of Morris's life. In turning to politics, in insisting on the connections between art and society, in organizing such pressure groups as the Society for the Protection of Ancient Buildings (known to Morris and his friends as 'Anti-Scrape', and still active today) and the Eastern Question Association, Morris was in effect returning to Ruskin. 'Rossetti', Morris noted after his old friend's death,

> took no interest in politics... The truth is he cared for nothing but individual and personal matters; chiefly of course in relation to art and literature, but he would take abundant trouble to help any one person who was in distress of mind or body; but the evils of any mass of people he couldn't bring his mind to bear upon. I suppose in short it needs a person of hopeful mind to take disinterested notice of politics, and Rossetti was certainly not hopeful.[8]

What Morris does not say here is that Rossetti's aversion to politics was probably due to over-exposure at an early age: his father, as an exiled revolutionary, attracted to their home an unending horde of hopeful or disappointed patriots. By all accounts, the two friends did indeed differ in the way Morris describes but, whatever the reason, while Rossetti's star was in the ascendant in Morris's life, Morris appeared content to regard the condition of England as 'a muddle' – or so he put it in a letter of 1856:

> I see that things are in a muddle, and I have no power or vocation to set them right in ever so little a degree. My work is the embodiment of dreams in one form or another.[9]

But Morris, being himself 'a person of hopeful mind' and a practical one at that, was always looking for ways of turning dream into practice. The endeavour began with what he referred to as 'the Firm', founded in 1861 with Rossetti, Burne-Jones, Ford Madox Brown and others as shareholders and contributors of designs. It went on to be a matter of the pressure groups I have cited, political and conservationist, and eventually the nascent Socialist movement. Rossetti was not practical and might almost be said to have cultivated the opposite condition. For him the whole point of dream was inwardness, the capacity of paintings or poems to reveal emotions and unconscious thoughts. Morris began by trying to emulate this quest for inwardness, but there was always something else in his work that was foreign to Rossetti: a natural vigour that informs his designs as well as the rhythms of his poetry. He has nothing of Dante Gabriel's languor. When he dreams up an incident in Froissart's France, his tone is far from dreamy. On the contrary, it is as if, having dreamed it, he knows how to make it real. Like Rossetti's, his poetry is full of intense and passionate kissing, which, quite as much as Grosvenor Gallery green, is a badge of the later phases of Pre-Raphaelitism. Yet I can think of no lines of Rossetti's that capture the raw sexual violence one finds in, for instance, this passage from 'Concerning Geffray Teste Noire':

> I saw you kissing once, like a curved sword
>   That bites with all its edge, did your lips lie,
> Curl'd gently, slowly, long time could afford
>   For caught-up breathings: like a dying sigh
>
> They gather'd up their lines and went away,
>   And still kept twitching with a sort of smile,
> As likely to be weeping presently;
>   Your hands too, how I watch'd them all the while![10]

Dante Gabriel is undoubtedly intense and deeply concerned with the sexual, but in such poems as 'Nuptial Sleep' or pictures like the *Paolo and Francesca* triptych, it is the emotional absorption he goes for rather than Morris's blunt physicality.

I want to suggest that this element of realism in Morris connects with his practical concerns and ultimately with his politics, for revolutionary politics is by its very nature a way of turning dream into reality. But as long as Morris accepted Rossetti as his mentor, politics stayed outside the frame. 'Dreamer of dreams, born out of my due time', he says in *The Earthly Paradise* (1868), 'Why should I strive to set the crooked straight?'[11] – which is much the same as 'I have no power or vocation to set them right'. Moreover, it was during the 1850s, the decade in which the two men became friends, that Rossetti's work was at its most inward and closest to Morris's poetry in intent. Some of Rossetti's finest lyrics belong to this phase of his life: 'The Woodspurge', 'Sudden Light', 'The Honeysuckle', 'During Music', 'Even So' and 'The Mirror'. So also do the very private sequence of drawings of Elizabeth Siddal and – most importantly – the 'medievalist' watercolours inspired by illuminated manuscripts. Between 1852 and 1859, Rossetti executed most of his illustrations to Dante's *Vita Nuova* and Malory's *Le Morte Darthur*, as well as other medievalist watercolours, like the celebrated *Wedding of St George and Princess Sabra* (1857) and such early instances of aesthetic abstraction as *The Blue Closet* (1856–7), which Morris owned and about which he wrote an equally abstract

Figure 7. 'Arthur's Tomb', by Dante Gabriel Rossetti

poem: 'stunning' in Rossetti's judgement.[12] Alicia Craig Faxon has summed up the elements in these pictures which seem indebted to illumination:

> Medieval illuminated manuscripts inspired certain stylistic conventions in Rossetti's works of the 1850s, such as the crowding of forms into a shallow space, the use of diapered backgrounds and elaborate patterns, the avoidance of classical perspective, the emphasis on jewellike colors, and the wealth of symbolic detail. Many of his watercolors of this time are small, like their medieval prototypes, with angular, unidealized figures.[13]

It is possible to argue that verbal equivalents for some of these characteristics are to be found in *The Defence of Guenevere*. The absence of narrative contextualization, partly indebted to Browning, might be compared to Rossetti's 'avoidance of classical perspective'. Pictorially speaking, it is not unrelated to the flattening of the picture-plane so often noted in Modernist painting. One might also compare the proto-Modernist aspects of Red House, the home designed for the Morrises in 1859 by Philip Webb, where the details, as Nikolaus Pevsner noticed, are 'deliberately rough and rustic' and often 'left fearlessly sheer, telling their tale without any borrowed phrases'.[14] Again, awkwardnesses of speech and metre in Morris's poems together with their forceful characterization may remind us of Rossetti's 'angular, unidealized figures'. Rossetti's colours and symbolic detail have obvious equivalents in Morris, and the latter's frequent compression of both plot and syntax can be quite as claustrophobic as Rossetti's pictorial space. For a time, Morris was clearly obsessed with his friend's pictures; *The Blue Closet* was neither the only one he owned nor the only one he wrote about. For instance, the very curious, even perverse, *Arthur's Tomb; or the Last Meeting of Launcelot and Guenevere* (1855)[15] – which incidentally was bought by Ruskin – must surely be the source of Morris's poem 'King Arthur's Tomb'.

Dante Gabriel's picture may be taken to typify his medievalizing work of this period. It follows Malory in showing the Queen, dressed as a nun, rejecting her lover's plea for a farewell kiss. Rossetti invents the idea of this last encounter taking place at the dead King's tomb, so that as Launcelot leans towards her, they almost embrace across her husband's praying effigy. The pictorial space, like that of the imagined Gothic reliefs on the sarcophagus, is extremely cramped, and this effect is exaggerated by the loaded branches of the fruit trees that seem to force the lovers down on to the tomb. The combination of 'shallow space' and 'jewellike colors' (in Faxon's words) is responsible for a more than usually claustrophobic feeling, which in its turn intensifies the emotion. This was a device Rossetti always favoured. One thinks of the awkward pose of the waking Virgin in *Ecce, Ancilla Domini* (1850), the compressed emotion enhanced by gracelessness of posture.[16] Rossetti's work is dreamlike and heavily dependent on artistic precedent – in this case, illuminated manuscript and medieval tomb sculpture – yet by these means he arrives at a kind of emotional authenticity we do not really meet again until the Post-Impressionists. Indeed, in some respects, it is closer to Expressionism.

Such emotional intensity is not absent from Rossetti's poetry. The deliberate overloading and opacity of *The House of Life* sonnets achieves something comparable, but the poems are too lush, by and large, to admit such awkwardness. Morris's poetry comes much closer, it seems to me, and it is not unreasonable to connect it to Rossetti's influence. Such poems as 'King Arthur's Tomb' are full of Rossettian vignettes. Here, for instance, is Guenevere speaking:

> Pray you remember how when the wind ran
>   One cool spring evening through fair aspen-tree,
>
> And elm and oak about the palace there,
>   The king came back from battle, and I stood
> To meet him, with my ladies, on the stair,
>   My face made beautiful with my young blood.[17]

This might be a description of a subject that recurs again and again in Rossetti, Burne-Jones and their imitators: the lady awaiting her knight's return from battle or, more commonly, bidding farewell to him as he departs

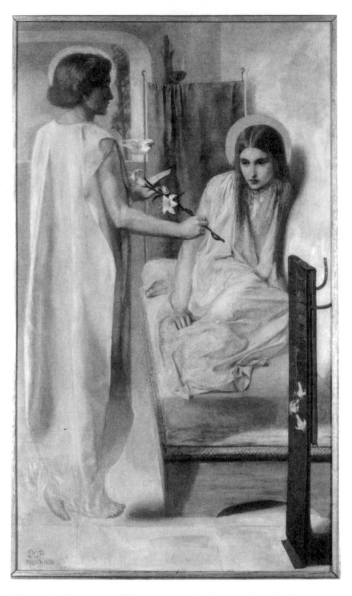

Figure 8. 'Ecce, Ancilla Domini', by Dante Gabriel Rossetti

for it. So common are these and related subjects that they almost deserve to
be classified together as a sub-genre of Victorian narrative painting. Rossetti's
watercolour *Before the Battle* (1858)[18] is a key example, as is Burne-Jones's beautiful pen-drawing of the same year, *Going to Battle*,[19] which, as Faxon says, 'has
a general subject related to Rossetti's "Froissartian" representations and a
style related to Rossetti's angular figures and detailed, cramped composi-

tions'.[20] It is perhaps worth noting that Pre-Raphaelite medievalism tended to focus on domestic, emotional and female subjects rather than on the more obvious knightly themes; the contrast resembles that between Alexandrian epyllion and the epic tradition it frequently refers to. This is certainly true of 'King Arthur's Tomb', which includes other motifs that recur in Rossetti's pictures: intense kisses again, loosened hair, fingers laid on lips. There is also an emphasis, characteristic of both men, on the decorative art and costume of the Middle Ages, something which obviously affected their work for the 'Firm' as well. Moreover, like Rossetti, Morris is constantly reminding us of medieval art and poetry, while writing in a manner that is inescapably modern. Browning again is the major influence. As in Browning, one hears distinctive tones of voice, a certain abruptness, a broken, even fragmentary quality, which makes at times for a gently tantalizing obscurity. The poem is written in rhymed quatrains, but the narrative runs across the stanzas, counterpointing them in a manner that never permits the reader to pause or rest, and Morris often deviates from the metrical norm in ways that are far from standard – the lines seem wilfully difficult to scan:

> Moreover she held scarlet lilies, such
>   As Maiden Margaret bears upon the light
>
> Of the great church walls, natheless did I walk
>   Through the fresh wet woods, and the wheat that morn,
> Touching her hair and hand and mouth, and talk
>   Of love we held, nigh hid among the corn.[21]

The way one stumbles through such passages calls to mind again the confined spaces and gauche poses that are found in Rossetti's pictures. And if that seems a somewhat forced comparison, think about a more accomplished passage which has also been more discussed, the opening of 'The Defence of Guenevere':

> But, knowing now that they would have her speak,
> She threw her wet hair backward from her brow,
> Her hand close to her mouth touching her cheek,
>
> As though she had had there a shameful blow,
> And feeling it shameful to feel ought but shame
> All through her heart, yet felt her cheek burned so,
>
> She must a little touch it...[22]

There is no Rossetti picture of Queen Guenevere on trial for adultery, but if there were, it would surely look like this. One can imagine the pose, the self-consciousness, the sense of isolation, that very private hand touching her cheek. Like 'King Arthur's Tomb', the poem is full of medieval things. I think especially of the angel the Queen imagines at a deathbed, asking the dying person to choose between two cloths, one of them standing for hell, the other for heaven. Yet the context in which such medievalisms occur could not have been more modern or less locked in the conventions of earlier art. Notice the beginning: 'But [comma]'. This is a Victorian poem but, like *The Cantos* of Ezra Pound, it starts with a coordinating conjunction. We know this to have been the result of a printer's error, but it takes a special sort of imagination to accept an error when it seems appropriate, and this harsh abruptness *is* appropriate to everything that follows. Paul Thompson has particularly commented on the expressively awkward movement of the poem. It is, he says, as if the language stammered – as it notably does in the fourth line of the passage quoted: 'As though she had had there a shameful blow'.[23] This strikes me as the rhythmic equivalent of the Virgin's angular shoulder pressed into the wall in *Ecce, Ancilla Domini*. The effect in the painting is to increase one's feeling of presence: no predetermined posture or arrangement is allowed to come between the viewer and the figure on the canvas. In a similar way, in the poem, the sudden and fragmentary opening abolishes the formalities of conventional exposition, so that the woman – very much a woman, hardly a queen – seems to be communicating directly with us. And communicating not so much with words – or not as yet – as with the posture of her body, especially fitting here, given the charge. There is something indefinably erotic about the description, as there is about many of the women described elsewhere in this young man's book: the wetness of her hair, the hand near the mouth, the burning cheek. And what is the nature of the shame that makes it burn? Is it the shame one feels for doing a wrong that one must now confess to? Or the shame of being so exposed, so unceremoniously thrust before knights and lords, to say nothing of readers? Moreover, to whom is a shameful blow shameful? To the person who receives it or the person who gives it? This question brings up what was, for its time, the shockingly unconventional outlook of the poem, for Morris's Guenevere, unlike Tennyson's, defends herself not against the charge of adultery, for she admits to that, but against the validity of such a charge. It is as if the twenty-three or twenty-four year-old Morris, soon to be married himself to a woman he sometimes identified with Guenevere, were already protesting against 'Our modern bourgeois property-marriage, maintained as it is by its necessary complement, universal venal prostitution'.[24]

What I am arguing is that 'The Defence of Guenevere' is in both method and content a modern poem. This is something that happens again and again in both Rossetti and Morris. An example of medieval art is admired, studied, imitated and, in the process of imitation, turned into something different – as often as not something challenging to contemporary orthodoxies. This is partly because the conventions of medieval art fall outside the norms of post-Renaissance culture and therefore suggest alternative ways of constructing modern works. The pattern is to be noticed in all aspects of the two men's activity – as much in tapestry and fine printing as in poems and paintings. In the case of Morris's poetry, though, a further complexity comes into play, for Morris's verbal world is sometimes filtered through the visual world of his friend. In the process another difference takes effect. To Rossetti's medievalist dreams Morris adds the realism I have referred to, a quality we may well miss in his friend the painter. Moreover, as Morris grew and acquired the confidence of a practical man endowed with many skills, he became impatient with Rossetti. This impatience was then exacerbated by resentment at what he could only have thought his friend's betrayal. In the late 1860s and the 1870s Morris found several ways of freeing himself from his failed marriage and a friendship that oppressed where it had once inspired and encouraged. The sequence begins in 1868 with his discovery of Icelandic literature, which (as his first biographer puts it)

> coincides with what might be called the final extinction of Rossetti's influence over him as an artist, and the gradual loosening which followed of the closer intimacy between them, though for several years more they still saw much of each other, and for three years, from 1871 to 1874, had a country house in common.[25]

The country house, of course, was Kelmscott Manor, Morris's serendipitously discovered earthly paradise. He loved Kelmscott, it might almost be said, passing the love of woman – with what in his *News from Nowhere* he describes as an 'intense and overweening love of the very skin and surface of the earth on which man dwells, such as a lover has in the fair flesh of the woman he loves'.[26] Morris's journeys to Iceland in 1871 and 1873, combined with the freedoms and delights that Kelmscott made possible, provided Rossetti and the Morrises with a temporary *modus vivendi*. Then, in 1874, Rossetti's attempted suicide and subsequent breakdown led to a final breach with both the Morrises. Soon afterwards, in 1875, Morris reorganized the 'Firm' as Morris and Company with himself as sole proprietor. This involved the deliberate exclusion of most of the original shareholders, notably Rossetti and his close friend Ford Madox Brown. In 1876 the Bulgarian massacre unexpectedly launched Morris into politics when, in disgust at Tory *realpolitik*, he founded the Eastern Question Association. A whole series of political, social and environmentalist commitments were to follow. Anti-Scrape, founded to resist the destruction of medieval buildings through what was known as 'restoration', was the most deeply Ruskinian of Morris's activities, inspired in particular by Ruskin's book *The Seven Lamps of Architecture* (1849). It is noteworthy that once he had succeeded in excluding Rossetti from his life, Morris returned to the kinds of issue that Ruskin's works had urged upon him as far back as his undergraduate days. Ruskin's insistence in *The Stones of Venice* on building as a *social* art had been instrumental in attracting Morris to architecture. Rossetti had drawn him away from it, yet the hidden current of his life had led him back to something closely related – interior design – and for the twenty or so years that remained to him he devoted himself to being something more than an artist. He lectured on the social value of art, he lobbied in favour of different kinds of conservation, he became one of the leaders of English Socialism.

When Morris began to read Icelandic literature, he discovered a new kind of medievalism. He found in the sagas and in the Icelandic way of life a virtue he felt he gravely needed amid the emotional pain of his own life. He referred to it as 'the religion of the Northmen' and characterized it as 'the worship of Courage'.[27] In it he had found, he said, 'a good corrective to the maundering side of medievalism'.[28] Maundering medievalism was, I would guess, what he rightly or wrongly saw as Rossetti's province: the realm of dreamers with no hope or desire to make their dreams reality. This may have been unfair to Rossetti. Nevertheless, it was something that even in their early friendship made their worlds distinct.

Notes

1 *The Collected Works of William Morris*, ed. May Morris, 24 vols (London: Longmans, Green, 1910), i, p. xl. Hereafter referred to as 'Morris'.
2 *Letters of Dante Gabriel Rossetti*, ed. O Doughty and JR Wahl, 2 vols (Oxford University Press, 1965), i, p. 312. Hereafter referred to as 'Doughty and Wahl'.
3 Tate Britain, London.
4 Paul Thompson, *The Work of William Morris*, 3rd edn (Oxford University Press, 1991), p. 10.
5 Most obviously in 'Scenes from the Siege of Troy' (Morris, xxiv, pp. 3–51) and the epic poem *Sigurd the Volsung* (Morris, xii). But Morris's preoccupation with these stories is also apparent elsewhere in his work, not least in his translations. At about the time of the Oxford adventure, he began writing a poem on the subject of his Union fresco, the unfinished 'Palomydes' Quest' (Morris, xxiv, pp. 70–1). Morris's most recent biographer, Fiona MacCarthy, has written with considerable insight on the largely impenetrable subject of Morris's obsession with sexual triangles. See *William Morris: A Life for our Time* (London: Faber, 1994); the Oxford fresco is discussed on p. 130.
6 Tate Britain, London.

7 *Inferno*, v, ll. 127–38.
8 *The Collected Letters of William Morris*, ed. Norman Kelvin, 4 vols in 5 (Princeton University Press, 1984–96), ii, p. 152. Hereafter referred to as 'Kelvin'.
9 Kelvin, i, p. 28. The word 'muddle' recalls Dickens's idealized working-class hero Stephen Blackpool and his hopeless attempt to account for the destructive force of class conflict: 'aw a muddle! Fro' first to last, a muddle!' (Charles Dickens, *Hard Times for these Times* (Oxford University Press, 1955), p. 272).
10 Morris, i, p. 80.
11 Morris, iii, p. 1.
12 Doughty and Wahl, ii, p. 688. Both *The Wedding of St George* and *The Blue Closet* are in Tate Britain, London.
13 Alicia Craig Faxon, Dante Gabriel Rossetti (London: Phaidon, 1989), pp. 86–7.
14 Nikolaus Pevsner, *Pioneers of Modern Design: From William Morris to Walter Gropius*, 3rd edn rev. (Harmondsworth: Penguin, 160), pp. 59–60.
15 The British Museum, London.
16 Tate Britain, London.
17 Morris, i, p. 17.
18 Museum of Fine Arts, Boston.
19 Fitzwilliam Museum, Cambridge.
20 Faxon, op. cit., pp. 219–20.
21 Morris, i, p. 13.
22 Morris, i, p. 1.
23 Thompson, op. cit., pp. 182 3.
24 William Morris, *Manifesto of the Socialist League* (1885). Reprinted as Appendix I in EP Thompson, *William Morris: Romantic to Revolutionary*, 2nd edn rev. (London: Merlin, 1977), p. 735.
25 JW Mackail, *The Life of William Morris*, 2 vols (London: Longmans, Green, 1899), i, pp. 200–1.
26 Morris, xvi, p. 132. *News from Nowhere* was serialized in *The Commonweal* between January and October 1890. It was published in book form in 1891.
27 Mackail, op. cit., i, pp. 334, 335.
28 Kelvin, ii, p. 229.

13

THE AESTHETICS OF MORBIDITY: DG ROSSETTI AND BUCHANAN'S *THE FLESHLY SCHOOL OF POETRY*

Gavin Budge

Recent work on the 'Fleshly School' controversy has tried to distance itself from the partisanship of earlier critical accounts. Christopher Murray, whose early 1980s articles remain the most thorough treatment, comments that 'some sympathy for Buchanan's point of view is necessary for a proper understanding of the controversy', and draws attention to the provocation Robert Buchanan had received from Swinburne and WM Rossetti. Despite this attempt to take a more impartial view, however, critics still persist in characterizing Buchanan's motivations as purely personal in nature. JB Bullen and Dennis Denisoff, for example, in their recent studies of the Pre-Raphaelites, present Buchanan's attack as the product of a sense of exclusion from the charmed circle of Rossetti's associates.[1]

This kind of characterization of Robert Buchanan seems in part to stem from lack of awareness of just how significant a figure he was in the literary culture of the late nineteenth century. Although Buchanan wrote a large number of potboiling novels and plays subsequent to the 'Fleshly School' controversy, he also published a very significant amount of poetry (as much or more than Robert Browning, John A Cassidy notes in his 1973 study of Buchanan). On his death in 1901 Chatto & Windus put out a two-volume *Poetical Works*, in small type and double columns; a lengthy biography and a critical study were also published. Above all, Buchanan was a literary professional who at the time of the 'Fleshly School' controversy had numerous contacts with the leading periodicals, and was altogether, as Murray notes, not an opponent to be lightly dismissed. [2]

Buchanan later publicly recanted his attack on Rossetti, describing him in

1883 as 'he who, more than perhaps many of his contemporaries, was the least objective, the least earthly, and the most ideal' – high praise in Buchanan's critical vocabulary. Much Rossetti criticism has taken its cue from WM Rossetti in seeing this as an admission on Buchanan's part that his earlier attack was unjustified, and in characterizing *The Fleshly School of Poetry*, both as an article and in its later pamphlet form, as a scurrilous attack which is below serious critical notice. JB Bullen sees Buchanan's later change of heart as an attempt to cash in on Rossetti's developing critical reputation – a somewhat implausible view, given that Buchanan in the 1880s was at the height of a very successful and lucrative literary career.[3]

Modern critics' general dismissal both of Buchanan's attack, and of his later volte-face, as opportunistic and insincere, is unconvincing, if only because Buchanan was well known for the bitterness and inveteracy with which he pursued literary feuds. Furthermore, it ignores the extent to which even Buchanan's pamphlet version of *The Fleshly School of Poetry* (which in the eyes of some recent critics oversteps the mark in comparison with the original article) met with a sympathetic response from contemporaries. The chord which Buchanan's criticisms of Rossetti struck cannot be put down to a Victorian 'puritanism' against which Rossetti was in revolt, because, as some commentators have pointed out, the *Fleshly School* pamphlet flaunts Buchanan's extensive acquaintance with erotic literature – he was later to write an attack on literary censorship.[4]

This failure to account satisfactorily for Buchanan's motivations in attacking Rossetti, I would suggest, is a major lacuna in critical understanding not only of Rossetti's career, but the cultural significance of Pre-Raphaelitism both in art and literature. Buchanan's emphasis in *The Fleshly School of Poetry* on the 'morbidity' of Rossetti and his associates reiterates a criticism made in many of the hostile reviews in the original Pre-Raphaelite controversy of seventeen years before. I will argue that the persistence of this accusation of 'morbidity' is indicative of a fundamental ambiguity in the Rossettian and Pre-Raphaelite aesthetic, one which may be exemplified in DG Rossetti's poem 'Jenny', which Buchanan singles out for special notice. 'Morbidity', with its related implications of inverted sexuality, forms part of a medicalized Victorian aesthetics in which art can be figured as a corruption of the artist's moral nature, in that it leads him to pay attention above all to his own sensations. Buchanan's accusations of 'morbidity', then, directly foreshadow the thematics of the Decadent Movement, and supply a way of relating them to the mid-Victorian preoccupation with 'sensation'.[5]

In order to understand Buchanan's criticisms of Rossetti, we must first have some idea of Buchanan's attitude to poetry. At the time of writing *The Fleshly School of Poetry*, Buchanan was an intensely political poet, engaged in writing an epic, *A Drama of Kings* (which later influenced Thomas Hardy's *The Dynasts*) on the revolutionary situation in contemporary France. Buchanan shared this interest in the events surrounding the Paris Commune with post-Chartist working class poets such as WJ Linton, much of whose intellectual background Buchanan shared. Although himself lower middle class rather than working class in origin, Buchanan was the son of a well-known 'missionary' for Owenite utopian socialism, and even after he renounced explicitly political poetry in the wake of the Paris Commune's failure, an attempt to formulate a modified, less rationalistic form of Owenism can still be seen to underlie much of his later work.[6]

Christopher Murray's articles have drawn attention to the important role played by Swinburne's various contemptuous references to Buchanan's childhood friend, the poet David Gray, in provoking Buchanan to write *The Fleshly School of Poetry*. Gray, who was from a working class background, had come down to London at the same time as Buchanan with the aim of making a living from literature, had quickly caught tuberculosis, and died. Buchanan's lyrically written memorial of Gray was really his first major breakthrough into periodical criticism, and Gray continued to represent his ideal of the poet throughout his literary career. What commentators on the Fleshly School controversy appear to have missed is that Buchanan's resentment of the public school Swinburne's slighting allusions to Gray had more than a merely personal dimension: in the highly charged political climate of the early 1870s (the second Reform Act had passed in 1867), the Swinburne-Rossetti clique must have appeared a vulnerable bastion of upper-class privilege.[7]

Poetically, Buchanan might be regarded as a successor to the ill-fated 'Spasmodic' school of working-class poets who had been dealt such a blow by WE Aytoun's *Blackwood's* review and by Arnold's 'Preface' to his poems in the early 1850s, a view which is strengthened by his contacts with Sydney Dobell, who had been connected with the Spasmodics. The political context of Buchanan's poetry makes it easy to understand why he was the first champion of Walt Whitman in Britain: for Buchanan, true poetry was essentially democratic in nature, a neo-Wordsworthian aesthetic which was shared, for example, by the Broad Church clergyman FW Robertson, who had claimed in the early 1850s that the greatest poetry would henceforth be written by the working classes. This context also suggests that Buchanan's antipathy towards WM Rossetti, against whom (rather than DG Rossetti), Murray argues, much of *The Fleshly School of Poetry* was directed, reflects internal tensions in leftist politics of the time – interestingly, WM Rossetti was also an early champion of Whitman's poetic reputation in Britain.[8]

Buchanan commented in *The Fleshly School of Poetry* that the subject of

DG Rossetti's poem 'Jenny' might have been suggested by his own widely read collection, *London Poems*, published in 1866. Although Dante Gabriel indignantly denied ever reading Buchanan's poetry, and we now know that drafts of 'Jenny' preceded the publication of Buchanan's collection by some years, it is revealing that Buchanan regarded 'Jenny' as so nearly allied to the themes of his own poetry – so few poems of urban realism were being published at this time that the suggestion might well have seemed plausible to a contemporary reader. In view of the comparison Buchanan suggests, some discussion of a couple of the poems from the collection will serve to illustrate the nature of Buchanan's poetics.[9]

In a two part poem entitled 'Tiger Bay: a Stormy Night's Dream', Buchanan describes two parallel dream visions, one of the jungle, where a black man who is sleeping is pounced on and killed by a tigress, and one where a woman, described metaphorically as a 'Tigress' in terms which closely parallel the first vision, watches a sleeping sailor with a view to killing him with the knife she holds, in order that she may rob him of the purse he clutches in his hand. Unlike the literal tigress, the woman finds she is unable to bring herself to kill the man she is watching, a moment which Buchanan describes in highly melodramatic terms:

> She gazeth on, – he does not stir –
> Her fierce eyes close, her brute lip quivers;
> She longs to strike, but she shrinks and shivers:
> The light on his face appalleth her.
> The Wind is wailing, the Rain is weeping:
> Something holds her – her wild eyes roll;
> His Soul shines out, and she fears his Soul,
> Tho' he lieth sleeping.[10]

Buchanan draws a political moral in the conclusion to the poem, which must have seemed highly topical in view of fears during the 1860s about starvation and political unrest in London:[11]

> I saw no more, but I woke, – and prayed:
> 'God! that made the Beast and the Woman!
> God of the tigress! God of the human!
> Look to these things whom Thou hast made!
> Fierce and bloody and famine-stricken,
> Knitted with iron vein and thew–
> Strong and bloody, behold the two!–
> *We* see them and sicken.

    Mark! mark!
  These outcasts fierce of the dark;
  Where murmur the Wind and the Rain,
  Where the Jungle darkens the plain,
    And in street and lane.'

God answer'd clear, 'My will be done!
  Woman-tigress and tigress-woman–
  I made them both, the beast and the human,
But I struck a spark in the brain of the one.
And the spark is a fire, and the fire is a spirit;
  Tho' ye may slay it, it cannot die
  Nay, it shall grow as the days go by,
For my Angels are near it–
    Mark! mark!
  Doth it not burn in the dark?
  Spite of the curse and the stain,
  Where the Jungle darkens the plain,
    And in street and lane.'

God said, moreover: 'The spark shall grow–
  'Tis blest, it gathers, its flame shall lighten,
  Bless it and nurse it— let it brighten!
'Tis scatter'd abroad, 'tis a seed I sow.
And the Seed is a Soul, and the Soul is the Human;
  And it lighteth the face with a sign and a flame.
  Not unto beasts have I given the same,
But to man and to woman...
    Mark! mark!
  A spark that grows in the dark;
  A spark that burns in the brain;
  Spite of the Wind and the Rain,
  Spite of the Curse and the Stain;
  Over the Sea and the Plain,
  And in street and lane.[12]

'Tiger Bay' is not one of the more successful pieces in *London Poems*, but per-haps for that reason it is quite revealing about the assumptions underlying Buchanan's poetry. Although to modern ears phrases such as 'His Soul shines out' and Buchanan's invocation of a 'spark in the brain' sound impossibly vague, a contemporary reader would have recognized that these signalled

Buchanan's allegiance to the philosophical intuitionism of the Scottish Common Sense school, who, although little read today, were a still a major intellectual influence in Victorian Britain at the time – Buchanan's Scottish education would have ensured that he was familiar at least with the work of William Hamilton, who was the contemporary representative of this tradition, and whose agnosticism would have appealed to Buchanan, who appears to allude to him in other contexts.[13]

Using the terms of reference provided by Common Sense philosophy, one can recognize that Buchanan's description of the inability of the 'tigress-woman' to kill the sailor dramatizes a moment of moral intuition which transcends her material surroundings, enabling her to perceive his 'Soul' and thus to realize the full horror of the act of murder she is contemplating. Buchanan's conclusion to the poem implies that social change, and the end of class division, will naturally come about as the sum of such transcendent acts of individual moral intuition grows – a process to which one might see the poem itself as contributing, since the aim of Buchanan's Wordsworthian poetic is to enable his readers to realize a moral intuition of this kind for themselves.[14]

Buchanan's reliance here on individual moral intuition as the motor of social reform (which is also apparent in his attitude towards charitable giving) can be paralleled in the work of Christian Socialist reformers in the East End: it is also, of course, intrinsic to Ruskin's social criticism. Buchanan's echo of Elizabeth Barrett Browning ('God of the human' recalls the title of her poem 'The Cry of the Human') indicates not only the affinity of their subject matter – some parts of Barrett Browning's *Aurora Leigh* form the nearest parallel to the kind of urban realism which Buchanan is attempting here – but also the affinity of their poetic theory, since Barrett Browning was influenced by the Common Sense philosophical tradition which I am suggesting forms the background to Buchanan's poetic. Buchanan cited Barrett Browning as the prime exemplar of the 'poetry of humanity' he is attempting to write in an essay on his poetic creed published soon after his *London Poems* collection.[15]

Interestingly, in the very year Buchanan published this poem WM Rossetti was defending Swinburne's *Poems and Ballads* by attempting to discredit exactly the linkage between poetry and moral intuition on which Buchanan's poetic is based. William Michael notes, in a comment which takes issue with attempts to identify poetry with moral intuition, that:

> Mr Swinburne's mind appears to be very like a *tabula rasa* on moral and religious subjects, so occupied is it with instincts, feelings, perceptions, and a sense of natural or artistic fitness and harmony... On these moral and religious subjects he seems to have no 'innate ideas', no

preconceptions, no prejudices. He has no sense of what moral philosophers call a 'sanction'. Dogmas and doctrines come warranted to him from outside; and there is nothing in him which leaps out to meet the warrant half-way.[16]

Rossetti's invocation of the empiricist figure of the *tabula rasa*, or blank slate, to describe Swinburne's mind is significant, since this stands for exactly the account of experience which the Scottish Common Sense school had opposed by arguing that fundamental intuitions formed the necessary basis for human knowledge. Rossetti's comment that 'dogmas and doctrines' do not correspond to anything intrinsic in Swinburne's experience, and that there is no evidence of a mental principle 'which leaps out to meet' them 'half-way', is particularly directed at the Common Sense school's account of the intuitive nature of morality, a point which Rossetti reinforces by repeated references to, and lengthy quotations from, the works of David Hume, the major philosophical opponent of the eighteenth-century Common Sense philosophers. In making these allusions, Rossetti places his defence of Swinburne in the context of JS Mill's concurrent assault on William Hamilton, the main mid-nineteenth century representative of the Common Sense tradition, which proposed an account of induction self-confessedly indebted to Hume's philosophy.[17]

The philosophical context in which Rossetti places his account of Swinburne is not merely designed to bolster his own critical authority, but is integral to his argument that 'moral and religious subjects' are not essential to great poetry. Rossetti accepts the Romantic position that the greatness of poetry is a function of its capacity to represent human nature, but is concerned to deny that religious and moral 'dogmas and doctrines' (which critics had found singularly lacking in Swinburne's poetry) are an inherent part of human nature. If, as Hume had claimed, all our ideas arose simply through experience (rather than being based on immediate and non-experiential intuitions, as the Common Sense school had argued), then it became possible for Rossetti to make a case for Swinburne's poetry as representative of human nature in general, rather than – as hostile critics characterized it – a freakish aberration.[18]

Buchanan's objections to the resolutely non-transcendent view of human experience presented by William Michael Rossetti are, I will argue, what underlie his criticisms in *The Fleshly School of Poetry*. Buchanan makes clear in the poem 'Liz' (one of the *London Poems*) that he regards as radically impoverished a life lived without transcendent intuitions of something beyond the material world. In the poem, Liz, a dying unmarried mother who has just given birth, is telling the story of her life to a parson. After mentioning the

Wordsworthian 'intimations of immortality' she had in her deprived child-hood (spent mainly in an attic), she describes the effects of London life:

> Ah, yes, it's like a dream; for time pass'd by,
>   And I went out into the smoky air,
> Fruit-selling, Parson – trudging, wet or dry–
>   Winter and summer– weary, cold, and bare.
> And when old mother laid her down to die,
> And parish buried her, I did not cry,
>   And hardly seem'd to care;
> I was too hungry and too dull; beside,
>   The roar o' streets had made me dry as dust–
> It took me all my time, howe'er I tried,
>   To keep my limbs alive and earn a crust;
> I had no time for weeping.[19]

Poverty in London (represented by 'The roar o' streets') has stifled in Liz the natural moral intuitions which we have seen Buchanan invoke in 'Tiger Bay'. This becomes apparent later in the poem, when in response to some attempt-ed consolation by the parson, Liz rejects the prospect of going to 'GOD's kingdom' on the grounds that it 'must be like the country – which I fear', and recounts in detail the single time she visited the country. After a somewhat Wordsworthian passage of nature poetry, the poem continues:

> How swift the hours slipt on! – and by and by
> The sun grew red, big shadows fill'd the sky,
>   The air grew damp with dew,
>   And the dark night was coming down, I knew.
> Well, I was more afraid than ever, then,
>   And felt that I should die in such a place, –
>   So back to London town I turn'd my face,
> And crept into the great black streets again;
> And when I breathed the smoke and heard the roar,
>   Why, I was better, for in London here
>   My heart was busy, and I felt no fear.
> I never saw the country any more.
> And I have stay'd in London, well or ill–
>   I would not stay out yonder if I could.
>   For one feels dead, and all looks pure and good –
> I could not bear a life so bright and still.
> All that I want is sleep,
> Under the flags and stones, so deep, so deep!

God won't be hard on one so mean, but He,
   Perhaps, will let a tired girl slumber sound
   There in the deep cold darkness under ground;
And I shall waken up in time, may be,
Better and stronger, not afraid to see
   The great, still Light that folds Him round and round![20]

Liz cannot bear the stillness of the countryside, because in the absence of the strong sensory stimulation there is in London (which keeps her heart 'busy') she feels 'dead', despite recognizing that 'all looks pure and good'. Her condition is like the one Coleridge had described in 'Dejection: an Ode': Liz can see, but not *feel*, the beauty of the country, and this is indicative of the condition of moral insensibility which has made her unable to weep for the death of her mother, and which makes her unable to envisage life after death except as a condition of perpetual slumber.

Buchanan's portrayal of the deadening of moral intuitions by the bustle of city life echoes the concerns of contemporary social reformers SA and HO Barnett, who organized the Whitechapel Exhibitions that eventually led to the founding of the Whitechapel Art Gallery. The Barnetts regarded the stifling of moral aspirations by material circumstances as one of the primary causes of 'pauperism' (or what we might call today the dependency culture); their work in organizing art exhibitions which were accessible to the poor was intended to break this vicious circle, in which the dominance of material circumstances over the mind resulting from poverty reinforced exactly those mental and moral tendencies which had led to the condition of poverty in the first place. Art, in their Ruskin-influenced view, could be a remedy for 'pauperism' because it embodied transcendent intuitions in a material form. The Barnetts also organized excursions from Whitechapel to the countryside for much the same reasons: they regarded the material forms of the countryside as representing expressions of the Divine mind in a way that utilitarian London buildings could not, so that contact with the countryside would be a morally ennobling experience for the poor, provided they were taught how to interpret it.[21]

The view, common to Buchanan and the Barnetts, of poverty as a morally degrading condition in which the mind was reduced to a condition of pure 'sensation' by the unremitting excitement of city life, had its antecedents in the characterization of 'cockneyism' in the Romantic period. It is significant in this connection that Dante Gabriel Rossetti himself was accused of indifference to the natural world by many late nineteenth-century critics, a complaint which links the city-dwelling Rossetti to Romantic condemnations of 'the cockney school of poetry'. Buchanan in *The Fleshly School of Poetry* seems

to be making a similar point about Rossetti's moral insensibility, and consequent recourse to purely sensuous stimulation, when he comments that the
narrator of 'Jenny' chiefly responds not to the moral dangers of her situation,
but to her physical attractions.[22]

This combination of apparent insensibility to moral feelings, with an
excessive sensitivity to physical influences, was known as 'morbidity' in the
Victorian period, a term which was borrowed from Brunonian ideas, which
flourished in the mid-nineteenth century, about nervous excitement as the
central object of medical diagnosis. 'Morbidity' is a word which constantly
recurs in reviews of Pre-Raphaelite art in the early 1850s, and these may be
usefully compared with Buchanan's response to Dante Gabriel Rossetti.
Ruskin's defence of the Pre-Raphaelites is particularly illuminating in this
regard, given Buchanan's later recantation of his attack on Dante Gabriel.
Ruskin admitted that he had changed his mind about Pre-Raphaelite art, but
denied accusations that he had contradicted his own critical principles, manifesting an ambivalence which anticipates Buchanan's own ambivalence about
Dante Gabriel Rossetti. Given the common influence of Scottish Common
Sense philosophy upon Ruskin and Buchanan, this ambivalence about Dante
Gabriel, I would suggest, testifies to a fundamental ambiguity in the category
of the aesthetic itself within the nineteenth-century British intellectual context.[23]

A suggestion that often accompanied complaints about the 'morbidity' of
Pre-Raphaelite art was that it was essentially materialistic: Edward Young,
for example, in his book-length attack *Preraffaelitism* (1857), links the Pre-
Raphaelite interest in medieval art to what he regards as the characteristic
materialism of Roman Catholicism.[24] Ruskin, in a discussion of Hunt's picture 'The Awakening Conscience', defends the Pre-Raphaelite concern with
minute depiction of realistic detail by suggesting that such detail is in fact
emblematic of a state of heightened perception:

> I can easily understand that to many persons the careful rendering of the
> inferior details in this picture cannot but be at first offensive, as calling
> their attention away from the principal subject... But without entering
> into the question of the general propriety of such treatment, I would only
> observe that, at least in this instance, it is based on a truer principle of the
> pathetic than any of the common artistical expedients of the schools.
> Nothing is more notable than the way in which even the most trivial
> objects force themselves upon the attention of a mind which has been
> fevered by violent and distressful excitement. They thrust themselves
> forward with a ghastly and unendurable distinctness, as if they would
> compel the sufferer to count, or measure, or learn them by heart.[25]

For Ruskin, Hunt's minute rendering of the furnishings of the living room conveys to the spectator the 'violent and distressful excitement' of the young woman's imagination. Hunt's attention to surface detail can be freed from the imputation of materialism because the source of this imaginative excitement is not in fact in the picture at all, but in the young woman's sudden moral intuition of the sinfulness of her condition as a 'kept woman'. The materiality of Hunt's pictorial rendering thus embodies something which is essentially immaterial, only to be identified by an act of moral intuition on the part of the spectator.

Dante Gabriel Rossetti, in his reply to Buchanan's criticisms in *The Stealthy School of Criticism*, seems to make a very similar argument in defence of his poem 'Jenny'. Although Rossetti's line of reasoning isn't easy to unpick from his rather tortuous prose, his point seems to be that the young man's recurrent references to Jenny's physical charms form a necessary part of the poem because they testify to the excitement of his imagination by the moral 'mystery' of prostitution: under the influence of this overwhelming moral intuition the physical details of Jenny's body become charged with transcendent significance in the same way as the hyper-realistic depiction of the living room in Hunt's 'The Awakening Conscience'. Buchanan's later 1881 praise of Rossetti as 'the least objective, the least earthly, and the most ideal' of poets presumably reflects his eventual acceptance of this interpretation of 'Jenny'.[26]

This defence of Pre-Raphaelite realistic detail as indicative of imaginative 'excitement' has a potential ambiguity, however, as the word 'excitement' itself suggests. For this defence to be effective, the concentration on physical detail has to be interpreted dramatically, as indicative of a state of imaginative excitement in the narrator or central figure with which the audience is expected to identify. Physical detail, in this line of argument, has to be suggestive of something beyond the senses, and this implies imaginative identification with another's personality. If, on the other hand, the audience are led to suspect that the 'excitement' is more properly to be attributed to the artist himself, rather than to a character within the work of art, then this defence of physicality will no longer avail. The work of art becomes merely physical, in the sense that it is non-transcendent: one might say, in view of William Michael Rossetti's references to Hume, that it becomes Swinburnian. Ruskin shows himself aware of this possibility when he comments that 'spurious imitations of Pre-Raphaelite work', which are *merely* detailed, have no 'infinity' or transcendent dimension.[27]

Obviously, this separation between artist and character is much harder to maintain in the case of Rossetti's poem than in Hunt's picture, and it is noticeable that Buchanan in *The Fleshly School of Poetry* entirely identifies Rossetti with the poem's narrator. Rossetti's use of physical detail in 'Jenny' is radically ambiguous in a way that is foreign to Hunt's essentially typological realism, and this ambiguity in Rossetti's practice might be said to reflect a fundamental ambiguity in the category of the aesthetic itself within Victorian culture. The aesthetic, as Ruskin (followed by Buchanan and the Barnetts) argued, could constitute the embodiment of immaterial, essentially moral, intuitions which would act to desensualize the perceptions of the spectator, but it could equally well corrupt the spectator by encouraging him to contemplate the material world for its own sake.[28] This fundamental ambiguity of the aesthetic also manifested itself in a concern that the very practice of art might tend to corrupt the artist, as FW Robertson argues:

> It is almost proverbial that the poetic temperament... is one of singular irritability of brain and nerve... And by this, too, we can understand, and compassionate, I do not say excuse, the force of that temptation of stimulants to which so many gifted natures have fallen a sacrifice. Poetry is the language of excited feeling: properly of pure excitement. But stimulants, like wine, opium, and worse, can produce, or rather stimulate, that state of rapturous and ecstatic feeling in which the seer should live; in which emotions succeed each other swiftly, and imagination works with preternatural power. Hence their seductive power.
>
> Our higher feelings move our animal nature; and our animal nature, irritated, can call back a semblance of those emotions; but the whole difference between nobleness and baseness lies in the question whether feeling begins from below or above. The degradation of genius, like the sensualising of passion, takes place when men hope to reproduce, through stimulus of the lower nature, those glorious sensations which it once experienced when vivified from above. Imagination ennobles appetites which in themselves are low, and spiritualises acts which are else only animal. But the pleasures which begin in the senses only sensualise.[29]

In an anticipation of the *poète maudit* invoked by Baudelaire and the decadents, poetry here figures in Robertson's account as a potential agent of moral corruption, as well as a morally improving influence. In fact, the practice of poetry can be morally corrupting for the poet for precisely the same reasons that it is a morally beneficial influence on the reader. Robertson at one point characterizes poetry as a 'safety valve' for emotions that readers cannot express in society, but Robertson's expressivist account of poetry demands that these be emotions which the poet has actually experienced, and it is this requirement that in Robertson's account may lead to a temptation to employ artificial stimulants such as opium. Although Robertson implies that this resort to artificial stimulation is doomed to failure, and cannot produce authentic poetry, it is clearly only a small step from this argument to Baudelaire's paradoxical characterization of the poet as a figure who, in a gesture of Christ-like self-sacrifice, deliberately seeks out the morally polluting influences of wine, drugs and prostitutes in order to obtain the maximum of sensory and emotional stimulation and so write the poetry which will morally ennoble his readers.

Buchanan's attack on Rossetti in *The Fleshly School of Poetry* is informed by exactly this kind of suspicion that the wish to write poetry has led Rossetti actively to seek out morally degrading 'sensation'. Buchanan puts a similar argument explicitly in his article, 'The Character of Goethe', published in the same 1883 volume as his laudatory essay on Rossetti, where he connects Goethe's strange insensitivity and remoteness with the aesthetic teaching of Arnold and Ruskin. Buchanan notes Goethe's many affairs, and comments that it wasn't necessary for these to be physically consummated for Goethe to be stimulated by them:

> God could not move Goethe, nor could Nature, nor revolution, nor
> aspiration, nor intellectual love. None of these could directly move him;
> but put him in the society of a fair woman... titillate him ever so slightly
> by sensuous means – and Goethe moved at once, expanded, soared,
> found a thousand ways of expending his activity on the world at large. In
> so far as this activity broke forth sensually, it impaired, paralysed, and
> limited his mental activity; but where it excited without fruition, where
> the homunculus, so to speak, agitated the back part of the brain, and the
> back part of the brain in its turn moved the mighty cerebral mass behind
> what the hero-worshipper called 'that impassive Jupiter-like brow' – this
> activity so engendered took an absolute form, begot issue as thoroughly
> in the way of nature as if the actual body had performed its part and
> directly engendered offspring. Out of the total virility of that wonderful
> mechanism called Goethe, not merely out of Goethe's brain, were born
> Mignon, and Faust, and Clärchen, and Lothario, all the troop of intellec-
> tual offspring, good, bad, and indifferent, just as certainly as was born
> Goethe's only son in the flesh by Christiane Vulpius.[30]

Goethe's moral insensibility, Buchanan implies, led him to seek mental, poet-ical stimulation from the physical sensation of sexual desire. This is a process, Buchanan suggests, which is purely physiological; the stimulus which doesn't issue as one kind of ejaculation is converted into mental activity, and issues in poetic form. Goethe's poetry thus represents for Buchanan a kind of mental masturbation. As Buchanan remarks, 'Science alone could have explained the

secret of his genius, if Science had been sufficiently advanced to explain sensuous cerebellic and consequent cerebral activity.'[31]

Buchanan's description of the role sensual titillation played in the production of Goethe's poetry parallels his emphasis in *The Fleshly School* on the presence of 'Leg' in the poetry of Rossetti – 'Leg' represents a fetishistic prelude to
sexual enjoyment, and by implication it is this sterile excitement, never issuing
in action, which is embodied in Rossetti's poetry. Christopher Murray has
drawn attention to the many coded references in *The Fleshly School* to Rossetti's
affair with Janey Morris, and the parallel with his description of Goethe suggests that Buchanan regarded this as an self-indulgent exercise in titillation.
There is also in *The Fleshly School* a direct parallel to the characterization of
Goethe in Buchanan's presentation of Baudelaire as 'that most unsympathetic
of all beings, a cold sensualist'. In Buchanan's view, Baudelaire is the baleful
influence that lies behind Rossetti's and Swinburne's 'fleshliness'.[32]

Buchanan's emphasis on the purely material and physiological nature of
the 'mechanism' involved in producing Goethe's poetry indicates that he
regards this poetry as inauthentic. Elsewhere in the same volume, Buchanan
comments that 'an atheistical *poet* is an anomaly, an impossibility', and characterizes 'the religious conception' as 'the source of nobler sentiments than the
conviction that Death merely robs us of sensation'. Goethe's and Rossetti's
sensualism is implicitly atheistic in its denial of any wider context to life than
the immediate sensation.[33]

Buchanan's invocation of physiology in his description of the sexual sources
of Goethe's imaginative activity indicates the derivation of the various ideas
about imaginative 'excitement' and 'irritability' which we have been explor-
ing in this essay from Brunonian medical theory, whose extensive influence in
the Victorian period may be seen from the fact that Brunonian ideas about
overstimulation of nervous fibres underlie the attacks of 'brain-fever' to which
characters in Victorian novels are subject. Something which strikingly illus-
trates the kind of radical ambiguity in Rossetti's poetic practice to which I
have been suggesting Buchanan responds both in *The Fleshly School* and his
subsequent recantation, is the extent to which Rossetti's poem 'Jenny' can be
read purely in terms of a Brunonian physiology of the brain. Such a materialist interpretation is not incompatible with the 'immaterialist' reading I have
suggested Dante Gabriel himself proposes, which sees the physical detail of
the poem as indicative of the young man's moral intuition of the 'mystery' of
prostitution: what this shows is that the poem aims to incarnate at the level of
its own interpretation the radical split between matter and spirit which in
most Victorians' view was constitutive of the human condition.[34]

Dante Gabriel's poem repeatedly draws attention to the rambling nature of
the narrator's thoughts, described as 'an empty cloud', and full of 'wasteful

whims more than enough'. The narrator has ended up in Jenny's room, in a manner which he can't really explain, because, tired of what seems fairly intensive study (he mentions his books and 'The hours they thieve from day and night') he has had a sudden urge to go out dancing.[35]

One can interpret the situation of the narrator in the context of mid-Victorian anxieties about the effects of cramming for examinations. According to Brunonian medical doctrine, writing and study involved intense and narrowly focused mental excitement which tended to debilitate the nervous fibres of the brain, leading to a condition of insensibility in the nerves which required stronger and stronger 'stimulants' in order to produce a response. The young man in 'Jenny' is thus in the condition which FW Robertson finds characteristic of the poet, tempted to seek stimulation in 'wine, opium, and worse' – the 'worse' presumably being that sexual excitement to which Buchanan suggests Goethe resorted. The search for sensory stimulation takes him out dancing, and also explains how he has ended up in Jenny's room. The activity of his thoughts thus reflects a purely sensory stimulus.[36]

This framing of the narrator's thoughts by a Brunonian physiology of the brain makes their status radically ambiguous. For example, the passage in the poem which seems most insistently to claim the status of a moral intuition that transcends surrounding material circumstances is the extended simile of the toad:

Yet, Jenny, looking long at you,
The woman almost fades from view.
A cipher of man's changeless sum
Of lust, past, present, and to come,
Is left. A riddle that one shrinks
To challenge from the scornful sphinx.

Like a toad within a stone
Seated while Time crumbles on;
Which sits there since the earth was curs'd
For Man's transgression at the first;
Which, living through all centuries
Not once has seen the sun arise;
Whose life, to its cold circle charmed,
The earth's whole summers have not warmed;
Which always – whitherso the stone
Be flung – sits there, deaf, blind, alone; –
Aye, and shall not be driven out

Till that which shuts him round about
Break at the very Master's stroke,
And the dust thereof vanish as smoke,
And the seed of Man vanish as dust; –
Even so within this world is lust.[37]

The toad to which lust is compared exhibits the kind of loveless self-absorption of which critics have often accused the poem's speaker (and which Buchanan found characteristic of Rossetti himself). One could interpret this simile as a moment of epiphany; it is presented as a consequence of the way in which the figure of Jenny has faded to a 'cipher', and could conceivably represent an intuition by the speaker of his own moral nature. According to this reading, the fading of Jenny into a 'cipher', or sign, would represent a moment of moral clarity and resolution where the 'cloud' of vague thoughts is broken, a point where the kind of intuition appealed to by the Common Sense school breaks through the sensual associative haze.[38]

Rossetti, however, refuses this reading:

Come, come, what use in thoughts like this:
Poor little Jenny, good to kiss, —
You'd not believe by what strange roads
Thought travels, when your beauty goads
A man tonight to think of toads![39]

The unlikeness of Jenny and the toad, instead of being, as a reader might expect, a marker for the moral authority of an intuition, is here used to relativize this image of lust: it becomes merely one bizarre association among many. Rossetti deflates the analogical and typological imagination the speaker displays here, reducing it to the status of a mere sensation. This deflation is marked by Rossetti's use of the word 'goads', which hints to the reader that the toad imagery should be regarded as merely one more physiological response to the sexual stimulus of Jenny's beauty.

The moment in the poem which seemed to transcend the physiological condition of 'excitability' in which Rossetti has situated the young man at the beginning of the poem, and so to represent an essentially immaterial intuition, is collapsed back into the materiality of the body. It was perhaps this feature of 'Jenny' which made Buchanan regard it as paradigmatic of the 'fleshly' quality of Rossetti's poetry in general.[40]

Notes

1   Christopher Murray, 'D G Rossetti, A C Swinburne and R W Buchanan. The Fleshly School Revisited: I', *Bulletin of the John Rylands University Library of Manchester* (Autumn

1982) vol. 65 (1) pp. 206–34, p. 207; Dennis Denisoff, *Aestheticism and Sexual Parody 1840–1940* (Cambridge: Cambridge University Press, 2001) pp. 27, 108; JB Bullen, *The Pre-Raphaelite Body: fear and desire in painting, poetry and criticism* (Oxford: Clarendon Press 1998), p. 158.

2 John A Cassidy, *Robert W Buchanan* (New York: Twayne Publishers, 1973) p. 80; Christopher Murray, 'D G Rossetti, A C Swinburne, and R W Buchanan. The Fleshly School Revisited: II', *Bulletin of the John Rylands University of Manchester Library* vol. 65 (2) pp. 176–207, 180–1.

3 Robert Buchanan, *A Look Round Literature* (London: Ward and Downey 1887), p. 153; William Michael Rossetti, *Dante Gabriel Rossetti as Designer and Writer* (London: Cassell and Co., 1889), p. 157, cf Oswald Doughty, *A Victorian Romantic: Dante Gabriel Rossetti*, 2nd ed. (London: Oxford University Press 1960), pp. 467–80; Denisoff, p. 27; Cassidy, p. 33.

4 Cassidy, p. 36; Brian and Judy Dobbs, *Dante Gabriel Rossetti: an Alien Victorian* (London: Macdonald and James 1977), p. 186; Cassidy, pp 51–2; ibid pp 53–4; cf Robert Buchanan, *On Descending into Hell: a letter addressed to the Right Hon Henry Matthews Q C Home Secretary concerning the proposed suppression of literature* (London: George Redway, 1889), passim.

5 Bullen, pp. 11–12, p. 37; cf Robert Buchanan, *A Look Round Literature* (London: Ward and Downey, 1887), pp. 81–2; Max Nordau, *Degeneration* (Lincoln, Neb.: University of Nebraska Press, 1993), p. 241; cf [HL Mansel] 'Sensation Novels', *Quarterly Review* (1863), 481–504, p. 482.

6 Robert Buchanan, *Poetical Works*, 2 vols (London: Chatto and Windus, 1901), vol. 1 p. 335; Anne Janowitz, *Lyric and Labour in the Romantic Tradition* (Cambridge: Cambridge University Press 1998), p. 213; Cassidy, pp. 19, 30.

7 Robert Buchanan, *David Gray and Other Essays, Chiefly on Poetry* (London: Simpson, Low, Son and Marston, 1868), pp. 61–114.

8 Isobel Armstrong, *Victorian Scrutinies* (London: Athlone Press 1972), p. 38; Murray (II), p. 192; Harriett Jay, *Robert Buchanan: Some Account of his Life, his Life's Work and his Literary Friendships* (London: Fisher Unwin 1903), pp. 66–7; Buchanan 1887, p. 188; cf Buchanan 1868, pp. 201–22; FW Robertson, *Lectures on the Influence of Poetry and Wordsworth* (London: Athenaeum 1906), pp. 77–8 (orig. pub. 1853); Murray (I), pp. 220, 226.

9 Robert Buchanan, *The Fleshly School of Poetry and Other Phenomena of the Day* (London: Strahan and Co., 1872), pp. 45–6; Dante Gabriel Rossetti, 'The Stealthy School of Criticism', in *The Pre-Raphaelites: writings and sources*, ed. Inga Bryden, 4 vols (London: Routledge/Thoemmes, 1998) vol. 1, pp. 251–7, pp. 254–5.

10 Buchanan, *Poetical Works*, p. 159.

11 Henrietta Olivia Barnett, *Canon Barnett: his Life, Work and Friends*, 2 vols (London: Murray, 1918), pp. 18–22.

12 Buchanan, *Poetical Works*, p. 159.

13 Rick Rylance, *Victorian Psychology and British Culture 1850–1880* (Oxford: Oxford University Press, 2000), pp. 44–7; Jay, p. 111.

14 Cf Richard Holt Hutton, 'The Genius of Wordsworth' in *Literary Essays* (London: Macmillan, 1908), pp. 90–132, pp. 125–9.

15 Gavin Budge, 'Poverty and the Picture Gallery: the Whitechapel Exhibitions and the Social Project of Ruskinian Aesthetics', *Visual Culture in Britain* vol. 1 (2) (2000), pp. 43–56, pp. 50–2; cf Elizabeth Barrett Browning, *Poetical Works* (London: Smith, Elder and Co., 1897), p. 48; Buchanan (1868), p. 297.

16 William Michael Rossetti, *Swinburne's Poems and Ballads: a criticism* (London: Hotten, 1866), p. 17.
17 SA Grave, *The Scottish Philosophy of Common Sense* (Oxford: Clarendon Press, 1960) pp. 114–16, 226–8; Michael St John Packe, *The Life of John Stuart Mill* (London: Secker & Warburg, 1954), pp. 440–1.
18 Clyde K Hyder, ed., *Swinburne: the Critical Heritage* (London: Routledge and Kegan Paul, 1970), p. 35.
19 Buchanan 1901, p. 121.
20 Buchanan 1901, p. 123.
21 Budge 2000, pp. 52–4.
22 William Hazlitt, *Works*, ed. PP Howe, 21 vols (London and New York: Dent and Dutton 1931), vol. 9, p. 67; cf William Tirebuck, *Dante Gabriel Rossetti: his work and influence* (London: Elliot Stock 1882), p. 23; Donald H Reiman, *The Romantics Reviewed: Contemporary Reviews of British Romantic Writers: Part C, Shelley, Keats and London Radical Writers*, 2 vols (New York: Garland, 1972) p. 768; Buchanan (1872), p. 47.
23 Michael Barfoot, 'Brunonianism under the Bed: an Alternative to University Medicine in Edinburgh in the 1780s' in *Brunonianism in Britain and Europe*, ed. WF Bynum and Roy Porter (*Medical History*, Supplement no. 8, 1988), pp. 22–45, p. 22, p. 34; Bullen, pp. 11–12, p. 37; John Ruskin, *Works*, ed. ET Cook and Alexander Wedderburn, 39 vols (London, Allan 1903–1912) vol. 12, p. xlv, pp. l–li; George Landow, *The Aesthetic and Critical Theories of John Ruskin* (Princeton: Princeton University Press, 1971), pp. 95–6, cited in Linda Dowling, *The Vulgarisation of Art: the Victorians and Aesthetic Democracy* (Charlottesville and London: University Press of Virginia 1996), p. 35.
24 Edward Young, *Pre-raffaellitism: or, a popular enquiry into some newly asserted principles connected with the philosophy, poetry, religion and revolution of art* (London: Longman, Brown, Green, Longmans & Roberts, 1857), p. 149.
25 Ruskin, vol. 12, p. 334.
26 Dante Gabriel Rossetti, in Bryden, vol. 1, pp. 251–7, 254–5.
27 Ruskin, vol. 12, pp. 330–2.
28 Ruskin, vol. 3, pp. 99–105.
29 Robertson, p. 25.
30 Buchanan 1887, pp. 81–2.
31 Buchanan 1887, p. 81.
32 Buchanan 1872, pp. 2–4; Murray (II), pp. 192–4; Buchanan, op cit, p. 19; pp. 29–31.
33 Buchanan 1872, pp. 50, 122.
34 Cf Charlotte M Yonge, *The Daisy-Chain, or, Aspirations* (www.blackmask.com: Blackmask Online 2001) PDF version (accessed 15/03/02), chap. 11, p. 89.
35 'Jenny', ll. 154, 56, 25.
36 Cf AR Grant, 'The Evils of Competitive Examinations' *The Nineteenth Century* vol. 8 (1880), pp. 715–23, pp. 716, 720; cf Walter Cooper Dendy, *The Philosophy of Mystery*, (London: Longman, Orme, Brown, Green and Longmans, 1841), p. 80; Robertson, p. 25; Buchanan 1887, pp. 81–2.
37 'Jenny', ll. 275–96.
38 Cf John P McGowran, "'The Bitterness of Things Occult': D G Rossetti's Search for the Real', *Victorian Poetry*, vol. 20, pp. 45–60 (p. 48).
39 'Jenny', ll. 297–301.
40 Buchanan 1872, p. 47.

PART V

LITERARY TRADITION AND THE ROSSETTI LEGACY

14

'IT ONCE SHOULD SAVE AS WELL AS KILL': DG ROSSETTI AND THE FEMININE

Catherinc Maxwell

In a discussion of decadent art in *Sexual Personae*, Camille Paglia asserts that Burne-Jones remarked of Dantc Gabriel Russelli, 'Gabriel was half a woman'.[1] Neither I nor Jan Marsh were able to find a source for this remark though we were both so tantalized by it as to spend some considerable effort trying to track it down; for whether the remark is authentic or not, the issue of Dante Gabriel Rossetti's relation to and identification with the feminine has clearly been a topic of considerable interest in the last twenty years. First fully broached by Barbara Charlesworth Gelpi in her 1982 essay 'The Feminization of D. G. Rossetti', the topic has been dilated on in various ways by a roll-call of eminent critics including David Riede, Griselda Pollock, J Hillis Miller, Martin Danahay and JB Bullen.[2] That there should be so much interest is hardly surprising in the light of our modern-day preoccupation with gender, but Rossetti himself made the issue of thc feminine central to his work, as signalled in his early fable *Hand and Soul* (1850) where the despairing painter Chiaro is comforted by a visionary woman, and 'it seemed that the first thoughts he had ever known were given him as at first from her eyes, and he knew her hair to be the golden veil through which he beheld his dreams'. As the woman tells him: "' I am an image, Chiaro, of thine own soul within thee"'.[3] In the year after his death, which saw the first major exhibitions of his paintings, Rossetti's investment in the feminine was noted by various contemporary critics. Characterizing Rossetti as the high-priest of Aestheticism in his 1883 essay 'Rossetti and the Religion of Beauty', FWH Myers commented: 'But with this newer school – with Rossetti especially – we feel at once that Nature is no more than an accessory. The most direct appeals, the most penetrating reminiscences, come to the worshipper of Beauty through a woman's eyes'. Rossetti's obsessive portrayal of Jane Morris was singled out by the popular art critic Harry Quilter, who remarked: 'There is probably no record of a painter whose personality grew to be so submerged in the form and face of one woman as did that of him of whom we are writing', adding that Rossetti was 'possessed by the strange beauty of the face he made so familiar to us'.[4]

When over a century later Barbara Charlesworth Gelpi reviewed the issue for a modern audience, she explored Rossetti's feminization through his placement in a 'Victorian, feminine, middle-class culture', stressing a number of factors: the artist's strong attachment to his mother and thus an interest in the maternal and the mother–child bond in his work, the feminization of artists in Victorian culture, where the arts were 'classified as activities proper to the domestic sphere', and the painter's identification of himself with the prostitute, economically dependent on the vagaries of the marketplace.[5] She also noted Rossetti's relationships with women artists, and his final hysterical illness, which evokes the hysterical illnesses suffered by his two great romantic loves, Elizabeth Siddal and Jane Morris. Various of these factors have generated further discussion, although critics after Gelpi have tended to concentrate more directly on representations of women in Rossetti's paintings and poems to show how he identified himself with such images, or used them defensively, perhaps aggressively, to identify a feminine otherness at once fascinating and fearful.

My own tack in this essay is somewhat different: I consider and acknowledge Rossetti's feminine identifications in the light of what they do for his poetic identity, how they make and mark him as a poet. In this way I align Rossetti with the patterns of male feminization I note in my recent book *The Female Sublime from Milton to Swinburne: Bearing Blindness* (2001), and show how his response to the feminine is not just a matter of a particular cultural epoch but a result of a long-meditated tradition of male feminization which stems from the crucial figure of Milton.[6] My argument is that Rossetti's ambivalence about some of his female images is less a narrow form of Victorian negativity towards women than an anxiety about the symbolic sacrifice he makes as a male poet.

My book proposes that Milton, the father of modern English poetry, is the crucial influence on Romantic and Post-Romantic verse. The allied figures of Miltonic blindness and the poet's inner illumination ground the eighteenth-century sublime, characterized by its 'progressive internalisation of the eye', a 'progressive interest in the subject rather than the object' and the imagination's transcendence of materiality.[7] Milton's symbolic language co-identifies blindness, castration and feminization as the necessary loss for the true compensatory vision that inspires song. Male poets after Milton struggle with an uncompromising legacy which tells them that in order to be strong poets they must undergo a form of disfiguration, that authentic poetic identity is achieved only through a sacrifice which is like a symbolic castration. In my view, male poets' adoption of feminine identities and images is less a matter of appropriation than of compulsion as they are driven towards feminization in order to attain vision. This castration is variously represented in Milton and in the poets who come after him by images of blindness and decapitation; images specifically singled out by Freud as representing castration. These and other related images of disfiguration and mutilation are taken up time and time again by poets after Milton as they work out their relation to his paradigms of loss and compensation through rehearsals of mythic narratives and personae. The principal sources are the interlinked myths of Philomela the nightingale, an unsurpassed songstress who makes poetry out of pain; of Orpheus, poetry's first singer who sings of his loss even after death; and of Sappho, history's most famous woman poet who supposedly kills herself out of unrequited love. However, other myths, particularly those concerned with looking and the dangers of looking are also important, and imitations of Narcissus, Perseus, Tiresias, Actaeon and Thamyris loom large.

Rossetti clearly has links with two of these mythic archetypes: Narcissus, the young man who falls in love with his own reflection and Perseus, who slays the Gorgon Medusa, avoiding her petrifying look by viewing her in his mirrored shield. Both these figures he inherits from Shelley, the poet who crucially mediates Milton's legacy to the Victorians. Rossetti can also be seen to bear a direct trace of Milton's Orpheus, the man who braves the Underworld to recover the woman he loves. However, before I trace the effects of the Miltonic legacy in Rossetti's work, I want to point out how, in a strangely literal way, a key episode in his career as a poet and painter is shaped by the Miltonic paradigm.

Max Beerbohm, who thought Rossetti one of the three most interesting Englishmen of the nineteenth century (the other two being Byron and Disraeli), wrote: 'I have known no man of genius who had not to pay, in some affliction or defect, either spiritual, physical or mental, for what the gods had given him'.[8] In 1865 Rossetti began to plan a painting entitled *Aspecta Medusa* depicting Perseus, Andromeda and the Gorgon's head, for which he composed a poem-inscription, and in July 1867 he was commissioned to undertake this design for the wealthy brewer C Matthews.[9] Rossetti abandoned the project in January 1868 on account of the squeamish reservations of his prospective purchaser. We have some preparatory drawings for the head of the gazing Andromeda and only a faintest sketch of the overall design in which the Medusa head is indicated by the vaguest of outlines with no corresponding reflection in the pool below. No trace of a painted work exists. Rossetti later promised the commission to another wealthy client, Frederick R

Leyland, in May 1868, but the painting never materialized, although Leyland had paid a considerable advance for it.[10] Rossetti's poem-inscription warns of the danger of the Medusa head which has the power to save and kill, and, significantly, the head itself is not described:

> Andromeda, by Perseus saved and wed,
> Hankered each day to see the Gorgon's head:
> Till o'er a fount he held it, bade her lean,
> And mirrored in the wave was safely seen
> That death she lived by.
>
>   Let not thine eyes know
> Any forbidden thing itself, although
> It once should save as well as kill: but be
> Its shadow upon life enough for thee.[11]

The poem breaks into two fragments: the first explaining the means by which Perseus shows the head to Andromeda, the second an admonition to the reader or prospective viewer or maybe even the poet-artist himself warning about the dangers of viewing a forbidden subject too directly or without mediation. As readers we are left to image for ourselves the occluded or censored face appearing as it were in the gap or the blank space between the two parts of the poem. Unlike Shelley, who in his famous poem on Leonardo's Medusa looks his subject straight in the face and describes its appearance in detail, Rossetti turns away from this encounter. Was there something about the Medusa which so unnerved him, that attracted though he was to the subject, he was unable to see the project through?

During the summer of 1867, when Rossetti proposed the subject to Matthews, he began to be plagued with the eye problems and 'confusion in the head' which were to prevent him for a period from painting. As his father had in fact gone blind, Rossetti believed his indisposition might be hereditary. Terrified by the thought of blindness, he consulted the leading oculists of the day who diagnosed the cause of his eye problems as not physical but psychical in origin.[12] It seems pertinent to point out that it was specifically these eye problems that made him turn from painting to poetry and to the eventual publication of *Poems* in 1870. Henry Campbell records:

> Rather dramatically, he reasoned that, if he were to be deprived of his painting, then, like blind Homer or Milton, he could live for his poetry. He had written little during the previous years, other than an odd sonnet for a picture, and now he began to gather together fragments of his work,

revise them, and to write again with renewed power. He began seriously
to concern himself with acquiring a literary reputation.[13]

What is also noticeable about this transition is that, as his sight fades,
Rossetti moves from painting's visible representations to an explicitly vision-
ary world, a symbolic if temporary shift from exterior to interior vision. On 18
December 1868 he produced the sequence of four sonnets known as
'Willowwood' which form the visionary heart of the sonnet series *The House of
Life*. Glossing the first sonnet of this sequence, Rossetti later explained that it
'describes a dream or trance of divided love momentarily re-united by the
longing fancy'.[14] In his diary entry for Friday 18 December, William Michael
Rossetti commented: 'Gabriel has just written a series of four sonnets –
Willow-wood – about the finest thing he has done. I see the poetical impulse is
upon him again: he even says he ought never to have been a painter, but a
poet instead'.[15] If the spectre of the symbolic castration that marks the poet's
embrace of the visionary mode is oddly literalized in 1867–8, one might also
note as another factor in this eerie literalization that at this time Rossetti had
also been much bothered by the hydrocele or testicular ailment which
afflicted him in his middle years and which, Jan Marsh has suggested, prevented him from consummating his relationship with Jane Morris.[16] The loss
of Elizabeth Siddal and the unattainability of the married Jane Morris which
may both mark 'Willowwood' also contribute in a larger sense to a Rossetti
haunted by a lost or out-of-reach woman who nonetheless confers him with a
sense of his own identity.

'I loved thee ere I loved a woman, Love' writes Rossetti in a verse fragment
entitled 'To Art',[17] yet addressing Art as a woman. Woman, Art and Rossetti's
sense of himself as an artist are inseparable. Griselda Pollock has pointed out
that Rossetti's later pictures are not portraits of the women they appear to
represent in that not only do they obsessively reproduce specific facial types
but they also realign the dimensions of the face in a completely fantastic way.
LS Lowry, a somewhat unlikely collector of Rossetti, remarked that 'his
women are very wonderful. I can't find anything quite like them. The Old
Masters didn't quite get them [...] wonderful creatures they are [...] unreal
pictures' and 'They are very queer creatures and I like him for it [...] What he
puts into the individual is all him, not the individual, they're probably all
ordinary people'.[18] William Gaunt notes Rossetti's 'superstitious aversion' for
the portrait, and Rossetti himself told Vernon Lushington in 1865 that 'whenever I have undertaken a portrait, I have always felt myself so encumbered
with anxiety as to getting a good likeness [...] that I have generally failed in
this more than in any other kind of work'.[19] Rossetti evidently then was
not painting 'good likenesses' of his female sitters but practising a form of

projection. But, as Camille Paglia declares, projection is no easy solution: 'Projection is a male curse: forever to need something or someone to make oneself complete. This is one of the sources of art and the secret of its historical domination by males. The artist is the closest man has come to imitating woman's superb self-containment'.[20] If the desire is to emulate woman's self-containment, or woman 'subtly of herself contemplative' as Rossetti puts it in a famous sonnet, then this process is also fraught with failure.[21] 'Why is it', asks J Hillis Miller, musing on the painting 'Lady Lilith' that partners this sonnet, 'that whenever we men contemplate not ourselves in the mirror but our own incongruous other self, a desirable woman contemplating herself, our own integrity is mutilated, destroyed?' Martin Danahay responds to Miller's question by suggesting that the 'threat' of mutilation 'exists precisely because the woman refuses to be a compliant mirror image', that the woman in the painting 'functions both as a mirror of masculine desire and as a threat to the imaginative unity and coherence of the masculine subject'.[22] I think this is right in that fear of non-compliance is one of the anxieties that inevitably accompany the desire for the reflecting female other.

Although Danahay doesn't say so, Rossetti's women derive directly from Shelley and his notion of the epipsyche, the reflecting female beloved, adumbrated in the essay 'On Love', the long poem *Epipsychidion* and other works such as *Alastor*, which show the protagonist in pursuit of a being like himself.[23] But Shelley himself borrows from Book 8 of Milton's *Paradise Lost*, where Adam encounters Eve and claims her as his own – 'I now see/Bone of my bone, flesh of my flesh, my self/Before me'[24] – and thus inaugurates the pattern whereby the male self claims the female beloved as an idealized projection of itself and as guarantor and reflector of its own male identity.[25] However, Adam's moment of confident self-identification through the other replaces a less reassuring mirror-scene narrated by Eve in which she explains that when she first woke to life she, like Narcissus, fell in love with her own image reflected in the nearby lake. When Adam presents himself to view, she is unimpressed by his less attractive appearance, preferring her own reflection, and he has to entreat her to stay. Though Adam finally secures Eve to be his 'other half', we are aware of how easily he might have lost her. Indeed both Shelley and Rossetti after him are aware that the female other may refuse her allotted role; that she might throw the male into confusion by her non-compliance. Rossetti's short poem 'The Mirror',[26] in which the male speaker realises that he has been mistaken in his momentary belief that he has found his epipsyche, is reminiscent of Shelley's sonnet 'To——':'Yet look at me – take not thine eyes away', in which the male speaker reveals his dependence on the woman's answering gaze and his anxiety that she may neglect him.[27]

However, woman's possible non-compliance is also accompanied by another threat. Woman, after all, is not a perfect reflection of man and her strange and troubling difference means that she always carries an element of threatened danger. If the male adult hallucinates woman as a self-affirming other, her image always carries an undertow of danger – castration, which 'the [male] look continually circles around but disavows'.[28] Disavowal may mean turning the woman into a fetish, building up her physical beauty into something reassuring rather than dangerous; however there is always the possibility that this beauty can turn dangerous, as in the fatal woman or where it begins to trouble the male gazer by becoming sublime. The mutilation Miller describes is thus not just the threat of the wayward woman whose non-returning look throws the male speaker into disarray, but the threat of castration imperfectly masked by beauty.

In his treatise *De Pictura* of 1435, Leon Battista Alberti writes of painting as a mirroring pool:

> Consequently I used to tell my friends that the inventor of painting, according to the poets, was Narcissus, who had turned into a flower; for, as painting is the flower of all the arts so the tale of Narcissus fits our purpose perfectly. What is painting but the act of embracing by means of art the surface of the pool?[29]

Shelley in *A Defence of Poetry* sees poetry as 'a mirror which makes beautiful that which is distorted', meaning, I think, not that distortion is corrected or erased by beauty but that distortion is itself made beautiful yet maintains its identity within beauty. When Shelley also asks why the reflection in the canal is more beautiful than the objects it reflects, he uses the idea of a reflection in water to suggest that the non-mimetic and idealizing mirroring carried out by art is itself a form of distortion.[30]

The mirror of art in Rossetti has a double function. It confirms and consolidates the poet-artist's representation of himself through an idealized representation but it also hints at the loss and sacrifice involved in that transformation. The mirror of art is simultaneously a scene of gratification and a scene of loss. The loss becomes conspicuous in a poem like 'Aspecta Medusa', in which the severed Medusa head, Freudian image of castration *par excellence*, is defensively mediated and effectively censored, although its shadow or reflection remains an indelible presence in the artist's life.[31] This poem is akin to a succession of key poems or poetic moments in the English literary tradition wherein a male observer comes face to face with a female figure or feminized object which represents the source of his imaginative inspiration and is either held hypnotized or, outfaced, is compelled to turn away. One thinks of Milton's visionary meeting with his dead wife, Shelley's gazer in his own Medusa poem, Keats's dreamer viewing Moneta or Tennyson's Lancelot on the verge of viewing the Grail. 'Aspecta Medusa' puts Rossetti among those who don't want to or can't look, bringing to mind Lacan's adage in the *Écrits*: 'Such is the fright that seizes man when he unveils the face of his power that he turns away from it even in the very act of laying its features bare'.[32]

Written after 'Aspecta Medusa', 'Willowwood',[33] the poem which marks Rossetti's new espousal of poetry, does something different as we shift from the mythic moment of Perseus to that of Narcissus. The mirroring of the water, which in 'Aspecta Medusa' substitutes for Perseus' original defensive shield and tames, stills and distances the Gorgonian reflection, here becomes a malleable screen which allows a repressed image to permeate and an observer momentarily to break the surface. In contrast to 'Aspecta Medusa', the drama of this reflection is acted out in slow motion and the male protagonist in this poem would like this mirror to give up even more than it does.

Considering that grey-eyed ethereal face in sonnet four, one might note for those interested in such things that both Elizabeth Siddal and Jane Morris were described as having grey eyes, but then so too was Rossetti himself; however, the poem evidently goes beyond any biographical context.[34] The many reflections of this poem which speak of the mixed and mixing identities of man, woman and Love remind us also of Rossetti's pledge to Art: 'I loved thee before I loved a woman, Love'. The meeting where the faces of man and woman coincide in the kiss and necessarily in a reflection also evokes Rossetti's dictum that 'Picture and poem bear the same relation to each other as beauty does in man and woman: the point of meeting where the two are most identical is the supreme perfection',[35] a statement significant in a poem which at a submerged level signals a transfer from painting to poetry. And here, to recast Alberti, it is visionary poetry rather than painting which acts out the artist's attempt to embrace the surface of the pool.

Rossetti's artfully narcissistic poem also contains another mythic reference which nonetheless underlines his desire for the reflecting beloved. His pursuit of the image of the unattainable beloved woman echoes Orpheus' attempt to see his dead wife Eurydice and, more specifically, Milton's implicit treatment of this myth in his sonnet to his 'late espoused saint'; a sonnet which influenced bereavement poems by Tennyson, Browning and Hardy.[36] Milton's poignant description of the beloved woman, who moves to embrace him but then flees as he wakes, evidently influences Rossetti's account of the woman who sinks back into the water after the shared kiss. Milton's sonnet in which he wakes to be reminded of his loss of sight ('day brought back my night') demonstrates how deprivation in the form of both bereavement and blindness generates the temporary compensation of imaginative vision. Milton's veiled woman represents the source of his visionary power; a power of which he is not totally in control and which might either elude or over-whelm him. As I hinted earlier when I mentioned this sonnet in relation to 'Aspecta Medusa', one can read the poet's waking as his incapacity to meet the full proximity and unveiled gaze of the visionary woman. Yet, as I have also remarked, the speaker in 'Willowwood' does not want to turn away.

According to William Allingham, Rossetti disliked Milton's poetry, and William Michael Rossetti suggests that Milton was 'comparatively neglected' by his brother along with various other poets such as Chaucer, Spenser, Dryden, Pope and Wordsworth. However, he adds, 'It should not be sup-posed that he read them not at all, or cared not for any of them'; and Rossetti certainly appears to have been familiar with Milton's poetry – an unsurprising detail considering his maternal grandfather Gaetano Polidori loved Milton and had translated his works into Italian.[37] In later life Rossetti revealed his admiration for Milton's sonnets which he discussed in letters with Hall Caine.[38] He also knew Shelley's beautiful recasting of Milton's sonnet in the deeply narcissistic *Alastor*, where the protagonist, the young poet, meets his epipsyche, a veiled visionary maid who vanishes as he tries to embrace her.[39] What is interesting about Rossetti's treatment of the encounter in 'Willow-wood' is that he, unlike Milton and Shelley, contrives to hold onto the last ves-tiges of the departing vision:

So when the song died did the kiss unclose;
   And her face fell back drowned, and was as grey
    As its grey eyes; and if it ever may
Meet mine again I know not if Love knows.

Only I know that I leaned low and drank
A long draught from the water where she sank,
   Her breath and all her tears and all her soul:
And as I leaned, I know I felt Love's face
Pressed on my neck with moan of pity and grace,
   Till both our heads were in his aureole.[40]

The speaker attempts to prolong his encounter: firstly through the kiss, and secondly through imbibing the remaining traces of his vision. As he drinks 'from the water where she sank', Love, standing behind him, presses down upon his neck 'Till both our heads were in his aureole.' The heads could be those of the speaker and Love (the speaker's reflected face occludes Love's reflected face, occupying the space encircled by Love's halo) or those of the speaker and his lost beloved (his reflected face is superimposed on the sub-merged and vanishing face of the woman who, in any case, is his female mirror-image; both are encircled by Love's reflected halo). These mingled images speak of narcissistic co-identities; temporarily suspended in a freeze-frame cameo, they represent a final attempt to stay the vision in the form of a memorial to enduring love. Yet there is something sinister about the way Love seems to push the speaker further down towards the water, suggesting his suicidal desire to follow the beloved into the Underworld of the pool and unite with her in death.

However, there are other, more restitutive, ways of reading this encounter and the wish to prolong it. The kiss in 'Willowwood' is important. As the psychotherapist Adam Phillips points out, 'of all self-comforting or autoerotic activities the most ludicrous, the most obviously unsatisfying and therefore infrequent, is kissing oneself'. Phillips reviews Freud's remarks on kissing in the *Three Essays on Sexuality*, which suggest that the infant replaces the original sensual pleasure of breast feeding with thumb-sucking and other substitutes:

> the child may stroke or suck himself, or kiss other people and things, but he will not kiss himself. Eventually, […] he will kiss other people on the mouth because he is unable to kiss himself there[…]. Because the mouth, unlike the body parts it sucks, is acutely alive to its own pleasure, it there-fore seeks, Freud seems to be suggesting, by that same narcissistic logic, its curious reunion through another person's lips'.[41]

'Finally', writes Phillips, 'Freud offers the intriguing, grotesque – almost unthinkable image of a person kissing his own mouth, and suggests that it is a narcissistic blow that he is unable to do so.' Kissing then for Freud is always something of a disappointment: an 'intensely evocative pleasure' which is also a 'disillusionment'.[42] Kissing is a form of loss and partial compensation like imaginative vision which compensates for blindness, castration and loss. It evokes something evanescent, out of reach, on the verge of disappearing – a ghostly double which itself is the shadowy substitute for a primary source of love and sustenance. But what then does Rossetti achieve in this uncanny poem? 'The 'corresponding part' of another person's body: the mouth' is also, as Phillips observes, the only part of oneself that one can 'kiss in the mirror', and the kiss, which ingeniously provides the only way for Rossetti's male pro-tagonist and his reflecting beloved to make a symbolic amatory connection, also allows him the pleasure of kissing his own mouth.[43]

In fact the 'unthinkable image of a person kissing his own mouth' had already been fantasized by Rossetti in his poem 'A Last Confession', in which the young girl has 'a mouth/Made to bring death to life, – the underlip/Sucked in, as if it strove to kiss itself',[44] and the kiss in 'Willowwood' could be seen as a softened version of the same thing: Narcissus kissing his own mouth in the mirroring pool.[45] And yet the mourned-for or unattainable woman with whom the speaker is briefly reunited in the kiss is, like Milton's 'late espoused saint', also the figure who is the source of his imaginative energy and his poetic identity, and, as she disappears, he literally drinks in and inspires himself with the traces of her presence: 'Her breath and all her tears and all her soul.' Such an act extends the aim of kissing by reminding us what the kiss originally replaces: 'There is something within us which from the instant that we live and move thirsts after its likeness,' writes Shelley in his essay 'On Love', adding that 'It is probably in correspondence with this law that the infant drains milk from the bosom of its mother'.[46] Unlike Milton, Rossetti's speaker pursues his visionary woman and tries to incorporate something of her essence. In this final sonnet he thus manages to kiss the elusive shade of his own mouth, fulfilling a complex fantasy in which he momentarily recovers his beloved, his creative origins and his earliest love. The broken kiss and the draught that follows it, although they mark an unavoidable deficiency and falling short, also recuperate something of the child's nutritive bond with the mother, making the kiss for Rossetti another one of those symbols which speak of an inextricable loss and compensation, mediated by a femininity which saves as well as kills.

Notes

1 Camille Paglia, *Sexual Personae: Art and Decadence from Nefertiti to Emily Dickinson* (Harmondsworth: Penguin, 1991), p. 494.

2 Barbara Charlesworth Gelpi, 'The Feminization of Dante Gabriel Rossetti', in *The Victorian Experience: The Poets*, ed. Richard A Levene (Athens, Ohio: Ohio University Press, 1982), pp. 94–114. See also David Riede, *Dante Gabriel Rossetti and the Limits of Victorian Vision* (Ithaca: Cornell University Press, 1983); Griselda Pollock, 'Woman as Sign: Psychoanalytic Readings', in *Vision and Difference: Femininity, Feminism and the Histories of Art* (London and New York: Routledge, 1988), pp. 120–219; J Hillis Miller, 'The Mirror's Secret', *Victorian Poetry*, 29:4 (1991), pp. 333–61; Martin Danahay, 'Mirrors of Masculine Desire', *Victorian Poetry*, 32:1 (1994), pp. 35–53; and JB Bullen, 'Dante Gabriel Rossetti and the Mirror of Masculine Desire', *Nineteenth-Century Contexts*, 21 (1999), pp. 329–52 (previously published as pp. 123–48 of Bullen's *The Pre-Raphaelite Body: Fear and Desire in Painting, Poetry and Criticism* (Oxford: Clarendon Press, 1998)).

3 *The Works of Dante Gabriel Rossetti*, ed. William Michael Rossetti (London: Ellis, 1911), p. 553. All subsequent references to this edition appear in the text as *Works*.

4 FWH Myers, 'Rossetti and the Religion of Beauty', *Essays Modern* (London: Macmillan and Co., 1908), p. 319; Harry Quilter, *Contemporary Review*, 43 (February 1883), p. 198.

5 Gelpi, 'The Feminization of Dante Gabriel Rossetti', pp. 96, 104.

6 Catherine Maxwell, *The Female Sublime from Milton to Swinburne: Bearing Blindness* (Manchester: Manchester and London, 2001).

7 Maxwell, *The Female Sublime*, p. 1, quoting from Angela Leighton, *Shelley and the Sublime: An Interpretation of the Major Poems* (Cambridge: Cambridge University Press, 1984), p. 18.

8 Max Beerbohm, *Rossetti and his Circle* (New Haven and London: Yale University Press, 1987), p. 48; and *Beerbohm: Literary Caricatures from Homer to Huxley*, selected by JG Riewald (London: Allen Lane, 1977), p. 66.

9 See Jan Marsh, *Dante Gabriel Rossetti: Painter and Poet* (London: Weidenfeld & Nicolson, 1999), p. 313, and *The Athenaeum* (11 November 1865), p. 658. See also Letters 723, 724 (20 and 25 July 1867) to Mrs Gabriele Rossetti and Ford Madox Ford, and Letters 756 (12 Nov 1867), 764 (3 January 1868), 765 (7 January 1868), Letter 766 (9 January 1868) to C Matthews in *The Letters of Dante Gabriel Rossetti*, eds Oswald Doughty and John Robert Wahl, 4 vols (Oxford: Clarendon Press, 1965–7), Volume 2: *1861–1870*, pp. 623, 624, 642–3, 647–9, 649–51, 651. Recent evidence dates the composition of the poem-inscription to October 1865. See the note on the composition of the poem in the Rossetti hypertext archive (http://jefferson.village.virginia.edu:2020/archive. html). This corroborates the date given by William Michael Rossetti, who placed the poem-inscription among the first pieces of verse Dante Gabriel Rossetti attempted after the death of his wife Elizabeth Siddal in 1862. See *Dante Gabriel Rossetti: Classified List of his Writings with the Dates*, comp. WM Rossetti (Privately printed, 1906), p. 41.

10 See William Michael Rossetti's diary for Monday 18 May 1868, in *Rossetti Papers 1862 to 1870*, compiled by William Michael Rossetti (London: Sands & Co., 1903), p. 308.

11 *Works*, p. 209.

12 William Sharp reports Gabriele practically blind in 1847 when Rossetti painted his portrait (according to Sharp, Rossetti's earliest production). See Sharp's *Dante Gabriel Rossetti: A Record and a Study* (London: Macmillan, 1882), p. 125. Gabriele finally resigned his professorship in this year. See Jan Marsh, *Christina Rossetti: A Literary Biography* (London: Jonathan Cape, 1994), p. 78. For Dante Gabriel Rossetti's concern about his sight, see William Michael Rossetti's diary entries throughout 1867–8 in *Rossetti Papers 1862 to 1870* and *Dante Gabriel Rossetti: His Family-Letters with a Memoir by William Michael Rossetti*, 2 vols (London: Ellis & Elvey, 1895), 1, pp. 264–70.

13 Henry Campbell, *Dante Gabriel Rossetti: Three Papers Read to the Rossetti Society of Birchington* (Birchington: Beresford Books, 1993), p. 19.

14 *Works*, p. 619.

15 William Michael Rossetti, diary entry for Friday 18 December 1868, in *Rossetti Papers 1862 to 1870*, p. 339.

16 Marsh, *Dante Gabriel Rossetti*, pp. 331, 333, 342, 351.

17 *Works*, p. 240.

18 Griselda Pollock, p. 132; LS Lowry, quoted in the Exhibition Catalogue *A Pre-Raphaelite Passion: The Private Collection of L. S. Lowry*, Manchester City Art Gallery, 1st April–31st May, 1977, p. 3.

19 William Gaunt, *The Pre-Raphaelite Tragedy* (London: Sphere, 1975), p. 96; Dante Gabriel Rossetti, Letter 620 (30 July 1865) in *The Letters of Dante Gabriel Rossetti*, 2, 562.

20 Paglia, *Sexual Personae*, p. 28.

21 The characterization is of Lilith in 'Body's Beauty', Sonnet 78 in *The House of Life* (*Works*, p. 100).

22 J Hillis Miller, 'The Mirror's Secret', *Victorian Poetry*, 29:4 (1991), p. 334; Martin Danahay, 'Mirrors of Masculine Desire', *Victorian Poetry*, 32:1 (1994), p. 41.

23 For Shelley's influence on Rossetti, see also Riede, *Dante Gabriel Rossetti and the Limits of Victorian Vision* (1983), pp. 122–37.

24 *Paradise Lost*, Bk 8, ll. 494–6.

25 *John Milton: Paradise Lost*, ed. Alastair Fowler (London: Longman, 1971), p. 422.

26 *Works*, p. 194.

27 *Shelley: Poetical Works*, ed. Thomas Hutchinson, rev. GM Matthews (Oxford and New York: Oxford University Press, 1970), p. 523.

28 Laura Mulvey, 'Visual Pleasure and Narrative Cinema', in *The Sexual Subject: A Screen Reader in Sexuality* (London and New York: Routledge, 1992), p. 29.

29 Leon Battista Alberti, *On Painting and on Sculpture: The Latin texts of De Pictura and De Statua*, ed. and tr. Cecil Grayson (London and New York: Phaidon, 1972), pp. 61, 62.

30 Shelley, *A Defence of Poetry*, in *Shelley's Poetry and Prose*, eds Donald H Reiman and Sharon B Powers (New York and London: Norton, 1977), p. 505; 'Three Fragments on Beauty' (Fragment 1), in *Shelley's Prose*, ed. David Lee Clark (London: Fourth Estate, 1988), p. 337.

31 Sigmund Freud, 'Medusa's Head' (1922), in *Collected Papers*, tr. A and J Strachey, 5 vols (London and New York: Hogarth Press and the Institute of Psycho-analysis, 1924–50), pp. 5, 105–6.

32 Jacques Lacan, *Écrits: A Selection*, tr. Alan Sheridan (London: Tavistock Publications, 1980), p. 34.

33 *Works*, p. 91–2.

34 For Siddal's grey eyes, see Walter Deverell's remarks cited by William Holman Hunt, *Pre-Raphaelitism and the Pre-Raphaelite Brotherhood*, 2 vols (London: Macmilllan & Co., Ltd, 1905), 1, p. 198; for Jane Morris's, see her obituary in *The Times* (28 January 1914), p. 9; for Dante Gabriel Rossetti's, see the remarks of Hunt, Hardinge and Caine in Marsh, *Dante Gabriel Rossetti*, pp. 40, 506, 514.

35 *Works*, p. 606.

36 'Sonnet XIX', in *Milton: Complete Shorter Poems*, ed. John Carey (London: Longman, 1971), pp. 413–14. Milton's sonnet explicitly refers to the myth of Admetus and Alcestis, but its denouement is clearly inspired by the Orphic myth. See my remarks on the sonnet in *The Female Sublime*, pp. 57–61, 65–6. See also Tennyson's *In Memoriam*, Canto 13, Browning's 'Eurydice to Orpheus' and Hardy's 'The Shadow on the Stone'. *In Memoriam* commemorates Arthur Henry Hallam while the other two poems were written after the deaths of the poets' wives: Elizabeth Barrett Browning and Emma Hardy (née Gifford).

37 *William Allingham: A Diary*, eds H Allingham and D Radford, intr. John Julius Norwich (Harmondsworth: Penguin, 1985), p. 162. William Michael Rossetti, Preface to *Works*, p. xvi. See also Kathleen Vejvoda, 'The Fruit of Charity: *Comus* and Christina Rossetti's *Goblin Market*', *Victorian Poetry*, 38:4 (2000), p. 558.

38 See *Dear Mr Rossetti: The Letters of Dante Gabriel Rossetti and Hall Caine 1878–1881*, ed. Vivien Allen (Sheffield: Sheffield Academic Press, 2000), pp. 52, 69–70, where Rossetti defends various of Milton's sonnets against Caine's criticisms.

39 'Alastor' (ll. 149–91), in *Shelley's Poetry and Prose*, pp. 74–5.

40 *Works*, p. 92.

41 Adam Phillips, Ch. 9: 'Plotting for Kisses', in *On Kissing, Tickling and Being Bored: Psychoanalytic Essays on the Unexamined Life* (London and Boston: Faber, 1993), pp. 100, 106, 101, 105.

42 Phillips, p. 106.

43 Phillips, p. 106.

44 *Works*, p. 48.

45 Jan Marsh suggests that the portrait of the young woman in 'A Last Confession' (including the detail of the lips) was inspired by Lizzie Siddal (*Dante Gabriel Rossetti*, pp.

88, 377). Other elements of 'A Last Confession' anticipate 'Willowwood' such as 'Her face was pearly pale, as when one stoops/Over wan water' (*Works*, p. 48) and the 'pool that once gave back/Your image, but now drowns it and is clear/Again' (*Works*, p. 52).

46 Shelley, 'On Love', *Shelley's Poetry and Prose*, p. 473.

15

PURSUING THE WELL-BELOVED: THOMAS HARDY, JOCELYN PEARSTON AND THE SCHOOL OF ROSSETTI

John Holmes

Writing in 1886 on 'The Sonnet: Its Characteristics and History', William Sharp declared of Dante Gabriel Rossetti:

> no critic of his work will have any true grasp of it who does not recognise that "Rossetti" signifies something of far greater import even than the fascinating work of, personally, the most dominant and fascinating man of his time—even as the historian of the brilliant period in question will work in the dark if he is unable to perceive one of the chief well-springs of the flood, if he does not recognise the relationship between certain radical characteristics of the time and the man who did so much to inaugurate or embody them.[1]

One of Rossetti's last friends and first biographers, Sharp is markedly partial. His hyperbole is not, however, entirely unjustified. Throughout his career Dante Gabriel was the willing centre and driving force of a succession of literary and artistic movements. In 1848, at the age of twenty, and together with William Holman Hunt and John Everett Millais, he founded the Pre-Raphaelite Brotherhood, soon drawing older painters and writers such as Ford Madox Brown, John Ruskin, William Bell Scott and Coventry Patmore into its orbit, and inspiring it to find a literary voice through the periodical *The Germ*. In the late 1850s and early 1860s he gathered around him a second generation of poets, notably William Morris, George Meredith and Algernon Charles Swinburne, and painters, including Edward Burne-Jones, Frederick Sandys and Simeon Solomon. When Dante Gabriel's *Poems* were finally published in 1870, even Meredith, who had not seen him for some years, wrote to him 'You are our Master, of all of us'.[2] Rossetti's cultural significance in these terms is widely acknowledged, as is his role as an inspiration to Pater, Wilde and the aesthetic movement. What is generally forgotten is the extent to which he continued to set the agenda for avant-garde poetry into the 1870s and 1880s.

As Dante Gabriel himself withdrew into seclusion and decline, a number of younger writers who were beginning to make their mark on the English literary scene were again taking their lead directly and often publicly from him. In 1880 the critic James Ashcroft Noble wrote, with reference to two of them:

> Mr. Philip Bourke Marston and Mr. John Payne have done some very exquisite sonnet-work; but their peculiar quality is to a large extent derivative. Their master is one who has many more followers than he perhaps cares to acknowledge—a poet of fine and subtle genius, and undoubtedly the greatest of living sonneteers—Mr. Dante Gabriel Rossetti.[3]

In spite of his rhetorical drum-roll, Noble's point about Dante Gabriel's followers remains well-observed. At the beginning of the 1870s, Marston, Payne and Arthur O'Shaughnessy were each publishing volumes of Pre-Raphaelite poetry. By the end of the decade the rising poet-critics Theodore Watts, Hall Caine and William Sharp had gathered themselves around Rossetti, each of them soon to contribute to building up the near-mythic status that 'Rossetti' would attain in the years following his death. In the interim, the primary form through which this third school of Rossetti – following on from the true Pre-Raphaelites, and the painters and poets of the 1850s and 1860s – sought to express itself was the sonnet, and in particular the sonnet sequence.

The first of these sequences to be published after Dante Gabriel's own 'Sonnets and Songs, towards a Work to be called *The House of Life*' was the title poem of Marston's first volume, *Song-Tide*, in 1871. This adolescent account of a love affair was followed in 1873 by Edmund Gosse's equally adolescent but more conspicuously incompetent sequence 'Fortunate Love', included in his volume *On Viol and Flute*. The same year a friend of Gosse's called Theophilus Marzials, who had made Rossetti's acquaintance and admired him, presented him with a copy of his new book *The Gallery of Pigeons and Other Poems*. This too contains a sonnet sequence, the darkly erotic 'Love's Masquerades', which transforms Rossetti's world of passion and personification into a series of sardonic vignettes anticipating the Rococo manner of Aubrey Beardsley's illustrative art. In 1875, as Marston brought out his second sequence, *All in All*, a number of shorter sequences appeared in the collection *Poems*, by the veteran poet and painter William Bell Scott, who was later to describe Rossetti as 'my dearest and, I may say, most attached friend, my admiration in poetry'.[4] *All in All* and *Poems* were followed in 1876 by *Annus Amoris*, yet another sonnet sequence by yet another member of Rossetti's circle, a painter of delicate Ruskinian landscapes called John William Inchbold. Inchbold was a friend of Swinburne's, and after an early hostility between him and Rossetti – 'I hate Inchbold' wrote Rossetti to Ford Madox Brown in 1856, 'Inchbold is less a bore than a curse' a few years later – Rossetti mellowed towards his friend's friend to the extent that by 1869 he was asking his brother William to join him in contributing to a subscription to help him find his feet financially.[5] Inchbold's book, published like Gosse's and Marzials's by Henry King, owes more to Wordsworth than the other sequences discussed above, yet remains characterized by a Rossettian style and a stress on the centrality of love.

Like their 'master', these five poets all employ the form of the sonnet sequence to explore love and death. From Rossetti they draw the form itself; his cast of vivid personifications, particularly the winged Love, who is reduced to the indignity of playing the organ at a wedding in the last sonnet of Gosse's sequence; a language heavy with archaisms and allegory; a preoccupation with mortality; and above all a technique for fusing the expression of sexual love with religious devotion.[6] Each of these sonneteers reproduces this legacy, following Rossetti's example without much extending his scope, and producing poems which, with the sole exception of Marzials's 'Love's Masquerades', and in stark contrast with those of earlier followers such as Swinburne, Morris and Meredith, have little originality or individuality. By the mid-1870s, however, this new Rossettian mode was being adopted and developed by writers who were less directly associated with Dante Gabriel himself. Wilfrid Scawen Blunt in his *Sonnets and Songs by Proteus* of 1875, mutating into *The Love Sonnets of Proteus* from 1881 onwards, Robert Bridges in successive versions of and contributions to *The Growth of Love*, first published in 1876, and John Addington Symonds in four volumes of original verse published at two-year intervals from 1878, all produced independent and considerable but nonetheless recognizable variations on the same theme. As the reputations of these writers and their works grew, so too did Rossetti's own. His death in 1882 removed the major obstacle to publicizing both the man and his work. As his new volume of poetry *Ballads and Sonnets* – including the finished *House of Life* – was going into its fourth edition, so retrospective exhibitions of his long-hidden but much talked-about paintings were held at the Royal Academy and the Burlington Fine Arts Club. Books of recollections by Sharp and Caine inaugurated what was to become an industry of biography surrounding Rossetti, an industry which was still in full steam ten years later, as William Bell Scott and Thomas Gordon Hake, both old friends of Rossetti, published auto-biographies trading on the public's interest not in themselves but in their friend.

It was at this time and in this context that Thomas Hardy's novel *The Pursuit of the Well-Beloved* was serialized in the *Illustrated London News*. Since the late 1970s, critics have been uncovering significant links between Hardy and Rossetti. LM Findlay, Joan Rees and Pauline Fletcher have traced Dante Gabriel's presence as a source or a model in the novels *Desperate Remedies*, *Tess of the d'Urbervilles* and *Jude the Obscure*, in numerous poems and in the short story 'An Imaginative Woman'. More recently, Paul Turner has added *The Return of the Native*, *Two on a Tower* and 'The Withered Arm' to this list.[7] Even allowing that some of these connections are less convincing than others, they combine to give an impression of a Hardy who knew his Rossetti and engaged creatively with him. This in turn supports Michael Ryan's suggestion, in his valuable essay 'One Name of Many Shapes: *The Well-Beloved*', that Rossetti is one of the aestheticists who together form the object of Hardy's satire in this late novel. According to Ryan, Hardy's primary targets are Walter Pater and Oscar Wilde. At the same time, he asserts that if the hero of Hardy's novel, Jocelyn Pierston, spelt Pearston in the original text of 1892, is 'a composite aesthete, then surely Rossetti is one of his components'.[8] On the face of it, Ryan's pointing the finger at Pater and Wilde, calling in Rossetti more as an accomplice than as an equal partner, appears entirely proportionate. Pater and Wilde were alive in 1892, when Hardy's novel was published, which Rossetti was not. Hardy had himself met them both, and they had both recently published novels concerned with aesthetic experience and the artistic temper – *Marius the Epicurean* and *The Picture of Dorian Gray*, in 1885 and 1890 respectively – whilst Rossetti had worked exclusively in other media.[9] On inspection, the case for choosing Pater and Wilde over Rossetti is little more than circumstantial. An alternative, more clearly documented case could be made to the opposite effect. In a letter of 1897 to Edmund Gosse, Hardy observed that 'the tale was sketched many years ago, when I was virtually a young man', and aspects of it are indeed prefigured in notes dated March 1884 and February 1889.[10] *The Pursuit of the Well-Beloved* is therefore as much a novel of the 1880s as it is of the 1890s when it was published, and during these years, the years of the novel's gestation, Dante Gabriel Rossetti was a markedly more prominent cultural presence than Wilde or even Pater. Indeed both Pater and Wilde contributed to the paean in praise and celebration of Rossetti which lasted for ten years and more after his death and was only beginning to show signs of discord by the time Hardy's novel was published.[11] Read in this context, and recalling the sonneteers and critics who extended Rossetti's influence and reputation, it seems, again circumstantially, that

Rossetti and his following would be the more, rather than the less, pertinent targets for Hardy's satire.

To pursue this line of argument further, it is worth briefly diverting from it to consider Hardy's short story 'An Imaginative Woman', first published in 1894 and linked by Rees to Rossetti and by Ryan to *The Well-Beloved*. Rees has convincingly identified Rossetti as a source for Robert Trewe, the poet who is the subject of fascination of the story's eponymous heroine. As Rees points out, both poets attempt suicide after a review damning their poetry as 'too erotic and passionate'; Rossetti's sonnet 'Stillborn Love' is quoted directly by Hardy in his story; and Trewe's 'mournful ballad on 'Severed Lives" is clearly Rossettian in its title and, as Pauline Fletcher has noted, in its form. But while Trewe is in part a reconstitution of elements of Rossetti – and indeed, as both Rees and Fletcher suggest, of Hardy himself – he is also a separate individual inhabiting a seemingly real world. As such, he takes his place alongside other, less fictional, contemporaries. Hardy outlines that place as follows:

> Trewe's verse contrasted with that of the rank and file of recent minor poets in being impassioned rather than ingenious, luxuriant rather than finished. Neither *symboliste* nor *décadent*, he was a pessimist in so far as that character applies to a man who looks at the worst contingencies as well as the best in the human condition. Being little attracted by excellencies of form and rhythm apart from content, he sometimes, when feeling out-ran his artistic speed, perpetrated sonnets in the loosely rhymed Elizabethan fashion, which every right-minded reviewer said he ought not to have done.[12]

Trewe is set apart by Hardy from the 'rank and file of recent minor poets', who are cast as symbolists and decadents, meticulous craftsmen elevating form above content and preferring ingenuity over enthusiasm. This is recognizable as a description of 'nineties poetry. But as Trewe himself dies more than two years before the last event in a story dated 1893, and as he has been writing and publishing for some time, he is clearly a member of a slightly earlier generation. This point is supported by a note by Hardy dated December 1893, in which he records that he 'Found and touched up a short story called "An Imaginative Woman"', implying that the story, like *The Pursuit of the Well-Beloved*, was first imagined some time before it saw publication.[13]

Trewe is marked out as a Rossettian not only through chronology but also through the imagined characteristics of his poetry itself. Eroticism, passion and luxuriance are all characteristic of the poetry of this school, from Rossetti himself onwards, as are Trewe's chosen forms, the ballad and the sonnet. His pessimism is akin to Rossetti's own, which was echoed by Payne and Marston among others, while his disregard for form, particularly in writing 'Elizabethan' sonnets, recalls not Rossetti himself but followers such as Inchbold and above all Blunt. Most significantly, he participates in the idealization of female beauty and love that is central to Rossettian poetry in the 1870s and 1880s, and that contrasts markedly with the homoeroticism of *The Picture of Dorian Gray* and the curious sexlessness of *Marius the Epicurean*. In the second version of his sonnet sequence *The Growth of Love*, privately printed in 1889, Robert Bridges sarcastically observes that:

> There's many a would-be poet at this hour,
> Rhymes of a love and truth he never woo'd.[14]

One self-confessed case in point would be Arthur O'Shaughnessy, in his sonnet 'Pentelicos':

> When, sometimes, mid these semblances of love,
>   Pursued with feverish joy or mad despair,
>   There flashes suddenly on my unrest
> Some marble shape of Venus, high above
>   All pain or changing, fair above all fair,
>   Still more and more desired, still unpossest.[15]

Another would be Robert Trewe, who declares in his suicide note:

> I have long dreamt of such an unattainable creature, as you know; and she, this undiscoverable, elusive one, inspired my last volume; the imaginary woman alone, for, in spite of what has been said in some quarters, there is no real woman behind the title. She has continued to the last unrevealed, unmet, unwon.[16]

It is this pursuit of 'an unattainable [...] undiscoverable, elusive [...] imaginary woman' that establishes a clear link not only from Trewe to the Rossettians, but also to Jocelyn Pearston and *The Pursuit of the Well-Beloved*.

As with Trewe, there are a number of biographical parallels which link Pearston to Rossetti. All three are the subject of 'spiteful criticism' and attempt suicide, although Pearston, like Rossetti, is unsuccessful in his attempt. Pearston is a both a poet – at least, he is the author of 'some attempts at lyric verse' – and a visual artist. For all that he is a sculptor rather than a painter, his characteristic traits as an artist are clearly reminiscent of Rossetti and his school. His precise attention to detail reflects the Pre-Raphaelite doctrine of truth to nature. As Ryan observes, his 'unconscious habit [...] of tracing likes in unlikes' recalls Rossetti's later portraiture. Then there are Pearston's 'beauty-chases':

> In the streets he would observe a face, or a fraction of a face, which seemed to express to a hair's-breadth in mutable flesh what he was at that moment wishing to express in durable shape. He would dodge and follow the owner like a detective; in omnibus, in cab, in steam-boat, through crowds, into shops, churches, theatres, public-houses, and slums.[17]

In a letter of 1897 to Florence Henniker, Hardy himself claimed that

> the plot of the story was suggested to me by the remark of a sculptor that he had often pursued a beautiful ear, nose, chin, &c, about London in omnibuses & on foot.[18]

Both here and in another letter, written earlier the same year to Gosse and making much the same claim, the sculptor remains anonymous. Nonetheless, Pearston's tendency to find beauty in the passer-by recalls how the Pre-Raphaelite Brotherhood reputedly discovered so many of their 'stunners', capitalizing on chance encounters – Fanny Cornforth met in the street, Lizzie Siddal traced back to her shop, Jane Burden spotted at the theatre – and paying little heed to questions of breeding and education when choosing and falling for their models.

Pearston's 'beauty-chases' reflect not only the artistic pursuits of the Pre-Raphaelite Brotherhood but also a recurrent motif in the sonnets of Rossetti and his later followers. John Payne speaks of seeking after hope in equivalent terms in 'Flitting Hope', while John Addington Symonds's short sequence 'In Absence' records the speaker's failure to bring together 'features caught/ From pictures, travels, and the dreams of night', as 'my careful heart/ Seeks, craving, through the wilderness of change/ The face she longs for':

> I have no power to bind
> These separate recollections, or impart
> Thy soul's life to the shadows of my mind.
> Eyes, lips, and brow, soft cheek, and braided hair,
> I see them all; for one by one they glide
> Into my memory, and vanish there,
> Leaving my seeking soul unsatisfied.[19]

Symonds' quest for an ideal of love, glimpsed in a number of different individuals and centred on details of form but ever unattainable, is foreshadowed in Rossetti's sonnet 'Soul's Beauty':

> This is that Lady Beauty, in whose praise
>   Thy voice and hand shake still,—long known to thee
>   By flying hair and fluttering hem,—the beat
>   Following her daily of thy heart and feet,
>   How passionately and irretrievably,
> In what fond flight, how many ways and days![20]

Incorporated into the text of *The House of Life* in 1881, this sonnet comes to act as a gloss on that sequence's idealizing love affairs. Like Pearston, Rossetti falls in love more than once. In order to understand their own behaviour, and to explain it to others, both shape images and metaphysical ideas into myths. For Rossetti in 'Soul's Beauty' the myth is one of an aesthetic ideal, existing beyond any given individual. For Symonds in his poem 'In Italy' chance encounters with passing strangers become a means by which 'the soul aspires to God above'.[21] For Pearston the quest is altogether more personal:

> To his intrinsic Well-Beloved he had always been faithful; but she had had many embodiments. Each individuality known as Lucy, Jane, Florence, Evangeline, or what-not, had been merely a transient condition of her. He did not recognise this as an excuse or as a defence, but as a fact simply. Essentially she was perhaps of no tangible substance; a spirit, a dream, a frenzy, a conception, an aroma, an epitomised sex, a light of the eye, a parting of the lips. God only knew what she really was; Pearston did not. He knew that he loved the Protean creature wherever he found her, whether with blue eyes, black eyes, or brown; whether presenting herself as tall, fragile, or plump. She was never in two places at once; but hitherto she had never been in one place long. She was indescribable, unless by saying that she was a mood of himself.[22]

Pearston's 'intrinsic Well-Beloved' is specific to him, but its details recall further attempts by the poets of the school of Rossetti to justify sexual disloyalty and promiscuity. Wilfrid Scawen Blunt declares in the Preface to *The Love Sonnets of Proteus*, 'The author of these sonnets, styling himself Proteus, acknowledges thereby a natural mood of change'.[23] Pearston's allusion to the Well-Beloved as 'Protean' calls Blunt's symbolic identity to mind, and even suggests that Blunt, by admitting that he himself is the locus of change, is more frank in his self-analysis than Pearston. Yet the appeal to a 'natural mood of change' elevates Blunt's Protean habit, like Pearston's Well-Beloved, into an established and unchanging 'fact'.

In the sonnet 'Affinities', moved by the death of his fiancée Mary Nesbit, Philip Bourke Marston imagines that his sonnets may yet win him the understanding and love of a woman akin to her:

> Somewhere, I do believe,—though where, who knows?—
>   One like my lady dwells. Should I not see,
>   If I could come upon her suddenly,
> The queenly face and eyes whose depths disclose
> Passionate rest, great thoughts, and the repose
>   Of natures wrought for wise, sweet mastery?
>   Yea, I do feel, though incommunicably,
> That round my life, in this life, hers yet flows,
>
> And she will read these lays, and all her soul
>   Will yearn toward me to comfort and sustain.
>   Others will read to find their truth in vain;
>   She only will entirely understand.
>   O soul twin-born with hers, stretch out thy hand
> And lead the pilgrim till he reach the goal.

Adopting the notion of the 'soul's birth-partner' from Rossetti's sonnet 'The Birth-Bond', Marston applies it not to the bond between the poet and his beloved, as Rossetti does, but rather to characterize a being who is to all intents and purposes identical to his deceased beloved.[24] Marston, unlike Rossetti, Symonds, Blunt and Pearston, is merely hoping for a second love, but he too employs a metaphysical, in effect mythic, construct to legitimize his desires.

The myth that is closest to Pearston's is Rossetti's own. It is most clearly encapsulated in 'The Love-Moon', in which the poetic persona is charged with failing to remember his dead beloved as he moves on to love another. He replies:

> "Nay, pitiful Love, nay, loving Pity! Well
>   Thou knowest that in these twain I have confess'd
> Two very voices of thy summoning bell.
>   Nay, Master, shall not Death make manifest
> In these the culminant changes which approve
> The love-moon that must light my soul to Love?"[25]

Rossetti's speaker remains constant, by his own account, to the constant moon of Love, although he knows it only through its changing surface. Strikingly, Pearston too chooses the moon as his tutelary goddess, 'representing, by her so-called inconstancy, his own idea of a migratory Well-Beloved'. Like Pearston's various 'individualities', each of Rossetti's beloveds becomes a vessel for a higher ideal of love. In *The Pursuit of the Well-Beloved* Pearston's metaphysical ideal undergoes a degree of slippage, as the Well-Beloved merges with the identity of its host in his mind. Over the course of the novel Pearston falls in love with three successive generations of women all called Avice Caro. What begins as the faint possibility 'that the migratory, elusive idealisation he called his Love was going to take up her abode in the body of Avice Caro' ends up as a conviction that not only are the Avices 'essentially the same person' but that each one is the 'present embodiment of Avice'. Thus when Pearston meets 'Avice the Third' she is both 'the thing itself' – the Well-Beloved – and 'the renewed Avice'.[26] A similar ambiguity of identity characterizes Rossetti's beloveds in *The House of Life*. While in 'The Love-Moon', as in 'Soul's Beauty', they seem to be different vessels for the same ideal, there is also the suggestion that they share the same soul. This is clearest in the song 'Sudden Light', included in the 1870 text of Rossetti's sequence:

> You have been mine before,—
> How long ago I may not know:
> But just when at that swallow's soar
> Your neck turned so,
> Some veil did fall,—I knew it all of yore.[27]

Here the speaker addresses both the 'individuality' and the transcendent soul that links her to its earlier manifestation. Read in the context of *The House of Life*, this poem suggests that the speaker sees his dead beloved alive again in the body of her successor.

One writer for whom such a reincarnation, even resurrection, of a dead love is distinctly troubling is Rossetti's sister Christina. In her sonnet-sequence 'Later Life' she echoes many of her brother's images, taking issue with his values and casting him as one who 'hankers after Heaven, but clings to earth'. In one of the last few sonnets of the sequence, she asks:

> For who that feel this burden and this strain,
> This wide vacuity of hope and heart,
> Would bring their cherished well-beloved again [...]?[28]

For Christina Rossetti it is both unkind and unchristian to wish to bring a loved one back to life again, as Gabriel does within his poetry. Like Hardy, the phrase she uses to describe this transcendent beloved is 'well-beloved'. This coincidence – if it is a coincidence – and the context in which it occurs, reinforce the suggestion made by Pauline Fletcher with reference to Hardy's poem 'The Well-Beloved' that 'the title alone could be taken as a reference to Rossetti'.[29]

Both in his stance on religion and morality, and in his frank approach to sex and sexuality within his writing, Hardy is far closer to Dante Gabriel than to Christina Rossetti. Yet he too is sceptical towards metaphysical ideals of earthly love. His satire is not cruel, and he ridicules Pearston rather than savaging him. In part, his derision is a good-humoured and perhaps self-mocking assault on 'an old boy' who still persists in paying court to 'a young girl'. In defining him in the novel's third and final part as 'A Young Man of Fifty-Nine', Hardy aligns himself with both Rossetti, who categorizes his love-sonnets under the heading 'Youth and Change', and Blunt, who declares himself to be 'closing for ever his account with youth' in publishing his.[30] But Pearston is not old throughout, and it is not, for the most part, his practices that Hardy objects to. Sexual openness is not something that offends Hardy, nor is the suggestion, which he makes himself in the poem 'The Well-Beloved', that allegiances in love will change and illusions be lost.[31] What Hardy reacts against in Rossetti and his school, and what he mocks through the figure of Pearston, is their moral and metaphysical pretensions, the myths by which they claim legitimacy for their solipsistic presentations of promiscuity.

When Hardy wrote *The Pursuit of the Well-Beloved* he had recently found himself under attack for the sexual and social immorality of *Tess of the d'Urbervilles*. Rossetti had of course suffered similar critical abuse in his turn, but by the time Hardy was writing these late novels he had been largely rehabilitated as an idealist for whom sensuality was not an end in itself but a conduit towards mystical and metaphysical enlightenment. Even Robert Buchanan, the author of 'The Fleshly School of Poetry', had turned apostate to his own cause, pronouncing Rossetti to be the founder of 'a kind of artistic religion' and vigorously repudiating his earlier criticisms:

> how false a judgement it was, how conventional, and Pharisaic a criticism, which chose to dub as 'fleshly' the works of this most ethereal and dreamy—in many respects this least carnal and most religious—of modern poets.[32]

It is in this climate and through the medium of satire that Hardy reasserts, in Pearston and his clearly Rossettian self-image, the case for reading Rossetti and his followers as motivated by sex for sex's sake. Hardy focuses his critique on three crucial elements in the idealistic myths that Rossetti and his followers construct. The first is the question, raised and dismissed by Pearston, of fickleness:

> he had escaped a good deal of ugly reproach which he might otherwise have incurred from his own judgment, as being the very embodiment of fickleness. It was simply that she who always attracted him, and led him whither she would, as by a silken thread, had not remained the occupant of the same fleshly tabernacle throughout her career so far.

Patricia Ingham observes that the phrase 'fleshly tabernacle' is an allusion to Milton on Christ; it is also clearly an echo of Buchanan's original attack on Rossetti. Whether or not the reader recalls this association, the issue of fickleness is raised again two instalments later by Pearston's friend, the painter Somers, who asserts:

> "You are like other men, only rather worse. Essentially, all men are fickle, like you; but not with such activity, such open-eyed perceptiveness."

Pearston replies:

> "My dear Somers, fickle is not the word. Fickleness means getting weary of a thing while the thing remains the same. But I am faithful to what I fancy each woman to be till I come to close quarters with her. I have ever been faithful to the elusive ideal creature whom I have never been able to get a firm hold of, unless I have done so now. And let me tell you that her flitting from each to each individual has been anything but a pleasure for me."[33]

Pearston is not in the least 'open-eyed' as regards his fickleness. Instead he is blinded to it by his obsession with his own emotional hurt and the myth he constructs to explain it. As with Rossetti and his school, his pursuit of a series of women in questing after his Beloved is justified in his own eyes. Hardy's satirical narrative suggests that such a self-deluding evasion of moral responsibility ought not to blind the reading public to the sculptor's nor the poet's foibles, nor indeed to their own.

The second feature of the Rossettian position targeted by Hardy is the appeal to spiritual or metaphysical myths to mask sensual appetite. Pearston perceives himself as idealistic, yet the metaphysics by which he justifies his inconstancy are unstable and haphazard, and the details by which he recog-

nizes his spiritual ideal are strictly physical. It is the 'sensation' of sexual
attraction that brings on the realization that 'a possible migration of the Well-
Beloved' is taking place. When Pearston himself, by now an old man, identifies his on-going pursuit with the curse of the wandering Jew, the narrator
adds, in a comically crude image of geriatric sexuality, 'or, in the phrase of the
islanders themselves, like a blind ram'. The reader is repeatedly reminded
that beneath Pearston's idealizing lies a simple sexual urge:

> All this time Pearston was thinking of the girl – that is to say, Nature was
> working her plans for producing the next generation under the cloak of a
> dialogue on linen.

What applies to the 'dialogue on linen' applies equally to the myth of the
Well-Beloved. Ultimately the idealist is a seducer, whose seemingly pure
intent is belied by his enthusiasm for 'the local custom' of premarital sex,
much as the supposedly ethereal poetry of Rossetti shows its true 'fleshliness'
in 'Nuptial Sleep'.[34]

In addition to exposing the fraudulence of the purely idealistic view of
Rossetti and his school on moral and metaphysical grounds, Hardy draws his
reader's attention to the social inequalities and hypocrisies which it embodies.
From one perspective Dante Gabriel was a progressive. Like Hardy's, his
writing puts across a number of models of female sexuality which are by no
means all judgemental and implicitly advocates greater sexual freedom for
women, while in his personal life he was noticeably unsnobbish. Yet the
legacy of his sonnets is an idealistic model of love which authorizes sexual
promiscuity on the part of upper- and middle-class men without extending
that liberty to women and the uneducated poor. It is this double standard to
which Hardy draws attention in a chapter entitled 'His Own Soul Confronts
Him'. In a satiric mirroring of Dante Gabriel's famous story 'Hand and Soul',
the artist meets an image of his own ideology in the person of an 'obscure and
almost illiterate girl', Avice the second:

> "I get tired o' my lovers as soon as I get to know them well. What I see in
> one young man for a while soon leaves him and goes into another
> yonder, and I follow, and then what I adore fades out of him and springs
> up somewhere else; and so I follow on, and never fix to one. I have loved
> *fifteen* already! [...] Of course it is really, to *me*, the same one all through,
> only I can't catch him!"

In this passage Hardy confronts Pearston, and the reader, with the realization
that 'this pursuit of the Well-Beloved was, then, of the nature of a knife which

could cut two ways'.[35] In reflecting the ideal back upon the idealist, he exposes both its unremarkableness as a habit of behaviour and its absurdity as an object of admiration. At the same time, he confronts the Victorian gentleman with his own hypocrisy, as the target of his satire expands beyond merely Rossetti and the Rossettians to the wider upper- and middle-class society with whose values their apparent idealism colludes.

Notes

1 *Sonnets of This Century*, ed. by William Sharp (London: Scott, 1886), pp. lxx–lxxi.

2 *The Letters of George Meredith*, ed. by CL Cline, 3 vols (Oxford: Oxford University Press, 1970), I, p. 418.

3 James Ashcroft Noble, 'The Sonnet in England', *Contemporary Review*, 38 (1880), pp. 446–71 (pp. 468–9).

4 *Autobiographical Notes of the Life of William Bell Scott*, ed. by W Minto, 2 vols (London: Osgood, 1892), II, p. 11.

5 *Letters of Dante Gabriel Rossetti*, ed. by Oswald Doughty and John Robert Wahl, 4 vols (Oxford: Clarendon Press, 1965–7), I, p. 285; II, pp. 497, 684.

6 Edmund W Gosse, *On Viol and Flute* (London: King, 1873), p. 38.

7 LM Findlay, 'D. G. Rossetti and *Jude the Obscure*', *Pre-Raphaelite Review*, 2:1 (1978), pp. 1–11; Joan Rees, *The Poetry of Dante Gabriel Rossetti: Modes of Self-Expression* (Cambridge: Cambridge University Press, 1981), pp. 56–7, 68, 73, 172, 197–8; Pauline Fletcher, 'Rossetti, Hardy, and the "hour which might have been"', *Victorian Poetry*, 20:3/4 (1982), pp. 1–13; Paul Turner, *The Life of Thomas Hardy: A Critical Biography* (Oxford: Blackwell, 1998), pp. 61–2, 89, 112.

8 Michael Ryan, 'One Name of Many Shapes: *The Well-Beloved*', in *Critical Approaches to the Fiction of Thomas Hardy*, ed. by Dale Kramer (London: Macmillan, 1979), pp. 172–92 (p. 188).

9 Florence Emily Hardy, *The Life of Thomas Hardy 1840–1928* (London: Macmillan, 1962), pp. 180, 182, 209.

10 *The Collected Letters of Thomas Hardy*, ed. by Richard Little Purdy and Michael Millgate, 7 vols (Oxford: Oxford University Press, 1978–88), II, p. 156; FE Hardy, pp. 164, 217.

11 Walter Pater, *Appreciations with an Essay on Style* (London: Macmillan, 1889), pp. 228–42; *The Uncollected Oscar Wilde*, ed. by John Wyse Jackson (London: Fourth Estate, 1995), pp. 96–9.

12 Rees, pp. 197–8; Ryan, pp. 172–3; Fletcher, pp. 2–3; Thomas Hardy, *Collected Short Stories*, ed. by Desmond Hawkins and FB Pinion (London: Macmillan, 1988), pp. 383, 387, 395–7.

13 FE Hardy, p. 260.

14 Robert Bridges, *The Growth of Love* (Oxford: Daniel, 1889), sonnet 11.

15 Arthur O'Shaughnessy, *Songs of a Worker* (London: Chatto and Windus, 1881), p. 107.

16 *Short Stories*, p. 396.

17 Thomas Hardy, *The Pursuit of the Well-Beloved & The Well-Beloved*, ed. by Patricia Ingham (Harmondsworth: Penguin, 1997), pp. 9, 42–3, 73, 114; Ryan, p. 187.

18 Hardy, *Letters*, II, p. 169.

19 John Payne, *Intaglios: Sonnets* (London: Pickering, 1871), p. 60; John Addington Symonds, *New and Old: A Volume of Verse* (London: Smith Elder, 1880), pp. 125–6.

20 *The Works of Dante Gabriel Rossetti*, ed. by William M Rossetti (London: Ellis, 1911), p. 100.
21 Symonds, p. 173.
22 *Pursuit of the Well-Beloved*, pp. 16–17.
23 Wilfrid Scawen Blunt, *The Love Sonnets of Proteus* (London: Kegan Paul, 1881), p. v.
24 *The Collected Poems of Philip Bourke Marston*, ed. by Louise Chandler Moulton (London: Ward, Lock, Bowden, 1892), pp. xxiv, 160; *Works*, p. 79.
25 *Works*, p. 87.
26 *Pursuit of the Well-Beloved*, pp. 13, 69, 119–20, 122.
27 *Works*, p. 200.
28 Christina Rossetti, *The Complete Poems*, ed. by RW Crump and Betty S Flowers (Harmondsworth: Penguin, 2001), pp. 356–7.
29 Fletcher, p. 10.
30 *Pursuit of the Well-Beloved*, pp. 111, 130; *Works*, p. 74; Blunt, p. v.
31 *The Complete Poems of Thomas Hardy*, ed. by James Gibson (London: Macmillan, 1978), pp. 133–5.
32 Robert Buchanan, *A Look Around Literature* (London: Ward & Downey, 1887), pp. 152, 154.
33 *Pursuit of the Well-Beloved*, pp. 17, 35, 340.
34 *Pursuit of the Well-Beloved*, pp. 18, 26, 73, 120; *Works*, p. 76.
35 *Pursuit of the Well-Beloved*, pp. 81–4.

16

DANTE GABRIEL ROSSETTI'S POETIC DAUGHTERS: *FIN DE SIÈCLE* WOMEN POETS AND THE SONNET

Florence S Boos

'On or about 1910', Virginia Woolf once remarked wryly, 'human character changed'[1] – a whimsical view which seemed at times to have become a kind of received wisdom about 'modernist' literature and its 'postmodern' reception. Temporal distance eventually enabled critics to discern some continuities in this alleged paradigm shift, however – in echoes of Morris's and Swinburne's poetry in the work of Hilda Doolittle, for example, or of Dante Gabriel Rossetti's art and criticism in the work of Yeats.[2] In this essay, I will explore a little-studied relationship between Rossetti's sonnet sequence *The House of Life* and two successive generations of work by British women poets,[3] among them Mathilde Blind, Augusta Webster, Catherine Dawson, Amy Levy, Olive Custance, 'Michael Field' and Rosa Newmarch. Further confirmatory instances might be found in the poetic work of Constance Naden, Edith Nesbit, Mary Coleridge, Annie Matheson, Katherine Tynan, Bessie Craigmyle, Margaret Woods and Rachel Annand Taylor, and I have gathered together a small sample of them in an appendix.

Such Rossettian filiations carry with them certain historical and ideological ironies, which can readily be appreciated by women in my generation, many of whom believed (or hoped) that on or about 1970, the 'situation of women' in Europe and North America changed in comparably deep ways. In *The Poetry of Dante Rossetti* (1976), for example, I commented on a number of sexist aspects of Rossetti's attitudes toward women, and subsequent criticism more or less confirmed this view. By contrast, many of the women poets mentioned in the last paragraph were committed feminists, some were lesbians, one or two were political radicals, and almost all could be described as 'new women'

– rather than exemplars of the 'True Woman' Rossetti invoked in sonnets 56–58 in *The House of Life*. What then did these poets find to respect or emulate in the work of Rossetti, in particular in his sonnets, whose images, patterns and preoccupations reverberated for more than a generation?

In 'Victorian Renascence: The Amatory Sonnet Sequence in the Late Nineteenth Century', Arline Golden notes that eight sonnet sequences appeared in the eighteenth century and thirteen between 1800 and 1830, but more than 147 between 1830 and 1900,[4] among them Elizabeth Barrett Browning's 'Sonnets from the Portuguese' (1850), Christina Rossetti's *Monna Innominata* (1881), and Dante Gabriel Rossetti's *The House of Life* (1881). Many critics and anthologists of the 1880s considered the latter one of the noblest examples of its genre, and Dante Gabriel's personal preferences guided many of his friend Hall Caine's choices in *Sonnets of Three Centuries* (1882), which included five sonnets by Christina Rossetti, eight each by Dante Gabriel Rossetti, Elizabeth Barrett Browning and John Milton, nine by Keats, eleven by Wordsworth and seventeen by Shakespeare.

In 1886 William Sharp prefaced his sumptuously printed anthology *Sonnets of This Century* (which contained twelve sonnets by Rossetti and thirteen by Wordsworth) with two dedicatory poems 'To D. G. R.', and his introduction asserted that Rossetti, 'the greatest master of sonnet-music posterior to the 'starre of poets' [Shakespeare]',[5]

> ... holds a remarkable place in the literary and artistic history of the second Victorian period, and no critic of his work will have any true grasp of it who does not recognise that 'Rossetti' signifies something of far greater import even than the fascinating work of, personally, the most dominant and fascinating man of his time.[6]

> Not a few among the best judges [...] consider [...] [Rossetti] the greatest sonneteer of our language, his sonnets having the fundamental brain-work of Shakespeare's, the beauty of Mrs. Browning's, the dignity and, occasionally, the sunlit transparency of Wordsworth's, with a more startling and impressive vehemence, a greater voluminousness of urgent music.'[7]

Such effusions pose natural critical questions about the attributes that elicited them. Rossetti arranged *The House of Life* in a progression of pointillist meditations which blurred or abstracted from plot or character, and refined individual sonnets' taut contrasts between octave and sestet through an alembic of unusually ornate polysyllabic imagery and Latinate diction. Allegorical figures – 'Life,' 'Love,' 'Death,' 'Passion,' 'Worship,' 'Past Selves' – offered ready-made higher-order representatives for lower-order personal experiences, periodic pointed questions to the reader formed a kind of vatic

counterpoint to the poems' elevated diction, and a composite sense of haunting regret seemed to transcend defining details in a blend of private interiority
and universal self-expression.

Two brief illustrations may represent something of the mannered
chiaroscuro of Rossetti's meditations on time and disembodied evanescent
presences. Consider, for example, the rhetorical question with which he
began 'Lovesight':

> When do I see thee most, beloved one?
>   When in the light the spirits of mine eyes
>   Before thy face, their altar, solemnize
> The worship of that Love through thee made known?
> Or when in the dusk hours, (we two alone),
>   Close-kissed and eloquent of still replies
>   Thy twilight-hidden glimmering visage lies,
> And my soul only sees thy soul its own?
>
> O love, my love! if I no more should see
> Thyself, nor on the earth the shadow of thee,
>   Nor image of thine eyes in any spring, –
> How then should sound upon Life's darkening slope
> The ground-whirl of the perished leaves of Hope,
>   The wind of Death's imperishable wing?

Not only did Rossetti's poem decline to 'answer' in the sestet the octave's
'question' (What if *both* memory *and* presence of the beloved were lost?), it elevated that unanswerability to an emblem of the inscrutable silence of death,
the poem's real underlying subject.

A few *House of Life* sonnets celebrated ostensible forms of sexual fulfilment,
but quickly sublated (or sublimated) them in a kind of dialectical realm east of
thwarted desire and anticipation, and west of resigned guilt and regret. 'The
One Hope,' *The House of Life*'s last sonnet, expresses something of this unstable
poetic equilibration between oscillating states of 'Hope', desire, anxiety and
irredeemable regret:

> When vain desire at last and vain regret
>   Go hand in hand to death, and all is vain,
> What shall assuage the unforgotten pain
> And teach the unforgetful to forget?
> Shall Peace be still a sunk stream long unmet, –
> Or may the soul at once in a green plain
>   Stoop through the spray of some sweet life-fountain
> And cull the dew-drenched flowering amulet?

Ah! when the wan soul in that golden air
  Between the scriptured petals softly blown
Peers breathless for the gift of grace unknown, –
Ah! let none other alien spell soe'er
But only the one Hope's one name be there, –
  Not less nor more, but even that word alone.

Few readers of *The House of Life*'s sonnets have failed to observe their solemn cadences, brocaded visual images, formally allusive and highly generalized diction, suspensive contrasts between octave and sestet, and adumbrations of religious doubt in gravely melancholic disclosures of ineffable despair. I wish to suggest that the women whose poems I will consider felt an affinity with Rossetti's sensuous ambivalence and conflict-ridden states of erotic contemplation, and that his 'feminine' preoccupations with personal grief and transience resonated with forms of loss and disillusionment in the inner lives of 'new women,' who negotiated 'aberrant' friendships, lesbian romances and unreciprocated passions in search of transcendence and inner peace. In support of such assimilations, I will consider the work (in roughly chronological order) of Mathilde Blind, Amy Levy, Catherine A Dawson and Augusta Webster, whose sonnets employed a Rossettian brush on different canvasses in the 1880s and 90s; and of Olive Custance, Rosa Newmarch, Edith Cooper and Katherine Bradley, whose sonnets a decade later evoked Rossetti's sense of numinous allegory, assimilation of different art forms, and preoccupation with liminal identities and passions.

The First Generation

Mathilde Blind (1841–96) wrote 'Rossettian' sonnets whose moral fervour, social conscience and assertive independence emancipated them from their prototypes. The daughter and stepdaughter of radical-democratic exiles, a childhood admirer of Mazzini and long-time friend and associate of Ford Madox Brown, Blind had close ties to William Michael Rossetti and other members of the Pre-Raphaelite circle, and cultivated Romantic and aesthetic sensibilities in the service of anti-clerical and reformist social views. She vigorously attacked Christian religious bigotry in *The Prophecy of Saint Oran and Other Poems* (1881); denounced the 'ethnic cleansing' of western Scotland in *The Heather on Fire: A Tale of the Highland Clearances* (1886); and published an extended poetic meditation on notions of evolution and the pervasiveness of natural and human violence in *The Ascent of Man* (1891).

She devoted the thirty-three sonnets of her *Songs and Sonnets* (1893), however, to more personal subjects of frustrated passion, the search for transcend-

Figure 9. **Mathilde Blind**

ence and the ache of irremediable loss. The very titles of Blind's sonnets suggest themes of *The House of Life* ('Hope,' 'The Dead,' 'Time's Shadow,' 'A Symbol,' 'Suffering,' '*Ananke*' ['Necessity'], 'Despair,' 'The After-Glow,' 'Beauty,' and 'Heart's Ease'), and she arranged them in *House of Life*-like recessions and progressions, from initial stages of remembered hope, through despair, loss and bereavement, to evocations of seasonal rebirth, renewed memory and immersion in wider forms of cosmic consciousness. 'Nirvana,' for example, the sequence's last sonnet, appealed to the reader to 'enter thy soul's vast realm as Sovereign Lord,' and like 'a ripple rounded by the sea,/ In rapture lost be lapped within the All' (compare, for example, the end of 'Astrophel and Stella').

Along similar lines, one might compare Blind's 'Beauty' with Rossetti's 'Portrait'; the bleak landscapes of 'To Memory' with those of Rossetti's 'Winged Hours', 'Ardour and Memory', or 'Barren Spring'; or the shrouded regret of 'Dead Love' with Rossetti's 'Lost on Both Sides':[8]

> Mother of the unfortunate, mystic form,
> Who calm, immutable, like oldest fate,
> Sittest, where through the sombre swinging gate
> Moans immemorial life's encircling storm.
> My heart, sore stricken by grief's leaden arm,
> Lags like a weary pilgrim knocking late,
> And sigheth – toward thee staggering with its weight –
> Behold Love conquered by thy son, the worm!
>
> He stung him mid the roses' purple bloom,
> The Rose of roses, yea, a thing so sweet,
> Haply to stay blind Change's flying feet,
> And stir with pity the unpitying tomb.
> Here, take him, cold, cold, heavy and void of breath!
> Nor me refuse, O Mother almighty, death.[9]

Here, Blind's Rossettian imagery (shrouded form, knocking pilgrim, tomb of dead love) expresses distinctly *un*Rossettian forms of acceptance and resignation, and her evocation of a powerful mother-figure as an emblem of fate is a distinctive alternative to Rosssetti's countless images of obscurely eroticized femininity.

The latter contrast was no accident, for Blind was an ardent feminist, who willed her possessions to Newnham College. She had no children, but one of her other sonnets offered a more hopeful tribute to the literal matrix of human evolution:

> From out the font of being, undefiled,
>   A life hath been upheaved with struggle and pain;
>   Safe in her arms a mother holds again
> That dearest miracle – a new-born child.

To moans of anguish terrible and wild –
    As shrieks the night-wind through an ill-shut pane –
    Pure heaven succeeds; and after fiery strain
Victorious woman smiles serenely mild.

Yea, shall she not rejoice, shall not her frame
    Thrill with a mystic rapture! At this birth,
The soul now kindled by her vital flame
    May it not prove a gift of priceless worth?
Some saviour of his kind whose starry fame
    Shall bring a brightness to the darkened earth.[10]

Blind's secularization of a traditionally religious subject and skilful uses of
astral and generative imagery also suggested Rossettian sacralizations of *eros*
and regeneration, but her central focus in the poem was quite remote from his
erotic preoccupations in *The House of Life*. Compare, for example, her focus on
the pain and triumph of a mother's gift of birth to her child with Rossetti's use
of the image of a child as an emblem of lost love:

Lo! Love, the child once ours; and Song, whose hair
    Blew like a flame and blossomed like a wreath;
And Art, whose eyes were worlds by God found fair;
    These o'er the book of Nature mixed their breath
With neck-twined arms, as oft we watched them there:
    And did these die that thou mightst bear me Death?[11]

Still another well-known Rossettian (and Shelleyan) motif appeared in
Blind's 'To the Obelisk: During the Great Frost, 1881,' an empathetic variation of Rossetti's address to the Assyrian bull, in which Blind expressed her
own idiosyncratic sympathy for the plight of exiled, alienated and displaced
statuary.

Thou sign-post of the Desert! Obelisk,
Once fronting in thy monumental pride
Egypt's fierce sun, that blazing far and wide,
Sheared her of tree and herb, till like a disk
Her waste stretched shawdowless, and fraught with risk
To those who with their beasts of burden hied
Across the seas of sand until they spied
Thy pillar, and their flagging hearts grew brisk:

Now reared beside our Thames so wintry grey,
Where blocks of ice drift with the drifting stream,
Thou risest o'er the alien prospect! Say,
Yon dull, blear, rayless orb whose lurid gleam
Tinges the snow-draped ships and writhing steam,
Is this the sun which fired thine orient day?

Rossetti's poem on a displaced Assyrian divinity had offered a vague but sweeping indictment of the verities of Victorian imperialist culture and its self-interested hegemonic greed. Blind's poem expressed wry but kindly empathy for an emblem of the Egyptian desert, forced to endure the physical and psychological chill of a wintry day by a remote river under an etiolated northern sun.

A similar image of wan crepuscular light appeared in 'The Red Sunsets, 1883', in which Blind exploited the contrasts of the Petrarchan form to refine and deepen Rossetti's fitful attention to oppression and social blight.[12] In Blind's poem, beneath the 'strange Apocalyptic glow/ On the black fringes of the wintry night',

...three factory hands begrimed with soot,
    Aflame with the red splendour, marvelling stand,
And gaze with lifted faces awed and mute.
    Starved of earth's beauty by Man's grudging hand...[13]

Amy Levy (1861–89), the first Jewish student admitted to Newnham College (in 1879), studied there for only two years, and published three novels and three volumes of verse (*Xantippe and Other Verse*, 1881; *A Minor Poet and Other Verse*, 1884; and *A London Plane Tree and Other Verse*, 1889) before she committed suicide at twenty-seven.

Best remembered now for her dramatic monologues 'Xantippe' and 'A Minor Poet,' Levy also experimented with a variety of lyric forms and published four sonnets. Her markedly introspective 'Sonnet' (1881) explicitly invoked Rossetti's initial and concluding personifications in *The House of Life*:

Two terrors fright my soul by night and day:
The first is Life, and with her come the years;
A weary, winding train of maidens they,
With forward-fronting eyes, too sad for tears;
Upon whose kindred faces, blank and grey,
The shadow of a kindred woe appears.
Death is the second terror; who shall say
What form beneath the shrouding mantle nears?

Figure 10. **Amy Levy**

Which way she turn, my soul finds no relief,
My smitten soul may not be comforted;
Alternately she swings from grief to grief,
And, poised between them, sways from dread to dread.
For there she dreads because she knows; and here,
Because she knows not inly faints with fear.[14]

Her final lines might be compared with the concluding tercet of 'Autumn Idleness':[15]

And here the lost hours the lost hours renew
While I still lead my shadow o'er the grass,
Nor know, for longing, that which I should do.

Similar 'waves of passion and of pain' in another early 'Sonnet' could only be assuaged by '... a kind of feeling.../ Which half a hope and half is a despair.'[16]

Levy's friends in her short life included activists and writers Vernon Lee, Olive Schreiner, Ada Radford Wallas and Clementina Black, and Levy also mocked orthodox religion, bourgeois marriage, and sexual double standards in her work. In 'Simphonia Eroica' (dedicated 'To Sylvia'), she also created an original variant of the sensuous descriptions of Rossetti's 'The Choice':[17]

> Then back you lean'd your head, and I could note
> The upward outline of your perfect throat;
> And ever, as the music smote the air,
> Mine eyes from far held fast your body fair.
> And in that wondrous moment seem'd to fade
> My life's great woe, and grow an empty shade
> Which had not been, nor was not.
>   And I knew
> Not which was sound, and which, O Love, was you.

Compare this poem's last lines with the conclusion to the octave of 'Heart's Hope':[18]

> Thy soul I know not from thy body, nor
> Thee from myself, neither our love from God.

Shortly before her death, Levy corrected the proofs of *A London Plane Tree and Other Poems* (1889), which contained a sonnet 'To Vernon Lee.' The octave of this stark evocation of companionship with a more favoured friend evoked the sublime horizons of 'The Choice, III',[19] and its sestet recalled Rossetti's angst-laden 'Woodspurge'.

> A snowy blackthorn flowered beyond my reach;
> You broke a branch and gave it to me there;
> I found for you a scarlet blossom rare.
> Thereby ran on of Art and Life our speech;
> And of the gifts the gods had given to each –
> Hope unto you, and unto me Despair.[20]

Less predictable echoes of Rossetti might be found in the work of Catherine Amy Dawson Scott (1865–1934), a novelist, short-story writer, and poet who was also the founder of PEN. *Sappho* (1889), her first published work, was a two-hundred-page blank verse epic in four books whose eponymous hero founds a woman's college, is immolated by enraged sexist priests and other coryphants, and dies in the sustaining hope that those of future centuries will resurrect and build on her ideals. Dawson prefaced this pointed rejoinder to Tennyson's hostility toward a woman's college in *The Princess* with an allegorical homage to female solidarity, in the form of a Petrachan sonnet which she dedicated to 'L. J.:'

> The lily bells were chiming reveries
> In the life-garden, and each swaying flower
> Deep-shadowed in the dusk of branchy bower
> Burgeoned into a maiden. Such as these –
> A sunrise vision under leafing trees –
> Have been those women of a parted hour
> Whose sorrows urged my song – a dim love-power
> Stretching from twilight of dead centuries,
> To thrill the hush of noon with echoes sweet.
>
> Oh thou! to me the noblest of that throng
> That ever passes with unceasing beat
> Of tireless footsteps – thou, white life and strong, –
> Receive of love, now learning at thy feet,
> And mistress of none other speech – a song.

Such transparently 'Rossettian' echoes ('deep-shadowed,' 'dim love-power,' 'none other speech') in a feminist dedicatory sonnet may serve to underscore the wider resonance of poetic devices and mannerisms Rossetti had employed to quite different ends in *The House of Life*.

Similar feminist reverberations appeared in the work of Augusta Webster (1837–94), more precisely in the posthumously published *Mother and Child* (1895), the century's only extended sonnet-celebration of maternal love.

To present-day readers Webster's best known work is probably the dramatic monologue 'The Castaway' (1870), a pointed reply to DG Rossetti's 'Jenny.' William Michael Rossetti wrote the introduction to *Mother and Child*, and Webster, who knew the Rossetti family well, also served as an early member of the London School Board, worked as an activist for women's suffrage and education, and wrote two novels, six dramas and five volumes of verse in all.[21]

She subtitled *Mother and Child's* twenty-seven sonnets 'An Uncompleted Sonnet-Sequence,' bound them with seven other sonnets arranged in small clusters after the manner of 'True Woman' or 'The Choice,' marked some of them with dates that ranged from 'Rome, November 1881' to 1882 and 1886, and arranged them (with a subsequence which focused on the exclusive depth of a mother's love for an only child) in a rough progression from celebrations

Photographed by Ferrando, Roma.

Figure 11. **Augusta Webster**

of her daughter's unqualified trust to expressions of sympathy and solidarity with mothers whose children have died, regret that the simplicity and immediacy of the parental bond must diminish with age, and bleak reflections on ultimate death.

An oblique but interesting comparison might be drawn between Webster's apprehensions about the inevitability of separation with age and the passage of time and analogous reflections in Shakespeare's sonnets to the beautiful young man and the dark lady. But Webster's 'Rossettian' images of vain regret, echoing footsteps and spectral traces of vanished hopes focused here on very different sorts of love and gradual estrangement.

A little child she, half defiant came
  Reasoning her case – 'twas not so long ago –
  'I cannot mind your scolding, for I know
However bad I were you'd love the same.'
And I, what countering answer could I frame?
  'Twas true, and true, and God's self told her so.
  One does but ask one's child to smile and grow,
And each rebuke has love for its right name.

And yet, methinks, sad mothers who for years,
  Watching the child pass forth that was their boast,
Have counted all the footsteps by new fears
Till even lost fears seem hopes whereof they're reft
And of all mother's good love sole is left –
  Is their Love, Love, or some remembered ghost?

Sonnet eleven, 'Love's Mourner,' deconstructed conventional ideals of 'womanly patience', and the cumulative tolls of abuse and neglect they imposed (and impose):

'Tis men who say that through all hurt and pain
  The woman's love, wife's, mother's still will hold,
  And breathes the sweeter and will more unfold
For winds that tear it, and the sorrowful rain.
So in a thousand voices has the strain
  Of this dear patient madness been retold,
  That men call woman's love. Ah! they are bold,
Naming for love that grief which does remain.

Love faints that looks on baseness face to face:
  Love pardons all; but by the pardonings dies,
  With a fresh wound of each pierced through the breast.
And there stand pityingly in Love's void place
  Kindness of household wont familiar-wise,
  And faith to Love – faith to our dead at rest.

The poem's brief examination of a dutifully 'loving' woman's inner alienation was unique in its genre and time, and utterly foreign to Rossetti's preoccupations. Given this, it may be interesting as well as ironic that Webster's bitter evocations of love's 'void space' and 'death' formally paralleled the arid disillusion which concluded Rossetti's sonnet 'The Sun's Shame'.[22]

I have argued in this section that young women such as Blind, Dawson and Levy found it useful to revalue Rossettian imagery of anxiety, memory and attachment in service to un-Rossettian aims. Webster's more experimental sonnet sequence reflected an idiosyncratic personal mixture of scepticism and ardent attachment, as well as careful study of Shakespeare, Barrett Browning's 'Sonnets from the Portuguese' and Rossetti's *The House of Life*. But she too drew on a common store of elegiac images for her more heterodox and independent meditations on broken attachments and generational loss.

The Second Generation

Dante Gabriel Rossetti's formal mannerisms gradually became part of a wider and more attenuated template of Pre-Raphaelite and 'decadent' antecedents as the turn of the century approached and passed, and a later generation of women modulated them in more 'imagist', 'symbolist' and proto-modernist directions. Extended sonnet-sequences became rarer, and capital-letter allegorical figurations faded away almost altogether as sensibilities evolved. But Pre-Raphaelite and Rossettian images of deliquescence and dissolution survived.

Olive Custance (1874–1944) married her 'Fairy Prince', Lord Alfred 'Bosie' Douglas, in 1902, and he published his own Rossettian sonnet sequence as a tribute *To Olive* in 1907. Custance herself wrote *Rainbows* (1902), *The Blue Bird* (1905) and two more volumes of verse before she fell silent in 1911, the year in which her father obtained control of her only child. A Rossettian undertow of intractable sadness sometimes modulated the scintillating surfaces of her eclectic poems, whose qualities also anticipated counterparts in the work of very different poets such as Angelina Grimke and May Cowdery in the Harlem Renaissance:

> In gorgeous plumage, azure, gold and green,
> They trample the pale flowers, and their shrill cry
> Troubles the garden's bright tranquillity!
> Proud birds of Beauty, splendid and serene,
> Spreading their brilliant fans, screen after screen
> Of burnished sapphire, gemmed with mimic suns –
> Strange magic eyes that, so the legend runs,
> Will bring misfortune to their fair demesne...
>
> And my gay youth, that, vain and debonair,
> Sits in the sunshine – tired at last of play
> (A child, that finds the morning all too long),

Tempts with its beauty that disastrous day
When in the gathering darkness of despair
Death shall strike dumb the laughing mouth of song.[23]

The sestet's 'darkness of despair' also recalled Rossetti's 'Lost Days',[24] and complemented the octave's more Keatsean and Shelleyan echoes.

Quite different and oddly arresting transmutations of Rossettian mannerisms and preoccupations with sexual transgression appeared in 'St. Sebastian' (*The Blue Bird*).

So beautiful in all thine agony!
So radiant in thine infinite despair…
Oh, delicate mouth, brave eyes, and curled bright hair…
Oh, lovely body lashed to the rough tree:
What brutal fools were those that gave to thee
Red roses of thine outraged blood to wear,
Laughed at thy bitter pain and loathed the fair
Bruised flower of thy victorious purity?

Marvellous Beauty… target of the world,
How all Love's arrows seek thy joy, Oh Sweet!
And wound the white perfection of thy youth!
How all the poisoned spears of hate are hurled
Against thy sorrow when thou darest to meet
With martyrdom men's mockery of the truth!

Among other things, St Sebastian's images recall counterparts in Rossetti's sonnets, such as 'Astarte Syriaca (For a Picture)', but Custance's celebrations of pain and androgyny are more 'decadent' than Rossetti's veiled references to adultery, and its sanguinary imagery ('red roses of thine outraged blood') more baroquely extravagant than Rossetti's carefully veiled metaphorical emblems of passion and loss.[25]

A music critic and translator who introduced Russian and Czech composers to the British public, Rosa Harriet Jeaffreson Newmarch (1857–1940) published seventeen other books in addition to *Horae Amoris: Songs and Sonnets* (1903) and *Songs to a Singer and Other Verses* (1906). *Mary Wakefield, A Memoir* (1912), for example, paid tribute to the founder of the Competition Festival movement, 'a noble worker and a dear friend'.[26] In *Horae Amoris*'s thirty-four sonnets, Newmarch, who had married in 1883, expressed her love and sympathy for an abused and deserted wife. The work's Latin title may have echoed references to assorted 'hours of love' in *The House of Life* (e.g. sonnet

19, 'This close-companioned inarticulate hour/ When twofold silence was the song of love'), and Rossettian titles for individual sonnets included 'Love Among the Ruins', 'The Vision', 'Men's Justice', 'Then and Now' and 'The New Iseult.'

In proper Rossettian fashion, the sequence's implicit metanarrative flowed from its initial premise that love for a fellow-woman 'dearer than all else beside' had been ill-fated, 'the child of bitterness and rue,/ Born in the wreckage of a fallen shrine' (I, 'Love Among the Ruins'). Newmarch followed this opening motive with expressions of anxious sympathy for a woman in flight from her abusive husband (VII, 'Men's Justice'), frustration with unreciprocated physical desire (XXV), pain at the loved one's indifference (XXXIII, 'The Problem') and resigned self-awareness mingled with stoic integrity (fidelity to 'a care/ I'd not have changed for all the world holds fair,' XXXIII).

The speaker of sonnet XXIII, for example, broods on the transience of her love:

> Should that day come – as come it surely must –
> When from her presence with sad steps and slow,
> Like a discharged steward I must go;
> Who, ere he quits, yields up each urgent trust,
> The deeds, the books, the keys he kept from rust,
> To one who in his place will sit and know
> All secrets of his mistress' weal and woe,
> And hear her wishes and her cares discussed: –
>
> When that dread day shall come, O let the grace
> And dignity of service keep me mute
> From bitter words; and let my unmoved face
> Conceal the inward wound that burns so sore;
> One parting blessing, and one grave salute:
> Then from her life I pass for evermore.

Likewise in 'God's Justice' Newmarch echoes *The House of Life*'s brooding sense of bereavement and poses counterparts of Rossetti's open questions in 'Michelangelo's Kiss' and 'Newborn Death'.[27]

Her concluding title-sonnet offered a small but accomplished and rather comprehensive cadaster of 'Rossettian' imagery:

> The day and night make up Love's book of Hours.
> Dawn comes, and with the shivering breeze that sighs,
> And with the weeping dews and paling skies,
> Returns the grief which bore this love of ours.

Noon-tide; the sun in all his solstice powers
Has kissed the parched and amorous earth that lies
In rapture throbbing, and with lifted eyes
My passion wakes and blooms like Clytie's flowers.

Sunset; and while I watch the rosy stain
Fade into starless dusk, a cold unrest
Warns me no sunrise rings her back again.
Midnight: long since I saw the tired moon climb
Down by a fleecy pathway to the West.
Good-night to Love for now, and for all time.[28]

In 'Men's Justice',[29] however, she abandoned this *ambiance* of music, shrines,
chimes, chants, chalices and festal robes for grimmer empyrean imagery:

Men's Justice

That day she came to me the sun went down
In a strong glare of wide, unbroken red,
Save at the eastern limit, where outspread
One straight black bar, as though the Heavens must frown
On men's harsh justice, who had overthrown
Her home, by right of law, of roof and bed
Bereaving her; while on her guiltless head
They set shame's stigma, worse than martyr's crown.

O fool, to dream that God traced in the sky
A sign of wrath because a woman crept
Heartbroken to your arms! That night on high
The stars swerved not from their accustomed course,
And men and women loved, or calmly slept,
Or revelled till the dawn, without remorse.

The mordant bitterness of 'Men's Justice' offered, in effect, another feminist
variant of 'The Sun's Shame', and Newmarch, like Rossetti, did not hesitate
to write large the flaming letters of indignation as well as sublimated personal
sorrow. In part perhaps because she was primarily a music historian,
Newmarch's sonnet sequence has vanished from the footnotes of literary
history, but *Hora Amoris*' precision and haunting honesty deserve a better fate.

'Michael Field' was the pseudonym of Katherine Bradley (1846–1914) and
Edith Cooper (1862–1913), an aunt and niece who together published twenty-
eight plays and eight volumes of 'aesthetic' poetry in a spirit of what Angela

Figures 12 and 13. **Katherine Bradley and Edith Cooper**

Leighton once called 'baroque unorthodoxy'. Bradley and Cooper were vigorous antivivisectionists and supporters of women's suffrage whose works celebrated their lesbian partnership, and they found various of their poetic antecedents in Sappho's lyrics, Browning's monologues, Rossetti's sonnets on paintings and the poetic narratives of Swinburne and Morris.

Most scholars prefer their early work to the volumes they published after the turn of the century, and especially after their conversion to Catholicism in 1907. But there are poignant and arresting qualities in later poems such as the

following, an uncannily 'decadent' (and posthumously published) evocation of
love beyond the grave.

> Let not a star suspect the mystery!
> A cave that haunts thee in the dreams of night
> Keep me as treasure hidden from thy sight,
> And only thine while thou doest covet me!
> As the Asmonaean queen perpetually
> Embalmed in honey, cold to thy delight,
> Cold to thy touch, a sleeping eremite,
> Beside thee never sleeping I would be.
>
> Or thou might'st lay me in a sepulchre,
> And every line of life will keep its bloom,
> Long as thou seal'st me from the common air.
> Speak not, reveal not… There will be
> In the unchallenged dark a mystery,
> And golden hair sprung rapid in a tomb.

The last line's image clearly echoed Rossetti's possible allusion to his wife's
disinterment at the end of 'Life-in-Love':[30]

> Mid change the changeless night environeth,
> Lies all that golden hair undimmed in death.

The preternatural 'imagist' clarity of this poem's declaration of eternal solidarity subserved distinctly Victorian emotional aims.

One of the Fields' most innovative works was 'Whym Chow, Flame of
Love', a sequence of thirty lyrics in a variety of verse forms composed to com-
memorate their dog's death in 1906, and published privately in 1914. This
idiosyncratic work blended fond evocations of Whym's fervour with unapolo-
getically epic seriousness, and some of its passages explicitly recall the tone
and diction of *The House of Life*:

> I did not love him for myself alone:
> I loved him that he loved my dearest love…
> So I possess this creature of Love's flame,
> So loving what I love he lives from me;
> O symbol of our perfect union, strange
> Unconscious Bearer of Love's interchange.[31]

'Wym Chow's best passages echoed the Anglican memorial service as well as Blake's 'Tyger' and Barrett Browning's 'Sonnets from the Portuguese.' But the desire to portray deep love through idealized ritual was also deeply Pre-Raphaelite, and Rossetti had likewise invoked a third mediating presence between two lovers – variously called 'Love,' 'Life' and 'Death' – so much so that Robert Browning once complained that 'Love' was a 'lubberly fellow' whose presence marred the poem.[32] (One instance of such mediation appeared in the lines 'Sometimes thou seem'st not as thy self alone,/ But as the meaning of all things that are…', from 'Heart's Compass'.[33])

The Fields may well have been the most original and arresting of the eclectic modernists I have mentioned, but other women of the period devoted sonnet sequences to cognate topics. Rachel Annand Taylor, for example, framed the sixty-one sonnets of *The Hours of Fiammetta: A Sonnet Sequence* (1910), with a prologue and epilogue in the voice of a 'dreaming woman,' and Grace Constant Lounsbery arranged *Love's Testament: A Sonnet Sequence* (1906) in twelve sections ('Of Love', 'Of Absence', 'Of Passion', 'Of Doubt', 'Of Philosophy', 'Of Content', 'Of Separation', 'Of Solitude', 'Of Reconciliation', 'Of Jealousy', and 'Retrospect').[34]

In Taylor's 'Soul and Body' (no. XXII of the *Hours of Fiammeta*), for example, Rossetti's recurrent preoccupation with soul and body reappeared (cf. 'The Heart's Compass' and 'The Soul's Sphere'):

Sometimes the Soul in pure hieratic rule
  Is throned (as on some high Abbatial chair
Of moon-pearl and rose-rubies beautiful)
  Within the body grown serene and fair:
Sometimes it weds her like a lifted rood;
  But she endures, and wills no anodyne,
For then she flowers within the mystic Wood,
  And hath her lot with gods – and seems divine:
Sometimes it is her lonely oubliet,
  Sometimes a marriage-chamber sweet with spice:
It is her triumph-car with flutes beset,
  The altar where she lies a sacrifice. –
Cold images! The truth is not in these.
Both are alive, both quick with rhapsodies.

Similarly, number twelve of one of Lounsbery's 'Absence'-sonnets (XII) echoed Rossetti's 'Lovesight' and 'Winged Hours',[35] though its cadences and prosody were more clearly Shakespearean:

If no night gave thee to mine arms again,
  If no day lent its taper to thy face,
  If the oblivion of thy deep embrace
Were but a memory invoked in vain;
If in the murmured melancholy rain,
  And in the spring I found of thee no trace,
  Banished thy love's sweet secret dwelling place,
Thy joys, thy sorrows, thy delight, thy pain:

If in the twilight of the wilted day,
  When each sheep nears its fold, each bird its nest,
  My weary head in vain should seek thy breast,
Thine answering hand, thy voice to soothe my way,
Life could not prison me, for each man hath
The right to pluck the ready grape of death.[36]

Conclusion

Dante Gabriel Rossetti was not the only poet whose crafted imagery and depressive introspection offered models for the writers whose work I have sketched. But the 'House of Life' was the paradigm love-sequence of its time, Rossetti's sonnets served as models for introspective lyrics on the frustration of desire, and many of these writers seemed to find a language or tonality in his forms, rhythms, diction and choices of imagery which helped them express elegiac and lucid resignation (Blind, Levy and Newmarch); liminal intimations of mortality (Levy, Custance and Field); and agapic or amorous solidarity with other women (Levy, Dawson, Newmarch and Field).

The boldness of Rossetti's celebration of a frankly erotic heterosexual love and desire, by contrast, quickly gave way in the hands of the women I have discussed to other, more varied and heterodox expressions of such love – for a daughter; for humanity; for a married person of the same sex; for a beloved dog; for a mouldering mummy; or for one's own elusive or half-fragmented identity.

Arline Golden, by contrast, has put rather bleakly the case against Rossetti's more conventional male imitators:

For although Rossetti's followers employ the devices of conventional symbolism and tropes to universalise their themes, they fail, for the most part, to achieve more than a narrowly personal expression. And although Blunt and Symons expand their sequences to represent modern love and even the perennial aspirations of youth, they, too, fail to attain the all-encompassing, transcendent vision of Meredith or Rossetti.[37]

None of Rossetti's female successors, not even the Fields, created from the precedents of Rossetti's sonnets a radically new language or poetic diction. But several gave new *substance* to these forms, and employed sonnet conventions in distinctive, original, revisionist, feminist and ingeniously parodic and 'deconstructive' ways. Surely, therefore, such successful efforts to decant new wine into old formal bottles manifested the 'fundamental brainwork' Rossetti once considered was essential to the sonnet – and presumably to its continued survival as a distinctive mode of creative poetic expression.[38]

In life, moreover, Rossetti was rigorously possessive in his claims to poetic and artistic originality, and often dismissive of the aspirations of 'new women' and other nineteenth-century feminists. In an afterlife of poetic collective memory, however, he might have been pleased as well as surprised to see some of the more haunting and creative aspects of 'his' forms and sensibility flourish in such paradoxically transmuted forms. If so, he might have learned to his pleasure that the 'gift[s] of grace unknown' had entered another century 'between the sculptured petals softly blown.'

Appendix: Ten More Rossettian Sonnets

Constance Naden

The Pessimist's Vision

I dreamed, and saw a modern Hell, more dread
   Than Dante's pageant; not with gloom and glare,
   But all new forms of madness and despair
Filled it with complex tortures, some Earth-bred,
Some born in Hell: eternally full-fed
   Ghosts of all foul disease-germs thronged the air:
   And as with trembling feet I entered there,
A Demon barred the way, and mocking said –

Through our dim vales and gulfs thou need'st not rove;
   From thine own Earth and from its happiest lot
    Thy lust for pain may draw full nourishment,
   With poignant spice of passion; knowest thou not
Fiends wed for hate as mortals wed for love,
   Yet find not much more anguish? Be content.'

Poet and Botanist

Fair are the bells of this bright-flowering weed;
   Nectar and pollen treasuries, where grope
   Innocent thieves; the Poet lets them ope
And bloom, and wither, leaving fruit and seed
To ripen; but the Botanist will speed
   To win the secret of the blossom's hope,
   And with his cruel knife and microscope
Reveal the embryo life, too early freed.

Yet the mild Poet can be ruthless too,
   Crushing the tender leaves to work a spell
   Of love or fame; the record of the bud
He will not seek, but only bids it tell
His thoughts, and render up its deepest hue
   To tinge his verse as with his own heart's blood.

from *Songs and Sonnets of Springtime*, 1881

Edith Nesbit

Pessimism

Not Spring – too lavish of her bud and leaf –
   But Autumn, with sad eyes and brow austere,
   When fields are bare, and woods are brown and sere,
And leaden skies weep their exhaustless grief:
Spring is so much too bright, since Spring is brief.
   And in our hearts is autumn all the year,
   Least sad when the wild pastures are most drear,
And fields grieve most robbed of the last gold sheaf.

For when the plough goes down the brown wet field,
   A delicate doubtful throb of hope is ours –
What if this coming Spring at last should yield
   Joy, with her too profuse unasked-for flowers?
Not all our Springs of commonplace and pain
Have taught us now that autumn hope is vain.

from *Lays and Legends*, 1887

Knowledge, I

I saw a people trampled on, oppressed,
    With helpless hands, and eyes of light afraid,
    With aching shoulders whereon burdens laid
By day and night choked hope and murdered rest;
A people sordid, sad, unloved, unblessed,
    Whose shroud by their own hands was ever made,
    Whose never-ending toil was only paid
By death-in-life – or death, of life's gifts best.

'What help,' I cried, 'for these whose hands are weak –
    Too weak to hold the weapons they should wield;
Too weak to grasp a helping hand, or seek
    With armed battalions to dispute the field,
And on the oppressors just revenge to wreak?'
    Then – as I cried – the helper was revealed.

from *Ballads and Lyrics of Socialism*, 1908

Bessie Craigmyle

A Wasted Day

Here in the dusky garden-plot I sit,
Laid in my lap are globed chrysanthemums,
Round which the gold-barred bee incessant hums,
And purple-winged butterflies still flit.
The night is near, the evening lamp is lit,
I have let day go by in dreamy thought,
But holding one poor day as less than nought
Have let it pass, taking no count of it.
But soon shall come a time, I know not when,
I shall go forth alone into the dark,
When my strained eyes no more on earth shall see
The face of lover or of friend; and then
At the bed-foot where I lie, stiff and stark,
This wasted Day shall stand, and laugh at me.

from *Poems and Translations*, 1886

Annie Matheson

The Ideal Wife
(Without Distinction of Nationality)

A wife whose love has vanquished doubt and fear,
   In faith and courage man's eternal mate,
     Of reason and of will commensurate!
A loveliness that time will but endear,
Whereof the flower, enfolding, year by year,
   A soul more beautiful, with light eleate,
     Steals sweetness from the winds of adverse fate –
Like snowy lilies fed with radiance clear!
Man's Home and Comrade, – passionate, pure and strong,
   Among the merry, gay with quip and jest,
     To all the sad and lonely, motherhood! –
The heart of him she loves, to war with wrong!
   He is her Strength and she to Him is Rest,
     Revealing, each to each, Truth, Beauty, Good.

from *Love Triumphant and Other New Poems,* 1898

Katherine Tynan

Fra Angelico at Fiesole, I

Home through the pleasant olive woods at even
He sees the patient mild-white oxen go;
Without his lattice doves wheel to and fro,
A great moon climbs the wan green fields of heaven
An hour since, the sun-vein whereon are graven
Gold bells and pomegranates in scarlet show
Parted, and lo! the city's spires of snow
Flushed like an opal, and the streets gold paven!
Then the night's purple fell and hid the rest,
And this monk's eyes filled with happy tears
That come to him beholding all things fair:
A bird's flight over wan skies to the nest;
The great sad eyes of beasts, the silk wheat ears,
Flowers, or the gold dust on a baby's hair.

from *Louise de la Valliere, and Other Poems,* 1885

Mary Coleridge

Companionship

The men and women round thee, what are they?
   Frail as the flowers, less lasting than the snow.
If there be angels flitting in the day,
   Who knows those angels? Who shall ever know?
Let them alone and go thou on thy way!
   They came like dreams; like dreams they come and go.

Nay, the companions of thy timeless hours
   Are dreams dreamt first for thee by them of old,
That thou mights't dream them after! These are powers
   Unending and unaging – never cold –
White as the driven snow, fair as the flowers.
   These be thy verities, to have, to hold!

Imagination

I called you, fiery spirits, and ye came!
Earth was the earth no more; the solid ground
Was as a maze of cloud-like glories found,
The sun was music and the wind was flame.
A rainbow shone about the sacred name
Of all the virtues. Thought in rapture drowned,
Wild ecstasy it was to hear the sound,
The fluttering of the wings of Love and Fame.
I called you, fiery spirits! When your task
Was over, faint, weary, and short of breath,
I would have driven you hence. I did but ask
The old life that I led, the life beneath.
In vain! The world henceforward seems a masque
Fit for the haunted rooms of dreamy death.

from *Poems,* 1908

Margaret Woods

The Earth Angel
(To a Child.)

Beloved spirit, whom the angels miss
   While those heaven-wandering wings thou foldest here,
Love musing on thee, Love whose shadow is fear,
Divines thee born of fairer worlds than this,
And fain ere long to re-assume their bliss.
Stay, winged soul! For earth, this human sphere,
Claims thee her own, her light that storms swept clear,
Her Righteousness that Love, not Peace, shall kiss.

'Twas out of Time thou camest to be ours,
And dead men made thee in the darkling years,
Thy tenderness they bought for thee with tears,
Pity with pain that nothing could requite,
And all thy sweetness springs like later flow'rs
Thick on the field of some forgotten fight.

from *Collected Poems*, 1914

Notes

1 'Characters in Fiction', *The Essays of Virginia Woolf*, ed. Andrew McNeillie (London: Harcourt Brace, 1988), vol. 3, p. 421.
2 Recent studies of the relationship between Victorian poets and their successors have included Carol Christ, *Victorian and Modern Poetics* (University of Chicago Press, 1984); and Cassandra Laity, *Hilda Doolittle and the Victorian Fin de Siècle: Gender, Modernism, Decadence* (Cambridge University Press, 1996).
3 Anthologies which have made the work of Victorian women poets more widely available include Angela Leighton and Margaret Reynolds, *Victorian Women Poets* (Blackwell, 1995); Isobel Armstrong and Joseph Bristow, *Nineteenth-Century Women Poets* (Oxford University Press, 1996) and Linda Hughes, *New Women Poets* (1890s Society, 2001).
4 Diss. Indiana University, 1970, p. 32.
5 *Sonnets of the Century* (London: Walter Scott, 1886), p. xlviii. The sonnets provide a pastiche of Rossettian imagery – compare 'The One Hope' with the sestet of 'To D. G. R., I':

> Hope dwelt with thee, not Fear; Faith, not Despair;
>   But little heed thou hadst of the grave's gloom.
> What though thy body lies so deeply there
>   Where the land throbs with tidal surge and boom,
> Thy soul doeth breathe some Paradisal air
>   And Rest long sought thou hast where amaranths bloom.

6 Op. cit., p. lvi.

7   Op. cit., p. 316. If later commentators were less partial, most recognized Dante
    Gabriel Rossetti's importance to the sonnet tradition. Arthur T Quiller Couch's 1897
    English Sonnets included five of his sonnets, more than from any other nineteenth-
    century poets except Wordsworth, Keats and Elizabeth Barrett Browning. A reflection
    of the sonnet's contemporary prestige may be seen in the fact that Evelyn Sharp's
    Women's Voices (1887), the first anthology of Victorian women poets, included no fewer
    than 38 sonnets by women. For comparison, *Great Sonnets,* ed. Paul Negri (NY: Dover,
    1994), included four each by DG Rossetti, Elizabeth Barrett Browning, Christina
    Rossetti, George Meredith and Gerard Manley Hopkins.

8   Nos 10, 25, 64, 83, 91.

9   'Dead Love'.

10 'Motherhood'.

11 No. 100.

12 cf. 'The Sun's Shame' (92) and 'Czar Alexander the Second (13th March 1881)'.

13 Her most anthologized poem is 'The Dead':

> The dead abide with us! Though stark and cold
>   Earth seems to grip them, they are with us still:
>   They have forged our chains of being for good or ill;
> And their invisible hands these hands yet hold.
> Our perishable bodies are the mould
>   In which their strong imperishable will –
>   Mortality's deep yearning to fulfil –
> Hath grown incorporate thorough dim time untold.
>
> Vibrations infinite of life in death,
>   As a star's travelling light survives its star!
>   So may we hold our lives, that when we are
> The fate of those who then will draw this breath,
>   They shall not drag us to their judgment-bar,
> And curse the heritage which we bequeath.

14 *Xantippe and Other Poems*, 1881.

15 No. 69.

16 *A Minor Poet* (London, 1891), 2nd ed., p. 89.

17 No. 71.

18 No. 5.

19 No. 71.

20 'To Vernon Lee'.

21 The most extensive study of Webster's work is Christine Sutphin, ed., *Augusta Webster:
    Portraits and Other Poems,* Peterborough, Ontario: Broadview, 2000. See also my
    'Augusta Webster', *Dictionary of Literary Biography,* ed. William E Fredeman and Ira
    Nadel, vol. 35 (Detroit: Gale Research, 1985).

22 No. 92.

23 'Peacocks: A Mood,' *Rainbows.*

24 No. 86.

25 Another trace of Rossetti's influence might be found in 'Beauty,' also in the 1905
    volume:

> I saw the face of Beauty – a pale rose
> In the gold dusk of her abundant hair...

A silken web of dreams and joys – a snare…
A bright temptation for gay youth that goes
Laughing upon his way without a care!
A shield of light for conquering Love to bear
Stronger than all the swords of all his foes.

O face of Beauty – O white dawn enshrined
In sunrise veils of splendid hair – O star!
Shine on those weary men who sadly wise
But guess thy glory faintly from afar –
Missing the marvel of thy smile – and blind
To the imperial passion in thine eyes!

26 *Mary Wakefield: A Memoir*, p. 120.
27 Nos 94, 99, 100.
28 'Horae Amoris,' 34.
29 No. 7.
30 No. 36.
31 V. Trinity.
32 *The Letters of Robert Browning*, ed. Th. H Hood (London, 1933), p. 137.
33 'Heart's Compass,' *The House of Life*, 27.
34 Rachel Annand Taylor, *The Hours of Fiammeta: A Sonnet Sequence* (London: Elkin Matthews, 1910). Other Rossettian sonnets in the sequence included XIII, 'The Voice of Love' and XXII, 'Soul and Body'. G Constant Lounsbery, *Love's Testament: A Sonnet Sequence* (London: The Bodley Head, 1906). Gertrude Witherby's *The Heart of Love: A Sonnet Sequence* (London, 1915), bears no apparent trace of Rossetti's influence, and I have tried without success to locate Edith Ellen Trusted's *Sonnet and Song* (London 1913).
35 Nos 4 and 25 respectively.
36 Other parallels may be found, e.g. in X, XVI, XVII, XXIV, XXXIV, XXXIX, XLIV, LX and LXIV.
37 Golden, p. 172.
38 Sharp, *Sonnets of the Century*, p. xlviii.

SELECTED BIBLIOGRAPHY

Arseneau, Mary, Antony H Harrison and Lorraine Janzen Kooistra, eds. *The Culture of Christina Rossetti: Female Poetics and Victorian Contexts* (Athens, Ohio: Ohio University Press, 1999).

Armstrong, Isobel and Joseph *Bristow*, eds, *Nineteenth-Century Women Poets* (Oxford: Oxford University Press, 1996).

Beerbohm, Max, *Rossetti and His Circle*, ed. by N John Hall (New Haven and London: Yale University Press, 1987).

Bullen, JB, *The Pre-Raphaelite Body: Fear and Desire in Painting, Poetry, and Criticism* (Oxford: Clarendon Press, 1998).

Burlinson, Kathryn, *Writers and their Work: Christina Rossetti* (Plymouth: Northcote, 1998).

Chapman, Alison, *The Afterlife of Christina Rossetti* (London: Macmillan, 2000).

Christ, Carol, *Victorian and Modern Poetics* (Chicago: University of Chicago Press, 1984).

Costantini, Mariaconcetta, *Poesia e sovversione: Christina Rossetti, Gerard Manley Hopkins* (Pescara: Edizioni Tracce, 2000).

D'Amico, Diane, *Christina Rossetti: Faith, Gender and Time* (Louisiana: Louisiana State University Press, 1999).

Denisoff, Dennis, *Aestheticism and Sexual Parody, 1840–1940* (Cambridge: Cambridge University Press, 2001).

Fraser, Hilary, *The Victorians and Renaissance Italy* (Oxford: Blackwell, 1992).

Harrison, Antony H, *Christina Rossetti in Context* (Brighton: The Harvester Press, 1988).

——, ed, *Letters of Christina Rossetti*, 4 vols (Charlottesville and London: University Press of Virginia, 1997–).

Jones, Kathleen, *Learning Not to Be the First: The Life of Christina Rossetti* (Adlestrop: The Windrush Press, 1991).

Jurlaro, Felicita, *Christina Georgina Rossetti* (London: Excalibur Press, 1990).

Kent, David A and PG Stanwood, eds, *Selected Prose of Christina Rossetti* (New York: St. Martin's Press, 1998).

Leighton, Angela, *Victorian Women Poets. Writing Against the Heart* (London and New York: Harvester Wheatsheaf, 1992).

Leighton, Angela, ed., *Victorian Women Poets: A Critical Reader* (Oxford: Blackwell Publishers, 1996).

Leighton, Angela and Margaret Reynolds, eds, *Victorian Women Poets* (Oxford: Blackwell, 1995).

L'Enfant, Julie, *William Rossetti's Art Criticism: The Search for Truth in Victorian Art* (Lanham, MD: University Press of America, 1998).

McGann, Jerome, *Dante Gabriel Rossetti and the Game that Must be Lost* (New Haven & London: Yale University Press, 2000).

Marsh, Jan, *Christina Rossetti: A Literary Biography* (London: Jonathan Cape, 1994).

——, *Dante Gabriel Rossetti: A Biography* (London: Weidenfeld & Nicholson, 1999).

Maxwell, Catherine, *The Female Sublime from Milton to Swinburne: Bearing Blindness* (Manchester: Manchester and London, 2001).

Palazzo, Lynda, *Christina Rossetti's Feminist Theology* (London: Palgrave, 2002).

Rossetti, WM, *Selected Letters of William Michael Rossetti*, ed. by Roger W Peattie (University Park and London: The Pennsylvania State University Press, 1990).

Rylance, Rick, *Victorian Psychology and British Culture 1850–1880* (Oxford: Oxford University Press, 2000).